BETTING SYNTHETIC SURFACES

A

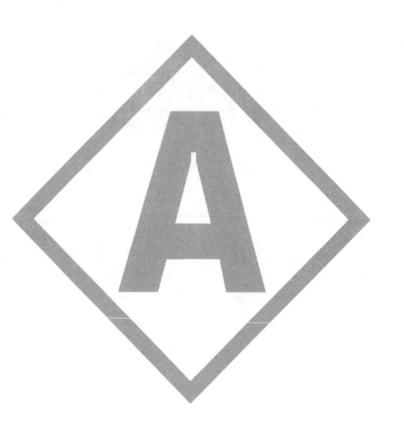

BETTING SYNTHETIC SURFACES:

Conquering Racing's Newest Frontier

BILL FINLEY

DRF Press
NEW YORK

Published by
Daily Racing Form Press
100 Broadway, 7th Floor
New York, NY 10005

ISBN: 978-1-932910-82-7
Library of Congress Control Number: 2008933442

Cover and jacket designed by Chris Donofry
Text design by Neuwirth and Associates

Printed in the United States of America

All entries, results, charts and related information provided by

EQUIBASE COMPANY

821 Corporate Drive • Lexington, KY 40503-2794 Toll Free (800) 333-2211 or (859) 224-2860; Fax (859) 224-2811 • Internet: www.equibase.com

The Thoroughbred Industry's Official Database for Racing Information

10 9 8 7 6 5 4 3 2 1

Table of Contents

Introduction

After nearly two years of researching and writing about the constantly developing and changing subject of synthetic racing surfaces, I've come to this conclusion: Synthetic surfaces are here and here to stay, and, sorry, but you're just going to have to deal with it. The only alternative is to never again place a bet on a race run at Keeneland, Arlington, Woodbine, Hollywood Park, Del Mar, Turfway, Golden Gate Fields, Santa Anita, or Presque Isle Downs, and who wants to do that? And even that won't exactly work. What do you do with the Santa Anita shipper coming into Belmont, or the Kentucky horse switching from Keeneland to Churchill?

And who's to say that the day won't come when there are dozens more converts to synthetic tracks? The synthetic revolution took a major step backward when the Cushion Track at Santa Anita caused so many problems during the winter of 2007–08, but proponents still believe that the pluses of synthetic surfaces outweigh the minuses. Though there is some evidence to the contrary, advocates say that synthetic surfaces are cheaper to maintain and result in fewer cancelations, but the biggest advantage may be their safety. The deaths of Barbaro, Eight Belles, and George Washington on some of the sport's biggest days have raised public consciousness about racing-related injuries, and many people feel that racing on conventional dirt surfaces could someday even become a thing of the past.

The biggest obstacle, of course, is money. Depending on the size of a racing surface, it costs about $10 million to put in a synthetic surface, a lot more than some tracks are willing to spend.

"We have spoken to a lot of tracks and they tell us they can't justify the investment," said Philip Bond, the overseas business-development manager for the manufacturers of Cushion Track, a company based in the United Kingdom. "So, we will always see dirt tracks, but the vast majority of tracks will be synthetic tracks in the future."

The modern horseplayer now has to learn the ins and outs of synthetic surfaces, which has some people horrified. Because they are not exactly dirt and they're certainly not grass, Cushion Track, Polytrack, Tapeta Footings—and now Pro-Ride, which will be in place at Santa Anita in time for the 2008 Breeders' Cup—may have their mysterious aspects, but there are those who seem to have overreacted to this, as if synthetics have created some sort of bizarre world where horse racing becomes an indecipherable mess.

Synthetic surfaces are indeed different, and a horseplayer must become acquainted with their nuances and individual characteristics. Many people feel, for example, that the Polytrack surfaces at Keeneland and Del Mar play differently from Cushion Track and Tapeta—and even from each other.

The good news is that synthetic surfaces are not *that* different. When dealing with handicapping synthetic tracks, the best course of action is a simple one: Stick to the basics. Many horses that run well on dirt will run just as well on a synthetic track and vice versa.

That may come as a surprise to some. I was among those who thought synthetic surfaces, at least initially, would create a nightmare for players. My guess was that some horses would love these new tracks and some would hate them, much the way some horses run like champions on turf but can't run a step on conventional dirt, and vice versa. If that were the case, in races where virtually all of the starters had never before raced on these newfangled tracks, form would probably be all but meaningless. Throwing darts at the pages of *Daily Racing Form* might work just as well as anything else.

The first North American race run over a synthetic surface probably did nothing to ease whatever fears people may have had about this strange new entity. Polytrack made its debut at Turfway Park on September 7, 2005, and the first race that day was a starter allowance with a $25,000 purse. The 2–1 favorite was a horse named Akanti, who was taking a drop in class after finishing fourth in a $40,000 stakes race at Louisiana Downs. At 3–1, the second choice was Mach Speed, who was coming in off a third-place finish in a $35,000 claimer at Saratoga.

It took one minute and 40.72 seconds for the one-mile race to be completed, and no doubt less than that for some horseplayers to vow never to bet on a synthetic-surface race again. Akanti finished next to last, beating just one horse, Mach Speed.

Meanwhile, the winner was a 13–1 shot named Regal Reproach, shipping in from Mountaineer Park. Though his form was good, he seemed outclassed after running in $10,000 starter races in West Virginia. He won by a half-length over 6–1 shot He's Awesome and the two produced a $215 exacta. Could it be that Regal Reproach was some sort of Polytrack freak and Akanti and Mach Speed were the first of what were sure to be many examples of horses that hated the new main track at Turfway?

One race isn't much to go on, but anyone paying close attention to the Turfway opener might have picked up on something that would, in time, become obvious about synthetic tracks, especially the one at Keeneland. Racing well back in the pack early behind slow fractions of 24.03, 48.53, and 1:14.14, the top two finishers were able to mow down the front-runners after making their moves late in the race. (See race chart, next page.) What happened was not some sort of coincidence. It soon became apparent that the Polytrack at Turfway, like most of the synthetic surfaces in North America, favored closers. (But more on that later).

It didn't take long for Turfway racing to return to some sense of normalcy. In the second race of the night, the 6–5 favorite won, the 8–5 second choice was second, and the 3–1 third choice was third. The exacta returned a whopping $10.20 and the trifecta paid $21.60. Perhaps the winning chalk players were then ready to give Polytrack another chance.

The first full card ever run on Polytrack in this country was about as normal as they come. Favorites won three of the 10 races and the remaining seven races were won by a mixture of longshots and medium-priced horses.

FIRST RACE
Turfway Park
SEPTEMBER 7, 2005

1 MILE. (1.35^{3}) STARTER ALLOWANCE . Purse $25,000 FOR THREE YEAR OLDS AND UPWARD WHICH HAVE STARTED FOR A CLAIMING PRICE OF $35,000 OR LESS IN 2004–2005. Three Year Olds, 119 lbs.; Older, 122 lbs. Non–winners Of Two Races Other Than Claiming At A Mile Or Over Since June 7 Allowed 3 lbs. A Race Other Than Claiming Since July 7 Allowed 6 lbs. (Highweights Preferred)(WILL BE RUN AS THE FIRST RACE). (Clear. 80.)

Value of Race: $25,000 Winner $15,000; second $5,000; third $2,500; fourth $1,250; fifth $250; sixth $250; seventh $250; eighth $250; ninth $250. Mutuel Pool $72,307.00 Exacta Pool $52,253.00 Trifecta Pool $47,888.00 Superfecta Pool $18,166.00

Last Raced	Horse	M/Eqt.	A.	Wt	PP	St	¼	½	¾	Str	Fin	Jockey	Odds $1
15Aug05 ^{3}Mnr^{2}	Regal Reproach	L	6	116	3	6	7^{2}	$6^{\frac{1}{2}}$	6^{2}	1^{1}	$1^{\frac{1}{2}}$	Diego I	13.10
17Jly05 ^{9}EIP^{1}	He's Awesome	L f	5	119	5	9	9	9	9	6^{hd}	2^{1}	Troilo W D	6.30
13Aug05 ^{8}EIP^{2}	On the Border	L f	5	116	6	3	$4^{1\frac{1}{2}}$	4^{2}	4^{hd}	$4^{\frac{1}{2}}$	3^{hd}	Borel C H	8.50
16Jly05 ^{3}Mnr^{1}	Hold Your Thought	L b	5	119	2	5	$5^{1\frac{1}{2}}$	$5^{1\frac{1}{2}}$	5^{hd}	3^{hd}	$4^{1\frac{1}{4}}$	Prescott R	4.00
31Jly05 ^{11}EIP^{3}	Honest Chance	L b	4	116	1	7	$6^{\frac{1}{2}}$	7^{2}	7^{2}	5^{1}	$5^{1\frac{3}{4}}$	McKee J	15.70
17Aug05 ^{8}Sar^{1}	Cat Stalker	L	3	116	9	8	$1^{1\frac{1}{2}}$	1^{1}	1^{hd}	$2^{1\frac{1}{2}}$	$6^{2\frac{1}{4}}$	Lanerie C J	12.90
19Aug05 ^{9}EIP^{4}	Next Step	L f	4	116	4	4	8^{4}	8^{5}	8^{4}	8^{2}	$7^{2\frac{1}{2}}$	Faulkner G	44.70
7Aug05 ^{6}LaD^{4}	Akanti-Ire	L f	5	116	8	1	$3^{1\frac{1}{2}}$	2^{hd}	$2^{\frac{1}{2}}$	$7^{1\frac{1}{2}}$	$8^{2\frac{1}{4}}$	Sarvis D A	2.10
20Aug05 ^{1}Sar^{3}	Mach Speed	L b	4	116	7	2	2^{hd}	$3^{\frac{1}{2}}$	3^{hd}	9	9	Castanon J L	3.30

OFF AT 7:00 Start Good For All But HE'S AWESOME. Won driving. Track fast.

TIME :24, :48^{2}, 1:14, 1:27^{1}, 1:40^{3} (:24.03, :48.53, 1:14.14, 1:27.31, 1:40.72)

$2 Mutuel Prices:

3 – REGAL REPROACH	28.20	10.20	4.60
5 – HE'S AWESOME		8.80	5.20
6 – ON THE BORDER			5.20

$2 EXACTA 3–5 PAID $215.00 $2 TRIFECTA 3–5–6 PAID $2,066.40
$2 SUPERFECTA 3–5–6–2 PAID $7,084.80

Ch. g, (Feb), by Regal Classic – Above Reproach , by Crafty Prospector . Trainer Reed Eric R. Bred by Prestonwood Farm LLC (Ky).

REGAL REPROACH reserved early, advanced four wide after a half, took over after six furlongs and held sway late. HE'S AWESOME broke in the air, was outrun for six furlongs, settled in upper stretch and closed fast to be rapidly getting to the winner. ON THE BORDER forced into the rail once on the first turn, recovered to race close up along the inside, angled out for the drive but lodged only a mild late bid. HOLD YOUR THOUGHT within striking distance off the inside, moved out four wide late on the second turn but lacked the needed closing bid. HONEST CHANCE unhurried along the inside, angled out four wide with a quarter mile to go but had little left late. CAT STALKER came in a bit entering the first turn, set the pace, moved in to be just off the inside, held on well to midstretch and tired. NEXT STEP unhurried three wide, could not menace. AKANTI (IRE) carried in entering the first turn, pressed the pace three wide, engaged the leaders approaching the stretch but gave way. MACH SPEED steadied when forced in on ON THE BORDER entering the first turn, raced close up while off the inside, challenged with a quarter mile to go but faded.

Owners– 1, Brumley Jerry S and Reed Kay; 2, Campbell Alex G Jr; 3, Nelson James E Sr; 4, Sydney Racing LLC; 5, Noriega Justo Jr; 6, Baker Robert C and Mack WIlliam L; 7, Oak Haven Farm; 8, Stone James H; 9, Overbrook Farm

Trainers– 1, Reed Eric R; 2, Register Alison; 3, Danner Doug; 4, Mogge Wayne D; 5, Hyland Angel; 6, Lukas D Wayne; 7, Frederick Isaac A; 8, Stall Albert M Jr; 9, Stewart Dallas

Turfway players soon learned that they didn't need to toss out the basics of handicapping they had always used. Class mattered. Beyer Speed Figures, Thoro-Graph sheets, and other speed figures were important. Good trainers won more than bad trainers. The same went for good jockeys versus bad jockeys. Trip handicapping was a good way to spot future winners. Money management was vital and finding value in the parimutuel pools was a must.

The 2005 fall meet at Turfway ran for 22 days and 219 races were run, all of them on Polytrack. At any given meet that runs for an extended period of time, favorites will win at a rate in the neighborhood of 30 percent. The percentage of winning favorites at Turfway? It was 29.7 percent.

At the corresponding meet the previous year, favorites won at a 31.8 percent clip. The difference between the 2004 and 2005 fall meets was negligible, especially when you consider that the larger fields in 2005 created more wide-open betting races and that in 2004, a dominant jockey (Rafael Bejarano) had ridden many winning favorites. The bottom line was that racing at Turfway was every bit as formful over Polytrack as it was over conventional dirt.

Woodbine was the next track to convert to a synthetic surface. A Polytrack strip debuted there August 30, 2006. With only six horses lining up for the first synthetic-surface race ever run in Canada and just one of them going off at more than 5–1, there was almost no chance that the race would turn out to produce a big payoff. It didn't. A 7–2 shot won, beating a 2–1 shot. The exacta (or exactor, as they say north of the border) paid $35.30.

Over the course of the Woodbine meet, form held up quite nicely, just as it had at Turfway. Favorites won at a 27.5 percent clip over the synthetic surface, and while that is a little lower than normal, it was not low enough to suggest that the switch to Polytrack threw form off wildly.

Keeneland was up next. Polytrack debuted there at the 2006 fall meet, and it was more of the same. Despite a strong bias favoring closers that lasted most of the meet, handicappers didn't seem to have much of a problem figuring out what was going on. Favorites won 42 of the 146 races run over the main track for a winning rate of 28.8 percent. Again, that was a little low, but well within the range of normalcy. Actually, favorites fared better over Polytrack in 2006 than they did over a conventional main track during the fall meet of 2005, when the chalk won at a rate of 26.7 percent on the dirt.

A different synthetic surface, Cushion Track, made its debut at Hollywood Park November 1, 2006, and the first race there pretty much summed up what was to come for the remainder of the meet. There was a small field and it was a generally formful race.

FIRST RACE
Hollywood
NOVEMBER 1, 2006

7 FURLONGS. (1.20^{2}) CLAIMING . Purse $34,000 (plus $4,080 CBOIF – California Bred Owner Fund) FOR FILLIES THREE YEARS OLD. Weight, 123 lbs. Non–winners Of Two Races In 2006 Allowed 2 lbs. A Race In 2006 Allowed 4 lbs. Claiming Price $50,000, if for $45,000, allowed 1 lb. (Maiden and Claiming races for $40,000 or less not considered). (Clear. 72.)

Value of Race: $36,440 Winner $22,440; second $6,800; third $4,080; fourth $2,040; fifth $680; sixth $400. Mutuel Pool $122,633.00 Exacta Pool $80,724.00 Quinella Pool $5,368.00 Trifecta Pool $78,589.00

Last Raced	Horse	M/Eqt.	A.	Wt	PP	St	¼	½	Str	Fin	Jockey	Cl'g Pr	Odds $1
9Oct06 ^{6}OSA^{11}	Matty G Whiz	LB b	3	113	5	2	$4^{1\frac{1}{2}}$	$4^{\frac{1}{2}}$	$1^{\frac{1}{2}}$	$1^{\frac{3}{4}}$	Garcia M^{5}	45000	3.60
15Sep06 ^{4}Crc^{5}	Your Quote	LB b	3	123	6	3	5^{1}	5^{2}	$4^{\frac{1}{2}}$	$2^{\frac{1}{2}}$	Espinoza V	50000	2.70
9Oct06 ^{6}OSA^{5}	More Angels	LB b	3	119	2	4	$1^{\frac{1}{2}}$	1^{1}	$2^{1\frac{1}{2}}$	3^{hd}	Baze M C	50000	4.70
9Oct06 ^{6}OSA^{4}	Itschelseagirl	LB b	3	121	3	5	3^{hd}	3^{1}	$5^{2\frac{1}{2}}$	$4^{3\frac{3}{4}}$	Nakatani C S	50000	3.00
11Oct06 ^{6}OSA^{5}	Princess Kinzie	LB	3	121	1	6	6	6	6	$5^{\frac{3}{4}}$	Valenzuela P A	50000	4.80
23Sep06 ^{11}Fpx^{7}	Mama Lula	LB	3	119	4	1	$2^{2\frac{1}{2}}$	2^{hd}	3^{1}	6	Cohen D	50000	8.50

OFF AT 12:31 Start Good. Won driving. Track fast.
TIME :23^{2}, :47^{3}, 1:12^{1}, 1:24^{3} (:23.42, :47.74, 1:12.29, 1:24.77)

$2 Mutuel Prices:

6 – MATTY G WHIZ	9.20	4.80	3.60
7 – YOUR QUOTE		3.80	3.20
2 – MORE ANGELS			3.20

$1 EXACTA 6–7 PAID $15.30 $2 QUINELLA 6–7 PAID $23.00
$1 TRIFECTA 6–7–2 PAID $45.60

Dk. b or br. f, (Feb), by Matty G – Contagious Love , by Graustark . Trainer Glatt Mark. Bred by Royal Match Stud Inc Thomas Birklid & Karen Murphy (Cal).

MATTY G WHIZ stalked the pace outside, went three wide then four wide on the turn, took the lead three deep into the stretch and gamely prevailed under urging. YOUR QUOTE chased outside, went four wide on the turn and into the stretch and gained the place. MORE ANGELS went up inside to duel for the lead, inched away into the turn, battled between foes nearing the quarter pole and along the rail into the stretch and held third. ITSCHELSEAGIRL stalked a bit off the rail then inside, tried to go through along the fence leaving the turn but steadied in tight nearing the quarter pole, came out a bit in the stretch and was edged for a minor award between foes late. PRINCESS KINZIE a bit slow to begin, settled inside, came a bit off the rail on the turn and into the stretch and did not rally. MAMA LULA broke out a bit, pulled her way to the early lead then dueled outside a rival, stalked between horses on the turn and into the stretch and weakened. Following a stewards' inquiry and a claim of foul by the rider of ITSCHELSEAGIRL against MORE ANGELS for alleged interference on the turn, no change was made when the stewards ruled the videotape inconclusive. A claim of foul by the trainer of MAMA LULA against the winner for alleged interference on the turn was not allowed by the stewards, who ruled the videotape failed to substantiate the claim.

Owners– 1, Portale Thomas and Xitco John and Mark; 2, La Canada Stables LLC; 3, Cummings Bob Equils James W and McCauley Bruce; 4, Craig Sidney H and Jenny; 5, Always Believe Inc; 6, Turf View Stables LLC

Trainers– 1, Glatt Mark; 2, Carava Jack; 3, Knapp Steve; 4, Spawr Bill; 5, Jones Martin F; 6, Hines N J

Scratched– Catch My Fancy (01Sep06 ^{7}Dmr^{4})

The rate of winning favorites over the main track during the inaugural Cushion Track meet at Hollywood Park was 32.7 percent. Southern California racing has a surfeit of races with small fields, no doubt the reason why favorites won at a higher percentage at Hollywood than they did at Turfway, Woodbine, and Keeneland.

In the early stages of the inaugural Polytrack meet at Arlington Park in 2007, handicappers were struggling a bit with dealing with the new surface. During the first 10 days of racing, favorites won only 20.7 percent of the races run over Polytrack. But just when it began to seem that racing at Arlington was a crapshoot, things straightened out. By the end of July, favorites were winning at a rate of 31 percent over Polytrack.

The bottom line is that synthetic surfaces are not that different from conventional dirt tracks. Generally, horses that run well on the dirt will handle the synthetic tracks. In addition, the type of versatile horse that runs well on grass but also runs well on dirt shouldn't have any problem with a synthetic surface. Turf horses are a different matter, which will be discussed in more detail later in this book, but for now, ignore those who tell you that grass horses love synthetic surfaces. It's not necessarily true. Horses that are successful only on the grass and don't run a lick on dirt will not, for the most part, run well over the synthetic tracks.

So far, handicappers have tended to overreact when it comes to synthetic surfaces, failing to realize that most horses will duplicate their dirt form on the new tracks. Take the case of Lava Man.

a Man
TD Racing Stable and Wood Jason

Dk. b or b. g. 6 (Mar)
Sire: Slew City Slew (Seattle Slew) $6,000
Dam: Li'l Ms. Leonard (Nostalgia's Star)
Br: Lonnie Arterburn, Eve & Kim Kuhlmann (Cal)
Tr: O'Neill Doug F(0 0 0 0 .00) 2007:(904 139 .15)

Life	43	17	8	3	$5,214,706	120	D.Fst	25	10	4	3	$4,047,002	120
2007	8	3	1	0	$1,410,000	109	Wet(375)	0	0	0	0	$0	-
							Synth	3	1	0	0	$470,000	105
2006	8	7	0	0	$2,770,000	113	Turf(288)	15	6	4	0	$697,704	107
	0	0	0	0	$0	-	Dst(0)	0	0	0	0	$0	-

-40OSA	fst	1⅛ ◈	:46	1:09 4	1:34 2	1:47 1	3↑ [S]CalCpClscH250k	92	9	41¼	2½	2½	2hd	62½	Nakatani C S	LB124 b	*1.60	-	-	BoldChieftin119½ ClticDrmin115¾ SminolNtiv116hd	Bid,led 1/4,wkend late	10
-6OSA	fm	1 Ⓣ	:23 1	:47 1	1:10 4	1:34	3↑ OakTrMl-G2	90	2	31½	31	62¾	63½	64¾	Nakatani C S	LB123 b	*1.30	89-	10	Out of Control123no Zann1191 Courtnall1191¾	Stalked rail,weakened	6
-8Dmr	fst	1¼ ◈	:49 3	1:14 4	1:40 3	2:07 1	3↑ PacifcCl-G1	89	1	32½	41½	2hd	32	67	Nakatani C S	LB124 b	*1.20	-	-	*StudentCouncil*124½ AwsomGm1244 HlloSundy1241½	Bid 3 wide, weakened	12
-40Hol	fst	1¼ ◈	:48 3	1:13 1	1:37 4	2:03 1	3↑ HolGldCp-G1	105	8	22½	21	2hd	2hd	1no	Nakatani C S	LB124 b	*1.40	-	-	Lava Man124no A. P. Xcellent116¾ Big Booster1134¼	Stalked,bid,gamely	9
-40Hol	fm	1¼ Ⓣ	:46 2	1:10 1	1:34 4	1:58 3	3↑ CWhtghmH-G1	101	8	38	38	11½	11	21½	Nakatani C S	LB124 b	*.90	100-	09	*After Market*1181½ *Lava Man*1242¾ Obrigado1181¾	3wd move,led,2nd best	8
Nad Al Sheba (UAE)	gd	*1⅛ Ⓣ LH	1:47 4				3↑ Dubai Duty Free-G1 Stk 5000000							1629½	Nakatani C S	126 b	-			Admire Moon126½ Linngari1264¼ *Daiwa Major*1262 *Pressed pace to 3f out,weakened.English Channel 12th*		16
ng Post Rating: 66																						

At least when racing in California, Lava Man had been one of the most consistent horses in the game for a long time, and had won on grass, dirt, and on a synthetic surface. But when he threw in a clunker in the Pacific Classic at Del Mar, many tossed the race out, opining that he simply hated the Polytrack.

"He tried hard. But he was struggling a bit out there. He wasn't really getting hold of the track," said his jockey, Corey Nakatani, after the Pacific Classic.

Actually, there was no reason that Lava Man shouldn't have handled the Del Mar surface. He had handled everything else thrown in his way in the past, including a synthetic track when he won the Hollywood Gold Cup over Cushion Track. The truth was that the track had nothing to do with his defeat in the Pacific Classic. Rather, he was a horse who had gone off form. Anyone who understood that probably made some money by throwing him out at 6–5 in the Oak Tree Mile.

So all these new and strange tracks might not be quite as strange or as revolutionary as everyone thought. But the synthetic surfaces are different enough. You simply cannot handicap new Keeneland the same way you handicapped old Keeneland. If you do, it won't be pretty. There are enough nuances and subtle differences with synthetic tracks that, in order for a handicapper to have a fighting chance, you are going to have to be well versed in the ins and outs of a new sort of racing. And it's going to take time for everyone—handicappers, jockeys, trainers, and track superintendents—to learn everything they need to learn about synthetic surfaces.

"I think we're on a three-year learning curve on how to ride on Polytrack, how to train on the artificial surfaces, and how to manage artificial surfaces," said Hall of Fame trainer Carl Nafzger, a two-time winner of the Kentucky Derby. "Right now, I don't think the riders know quite how to ride it. Trainers don't know quite what to expect. And track management is still learning how to maintain it. We've got to wait and see how it's going to play."

Still, we do know some things.

Actually, handicapping races run on synthetic tracks can be less tricky than handicapping races on dirt tracks. Normally, the best horse wins—not the horse that finds the best part of a biased track or the horse that moves up 10 lengths in the slop or the horse that gets clear, sets a slow pace, and steals the race.

"You should just pick the best horse," said former trainer Michael Dickinson, the inventor of the Tapeta synthetic surface. "There's nothing radical about it. It will be a more level playing field and, I daresay, more predictable. Horses will become more consistent. But there will be fewer sore horses, and that's the good news for handicappers. How do you handicap a sore horse? You can't. You can have the best speed and pace figures in the world, but if the horse you're betting on is sore it's not going to matter."

The goal of this book is to teach you about playing the horses at the synthetic tracks and give the best answers possible concerning the many handicapping riddles they have posed. I want to demystify the process of handicapping on synthetic tracks. Although there simply isn't enough data available yet to give definite answers to the many questions raised by their existence, enough synthetic-surface races have been run that we can start to offer preliminary answers to some of the most important questions.

Can you read this book and go out and get rich betting the horses? That's very doubtful. Winning at the racetrack is an immensely difficult proposition and there are no easy ways to beat the game. Synthetic tracks are just one more piece of an already complex puzzle.

In the chapters that follow, I will try to answer some of the questions many handicappers have been asking about synthetic surfaces. In some cases, the answers may disappoint you. I had hoped to find numerous handicapping angles where the sharp player could take advantage of the synthetic revolution and use this knowledge to make a fortune. Of course, it's never that easy. A lot of my research took me a down a dead end.

I have been writing about horse racing for nearly 25 years and I started playing the horses when I was 8. (Okay, so I cried the first time I lost a $2 show bet, which would have been back in 1969 at Garden State Park. My father felt so bad for me, he gave me my $2 back. No wonder I used to think this was an easy game.) One of the proudest moments of my young life was when my opinion that Affirmed was a superior horse to Alydar was verified in the 1978 Kentucky Derby, the first Derby I attended in person. Clutching a $5 win ticket on Affirmed, which was worth $14, I felt like the king of the world.

I played the horses with gusto for many years, especially during the 14-year span I regularly covered New York racing, first for the *New York Post* and then for the *Daily News.* I had a few winning years, but could not consistently beat the game. That doesn't make me a bad handicapper; it makes me the same as 99.9 percent of the people who play the races.

I have never before written a handicapping book, nor was I even tempted to write one. I didn't think I had anything to say that could legitimately help a handicapper win, so I didn't see any justification for writing a book.

I have had many good days at the track and many bad days at the track. I have gone through periods where I thought I had this game all figured out and was on my way to Easy Street. There is nothing like the feeling of loving an 18–1 shot and watching him pull clear in the final yards. It makes you feel like you are the smartest guy in the world, at least until they run the next race.

Then again, I have had periods where I thought I might never cash another bet. It's a terrible, helpless feeling. I have always found this game to be fascinating and challenging, yet a struggle, a roller coaster that pitches you back and forth, up and down and takes you on a wild, exhilarating and, unfortunately, bumpy ride.

Right now, I don't bet. Having quit the *Daily News* in 2000, I am a freelance racing journalist whose stories often appear in *The New York Times*, and the *Times* believes that betting presents a conflict of interest. Supposedly, I might be tempted to unfairly malign a jockey in print after he had gotten left at the gate, rushed up into a fast pace, and gone eight-wide on the horse I had just bet my $2 on.

I don't agree, but I respect that policy and abide by it. Still, I am fascinated by the handicapping aspects of the sport, and enjoy going through yellowed *Racing Form*s looking for the keys that will unlock the secrets of this mysterious game.

Reading this book does not mean you will turn into a consistent winner at the synthetic or non-synthetic tracks. It should, however, give you a better chance of winning and a better chance of conquering a new era, one that represents one of the most significant changes ever for horse racing and horseplayers. A smart horseplayer has a better chance than a dumb horseplayer. Keep reading. That might not help make you any richer, but it will make you smarter. That's my promise.

1

Synthetic Surfaces: A History Lesson

Since the beginning of time, or at least from the point when mankind decided to race horses against one another, horses have pretty much run and trained on just two kinds of surfaces—grass and dirt. That may not have been a good idea, but this sport is notoriously slow to adapt and change. In fact, change is sometimes regarded as a radical concept.

But several centuries into the sport's history, a few open-minded individuals began to consider that perhaps there were better surfaces to train over and race over, particularly compared to the dirt tracks that are so common in North America.

Dirt tracks are primarily made of sand, silt, clay, and loam. All of them are a little bit different and some are better than others, but there's not a one out there that doesn't create problems. When it rains or snows, they get wet, sloppy, muddy, messy. In the worst cases, they can freeze. Too often, there is some sort of problem with dirt tracks and they create adverse racing conditions, which isn't good for anybody or anything. Many are uneven, deep in some areas, hard in others.

On rare occasions, entire cards can be canceled when the tracks get so sloppy or messy that they are unsuitable for racing. Even if racing isn't canceled, many trainers would rather scratch their horses than have them run over a track that is in lousy shape. Small fields usually mean uninteresting racing, and uninteresting racing means bettors will stay away.

Synthetic tracks are able to stand up to virtually any kind of weather and are never anything but fast. With the way they are constructed, they are virtually waterproof. Turfway Park, in northern Kentucky, used to be at the mercy of the weather, particularly in the winter, when snow, sleet, and freeze-and-thaw conditions caused all sorts of problems. Now, with Polytrack in place, Turfway only has to cancel when the weather makes it impossible for fans, employees, horses, and horsemen to get to the track.

During its first full six months of Polytrack racing, Turfway canceled only once, on a day when a snowstorm prevented horses from shipping in from other tracks and training centers.

That doesn't mean that Turfway's Polytrack surface has been perfect. Like most synthetic surfaces, it has had its share of snags. At one point, after the surface was reconfigured to include more wax, the track would tend to form balls or clumps that would collect inside the horses' hooves.

In addition to the purely economic argument for synthetic surfaces, the larger issue, and one that is getting a tremendous amount of attention these days, may turn out to be safety. An injured horse can't run and can't make money for its owner or trainer, but more importantly, no one wants to see a horse or jockey get hurt.

In recent decades, popular champions such as Ruffian, Go for Wand, and Barbaro suffered fatal injuries on the track, but the death of the filly Eight Belles in the 2008 Kentucky Derby shook the racing industry to an unprecedented degree and fueled outrage among many people outside the sport.

While no one will ever know what caused Eight Belles to fracture both front ankles just seconds after running the best race of her life, her death spurred tremendous debate about the safety of racing in general and prompted demands that everything possible be done to avoid such injuries in the future.

Perhaps these catastrophic breakdowns would have happened on any kind of surface, no matter how safe. In certain cases, though, a dirt track can seem to be the culprit.

Some people believe that had the 2007 Breeders' Cup been run on a synthetic surface, and not the sloppy mess that was the main track at Monmouth Park, George Washington would not have broken down and had to be destroyed.

Prominent veterinarian Dr. Wayne McIlwraith speculated that the track condition could have caused George Washington's fatal injury.

A conventional racetrack has a base that provides support and drainage, topped with a deep, soft top layer, or cushion. After long periods of rain and after several races, horses can tend to run on the base of conventional dirt tracks, which creates a dangerous situation. "Obviously, the base is not made for them to be running on directly," McIlwraith said. "The rest of the races went off well, but it's always a concern."

Some injuries, maybe even many injuries, are unavoidable. As long as horses are raced, they will get hurt, sometimes seriously. But it is possible that many injuries have something to do with the nature of the dirt tracks over which the vast majority of North American races are held. Largely because water on dirt tracks drains toward the inside rail, the conventional surfaces can become very uneven. And even on a dry day, dirt surfaces can become hard or jarring.

Remember, a Thoroughbred is a huge animal running on narrow, spindly legs that strike the ground with a great deal of force. It's as if they were put together all wrong; massive beings capable of traveling at great speeds but having to do so on legs no thicker than a ballerina's.

"At the moment, most of our horses are racing on a three-inch loose cushion of sand and dirt," said Michael Dickinson, creator of Tapeta Footings. "When a person walks on that track, like Belmont or any dirt track, your foot is flat. But take something like an umbrella and push it through the track. You'll see that it suddenly hits the bottom and it jars you. You don't realize how close that bottom is and how hard it is. A horse going at 40 miles per hour with a sharp foot goes straight through to that bottom. He's only running over 3½ inches."

That's a problem, one synthetic-surface manufacturers hope to solve. Here's what Mick Peterson, a mechanical engineer at the University of Maine, had to say on the topic: "We have found that there is not a bad step on these [synthetic] tracks," he said. "On dirt, there is more variability. Horses can adapt to different surfaces, but they cannot adapt stride by stride at the speeds they travel."

Catastrophic breakdowns have always been a serious issue in this sport. Although racing did not keep actual statistics on this in the past, these days, it is estimated that 1.5 out of every 1,000 starters will suffer a fatal injury.

"We are part of the Sport of Kings, which too often has meant that we let the past carry us," trainer Patrick Biancone told *The New York Times*. "No one has had the guts to look forward and take advantage of the science and technology available. There has to be a better way to keep these animals and these riders safe. [Polytrack] is one of them."

Dickinson agrees.

"[Track superintendents] are having to work with tracks where they are using technology from a hundred years ago," he said. "Farming in the last 20 years has had to reinvent itself, even Las Vegas has reinvented itself over the last few years. Why didn't horse racing?"

At last, horse racing is also reinventing itself, at least when it comes to track surfaces. Better late than never, as they say. People have figured out that there may be a better way.

The installation of synthetic surfaces at North American racetracks, whether Polytrack, Cushion Track, Tapeta Footings, or the latest addition, Pro-Ride, has been among the major news stories in racing during the young century and some people are hailing them as the surface of the future. Yet synthetic racetracks aren't entirely new and revolutionary. They've actually been around since the early 1960s.

John Nerud has always been one of the great thinkers in horse racing. A Hall of Fame trainer, he directed the careers of Dr. Fager, Ta Wee, and dozens of other outstanding horses for William L. McKnight's Tartan Farms. After he retired from training, he continued to play several important industry roles and was one of the primary forces behind the advent of the Breeders' Cup.

As early as 1959, Nerud told McKnight that the time had come for racing to develop an artificial surface that would be safer than the conventional dirt tracks and would also be impervious to rain. Because McKnight was the chairman of the 3M corporation at the time, he was just the type of person who could get the job done. McKnight went to his best researchers at 3M and told them to develop such a track. The team included Dick Drew, the inventor of 3M's most popular product, Scotch tape.

After several tests and trials, a 3M synthetic track was laid down at a harness-racing training facility in Pennsylvania.

In 1963, the first horse race of any kind was held over a synthetic surface. The 3M track, which would be christened Tartan, was in place when a new harness track named the Meadows opened near Pittsburgh.

Another Tartan track would eventually be put down at Windsor Raceway, a harness track in Ontario.

Here's how *The New York Times* reported the story on opening day 1963 at the Meadows:

"What seems to be the world's fastest, bounciest harness-racing oval opened for business here last night, and the men who put it into operation hope it will make dirt obsolete at the nation's horse parks.

"Maybe it will; probably it won't. It certainly has given racetrack managements something to think about.

"The new racing strip is in use at a brand-new $5,000,000 track called the Meadows. The track's president is Delvin Miller, who has won fame as a driver, trainer, owner and breeder of pacers and trotters.

"Now he's winning new prominence in the horse-and-buggy sport as (a) the operator of Western Pennsylvania's first parimutuel racing plant, and (b) the first racetrack operator to make use of a drip-dry, all-weather, no-dirt surface."

The article noted that the final times that night were all a second or two faster than normal.

In 1966, Tartan made its debut in Thoroughbred racing. Built for $1 million, a Tartan surface was installed inside the main dirt course at old Tropical Park in south Florida. The plan was to hold two races a day over it.

"The Tartan synthetic course was developed by the 3M Company for the purpose of providing consistent, uniform footing and thereby removing one of the greatest single problems of racing—the changing texture of the soil," Tropical Park Racing Secretary Tommy Engleman wrote in a 1967 column for *The Backstretch* magazine. "To this end, 3M Company has invested millions of dollars in coming up with the right combination of materials and concomitantly the perfect resiliency to absorb the strides of racing horses and provide the animals with the ideal footing."

For the record, the first Thoroughbred ever to win a U.S. race over a synthetic surface was named Barricado.

Nerud and McKnight were convinced that synthetic tracks were the future. McKnight became the chief financial backer of Calder Race Course, which opened in 1971, and was responsible for that track also putting in a synthetic surface. They called the Calder track Saf-T-Turf and it was the only dirt track at Florida's summer racetrack. Ironically, it was a speed-favoring surface, which has been far from the case with the modern synthetic tracks.

"It would seem to favor speed horses and the results of the first six days of racing made it clear that a horse not in contention going to the half-mile pole—in both sprints and distance races—had virtually no chance to win," reported *The Blood-Horse* magazine in 1971.

Like many concepts that arrive before their time, the Tartan track proved to be a failure. According to Stan Bergstein, the executive vice president of Harness Tracks of America, the synthetic track at the Meadows only lasted about one year.

"After a year, it became obvious that there were serious problems with the track at the Meadows," Bergstein said. "Chunks of material would break loose and come up, which created dangerous conditions. They had to tear it out right down to the base and put down a new dirt racetrack."

Tropical Park closed in the early 1970s, but the synthetic era would continue at Calder. The rubbery Saf-T-Turf surface at Calder created more problems than it solved. It was overly hard, and horses couldn't handle the pounding. Trainers complained constantly to Calder management and many threatened to take their horses elsewhere. Something had to be done, and within two months of the track's opening, a normal sand-based track was put down on top of Saf-T-Turf.

The dirt/synthetic surface was an improvement, but far from the optimal solution. In 1991, Calder went back to square one, tore out the synthetic base, and put down a conventional dirt track. Part of the problem was that many trainers were reluctant to race their horses over what was, back then, looked at as an oddball surface.

"We have concluded, after researching the issue, that a natural surface will attract a significantly wider range of entries to Calder as more of the nation's top horsemen choose the track to race their horses," said Bertram Firestone, then the owner of Calder, in a prepared statement released at the time.

The next phase for synthetic surfaces came in 1988 when Remington Park opened in Oklahoma City. Remington featured something called Equitrack, which had been developed in England and was essentially a wax-coated dirt. The idea was to produce a track that never got sloppy or muddy and one that would be safer for horses and jockeys. Equitrack worked and it didn't work. It was impervious to water and was always fast. But the brutal summer heat in Oklahoma caused serious problems. The wax would melt, which caused all sorts of woes. Remington also had problems attracting shippers, since many trainers were reluctant to race over an unfamiliar and largely untested surface. After three years of Equitrack, Remington shifted to a conventional dirt surface.

"We're still learning about how to best maintain it," said Remington's general manager, David Vance, in explaining the decision to take out Equitrack. "There have been some difficulties associated with changes in the characteristics of the material from morning training to racing in the heat and sun of the Oklahoma afternoon. It has been very frustrating when it comes to recruiting horses. This was especially frustrating when recruiting for the Remington Park Derby. I believe in the concept of Equitrack and I believe that it is absolutely the best training surface in the history of the sport."

With Equitrack's widely publicized failures, all-weather surfaces seemed to be a forgotten matter. U.S. racing continued to be held on dirt and grass and nothing else. Racing wasn't the type of business where people went back to the drawing board.

But, fortunately, not everyone gave up on the idea of producing a new and improved track surface.

According to Dickinson, also known as the Mad Genius for his unconventional and sometimes brilliant training feats, the first person to come up with an all-weather racing surface that truly worked was none other than the legendary Irish trainer Dr. Vincent O'Brien. That O'Brien would be ahead of the curve should come as no surprise. O'Brien was a genius and one of the greatest horsemen ever. He trained such horses as Nijinsky, Roberto, and The Minstrel and won the Epsom Derby six times. He also won the 1990 Breeders' Cup Mile at Belmont Park with Royal Academy.

According to Dickinson, O'Brien installed a wood-chip track in the seventies at Ballydoyle, his training center in County Tipperary. O'Brien's goal was to create a track his horses could train over during rainy spells, often a serious problem in Ireland.

"Dr. O'Brien is the person who invented the all-weather gallop [training track]," Dickinson said. "He was way ahead of everyone. After he did this, a lot of people in England copied him."

About the same time that Vincent O'Brien was tinkering with ways to improve the gallops at his yard, a young equestrian in England named Martin Collins was trying to develop a better surface for show jumpers and other performance horses to train on. Like racehorses, show horses need safe and dry footing to school over. Collins also had a building company and saw several innovations in that industry.

So, Collins went to work.

"I just started messing around with different things," he said. "It's a bit like making a cake. You chuck something in, you stir it around, and eventually you come up with something. I'm a hands-on guy; I've never been the type who likes to sit around in an office. I was always looking and watching products to see why you should do this and why you shouldn't do that. Being a horse person was definitely important. If you're not a rider and you can't feel things from sitting on a horse, then how the hell can you produce something that's going to be effective? It's almost an impossibility."

Collins's initial efforts ran into problems. Everything he produced would end up freezing in cold weather. Eventually, a light bulb went on in his head. Collins decided to take the plastic strippings from electric cable and add them to his recipe. The stuff stopped freezing in the winter. But he wasn't there yet. The surface would dry out in the summer, so he kept tinkering, kept trying to bake the perfect cake.

"I looked at producing a total synthetic surface where, along with the plastic strippings, we added bits of emulsion, synthetic latex, natural latex. We made that 20 years ago and it was expensive. There really wasn't a market for it."

Collins, who would eventually expand beyond the equestrian world and attempt to sell his product to racetracks and training facilities, was finding out firsthand that people in horse racing don't like change or anything that is different from the standard fare. "Nobody likes change in this sport," he said. "It's all old school."

But Collins kept working on his project, trying to make it cheaper and even better. He found an important advocate and financial backer in the Australian publishing, media, and gaming tycoon Kerry Packer, who was also a serious polo player and wanted Collins to develop ideal footing for his polo ponies. Collins knew he was on to something good and that eventually the equestrian and racing worlds would see that his new surface was a win-win for everyone.

In 1987, Collins, whose product would become known as Polytrack, installed his surface at the training facility of English trainer Richard Hannon. But things seemed to stall from there. Seven years later, he had the major breakthrough he needed. It was then that highly respected trainer John Gosden had Polytrack installed at his Stanley House Stables. After that, the orders started coming in, including one from the Horse of the Year Show in Wembley, England.

Meanwhile, actual racing on all-weather tracks was under way in England. The English had been looking for an alternative to steeplechase racing, which had, traditionally, been the only kind of racing held in the winter. Not only were some punters clamoring for more "flat" racing, but bookies needed a product to keep their customers busy on the many occasions when winter weather made it impossible to conduct steeplechase meets. The obvious answer was flat racing that could be conducted no matter the weather conditions, which is why synthetic surfaces in England are known as all-weather tracks.

In 1989, the English track Lingfield began the first all-weather meet, conducting flat racing in the winter months over a synthetic Equitrack surface. Over the next few years, synthetic surfaces would also be installed in England at Southwell Race Course and at Wolverhampton. The Southwell and Wolverhampton tracks were composed of something known as Fibresand. These surfaces worked, but not nearly as well as the English racing industry had hoped. The tracks did not hold up during severe weather, and the tracks that were never supposed to cancel racing often canceled racing.

With the all-weather tracks in England having obvious flaws, racing officials there started to look for something better. The answer was Martin Collins's Polytrack.

"They used to jump on Fibresand and Equitrack but they just weren't suitable," Collins said. "You need a surface with cut and you can get it with Polytrack."

The next chapter in the history of all-weather surfaces began in November 2001 when racing at Lingfield was first conducted over the Polytrack surface. One race into the inaugural Polytrack card, jockeys were giving it high marks.

"It is a perfect racing surface, with lots of bounce, which horses will enjoy," jockey Martin Dwyer told British reporters. "There is very little kickback, which is good for the horses and jockeys. It is like a carpet to ride on."

The first day, however, was not perfect. A horse named Ahouod, a 5-year-old mare, shattered a pelvis during the running of a race and had to be put down. At least for one day, Polytrack did not deliver on its promise that it would be the world's safest racing surface.

But it soon became apparent that the death of Ahouod was an aberration. Lingfield's Polytrack proved to be a safe surface. Buoyed by the favorable results at Lingfield, Wolverhampton also switched over to Polytrack. Kempton Race Course in England would also put in its first synthetic track, opening a Polytrack course in 2006.

Horsemen were impressed and Polytrack began to appear at the training facilities of several of Europe's top trainers. In 2003, a Polytrack training track was installed at Ballydoyle, where Aidan O'Brien—no relation to Vincent O'Brien—trains for the powerful Coolmore operation.

Synthetic-surface racing would also come to other parts of the world. France, Italy, and Australia are among the countries that have tracks with synthetic-dirt surfaces. However, turf remains the preferred surface in Europe, and the vast majority of the top-class races there are run on grass.

Is Collins solely responsible for taking synthetic surfaces to the next level? We'll let others decide that one. But he was not the only one who saw the possibilities, economic and otherwise, in creating a surface that was both extremely safe and able to stand up to the worst possible weather conditions.

In another part of England, a company called Equestrian Surfaces was busy developing its own product, primarily for other areas of equestrian competition. But Equestrian Surfaces would branch out and develop Cushion Track, which was eventually installed at Hollywood Park and Santa Anita.

Then there was the Mad Genius. Dickinson, always trying to reinvent the wheel, was constantly trying to come up with the perfect racing surface to train his horses over. Eventually, he would perfect something he calls Tapeta Footings, which debuted at his training facility in Maryland and later became the surface of choice at Golden Gate Fields and at Presque Isle Downs, a new racetrack in Pennsylvania.

Still, the U.S. figured to be a tough sell for makers of synthetic tracks. The Remington failure was still fresh in everyone's mind, and convincing racing people to try something new and different figured to be next to impossible.

It used to be that Keeneland was the most tradition-bound racetrack in the country. It didn't even have an announcer until 1997. But major changes in management signaled a new era at the elegant old track in Lexington, Kentucky. Keeneland became a forward-thinking racing organization, which made it the perfect candidate to try something new, different, and potentially revolutionary.

Keeneland Association President and CEO Nick Nicholson knew that there had to be something better out there than the traditional dirt tracks that kept producing an unacceptable amount of injuries to horses and jockeys. He became convinced that the answer was synthetic surfaces.

"The gut-wrenching agony of seeing a jockey that you know and care about, and know their families and know them as a human being, get hurt or, God forbid, killed, is something that haunts you," Nicholson said. "You can't imagine the nauseousness involved. To a lesser degree, it's the same with the horses. To see a horse die right in front of you is awful. That has held this sport back and continues to be one of the great deterrents to growth of Thoroughbred racing; the horribleness of someone coming to the races and seeing this happen in front of them and not ever wanting to come back. And I don't blame them."

Nicholson sold the Keeneland board of directors on the merits of synthetic surfaces and, in particular, Polytrack. Keeneland became partners with Polytrack manufacturer Martin Collins Surfaces and Footings and began to formulate plans for Keeneland and sister track Turfway Park, which is co-owned by Keeneland and the Harrah's casino company, to go synthetic.

"[The partnership] was set up to facilitate the surface coming to North America," Nicholson said. "We found the surface before we knew Martin. We were introduced to it first at Newmarket. It impressed us that those horsemen who had access to the greatest gallops in the world were choosing to work on this all-weather surface; there must be something to it. So then we started watching the races at Lingfield closely for about a year. We would even tape them particularly when it was raining. Only after we were pretty knowledgeable about the surface and knew that it was the one we wanted did we contact Martin."

In 2004, Keeneland converted its five-eighths-of-a-mile training track to Polytrack. It was a way to test the waters, to see how the new surface would hold up through an assortment of weather conditions and, more importantly, how horsemen would accept it.

It was an instant hit.

"I thought it would take maybe years and certainly months,"

Nicholson said when asked how long he thought it would take trainers to accept Polytrack. "But by the end of the first October meeting, virtually every trainer on the grounds was not only galloping their horses on the training track but they were working them on the training track. There probably were more breezes and more serious works on that training track that one month than there had been in the previous 40 years.

"It's just a galloping track and it's only five-eighths of a mile. It has tight turns. Everything is wrong with it. That was one of the first signs that we were on to something. We thought trainers would watch this thing for years before they put their valuable horses on it. Instead, the winners of several stakes that first meet worked on the training track, particularly when there was bad weather. They'd get their last works in on the training track, where they otherwise would have had to work in the slop on the main track."

Keeneland had planned to take a cautious approach and wait at least one year before making any firm decisions about Polytrack's future. But two things fast-tracked its installation for racing. Trainers loved it and Turfway Park needed it. Turfway, which runs throughout the winter and can be crippled by erratic winter weather in northern Kentucky, needed Polytrack not just because of the safety factor but also because the old dirt track wasn't working. It had so many problems in the winter that Turfway frequently had to cancel cards, which was hurting its business.

With Tartan, Saf-T-Turf, and Equitrack long forgotten, the Polytrack era began at Turfway on a September evening in 2005, when a field of nine competed in a starter-allowance event that ushered in the new synthetic era.

Turfway's Polytrack surface passed every test. Buoyed by Turfway's success, Keeneland pushed ahead and converted its main track to a Polytrack surface before the 2006 fall meet, the first major Thoroughbred meeting run over a synthetic surface in this country.

Racing in the U.S. and Canada would never again be the same.

2

Track Bias in the Synthetic Era

In the seminal book *Winning at the Races*, author William Quirin deducted that the easiest way to win a horse race run on the dirt in this country was to get to the front early and keep going.

"An old racetrack adage states that the advantage in a race lies with the horses that have early speed," Quirin wrote. "It is truer than most horseplayers realize. You might go as far as to say that it is the key to handicapping a race."

Quirin's research, which consisted of more than 15,000 races run at a variety of distances, revealed that 57 percent of all races were won by horses that were first, second, or third at the first-call position in the charts. Conversely, only 8.5 percent of the races he studied were won by horses racing eighth or worse at the first call.

He also found that if you could somehow figure out which horse was going to get to the lead, you could beat the races. The horse that had the lead at the first call won 26.6 percent of the time and produced a healthy $3.38 return on investment (ROI). Of course, figuring out who is going to get the lead is sometimes as difficult as figuring out who is going to win.

Quirin offered conclusive proof of what most handicappers had long suspected: that speed horses had a pronounced, built-in advantage over horses that came from off the pace.

It probably didn't happen overnight, but by 1979, when *Winning at the Races* was published, early speed clearly had become the single most dominant factor in racing in North America, at least when it came to dirt racing. Twenty-six years later, Steve Klein's *The Power of Early Speed* showed an even higher percentage of front-running winners—28.4 percent, with a $3.12 ROI.

Even the breeding industry got in on the act. Top breeders were no longer looking for the type of stout, late-developing horses bred to go the classic distances and hit their peak at ages 4 or 5. Instead, it became fashionable to shoot for precocious horses who would turn out to be good 2-year-olds and who had the type of brilliant early speed that could make them world-beaters at seven furlongs and a mile.

There was no track in the country more speed-favoring than Keeneland. For reasons that remain unclear, some seven or eight years ago, the main track at Keeneland turned into the type of surface that gave front-runners, particularly those staying on the rail, a huge advantage. Conversely, horses coming from off the pace seemingly had no chance.

Never was this more evident than in the 2006 Blue Grass. The modestly talented Sinister Minister, who was coming off a second-place finish in the California Derby, got to the front and drew away to an astounding 12¾-length win. Knowing that his Blue Grass victory was aided by the bias, smart handicappers dismissed him three weeks later in the Kentucky Derby, where he finished 16th. Sinister Minister went 0 for 8 after his Blue Grass win and was eventually retired to stand at stud in Japan.

Winning at the Races was published long before anyone had ever heard of Polytrack, Cushion Track, and the rest. All these years later, synthetic surfaces are threatening to change racing from a speed game to something entirely different. At the first two Keeneland meets run over Polytrack, showing early speed was the surest way to lose. At other tracks using synthetic surfaces, speed horses fared better than they did at Keeneland, but there were still some noticeable shifts away from the good old days when speed dominated.

Turfway Park is not the type of track that receives a lot of attention, so few noticed the way races were unfolding there when its Polytrack surface debuted September 7, 2005. Had they, they might have been prepared for what was to come when Keeneland unveiled its Polytrack at the 2006 fall meet. Within the first few days of Keeneland, a meet that everybody watches, it had become apparent that speed horses were going to have a very difficult time there.

In the first race run over Keeneland's Polytrack, trainer Todd Pletcher had a horse that looked unbeatable on paper, Maizelle, who was sent off at 2–5. She didn't show much speed in her debut, but it had come in a six-furlong race at Saratoga. Going long (a mile and a sixteenth) for the first time, she figured to race close to the pace from post 4.

Maizelle stalked the early pace before taking control midway on the turn while still under wraps. Just as it appeared that she was going to pull clear to an easy win, a 31–1 shot named Lordly started making a bold move from ninth, drew even with the favorite near the top of the stretch, and outbattled her to the wire. Considering what was to come at Keeneland, Maizelle's performance was actually an accomplishment. Few speed horses would hang on as well as she did. Back on conventional dirt when making her next start at Churchill Downs, she romped by 8½ lengths.

The Keeneland 2006 fall meet featured one of the most severe track biases in racing history. At the same racecourse where speed used to dominate, front-runners kept hitting the proverbial brick wall in the stretch. The bias was at its worst in the early part of the meet. No matter how good a horse looked on paper, no matter how easy a lead he got, no matter what the pace was, speed horses just weren't winning.

During the first six days of the meet, only one horse won wire to wire on the Polytrack. That winner, Cat and a Half, was taking a huge class drop from an allowance race at Arlington Park to a $16,000 claimer and was, obviously, simply too good for his rivals. At the same track where speed had been king, front-runners won only one of the first 48 races run at the 2006 fall meet over Polytrack.

In any race, there are three basic kinds of running styles: front-runners, stalkers, and closers. In an attempt to keep things simple, let's consider a wire-to-wire winner as any horse who had the lead at the first call and won the race; a winning stalker as any horse who was second or third at the first call; and a winning closer as any horse who was fourth or worse at the first call. There were 136 races run on the Polytrack at the Keeneland fall meet and the winning running styles were as follows:

	WTW	STALKER	CLOSER
Sprint	10 (12%)	18 (22%)	54 (66%)
Route	3 (6%)	12 (22%)	39 (72%)
Total	13 (10%)	30 (22%)	93 (68%)

For 68 percent of all races to be won by horses that were not among the first three at the first call is an inordinately high number, completely out of whack for what is customary on conventional dirt surfaces. Below are the winning running styles at the 2006 Keeneland spring meet, the last run there on conventional dirt.

	WTW	STALKER	CLOSER
Sprint	31 (44%)	19 (27%)	21 (30%)
Route	13 (43%)	6 (20%)	11 (37%)
Total	44 (44%)	25 (25%)	32 (32%)

With both sets of figures, keep in mind that, nationwide, about 28 percent of all races run on conventional dirt are won wire to wire.

Anyone betting strictly on closers and eliminating speed horses in the early days of Polytrack at Keeneland was probably making a fortune. Eventually, the trend shifted somewhat, but not because the track was necessarily playing any differently. Jockeys began to figure out that going to the front would compromise their chances, so nobody wanted the lead. The result was that the occasional horse would get in front unchallenged, lope along through very slow fractions and, with those advantages, manage to hold on.

That's exactly what happened in the second race on October 27, the next-to-last day of the 2006 fall meet. There wasn't much early speed in the race to begin with and 10 of the 11 jockeys involved, no doubt influenced by the anti-speed bias, wanted no part of the lead. The exception was jockey Brian Hernandez. He got 20–1 shot Ready Ruler to the front and coasted through fractions of 24.83 and 50.10. With such an easy trip, he was able to hold on.

SECOND RACE
Keeneland
OCTOBER 27, 2006

$1\frac{1}{16}$ MILES. (1.41^{3}) CLAIMING. Purse $22,000 FOR THREE YEAR OLDS AND UPWARD. Three Year Olds, 121 lbs.; Older, 124 lbs. Non–winners Of Two Races Over A Mile Since August 27 Allowed 2 lbs. One such race since then Allowed 4 lbs. Claiming Price $16,000 (Races Where Entered For $12,500 Or Less Not Considered).

Value of Race: $22,000 Winner $13,640; second $4,400; third $2,200; fourth $1,100; fifth $660. Mutuel Pool $228,649.00 Exacta Pool $194,367.00 Trifecta Pool $139,394.00 Superfecta Pool $72,448.00

Last Raced	Horse	M/Eqt.	A.	Wt	PP	St	¼	½	¾	Str	Fin	Jockey	Cl'g Pr	Odds $1
11Oct06 ^{5}Lrl^{5}	Ready Ruler	L b	4	120	7	3	$1^{2\frac{1}{2}}$	$1^{2\frac{1}{2}}$	1^{hd}	1^{1}	1^{nk}	Hernandez B J Jr	16000	20.10
18Oct06 ^{6}Kee^{8}	Forth and Forever	L bf	5	115	10	10	8^{hd}	10^{hd}	$8^{\frac{1}{2}}$	2^{1}	$2^{2\frac{1}{2}}$	Lebron V^{5}	16000	6.80
14Sep06 ^{6}TP^{2}	Clever Dude	L	4	120	8	6	$7^{\frac{1}{2}}$	8^{hd}	3^{1}	$3^{1\frac{1}{2}}$	$3^{\frac{1}{2}}$	Leparoux J R	16000	3.40
20Sep06 ^{4}TP^{1}	Awesome Pro	L b	4	120	2	1	$5^{\frac{1}{2}}$	7^{hd}	1^{1}	6^{hd}	4^{hd}	Castanon J L	16000	2.80
26Sep06 ^{8}KD^{6}	Hero Act	L	4	120	3	2	$2^{1\frac{1}{2}}$	$2^{\frac{1}{2}}$	4^{hd}	4^{2}	5^{nk}	Solomon N G	16000	26.20
11Oct06 ^{4}Kee^{9}	Plumwood	L b	4	113	6	7	4^{hd}	4^{hd}	6^{hd}	5^{1}	$6^{1\frac{1}{2}}$	Bourque D L^{7}	16000	46.70
30Sep06 ^{3}TP^{3}	Devil in Excess	L	4	120	5	9	9^{hd}	11	10^{hd}	$8^{1\frac{1}{2}}$	7^{1}	McKee J	16000	6.30
15Sep06 ^{6}TP^{5}	Storm'n J R	L f	8	120	1	4	$6^{\frac{1}{2}}$	5^{hd}	5^{hd}	$7^{1\frac{1}{2}}$	8^{1}	Bejarano R	16000	4.30
1Sep06 ^{1}EIP^{1}	South of Here	L bf	4	122	9	8	10^{hd}	9^{2}	$9^{\frac{1}{2}}$	$9^{2\frac{1}{2}}$	$9^{3\frac{1}{2}}$	Castro E	16000	11.00
30Sep06 ^{1}TP^{6}	Parioli's Delight	L b	4	120	4	5	3^{1}	$3^{\frac{1}{2}}$	2^{1}	10^{hd}	10^{nk}	Martinez W	16000	29.10
30Aug06 ^{6}EIP^{7}	Ravencliff	L bf	3	117	11	11	11	$6^{\frac{1}{2}}$	$7^{\frac{1}{2}}$	11	11	Lanerie C J	16000	27.10

OFF AT 1:47 Start Good For All But RAVENCLIFF. Won driving. Track fast.
TIME :24^{4}, :50, 1:14^{4}, 1:39^{2}, 1:45^{2} (:24.83, :50.10, 1:14.95, 1:39.46, 1:45.46)

$2 Mutuel Prices:				
	7 – READY RULER	42.20	19.20	10.40
	10 – FORTH AND FOREVER		8.00	5.40
	8 – CLEVER DUDE			3.40

$2 EXACTA 7–10 PAID $332.20 $2 TRIFECTA 7–10–8 PAID $2,422.80
$2 SUPERFECTA 7–10–8–2 PAID $14,980.80

Dk. b or br. g, (Mar), by More Than Ready – Reina Victoriosa-Arg, by Interprete-Arg. Trainer Potts Ron G Jr. Bred by Vinery LLC (Ky).

READY RULER gained a clear advantage on the first turn, went along under careful handling, shook off a challenge from PARIOLI'S DELIGHT on the far turn, then was fully extended to last. FORTH AND FOREVER, unhurried to the far turn, commenced a sweeping rally five or six wide approaching the stretch, had aim at the winner but couldn't get up. CLEVER DUDE, never far back and four wide, loomed prominently for the last eighth but couldn't respond. AWESOME PRO, well placed near the inside early, lost position on the far turn, angled five entering the stretch and managed a mild gain. HERO ACT chased the winner three or four wide, moved to the inside leaving the second turn and was empty in the final furlong. PLUMWOOD raced in contention between horses four wide to the stretch and came up empty. DEVIL IN EXCESS settled in behind rivals early, worked his way out eight wide leaving the second turn but lacked a serious late bid. STORM'N J R raced in a striking position near the inside between foes to the stretch and weakened. SOUTH OF HERE never menaced. PARIOLI'S DELIGHT forced the pace from between foes three or four wide for six furlongs and tired. RAVENCLIFF broke awkwardly in the air, trailed briefly early, moved up five wide on the backstretch, continued in contention for six furlongs and weakened gradually.

Owners– 1, Potts Ron G; 2, Chudzik Keith; 3, Lenihan Thomas F Kerr Rick and Dalby Ed; 4, Castanon Jose L; 5, Nemann Fred A; 6, Sano Park LLC; 7, England David P and Wright James; 8, Vaudo Joseph; 9, Montgomery Glenn and Sara; 10, 4-D Stable (Arnold Donna); 11, Davis Joseph E

Trainers– 1, Potts Ron G Jr; 2, Chudzik Keith; 3, Connelly William R; 4, Simpson Rolanda; 5, Nemann Kris; 6, White Vince; 7, England David P; 8, Sims Phillip A; 9, Montgomery Gary W; 10, Lopresti Charles; 11, Crescini Joseph D

Forth and Forever was claimed by Musselman Thomas and Foley, Vickie L; trainer, Foley Vickie L,
Clever Dude was claimed by Goldsmith Gus; trainer, Talley Jeff,
Awesome Pro was claimed by Smoke and Mirrors Racing LLC; trainer, Vance David R,
Hero Act was claimed by Johnson Kyle B; trainer, Schuh Tim,
Devil in Excess was claimed by Calabrese Frank C; trainer, Catalano Wayne M.
Scratched– Irish Bulldog (09Oct06 ^{9}Mnr^{3})

$2 Daily Double (1–7) Paid $1,176.60; Daily Double Pool $82,912.

Playing Keeneland can, at times, be frustrating. While you usually don't want to play front-runners, you can also wind up using closers who get caught behind ridiculously slow paces, which puts them at a disadvantage. It's a scenario that can have you praying for more grass races.

Still, as long as the track remains biased in favor of closers, there will be opportunities to cash in. One of them came in the first race on April 11, 2007. As the betting public is wont to do, it pounded a Todd Pletcher horse, Sarah Supreme, making her the even-money favorite. But she had two huge strikes against her: She looked like the obvious candidate to take the early lead and she appeared to be better on turf, meaning there were no guarantees she would run to the best of her abilities on the Polytrack.

To me, Cambridge Belle looked like a stickout. She had the best dirt or Polytrack Beyer Speed Figures of any horse in the field and she was sure to come from off the pace.

1 **Keeneland** Ⓕ**Md Sp Wt 50k** — 1 1/16 MILES

1 1/16 MILES (1:41³) **MAIDEN SPECIAL WEIGHT. Purse $50,000 (include $6,000 KTDF – KY TB Devt Fund)**
For Maidens, Fillies And Mares Four Years Old And Upward. Weight, 122 lbs.

Coupled – Cambridge Belle and Succeed

Cambridge Belle
Own: G Watts Humphrey Jr
Green, White Diamonds, White Stripes On
BEJARANO R (7 2 1 0 .29) 2007: (459 67 .15)
Dk. b or br f. 4 (Feb) FTSAUG04 $200,000
Sire: Dixie Union (Dixieland Band) $50,000
Dam: Brittan Lee (Forty Niner)
Br: William Diamant (Ont-C)
Tr: Oliver Victoria(—) 2007:(15 0 .00)
L 122

Life	5	M	1	0	$12,740	74	D.Fst	1	0	0	0	$360 2
2007	1	M	0	0	$380	71	Wet(378)	0	0	0	0	$0 –
2006	4	M	1	0	$12,360	74	Synth	2	0	1	0	$10,250 74
Kee	1	0	1	0	$8,500	74	Turf(219)	2	0	0	0	$2,130 71
							Dst(347)	2	0	1	0	$10,250 74

1Mar07-3GP	fm	1⅛ Ⓣ	:484 1:123 1:354 1:472	ⒻMd Sp Wt 38k	71	2	52½	54	53	43	54	Bejarano R	L123 f	4.00e	82- 15	Greenery1231¾ Treasure Chest123hd Bobbin1232	Lacked a rally	8
11Nov06-1WO	fst	1 1/16 ◈	:242 :491 1:142 1:47	3↑ⒻMd Sp Wt 66k	60	7	55	55	32	513	514½	McAleney J S	L116 f	*1.50	- -	*Lien On Me*11610¼ *Go Marching Thru*1163 *Val Gardena*114nk	4w,evened out	7
15Oct06-3Kee	fst	1 1/16 ◈	:241 :482 1:131 1:433	3↑ⒻMd Sp Wt 47k	74	7	73¼	64¾	65	43	2hd	Bejarano R	L118 f	5.60	- -	Divine Rahy118hd Cambridge Belle118nk *Quaderna*1182	5w bid,going well	11
21Sep06-6Mth	fm	1 1/16 Ⓣ	:224 :464 1:111 1:412	+3↑ⒻMd Sp Wt 35k	62	8	73¼	87¼	63	54	43½	Garcia Alan	L118 f	14.60	89- 05	ForvrGrtfl118hd Yoknowshsrght118no InSconds1183¼	Passed tiring rivals	8
6Aug06-2Mth	fst	6f	:22 :452 :581 1:11	3↑ⒻMd Sp Wt 36k	2	3	9	95¾	1010	109½	1026¾	Garcia Alan	L118 f	12.00	58- 09	Strelladar1187½ Eleven Eleven118no Vonnegut1182¾	No speed	10

WORKS: Apr6 Kee ◈4f fst :49 B *52/68* Mar30 Pay 4f fst :504 B *16/26* Feb26 Pay 4f fst :502 B *9/26* Feb19 Pay 4f fst :51 B *6/14* Feb13 Pay 4f fst :502 B *6/14* Jan31 Pay 4f fst :52 B *13/17*
TRAINER: 2Off45-180(16 .12 $1.56) Synth(9 .11 $2.31) Turf/Synth(3 .33 $6.93) 31-60Days(30 .10 $2.83) Routes(91 .13 $2.68) MdnSpWt(29 .14 $3.48) J/T 2006-07 KEE(11 .27 $3.55) J/T 2006-07(23 .22 $3.68)

Succeed
Own: G Watts Humphrey Jr and St George Far
Navy, Red Cross, Navy Cap
BRIDGMOHAN S X (3 0 0 0 .00) 2007: (197 23 .12)
Ch. f. 4 (Mar)
Sire: Coronado's Quest (Forty Niner)
Dam: Policy Setter (Deputy Minister)
Br: G Watts Humphrey Jr & Louise I Humphrey (Ky)
Tr: Oliver Victoria(—) 2007:(15 0 .00)
L 122

Life	3	M	2	0	$21,120	72	D.Fst	1	0	1	0	$9,600 69
2007	1	M	0	0	$1,520	68	Wet(384)	0	0	0	0	$0 –
2006	2	M	2	0	$19,600	72	Synth	1	0	1	0	$10,000 72
Kee	1	0	1	0	$10,000	72	Turf(290)	1	0	0	0	$1,520 68
							Dst(373)	0	0	0	0	$0 –

8Feb07-9GP	fm	1 Ⓣ	:232 :471 1:111 1:35	ⒻMd Sp Wt 38k	68	3	52½	63¼	52¾	63	43½	Bejarano R	L123 f	4.90	78- 19	Gone Overboard123nk Inavision1231¾ War Charm1231½	No late response	12
22Nov06-3CD	fst	7f	:223 :46 1:111 1:233	3↑ⒻMd Sp Wt 48k	69	7	5	42½	33	22	24¼	Bejarano R	L122 f	2.10	80- 14	StorminMon1224¼ Succed1223 RunningQuitly1221¾	Bmp start,2ndbest,4w	12
28Oct06-5Kee	fst	7f ◈	:222 :45 1:10 1:23	3↑ⒻMd Sp Wt 50k	72	6	10	96¼	75½	21½	2hd	Bejarano R	L118 f	*3.00	- -	MrgysForest118hd Succeed1181½ SummerShowr1181¼	6w bid,gaining late	12

WORKS: Apr6 Kee ◈4f fst :483 B *36/68* Mar17 Pay 4f fst :50 B *4/29* Mar11 Pay 4f fst :51 B *2/12* Mar6 Pay 4f fst :513 B *10/14* Feb4 Pay 4f fst :501 B *3/8* Jan29 Pay 4f fst :51 B *12/21*
TRAINER: 61-180Days(18 .11 $0.71) Synth(9 .11 $2.31) Turf/Synth(3 .33 $6.93) Routes(91 .13 $2.68) MdnSpWt(29 .14 $3.48) J/T 2006-07 KEE(3 .00 $0.00) J/T 2006-07(7 .00 $0.00)

Moneypenny
Own: Glencrest Farm LLC
Yellow, Green Hoops, Green Cap
QUINONEZ A (7 0 0 0 .00) 2007: (437 75 .17)
Ch. f. 4 (Mar) KEEAPR05 $180,000
Sire: Monarchos (Maria's Mon) $7,500
Dam: My White Corvette (Tarr Road)
Br: Fletcher Gray Carolyn Gray & John Youngblood (Ky)
Tr: Arnold George R II(—) 2007:(44 6 .14)
L 117⁵

Life	7	M	3	1	$26,250	69	D.Fst	4	0	2	1	$19,550 61
2006	7	M	3	1	$26,250	69	Wet(382)	0	0	0	0	$0 –
2005	0	M	0	0	$0	–	Synth	0	0	0	0	$0 –
Kee	0	0	0	0	$0	–	Turf(296)	3	0	1	0	$6,700 69
							Dst(348)	3	0	2	1	$17,400 61

Previously trained by Pletcher Todd A 2006(as of 9/13): (866 233 166 99 0.27)

13Sep06-5Del	yl	1 1/16 Ⓣ	:261 :531 1:18 1:494	3↑ⒻMd 40000(40-35)	50	8	62¾	52½	74½	96¾	85¾	Dominguez R A	L120	*.70	47- 47	City Glitter120¾ Rookery120nk Nautical Agent120no	Failed to menace	9
17Aug06-6Sar	fm	1⅛ Ⓣ	:484 1:131 1:371 1:493	3↑ⒻMd 40000(45-40)	68	7	55	41½	4¾	36	23¼	Velazquez J R	L118	3.00	80- 17	Hey Gorgeous1203¼ Moneypenny118½ Litethenight1201¼	Rallied for place	8
1Jly06-3Del	fst	1 1/16 ⊗	:242 :49 1:142 1:48	3↑ⒻMd 40000(40-35)	54	5	63	64½	41½	23½	21	Carmouche K	L118	*2.00	72- 17	StreetKid1181 Moneypenny1181½ HevnlyCrtion1086	Angled o 4w, gaining	10
29Apr06-4Aqu	fm	1 1/16 Ⓣ	:241 :504 1:153 1:452	3↑ⒻMd Sp Wt 44k	69	3	73¾	71¾	53½	52¼	43½	Santos J A	L118 b	5.90	76- 15	Hostess118nk *Moya*1181¾ Marias Locket1171½	Between foes, rallied	10
26Mar06-2Aqu	fst	170 ⊡	:232 :49 1:143 1:441	ⒻMd Sp Wt 44k	56	8	54	41	2hd	3½	32	Santos J A	L120 b	2.40	77- 15	A Bit of Pressure1201½ Hi Lili120¾ Moneypenny1204¼	3 wide move, faded	9
26Feb06-3Aqu	fst	170 ⊡	:233 :474 1:14 1:454	ⒻMd Sp Wt 44k	61	6	55½	54½	79	69½	24¼	Santos J A	L120	2.80e	67- 27	Red Damask1204¼ Moneypenny120¾ Berkshire Cat120½	Rallied inside	7
22Jan06-2Aqu	fst	6f ⊡	:224 :471 :594 1:132	ⒻMd Sp Wt 43k	57	8	4	66½	57½	58½	44½	Morales P5	L114	2.90e	68- 21	*Ring True*119hd Ok to Pay1192¾ Southfield1191½	3 wide, mild rally	8

WORKS: Apr7 Kee ◈5f fst 1:014 B *26/39* Apr1 Kee ◈5f fst 1:03 B *22/24* Mar17 Kee ◈5f fst 1:004 B *7/17* Mar10 Kee ◈5f fst 1:012 B *4/8* Feb28 Kee ◈5f fst 1:02 B *5/11* Feb19 Kee ◈4f fst :49 B *2/8*
TRAINER: 1stW/Tm(7 .14 $0.89) +180Days(11 .00 $0.00) Synth(54 .15 $1.49) Turf/Synth(16 .06 $0.58) Routes(153 .16 $1.69) MdnSpWt(94 .20 $2.14) J/T 2006-07(5 .00 $0.00)

Sarah Supreme
Own: Zayat Stables LLC
Turquoise, Gold Ball Sash, Gold 'Z'
VELASQUEZ C (5 0 1 0 .00) 2007: (494 76 .15)
Ch. f. 4 (Apr) KEESEP04 $10,000
Sire: Golden Missile (A.P. Indy) $10,000
Dam: Societe Royale*GB (Milford*GB)
Br: Kilboy Estate (Ky)
Tr: Mott William I(2 1 0 0 .50) 2007:(163 32 .20)
L 122

Life	2	M	1	1	$12,160	81	D.Fst	1	0	0	1	$4,180 56
2007	2	M	1	1	$12,160	81	Wet(255)	0	0	0	0	$0 –
2006	0	M	0	0	$0	–	Synth	0	0	0	0	$0 –
Kee	0	0	0	0	$0	–	Turf(187)	1	0	1	0	$7,980 81
							Dst(261)	0	0	0	0	$0 –

18Mar07-5GP	fm	1 1/16 Ⓣ	:224 :47 1:111 1:411	Md Sp Wt 38k	81	1	21	52	42	32	2nk	Velasquez C	L119	5.00	84- 21	TrickyCusewy124nk SrhSuprem119nk ThCubnHwk124½	Bumped hard late	8
24Jan07-1GP	fst	7f	:223 :451 1:11 1:234	ⒻMd Sp Wt 38k	56	7	2	2hd	3nk	33	310	Velasquez C	L123	12.20	76- 11	WestSideDancer1235¾ Pension1234¼ SarhSupreme123¾	Vied 3 wide, tired	7

WORKS: Apr7 Kee ◈5f fst :593 B *4/39* Mar30 Pay 4f fst :523 B *24/26* Mar12 Pay 4f fst :504 B *13/26* Mar5 Pay 4f fst :501 B *6/23* Feb26 Pay 4f fst :504 B *13/26* Feb20 Pay 4f fst :50 B *2/19*
TRAINER: 2Off45-180(112 .19 $1.29) Synth(18 .06 $0.39) Turf/Synth(6 .00 $0.00) Routes(613 .18 $1.47) MdnSpWt(296 .16 $1.43) J/T 2006-07 KEE(6 .00 $0.00) J/T 2006-07(274 .19 $1.82)

Le Peaks
Own: Dana Powell
Yellow, Blue Belt, Blue Sleeves, Yellow
ALBARADO R J (6 0 3 0 .00) 2007: (355 85 .24)

Dk. b or br m. 5 (Apr) KEEJAN03 $8,500
Sire: Peaks and Valleys (Mt. Livermore) $8,000
Dam: Flying Clear (Cryptoclearance)
Br: Ruth Fitzgerald (Ky)
Tr: Moore John(—) (—)

L 122

Life	10	M	3	3	$23,535	71	D.Fst	4	0	1	0	$8,000	53
2007	5	M	2	3	$14,325	71	Wet(337)	1	0	0	0	$1,210	42
2006	5	M	1	0	$9,210	53	Synth	5	0	2	3	$14,325	71
							Turf(206)	0	0	0	0	$0	–
Kee	0	0	0	0	$0	–	Dst(348)	1	0	0	0	$1,500	41

Previously trained by Lake James 2006: (49 3 5 4 0.06)
23Mar07–7TP fst 1 ◈ :24 :473 1:122 1:384 3↑ⒻMd Sp Wt 24k 67 6 56½ 47½ 35½ 22½ 22½ ♦Prescott R L124 fb 8.20 81–17 Philips Pride124²½ DH Miss Trinidad124 DH Le Peaks124¹ 3 wide run, hung 7
9Mar07–7TP fst 1 ◈ :25 :492 1:141 1:383 3↑ⒻMd Sp Wt 25k 56 2 31½ 31 2½ 33 38¾ Prescott R L124 fb 3.20 77–19 Dezba117¹ **Biblical Point**124⁷½ Le Peaks124³¾ Inside trip 6
23Feb07–8TP fst 1 ◈ :243 :484 1:143 1:402 3↑ⒻMd Sp Wt 17k 65 1 74½ 85½ 52½ 38 39 Prescott R L124 fb 6.20 67–29 Gospel Singer124⁸¾ **Biblical Point**124nk Le Peaks124⁴¾ Evenly drive 8
9Feb07–10TP fst 1 ◈ :243 :484 1:144 1:41 3↑ⒻMd Sp Wt 21k 71 5 86½ 44½ 42½ 22 2¾ Prescott R L124 fb 13.40 72–31 Mia Bella124¾ Le Peaks124⁴½ Number One Girl124²¾ Mild late bid 8
7Jan07–5TP fst 1 ◈ :253 :50 1:144 1:403 4↑ⒻMd 25000(30-20) 52 6 65½ 52½ 5¾ 31½ 3¾ Quinonez A5 L117 11.00 74–16 MinnieMillie124hd BeckyBeckyBecky124¾ LePks117²½ 5 wide run, gamely 6
26Dec06–4Mnr my 1⅛ :492 1:161 1:443 1:583 3↑ⒻMd Sp Wt 24k 42 8 611 67 43 46 414½ Pereira O M L121 f 18.00 23–50 RedytoGos121⁶ FondRondTwo118⁶¼ SoftHit121²¼ Mild move, leveled off 8
Previously trained by Craddock Kari 2006(as of 11/21): (97 11 13 13 0.11)
21Nov06–1RP fst 170 :233 :464 1:113 1:411 ⒻMd Sp Wt 25k 41 7 73½ 611 415 412 423 Murphy B G L121 5.40 76–10 Molly's Pride117⁹ Miss McFleet117⁴¾ America's Quest117⁹½ No factor 8
6Nov06–5RP fst 6f :22 :454 :584 1:122 ⒻMd Sp Wt 25k 43 10 5 78 811 76½ 67 Murphy B G L123 5.70 75–17 SkylrsRnbow119hd MdowlkMn123½ WhplshWrnng119¹¼ Wide, no menace 10
2Oct06–1RP fst 7f :224 :454 1:112 1:244 ⒻMd Sp Wt 25k 53 1 4 52½ 43½ 41½ 24¾ Murphy B G L123 2.40 83–08 IndinHeiress119⁴¾ LePeks123hd AmericsQuest119no Rail,rallied for place 8
15Sep06–7RP fst 6f :22 :45 :572 1:10 ⒻMd Sp Wt 25k 47 1 9 93¾ 96¾ 79½ 415¾ Murphy B G L123 4.00 78–11 NtivDlits119⁶½ WdnsdysOut119½ WhiplshWrnng119⁸¾ Inside, imp position 11

Artistic Escape
Own: Bruce Lunsford and William I Mott
Black, Hot Pink Sash, Hot Pink Stripes
ROSARIO H L JR (1 0 0 0 .00) 2007: (156 16 .10)

Dk. b or br f. 4 (Jan) FTSAUG04 $400,000
Sire: Kris S. (Roberto) $150,000
Dam: Essence of Success (Deputy Minister)
Br: WinStar Farm LLC (Ky)
Tr: Mott William I(2 1 0 0 .50) 2007:(163 32 .20)

L 122

Life	2	M	0	0	$1,900	69	D.Fst	0	0	0	0	$0	–
2007	2	M	0	0	$1,900	69	Wet(401)	0	0	0	0	$0	–
2006	0	M	0	0	$0	–	Synth	0	0	0	0	$0	–
							Turf(352)	2	0	0	0	$1,900	69
Kee	0	0	0	0	$0	–	Dst(382)	0	0	0	0	$0	–

1Mar07–3GP fm 1⅛ Ⓣ :484 1:123 1:354 1:472 ⒻMd Sp Wt 38k 62 5 2½ 21 2½ 53½ 78¼ Velasquez C L123 3.70 78–15 Greenery123¹¾ Treasure Chest123hd Bobbin123² Prompted, tired 8
18Jan07–6GP fm 1 1/16 Ⓣ :233 :474 1:121 1:413 ⒻMd Sp Wt 38k 69 1 65½ 66 54½ 44 44¾ Velasquez C L123 12.70 77–19 St. Hildegard123² *Greenery*123nk Bobbin123²½ No late response 12
WORKS: Apr7 Kee ◈4f fst :483 B *36/72* Mar28 Pay 4f fst :52 B *10/13* Mar20 Pay 4f fst :50 B *3/17* Mar12 Pay 4f fst :513 B *17/26* Feb22 Pay 4f fst :51 B *8/22* Feb15 Pay 4f fst :492 B *2/30*
TRAINER: Synth(18 .06 $0.39) Turf/Synth(6 .00 $0.00) 31-60Days(271 .18 $1.76) Routes(613 .18 $1.47) MdnSpWt(296 .16 $1.43)

Biblical Point
Own: Tracy Farmer
Black, White Diamond Frame, White Band
LEPAROUX J R (8 2 2 0 .25) 2007: (366 83 .23)

Ch. f. 4 (Apr) KEENOV03 $125,000
Sire: Point Given (Thunder Gulch) $30,000
Dam: Bibical Sense (Blushing Groom*Fr)
Br: Barry Stein Stephen A DiMauro & The Thoroughbred Cor (Ky)
Tr: McKeever Andrew(1 0 0 0 .00) 2007:(10 1 .10)

L 122

Life	8	M	4	2	$29,173	73	D.Fst	0	0	0	0	$0	–
2007	3	M	3	0	$13,860	69	Wet(425)	0	0	0	0	$0	–
2006	5	M	1	2	$15,313	73	Synth	5	0	4	0	$17,985	69
							Turf(299)	3	0	0	2	$11,188	73
Kee	0	0	0	0	$0	–	Dst(393)	1	0	1	0	$4,020	69

9Mar07–7TP fst 1 ◈ :25 :492 1:141 1:383 3↑ⒻMd Sp Wt 25k 69 6 52 42 3½ 2½ 21 Mojica O L124 b 1.90 84–19 Dezba117¹ Biblical Point124⁷½ **Le Peaks**124³¾ 4 wide bid, 2nd best 6
23Feb07–8TP fst 1 ◈ :243 :484 1:143 1:402 3↑ⒻMd Sp Wt 17k 65 2 41¾ 52¾ 41½ 24 28¾ Mojica O L124 b 2.80 67–29 Gospel Singer124⁸¾ Biblical Point124nk **Le Peaks**124⁴¾ Lacked closing bid 8
27Jan07–7TP fst 1 ◈ :233 :472 1:132 1:392 4↑ⒻMd Sp Wt 15k 58 7 57 47½ 42½ 42¾ 25½ Mojica O L124 b 2.30 75–22 GorgeousTrist124⁵½ BiblclPoint124hd BckyBckyBcky124¹½ 3 wide, no bid 11
28Dec06–10TP fst 1 1/16 ◈ :24 :48 1:123 1:444 3↑ⒻMd Sp Wt 20k 69 8 85¾ 86½ 42½ 11½ 2no Mojica O L123 b 5.20 98–10 *Rashaund*124no Biblical Point123½ **Neon Lipstick**123³ In tight early 12
24Nov06–7CD fm 1⅜ Ⓣ :503 1:17 1:431 2:21 3↑ⒻMd Sp Wt 48k 60 5 51¼ 32 3½ 21 55¾ Blanc B L121 b 5.10 59–27 BrdStsSl121½ MyOwnStory121hd StrsIndySks121²¾ Bmp start,bid,weaken 11
29Jun06–6CD gd 1 Ⓣ :242 :484 1:141 1:383 3↑ⒻMd Sp Wt 50k 73 9 64½ 75½ 86¼ 53½ 31¾ Jacinto J L117 b 4.50 74–19 BnkinOnCndy117nk MinnhhChc124¹½ BblclPont117nk Carried out 1st turn 10
24May06–9CD fm 1⅛ Ⓣ :474 1:131 1:38 1:50 3↑ⒻMd Sp Wt 50k 62 3 31 32 31½ 41¾ 33 Jacinto J L117 56.80 80–08 Glorious Girl124¹¼ *Royal Dazzle*117¹¾ Biblical Point117²¾ Rail,no final gain 10
11Mar06–7TP fst 5½f ◈ :223 :46 :582 1:043 ⒻMd Sp Wt 21k 18 8 5 44 65¾ 713 720¼ Teator P A L122 51.20 80–07 Brilliant Star122⁵¼ Nightmare122½ Chacana122⁵½ 4 path turn 8
WORKS: Apr4 Kee ◈5f fst 1:022 B *15/20* Feb10 Kee ◈3f fst :382 B *7/7* Jan19 Kee ◈4f fst :51 B *17/18* Jan12 Kee ◈4f fst :484 B *10/21*
TRAINER: Synth(42 .12 $1.24) 31-60Days(20 .10 $0.91) Routes(42 .05 $0.37) MdnSpWt(23 .04 $0.24)

Neon Lipstick
Own: Charles Zeidler III
Blue, Yellow Flying 'Z', Yellow Sleeves
MENA M (2 0 0 0 .00) 2007: (369 70 .19)

Dk. b or br f. 4 (Jan) KEESEP04 $12,000
Sire: Royal Anthem (Theatrical*Ire)
Dam: Classy Ensign (Polish Navy)
Br: Tony Holmes (Ky)
Tr: Harrington Glen(—) 2007:(1 0 .00)

Blinkers OFF

L 122

Life	8	M	0	3	$13,985	71	D.Fst	0	0	0	0	$0	–
2007	1	M	0	0	$1,005	55	Wet(275)	0	0	0	0	$0	–
2006	7	M	0	3	$12,980	71	Synth	3	0	0	1	$3,015	68
							Turf(307)	5	0	0	2	$10,970	71
Kee	1	0	0	0	$0	62	Dst(319)	2	0	0	1	$2,010	68

27Jan07–7TP fst 1 ◈ :233 :472 1:132 1:392 4↑ⒻMd Sp Wt 15k 55 1 33 33½ 2hd 32½ 47 Sarvis D A L124 b 5.90 74–22 GorgousTrist124⁵½ **BblclPont**124hd BckyBckyBcky124¹½ Bid, tired stretch 11
28Dec06–10TP fst 1 1/16 ◈ :24 :48 1:123 1:444 3↑ⒻMd Sp Wt 20k 68 10 41½ 21½ 21 32 3½ Sarvis D A L123 b 28.10 97–10 *Rashaund*124no **Biblical Point**123½ Neon Lipstick123³ 4 path 2nd turn 12
12Nov06–6CD fm 1 1/16 Ⓣ :233 :48 1:134 1:454 3↑ⒻMd Sp Wt 42k 19 3 52¾ 44½ 87 1120 1126¼ Blanc B L121 7.60 51–23 Quaderna121⁴ Royal Rosanna121¹¾ DH Rashaund124 Near inside,tired 12
15Oct06–3Kee fst 1 1/16 ◈ :241 :482 1:131 1:433 3↑ⒻMd Sp Wt 47k 62 9 105 109½ 75¼ 66½ 67 Blanc B L118 23.50 – – Divine Rahy118hd **Cambridge Belle**118nk *Quaderna*118² 5w trip,empty 11
Previously trained by Wiggins Lon 2006(as of 8/31): (60 2 9 14 0.03)
31Aug06–6AP sf *1 1/16 Ⓣ :232 :483 1:142 1:474 3↑ⒻMd Sp Wt 27k 59 4 69½ 611 77¾ 45 38 Martin E M Jr L121 3.60 63–27 GrndmsGirl121hd MrsStephens121⁸ NonLipstick121½ Angled out, late bid 7
10Aug06–5AP fm *1 Ⓣ :242 :49 1:141 1:373 3↑ⒻMd Sp Wt 30k 60 3 54 55 53 42½ 45 Martin E M Jr L121 4.70 86–09 *Bridge Game*121¹¾ Y Seven121¹¼ Quaderna121² Off rail, no rally 9
Previously trained by Harrington Glen 2006(as of 7/14): (16 0 1 4 0.00)
14Jly06–7CD yl 1 1/16 Ⓣ :251 :501 1:153 1:461 3↑ⒻMd Sp Wt 48k 66 9 42½ 31½ 31 41¼ 32¼ Blanc B L118 6.50 73–23 Rose'sJewel118¹½ Quaderna118¾ NeonLipstick118no Track,4w,no late gain 10
29Jun06–6CD gd 1 Ⓣ :242 :484 1:141 1:383 3↑ⒻMd Sp Wt 50k 71 7 87 98¼ 108¾ 75¾ 52½ Blanc B L117 16.00 73–19 BnknOnCndy117nk MnnhhChc124¹½ **BblclPont**117nk Improved position,9w 10
WORKS: Mar30 Sky 4f fst :522 B *1/3*
TRAINER: 61-180Days(2 .50 $5.00) Synth(10 .00 $0.00) BlinkOff(1 .00 $0.00) Routes(23 .04 $1.72) MdnSpWt(6 .00 $0.00)

Shine Like the Sun
Own: Sam–Son Farms
Red, Gold Sleeves, Red Cap
GRAHAM J (6 0 0 0 .00) 2007: (414 45 .11)

Dk. b or br f. 4 (Feb)
Sire: Seeking the Gold (Mr. Prospector) $125,000
Dam: Radiant Ring (Halo)
Br: Sam–Son Farm (Ont–C)
Tr: Frostad Mark(—) 2007:(35 5 .14)

L 122

Life	7	M	1	1	$23,176	80	D.Fst	2	0	0	0	$361	58
2007	2	M	1	1	$15,790	80	Wet(391)	1	0	0	0	$6,312	47
2006	4	M	0	0	$1,074	74	Synth	1	0	0	0	$357	45
							Turf(277)	3	0	1	1	$16,146	80
Kee	1	0	0	0	$0	58	Dst(363)	3	0	0	0	$7,030	47

18Mar07–5FG fm *1 Ⓣ :241 :49 1:15 1:393 ⒻMd Sp Wt 58k 80 12 44 43½ 31½ 21½ 21¼ Melancon G L121 3.60e 78–21 PrkAtDrk116¹¼ ShineLikthSun121³¼ CloptrsNdl121²½ Could not overtake 12
11Jan07–6FG fm *7½f Ⓣ :253 :493 1:162 1:343 ⒻMd Sp Wt 40k 62 7 7 31 42½ 31½ 32¼ Wilson E L123 3.40 75–21 Belwood123hd Wishrt123²¼ ShineLiketheSun123½ Loomd 4w,no final kick 9
16Sep06–6WO fst 1 1/16 ◈ :233 :472 1:114 1:452 3↑ⒻMd Sp Wt 67k 45 8 75 65¼ 79 718 721¼ Cruise G L116 26.15 – – TheNigrQueen116⁵¼ Wishforemore116¾ CorlBch118²¼ 3-wide,lacked rally 8
13Aug06–10WO fm 1⅛ Ⓣ :47 1:111 1:351 1:481 3↑ⒻMd Sp Wt 67k 74 4 42 31½ 42 57 65¾ Cruise G L116 24.85 85–07 FeistyWoman116½ FinlMelody116nk StormRoyle116²¾ Stalked rail,all out 9
27May06–3WO fst 1 1/16 :232 :464 1:121 1:48 3↑ⒻMd Sp Wt 66k 25 1 42 52¾ 58¼ 613 621½ Landry R C L117 2.90 48–23 *Rosa Rose*116¹¼ Arden Belle117¹½ Brahms Affair111⁵¾ Faded rail far turn 6
8Apr06–6Kee fst 1⅛ :484 1:141 1:394 1:531 ⒻMd Sp Wt 44k 58 6 75 73¼ 53½ 79½ 713½ Graham J L120 12.30e 53–19 Feathered Diamond120²½ Peig Sayers120¹¾ Sugar Shake120³½ No threat 9
22Oct05–8WO gds 1 1/16 :231 :474 1:141 1:50 ⒻⓇPrncssEliz251k 47 6 98¾ 910 811 514 515½ Cruise G 119 25.75 45–34 Sugar Swirl119¹¼ *Kimchi*119⁶½ Classical Miss119⁵¾ Gained, no menace 9
WORKS: Mar31 Kee ◈5f fst 1:003 B *11/45* Mar12 FG 5f fst 1:022 B *7/16* Mar5 FG 5f fst 1:03 B *22/32* Feb19 FG 6f fst 1:15 B *3/7* Feb5 FG 5f fst 1:011 B *4/54* Jan28 FG 5f gd 1:05 B *22/28*
TRAINER: 2Off45-180(27 .11 $0.78) Synth(69 .20 $1.69) Turf/Synth(23 .22 $2.20) Routes(137 .14 $1.33) MdnSpWt(85 .15 $1.57)
J/T 2006-07 KEE(5 .20 $1.04) J/T 2006-07(23 .13 $1.04)

More to Prove
Own: Roger L Attfield and William Werner
Black, White 'Wa', Black And White
PRADO E S (6 3 1 1 .50) 2007: (371 72 .19)

B. f. 4 (Apr) ONTSEP04 $31,076
Sire: With Approval (Caro*Ire)
Dam: Alyette (Alydeed)
Br: Kinghaven Farms Limited (Ont–C)
Tr: Attfield Roger L(2 0 0 0 .00) 2007:(17 2 .12)

L 122

Life	2	M	0	0	$760	67	D.Fst	1	0	0	0	$380	–
2007	2	M	0	0	$760	67	Wet(335)	0	0	0	0	$0	–
2006	0	M	0	0	$0	–	Synth	0	0	0	0	$0	–
							Turf(290)	1	0	0	0	$380	67
Kee	0	0	0	0	$0	–	Dst(318)	0	0	0	0	$0	–

21Mar07–3GP fm 1 1/16 Ⓣ :234 :483 1:13 1:413 ⒻMd Sp Wt 38k 67 9 115¾ 116½ 93¾ 86 75¾ Castro E L123 40.30 76–20 Roshani123¹ Judith Basin123¹ Brantley123½ Steadied early 12
24Jan07–1GP fst 7f :223 :451 1:11 1:234 ⒻMd Sp Wt 38k – 6 4 71¾ 710 726 – Castro E L123 5.40 – 11 West Side Dancer123⁵¾ Pension123⁴½ **Sarah Supreme**123¾ Trailed, eased 7
WORKS: Mar31 Pay 5f fst 1:041 B *10/17* ●Mar16 Pay 5f fst 1:031 B *1/14* ●Mar9 Pay 4f fst :49 B *1/18* Feb27 Pay 4f fst :503 B *9/19* ●Feb17 Pay 5f fst 1:03 B *1/5* Feb10 Pay 5f fst 1:05 B *5/5*
TRAINER: 2Off45-180(29 .10 $0.68) Synth(94 .11 $1.49) Turf/Synth(21 .24 $3.55) Routes(154 .15 $2.48) MdnSpWt(82 .16 $1.55)
J/T 2006-07 KEE(4 .25 $0.85) J/T 2006-07(11 .09 $0.31)

At 3–1, Cambridge Belle was an overlay because people were betting on a false favorite in Sarah Supreme. (With Shine Like the Sun's best races having come on the grass, there's no way I would have had the exacta.)

FIRST RACE
Keeneland
APRIL 11, 2007

1$\frac{1}{16}$ MILES. (1.41^{3}) MAIDEN SPECIAL WEIGHT. Purse $50,000 (includes $6,000 KTDF - Kentucky TB Devt Fund) FOR MAIDENS, FILLIES AND MARES FOUR YEARS OLD AND UPWARD. Weight, 122 lbs. (Preference To Horses That Have Not Started For Less Than $30,000). (Rainy. 51.)

Value of Race: $44,900 Winner $27,280; second $8,800; third $5,000; fourth $2,500; fifth $1,320. Mutuel Pool $183,305.00 Exacta Pool $152,462.00 Trifecta Pool $107,221.00 Superfecta Pool $46,397.00

Last Raced	Horse	M/Eqt.	A.	Wt	PP	St	¼	½	¾	Str	Fin	Jockey	Odds $1
1Mar07 ^{3}GP^{5}	Cambridge Belle	L f	4	122	1	2	5½	6$1\frac{1}{2}$	4^{1}	1^{hd}	1¾	Bejarano R	3.00
18Mar07 ^{5}FG^{2}	Shine Like the Sun	L	4	122	8	6	6$1\frac{1}{2}$	5^{hd}	3^{hd}	4^{1}	2^{nk}	Graham J	7.40
1Mar07 ^{3}GP^{7}	Artistic Escape	L	4	122	5	8	8	7½	7^{hd}	6½	3$1\frac{1}{2}$	Rosario H L Jr	17.10
23Mar07 ^{7}TP^{2}	Le Peaks	L bf	5	122	4	7	7$1\frac{1}{2}$	8	8	8	4no	Albarado R J	30.00
9Mar07 ^{7}TP^{2}	Biblical Point	L b	4	122	6	5	4^{hd}	4^{hd}	6$1\frac{1}{2}$	3^{hd}	5½	Leparoux J R	5.20
18Mar07 ^{5}GP^{2}	Sarah Supreme	L	4	122	3	4	1^{hd}	2½	1^{hd}	2^{1}	6^{hd}	Gomez G K	1.00
13Sep06 ^{5}Del^{8}	Moneypenny	L	4	117	2	1	2½	3½	5½	7$2\frac{1}{2}$	7^{nk}	Quinonez A^{5}	15.70
27Jan07 ^{7}TP^{4}	Neon Lipstick	L	4	122	7	3	3$1\frac{1}{2}$	1^{hd}	2$1\frac{1}{2}$	5^{hd}	8	Mena M	25.50

OFF AT 1:15 Start Good. Won driving. Track fast.

TIME :25, :50^{4}, 1:16^{1}, 1:40^{2}, 1:46^{2} (:25.13, :50.86, 1:16.30, 1:40.50, 1:46.48)

$2 Mutuel Prices:

1 – CAMBRIDGE BELLE	8.00	4.60	4.20
8 – SHINE LIKE THE SUN		7.20	5.00
5 – ARTISTIC ESCAPE			8.40

$2 EXACTA 1–8 PAID $60.00 $2 TRIFECTA 1–8–5 PAID $521.80
$2 SUPERFECTA 1–8–5–4 PAID $4,960.40

Dk. b or br. f, (Feb), by Dixie Union – Brittan Lee, by Forty Niner. Trainer Oliver Victoria. Bred by William Diamant (Ont-C).

CAMBRIDGE BELLE, in hand and saving ground from early on, inched forward between foes on the far turn, split horses into the stretch, took over, then was hard ridden to hold sway. SHINE LIKE THE SUN, within striking distance always and following the leaders five wide, was fully extended to earn the place. ARTISTIC ESCAPE broke slowly, was unhurried, raced two or three wide most of the way and offered a mild gain. LE PEAKS settled near the inside early, swung out five wide leaving the second turn and managed a mild gain. BIBLICAL POINT, in a striking position and between foes four wide to the upper stretch, flattened out in the late going. SARAH SUPREME gained a slight edge near the inside while dueling with NEON LIPSTICK, alternated with that one through pedestrian fractions and faltered in the drive. MONEYPENNY raced near the inside from the outset, was never far back, grazed the inner railing in the upper stretch and was steadied. NEON LIPSTICK vied for the lead three or four wide to the head of the stretch and weakened.

Owners– 1, Humphrey G Watts Jr; 2, Sam-Son Farms; 3, Mott W I and Lunsford Bruce; 4, Powell Dana; 5, Farmer Tracy; 6, Zayat Stables LLC; 7, Glencrest Farm LLC; 8, Zeidler Charles III

Trainers– 1, Oliver Victoria; 2, Frostad Mark; 3, Mott William I; 4, Moore John; 5, McKeever Andrew; 6, Mott William I; 7, Arnold George R II; 8, Harrington Glen

Scratched– Succeed (08Feb07 ^{9}GP ^{4}), More to Prove (21Mar07 ^{3}GP ^{7})

The 2007 Keeneland spring meet, the second at that track held over Polytrack, was, for the most part, a case of more of the same. Below is the breakdown of the winning running styles. Because they bear little resemblance to the other races run at Keeneland, the 4½-furlong 2-year-old races, a staple of the spring meet, are not included in the data I've used for Keeneland's spring sessions.

	WTW	STALKER	CLOSER
Sprint	8 (13%)	18 (28%)	38 (59%)
Route	2 (5%)	11 (26%)	30 (70%)
Total	10 (9%)	29 (27%)	68 (64%)

While the figures for the fall and spring meets were nearly identical, a strange thing did happen during the middle of the spring meet. From out of nowhere, the track had a pair of speed-favoring days and then reverted right back to favoring closers. On April 18, several horses that either went to the front or stalked the pace won. The next day, speed fared even better. Of the seven races run that day on the main track, three were won wire to wire and three other winners were second or third at the second call. Go figure.

There is a theory that synthetic tracks become more speed-favoring in colder weather. Perhaps it was not a coincidence that it was just 45 degrees on April 19, the day Keeneland turned speed-favoring.

"The wax changes in cold weather," explains Michael Dickinson, who is the producer of the Tapeta surface. "It tends to be a little more sticky and more solid. In the other extreme, when it gets really hot, wax doesn't melt but it becomes more liquid and less sticky. In the cold weather, the track tightens up and the track is faster. When the wax isn't as sticky, it is a bit looser and a bit slower."

Irwin Driedger, Woodbine's director of racing surfaces, has also found that weather will have an impact on a track, particularly the heat, which can cause the wax to loosen. It's no different from what would happen if someone left a candle out in the blazing sun. The candle wouldn't stay the same. Driedger has not, however, found any correlation as far as the weather creating bias situations.

"When it gets real hot out the wax gets somewhat thinner," he said. "The material becomes a little bit looser. When the sun is down and there is rain, the opposite happens. I haven't seen any evidence that any of this makes the track more or less favorable to speed. The other day, we had rain and the majority of the races were won from off the pace. But I've seen it also go the other way. It's really hard to say. I haven't seen a consistent bias of any sort. But when it's cloudy or it rains it seems like the track is a little bit quicker. The reason is the wax tightens up a bit."

Keeneland's track superintendent, Mike Young, said he has done his best to create a uniform track, but admits he's still learning how to deal with Polytrack.

"The first part of [the spring 2007] meet, it seemed like most of the horses were winning from behind," Young said. "I'm not sure why. It might have been the way the jockeys were riding more than it was the track. Also, we had some awful cool weather during the first part of the meet. It seemed liked that caused the track to get a little stiffer and maybe that had something to do with it."

Keeneland President and Chief Executive Officer Nick Nicholson has still another theory—that jockeys riding at Keeneland have been so influenced by the biases there over the years that they ride Keeneland unlike any other track.

"The first week in October of 2006 when the jockeys came in, they knew it was a new surface," Nicholson said. "Yet, many of the top jockeys had never ridden at Turfway. They never had been on a Polytrack surface. I was surprised that several of them hadn't even worked horses on it. They came in thinking it's the same track, the same place. I think to a degree, they rode horses the way they would at the old Keeneland track. They would rush to the rail. They'd fight like hell going into that first turn. But you can't use your horse up on this track. It was not the old golden-rail Keeneland racetrack. What would happen is that horses who were ridden that way would falter in the stretch and lose.

"In a matter of days, the track got the reputation of being the converse of the old Keeneland," Nicholson continued. "I'm convinced part of it was the way they rode here that first week. Then it dawned on them that it was not the old Keeneland.

"Then they would come in here in April and they had it in their head from the prior October that it was a come-from-behind, grass-type track and they rode exactly the opposite of the way they did in October and everybody took their horses back. A lot of the biases here are caused by external circumstances and self-fulfilling prophesies."

Nicholson admits, however, that the track's management must continue to look at the biased nature of its synthetic surface and find solutions if the problem persists.

"We are going to try to get better and better at statistical gathering," he said. "We want to gather the right statistics the right way. It's very important to us to keep blinkers off, to be objective, analytical, and almost scientific as far as data gathering goes and not be defensive. It would be unreasonable to expect that we could do something this revolutionary and get every single aspect of it exactly right the first time. We need to monitor everything, we need to analyze, and we need to look at all the variables."

Between its spring and fall meets in 2007, it appeared that Keeneland made some progress toward solving its bias problems. The thing about Keeneland, though, is the place never seems to stop throwing you curveballs. Just when everyone had concluded that speed horses were at a huge disadvantage there, the 2007 fall meet turned out to be something entirely different from the two previous Polytrack meets. All of a sudden, speed horses started doing much better. Here are the numbers for that meet:

	WTW	STALKER	CLOSER
Sprint	17 (20%)	27 (31%)	42 (49%)
Route	6 (14%)	3 (7%)	34 (79%)
Total	23 (18%)	30 (23%)	76 (59%)

All we can do for now is to continue to watch the trends at Keeneland, but I would still be hesitant to play any horses that look like they are going to get the early lead.

Turfway Park also had a reputation as a speed-favoring track before Polytrack was installed there. There was many a day at Turfway when an entire card consisted of a parade of front-runners winning race after race.

Here is the breakdown of the winning running styles for the last 200 races run over Turfway's old dirt surface.

	WTW	STALKER	CLOSER
Sprint	45 (41%)	38 (34 %)	28 (25%)
Route	32 (36%)	26 (29%)	31 (35%)
Total	77 (39%)	64 (32%)	59 (29%)

Though Turfway has yet to be as consistently biased toward closers as Keeneland has been, the Polytrack definitely shifted the balance toward late-runners.

Here is the breakdown of winning running styles for the first 200 races run on Turfway's Polytrack:

	WTW	STALKER	CLOSER
Sprint	23 (21%)	35 (32%)	53 (48%)
Route	19 (21%)	19 (21%)	51 (57%)
Total	42 (21%)	54 (27%)	104 (52%)

Before the 2006 fall meet, Turfway management decided to tweak the Polytrack. The change involved removing the top two inches of the surface and replacing it with a different mixture of materials. The idea was to reduce the amount of kickback the track produced.

The old and new surfaces were then mixed together. As far as how the track played, there was hardly any difference. Below is the breakdown of winning running styles for the first 200 races run over the revamped Polytrack surface at Turfway.

	WTW	STALKER	CLOSER
Sprint	25 (24%)	29 (28%)	51 (49%)
Route	16 (17%)	24 (25%)	55 (58%)
Total	41 (20%)	53 (26%)	106 (53%)

Several hundred miles north of Keeneland and Turfway, handicappers in Canada were also dealing with the advent of the Polytrack era in the summer of 2007. The old Woodbine had always seemed like a reasonably fair track. Speed horses won their share of races, but never dominated the way they had over the old Keeneland dirt surface.

Woodbine had opened its Polytrack August 30, 2006, and, just as had happened at Turfway, the new synthetic surface gave frontrunners a bit of a hard time. Interestingly, though, the Woodbine surface was not nearly as biased as Keeneland's Polytrack would turn out to be. Below is the breakdown of winning running styles for the first 200 races run over Polytrack at Woodbine.

	WTW	STALKER	CLOSER
Sprint	32 (23%)	30 (22%)	75 (55%)
Route	12 (19%)	14 (22%)	37 (59%)
Total	44 (22%)	44 (22%)	112 (56%)

However, the Polytrack track at Woodbine was, as usual,

considerably less speed-favoring than the old main track at Woodbine, which was last used on July 3, 2006. For a short time afterward, the Thoroughbreds at Woodbine raced on the harness track while the main track was being converted to Polytrack.

Below is the breakdown of winning running styles for the last 200 races run over the main dirt track at Woodbine.

	WTW	STALKER	CLOSER
Sprint	44 (32%)	44 (32%)	48 (35%)
Route	16 (25%)	23 (36%)	25 (39%)
Total	60 (30%)	67 (34%)	73 (37%)

Dirt-track racing in southern California has been known to be a speed-dominated game. Jockeys traditionally let their mounts break running from the gate and go as fast as they can for as long as they can. Pat Valenzuela perfected that style and it helped make him one of the most successful riders on the circuit. During the last 200 races run on the conventional dirt track at Hollywood, California racing's reputation for being speed crazy didn't necessarily hold up. Speed horses did fine, but not great. Below is the breakdown for those 200 races.

	WTW	STALKER	CLOSER
Sprint	34 (22 %)	54 (35%)	65 (42%)
Route	10 (21%)	16 (34%)	21 (45%)
Total	44 (22%)	70 (35%)	86 (43%)

Hollywood's synthetic surface debuted November 1, 2006. It was built by one of Polytrack's competitors and was christened Cushion Track. Speed didn't do quite as well as it had been doing over the old Hollywood track, but the difference was relatively minor. Below is the breakdown of the winning running styles for the first 200 races run over Cushion Track.

	WTW	STALKER	CLOSER
Sprint	35 (23%)	39 (26%)	75 (50%)
Route	9 (18%)	13 (25%)	29 (57%)
Total	44 (22%)	52 (26%)	104 (52%)

Why was Hollywood's Cushion Track so much kinder to speed than Keeneland's Polytrack? Corey Nakatani, who rode at both tracks, offered an explanation.

"It has a lot to do with how much they water it," Nakatani said. "The synthetic tracks still have a lot of sand. To put it in terms that people can understand, say it's like a beach. When the waves come in, the sand is tight and wet. When they fluff it up, it's dry and it's loose.

"It seems like they keep a little more moisture on Cushion Track than they do at Keeneland. They don't seem to water the track at Keeneland much. Does a front-runner have a better chance at Keeneland than Hollywood? It depends on what they do at Keeneland. They've been experimenting with it and everybody's in a learning process. I think they know how to make it fast and how to make it so speed can carry. There were a couple of days at Keeneland where they ran 6½ furlongs in 1:14. They showed they know how to make it fast and speed-favoring. A happy medium would be best."

Kentucky-based jockey Dean Butler, who rides over Polytracks at Turfway and Keeneland, agrees that the amount of water in the surface will dictate whether or not speed holds up. Perhaps the astute handicapper should be watching whether or not the water trucks are out between races.

"A lot of it depends on how much water they put on it or how much rain we get," Butler said. "The water settles it down and tightens it up. Speed has held a lot better when there's more water on it, but not always. There were a few days when more or less you got to the lead and you hung on."

Dickinson says that water has a cooling effect on a track and that is why synthetic tracks tend to be faster when wet.

Garrett Gomez, another jockey with experience at both Keeneland and Hollywood, had an interesting take on Polytrack, Cushion Track, and the infamous Keeneland closers' bias.

"Cushion Track and Polytrack are different kinds of racetracks with the same purpose," he said. "They're both meant to be very kind to the horses and they're very cushiony. One thing I noticed is that Cushion Track at Hollywood Park has a lot of rubber in it. The Polytrack at Keeneland doesn't. It has a lot more of the wax and the fibers in it, so it's a little more fluffy. Even when it does tighten down, it doesn't seem to hold speed very well.

"Most of us who have ridden on it, we're still trying to figure out why the speed isn't holding. All of a sudden, there'll be one or two days, like there were at Keeneland, where three-quarters of the races are won wire to wire. Then, the opposite will happen. It has us scratching our heads, too. It does feel like it gets a little tighter when it gets cooler, but I don't think speed necessarily does any better on those days."

Gomez agrees that jockeys ride differently at Keeneland. No one, he said, wants to go to the front there.

"Everyone just kind of sits there trying to get someone else to go to the lead," he said. "You wind up waiting and waiting. The horse who winds up making the lead is a horse who doesn't relax as well as some of the other horses. When you start having races where they go a half-mile in 50 and three-quarters in 1:16, you have a situation where the closers wind up right in behind the speed horses. A closer is going to outkick a speed horse any day of the week. You can get to the front in a real slow pace and everyone is chasing you and your horse still collapses. It's mind-boggling. You can ask your horse to quicken and it feels like he's running and they run by you like you're on a dead horse. [The jockeys] can't figure it out."

Here's still another theory, this one from Kentucky-based jockey Bill Troilo, who rides regularly at Keeneland and Turfway.

"What they've done with the Polytracks here is they've taken out the crown of the racetrack, so the racetrack is level all over," he said. "I don't know if that has anything to do with horses in the middle of the track doing well, but when you have a crown you get up on that crown and you're losing all the ground and it's like you're going uphill. With no crown, it's enabled horses to come nine- and 10-wide and win from off the pace. On Polytrack, there's a certain point in the races where things bottle up. If you're stuck on the inside, you might never get out. If you stay outside, you might lose a lot of ground and that will cost you. It's a decision you have to make out there."

Perhaps Cushion Track is simply kinder to speed horses than Polytrack is. Several handicappers started to draw that conclusion after watching front-runners do well over the Cushion Track at Hollywood. When North America's second Cushion Track debuted

September 26, 2007, at the Oak Tree at Santa Anita meet, that theory was put to the test.

In the early going of the Cushion Track era at Santa Anita, it looked as if the track was as fair as a track can be. With 36 horses winning wire to wire in sprints at the Oak Tree meet, it certainly couldn't be said that front-runners were at a disadvantage, at least not in sprints. They were winning at a rate above the traditional 28 percent average on dirt tracks.

In the first race on October 25, 2007, for instance, Wild Diplomat dueled through wicked early fractions of 21.75 and 44.54. Though favored, that should have been enough to slow him down. Instead, he shook off Stormy Woods and drew away to a 3¾-length win. That's not the type of race you are ever going to see on a closer-biased track.

Below is the breakdown on the winning running styles at the 2007 Oak Tree meet. You could make a case that speed was at a disadvantage in routes, but my guess is the figures are skewed because of an insufficient number of races available for data.

	WTW	STALKER	CLOSER
Sprint	36 (27%)	39 (30%)	57 (43%)
Route	5 (9%)	16 (28%)	36 (63%)
Total	41 (22%)	55 (29%)	93 (49%)

Though the Santa Anita Cushion Track may not have had a bias, it was a lot different from the old conventional dirt track. Below is the breakdown for the winning running styles at the 2006 Oak Tree meet. Note the change in the percentage of wire-to-wire winners between Oak Tree 2006 and Oak Tree 2007.

	WTW	STALKER	CLOSER
Sprint	38 (36%)	33 (31%)	34 (32%)
Route	12 (27%)	14 (32%)	18 (41%)
Total	50 (34%)	47 (32%)	52 (35%)

Illinois racing entered the synthetic era when Polytrack debuted at Arlington on May 4, 2007. Once again, the story was pretty much the same as it had been at other synthetic tracks. Speed was not quite as good as it had been over Arlington's old dirt track, but the new Arlington was nowhere near as biased at Keeneland was during the first two Polytrack meets there.

Below is the breakdown of winning running styles for the first 200 races run over Polytrack at Arlington Park.

	WTW	STALKER	CLOSER
Sprint	21 (18%)	25 (20%)	74 (62%)
Route	20 (25%)	18 (23%)	42 (53%)
Total	41 (21%)	43 (22%)	116 (58%)

Below is the breakdown for the winning running styles for the final 200 races run over the conventional dirt surface at Arlington.

	WTW	STALKER	CLOSER
Sprint	35 (27%)	52 (40%)	43 (33%)
Route	23 (33%)	23 (33%)	24 (34%)
Total	58 (29%)	75 (38%)	67 (34%)

After Arlington, it was Del Mar's turn to unveil a synthetic track, in this case Polytrack. Within the first few days of the meet, trainers, in particular Bob Baffert, began to complain about the racing surface. On behalf of one of his most prominent owners, Ahmed Zayat, Baffert pulled several horses out of Del Mar, taking many to Saratoga. According to a report by *Daily Racing Form*'s Steve Andersen, "Baffert, Zayat, and several trainers have said Polytrack is firm in the morning, when coastal fog keeps temperatures mild, but loose and tiring in the afternoon, when the sun beats down on the surface." In addition, Baffert and Zayat felt that many of their horses were at a disadvantage because the Polytrack surface was unkind to speed horses.

Zayat also said, "What distinguishes American racing is speed," adding that Polytrack was "artificially slowing down" brilliant horses. "The way the Thoroughbred runs is so majestic," he said. "Why are we doing this?"

On the subject of whether or not the Del Mar track put speed horses at a disadvantage, Zayat wasn't wrong. The Polytrack at Del Mar had a pronounced anti-speed bias throughout the 2007 meet. Here is the breakdown:

	WTW	STALKER	CLOSER
Sprint	37 (18%)	71 (34%)	98 (48%)
Route	10 (14%)	17 (23%)	47 (64%)
Total	47 (17%)	88 (32%)	145 (52%)

Once again, a synthetic surface turned out to be less kind to front-runners than the conventional dirt track it replaced. Here is the breakdown for the winning running styles on the dirt at the 2006 Del Mar meet.

	WTW	STALKER	CLOSER
Sprint	49 (24%)	67 (33%)	90 (44%)
Route	13 (19%)	26 (39%)	28 (42%)
Total	62 (23 %)	93 (34%)	118 (43%)

Still another synthetic track debuted just a few days after Del Mar closed. A new track, Presque Isle Downs in Erie, Pennsylvania, opened September 1, 2007, marking the first time that Tapeta Footings was used for a race anywhere. Because Presque Isle had never raced before, there was no corresponding data to compare Tapeta racing to normal dirt racing. Nonetheless, Tapeta seemed to be like most synthetic tracks. Speed didn't fare quite as well as it does over conventional dirt tracks. The Presque Isle stats, for the entire 25-day meet, looked like this:

	WTW	STALKER	CLOSER
Sprint	32 (24%)	44 (33%)	56 (42%)
Route	13 (19%)	12 (18%)	43 (63%)
Total	45 (23%)	56 (28%)	99 (50%)

Why are some synthetic tracks more speed-favoring than others? Cushion Track's Philip Bond believes that the way a synthetic track is maintained will determine how fast it is and whether or not it favors closers. He has found that when the track crew uses light equipment on the Cushion Track and does little more than remove the hoof and tire marks from the surface, the track seems to favor closers. When heavier equipment is used and the track is aggressively harrowed it will become more speed-favoring.

Bond regrets that more of this information isn't made available to the betting public.

"It's hard to predict how the track will play unless you know how it was prepared," Bond said. "We'd love to see the bettor be given more information on how the track has been maintained."

While it may be a long time before anyone solves the ins and outs of synthetic tracks and the types of biases they produce, it seems that Cushion Track is a better surface for speed horses than Polytrack. Stay tuned.

It wasn't that hard to predict that, in general, synthetic tracks would turn out to be less speed-favoring than dirt tracks. One of the advantages front-runners have on dirt tracks is that they are the only horses in the race not getting dirt and sand kicked in their faces, which is obviously uncomfortable. The problem becomes even worse on sloppy and muddy tracks when all sorts of wet, messy muck is being thrown in the faces of the closers. That's one of the reasons speed tends to hold up better in the slop than on fast tracks.

Not only do synthetic surfaces eliminate sloppy tracks, but most produce far less kickback than dirt surfaces. For that reason, come-from-behind horses are competing on a more level playing field when it comes to the artificial tracks.

"Gary Stevens once told me that few realize how big a negative impact kickback has on horses," Tapeta inventor Michael Dickinson said. "The stuff thrown back at these horses can be bloody hard and it makes a lot of them spin their wheels. With a synthetic surface, there's virtually no kickback because it is bound together."

And even when there is kickback, it's not the same as being hit by a hard clod of dirt and sand; jockeys say that the synthetic material dissolves on contact instead of stinging.

When Polytrack was first introduced in this country it came with the promise that it would end track biases as we knew them. The irony is that Polytrack created a colossal bias at Keeneland.

What you will see, though, is fast times. Before the first synthetic race was run in this country, it was widely believed that races on the artificial dirt would generally be much slower than races run on the real stuff. That hasn't been the case. In fact, at times, Keeneland's Polytrack surface has been exceptionally fast. During the 2007 spring meet, a 2-year-old named One Hot Wish set a world record when running 4½ furlongs in 48.87. At the same meet, a six-furlong race went in 1:08.30 and a 6½-furlong race in 1:14.41. That's fast, on any surface.

A synthetic surface was also responsible for what was surely the fastest racing surface in history. The 2008 winter-spring meet at Santa Anita was a fiasco. The Cushion Track there wouldn't drain properly and management tried everything it could think of to create a usable racetrack. Even so, the Cushion Track resulted in 11 cancelations.

For a period of about three weeks, the various experiments created a track that seemed like and played like the Santa Monica Freeway. Speed dominated and times were ridiculously fast. It was over this stuff that Bob Black Jack set a world record for six furlongs, running the distance in 1:06.53 in the Sunshine Millions Dash. What happened at Santa Anita was an aberration and in no way should change the closer-biased image of synthetic tracks.

By the second week of February, after calling in consultants from a competing manufacturer, the Australian company Pro-Ride, and reformulating the surface, Santa Anita officials had the track back under control and producing races that bore some semblance of normalcy.

Then again, some synthetic tracks have been much slower than others. Horses at Del Mar looked like they were running over a plowed field for much of the inaugural Polytrack meet there. Never was this more evident than in the running of the track's signature race, the Pacific Classic, which was being run for the 17th time.

EIGHTH RACE
Del Mar
AUGUST 19, 2007

1¼ MILES. (2.071) 17TH RUNNING OF THE PACIFIC CLASSIC. Grade I. Purse $1,000,000 (includes $120,000 BC – Breeders' Cup) FOR THREE-YEAR-OLDS AND UPWARD. The winner of this race will be entitled to automatic entry into the 2007 running of the Breeders' Cup Classic. Three-year olds, 117 lbs. ; older 124 lbs.

Value of Race: $1,120,000 Winner $600,000; second $200,000; third $120,000; fourth $60,000; fifth $20,000; sixth $20,000; eighth $20,000; ninth $20,000; tenth $20,000; eleventh $20,000; twelfth $20,000. Mutuel Pool $1,424,642.00 Exacta Pool $684,356.00 Quinella Pool $44,465.00 Trifecta Pool $650,572.00 Superfecta Pool $396,166.00

Last Raced	Horse	M/Eqt.	A.	Wt	PP	¼	½	¾	1	Str	Fin	Jockey	Odds $1
8Jly07 6CD2	Student Council	LB	5	124	5	6½	51½	52½	3½	12	1½	Migliore R	23.40
21Jly07 9Dmr2	Awesome Gem	LB b	4	124	4	91½	93	92	84	42½	24	Flores D R	10.30
19Jly07 7Dmr1	Hello Sunday-FR	LB	4	124	12	2½	21½	21	1hd	2hd	31½	Blanc B	13.40
21Jly07 9Dmr6	Arson Squad	LB	4	124	8	72	72½	73½	61	52	4½	Solis A	11.60
30Jun07 10Hol3	Big Booster	LB b	6	124	9	10½	101½	103	9½	7½	5½	Gomez G K	8.00
30Jun07 10Hol1	Lava Man	LB b	6	124	1	4hd	3hd	42	2hd	31½	63	Nakatani C S	1.20
30Jun07 10Hol4	Porfido-Chi	LB	5	124	6	8½	81	8½	103	92	71¾	Rosario J	51.40
14Jly07 8Hol2	Albertus Maximus	LB	3	117	2	32	42½	3hd	52½	8hd	81¼	Talamo J	17.30
1Aug07 2Dmr5	A. P. Xcellent	LB b	4	124	10	11	11	1½	41½	61½	91¾	Espinoza V	14.60
14Jly07 9AP2	Time Squared	B bf	3	117	11	51½	61½	61	72½	102	101¼	Leparoux J R	31.30
21Jly07 9Dmr3	Salty Humor	LB bf	5	124	7	12	12	12	115	1115	1129½	Court J K	69.40
21Jly07 9Dmr1	Sun Boat-GB	LB b	5	124	3	111½	11hd	11hd	12	12	12	Baze M C	5.10

OFF AT 4:49 Start Good. Won driving. Track fast.

TIME :244, :493, 1:144, 1:403, 2:071 (:24.95, :49.75, 1:14.81, 1:40.65, 2:07.29)

(New Track Record)

$2 Mutuel Prices:

5 – STUDENT COUNCIL	48.80	31.80	20.60
4 – AWESOME GEM		12.40	8.20
13 – HELLO SUNDAY-FR			9.40

$1 EXACTA 5–4 PAID $177.60 $2 QUINELLA 4–5 PAID $227.60
$1 TRIFECTA 5–4–13 PAID $2,513.90 $1 SUPERFECTA 5–4–13–8 PAID $18,027.30

B. h, (May), by Kingmambo – Class Kris, by Kris S.. Trainer Cerin Vladimir. Bred by W S Farish (Ky).

STUDENT COUNCIL stalked the pace inside then a bit off the rail leaving the backstretch, bid four wide leaving the second turn, took the lead into the stretch, kicked clear under urging, drifted out in the final furlong but held gamely. AWESOME GEM chased inside then off the rail into the backstretch, ranged up four wide into the stretch and finished well to just miss. HELLO SUNDAY (FR) pulled his way along and angled in early, stalked off the rail, bid alongside the pacesetter on the backstretch and into the second turn, put a head in front between foes leaving that turn, continued inside in the stretch and held third. ARSON SQUAD chased outside a rival or off the rail, came three deep into the stretch and had a mild bid. BIG BOOSTER settled outside a rival then off the rail, came three wide into the stretch and was not a threat. LAVA MAN stalked inside then outside a rival on the first turn and backstretch, bid three deep on the second turn and between horses a quarter mile out and weakened in the stretch. PORFIDO (CHI) pulled between horses early then angled in and saved ground off the pace and did not rally. ALBERTUS MAXIMUS between horses early, stalked outside a rival then inside, dropped back into the stretch and weakened. A. P. XCELLENT wide early, took the early lead and angled in, set the pace inside, dueled along the rail on the backstretch and second turn, dropped back into the stretch and also weakened. TIME SQUARED pulled early, angled in and chased outside a rival then along the inside, came out into the stretch and lacked a further response. SALTY HUMOR a bit awkwardly into stride, settled off the pace outside a rival then angled in on the second turn and failed to menace. SUN BOAT (GB) saved ground off the pace, dropped well back on the second turn, came out into the stretch, gave way and was eased in the drive.

Owners– 1, Millennium Farms; 2, West Point Thoroughbreds Arudel Patrice Blavin Paul et al; 3, Tanaka Gary A; 4, Jay Em Ess Stable; 5, Anastasi S and W and Ukegawa; 6, STD Racing Stable and Wood Jason; 7, Sumaya Us Stables; 8, Chase Brandon L and Marianne; 9, Fulton Stan E; 10, Fab Oak Stable Giacopelli Lakin Et Al; 11, Totally Platinum LLP; 12, Bongo Racing Stable Capen and Tjosvold

Trainers– 1, Cerin Vladimir; 2, Dollase Craig; 3, Frankel Robert; 4, Headley Bruce; 5, Mitchell Mike; 6, O'Neill Doug; 7, Frankel Robert; 8, Mandella Gary; 9, Shirreffs John; 10, Biancone Patrick L; 11, McCarthy Sean; 12, Mitchell Mike

Scratched– Tiago (14Jul07 8Hol1)

$2 Daily Double (6–5) Paid $185.60 ; Daily Double Pool $112,546 .
$1 Pick Three (9–6–5) Paid $758.60 ; Pick Three Pool $209,562 .

The final time of 2:07.29 for the mile and a quarter was the slowest in the race's history. The slowest time for the Pacific Classic over conventional dirt was 2:01.62.

Many trainers thought that the Del Mar surface was uniform and even glib in the mornings, when it tended to be moist because it is so near the ocean, but it changed character in the hot afternoon sun, and track management was reluctant to use water on a surface that was supposed to be practically maintenance free.

Del Mar officials responded to that problem in time for the 2008 meeting—which was getting under way just as this book went to press—by adding a new, more heat-resistant wax to the surface. They also planned to water the track during the afternoon races in an attempt to keep it cooler and more consistent.

I've never been at all concerned with whether or not a track is producing fast or slow times, which is why I've glossed over this subject when it comes to conventional surfaces. I leave that to the people who make published speed figures to worry about, and have confidence that they'll figure out the variants and par times for the various synthetic surfaces and come up with an accurate figure.

Summary

Having thrown so many numbers at you, a summary would probably be helpful. When it comes to biases and synthetic surfaces, here is what you need to know: While all tracks are different, there is no doubt that, in general, speed horses do not perform as well on synthetic surfaces as they do on conventional dirt tracks. It also appears that the closers' bias is less pronounced on Cushion Track than it is on Polytrack. (It's too early to tell about Tapeta.) Below is the breakdown on winning running styles for 2,039 races run on synthetic surfaces at all distances. "WTW" is a horse who led at the first call and won. "Stalker" is a horse that was second or third at the first call and won. "Closer" is a horse that was fourth or worse at the first call and won. Note that the rule of thumb on conventional dirt tracks is that about 26 percent of all races are won wire to wire.

WTW	STALKER	CLOSER	TOTAL RACES
390 (19%)	533 (26%)	1,116 (55%)	2,039

I studied 1,323 conventional dirt races at tracks that have since converted to synthetic surfaces. Using the same categories, here is the breakdown of winning running styles. It's obvious, dirt racing and synthetic-surface racing are two very different things.

WTW	STALKER	CLOSER	TOTAL RACES
395 (30%)	441 (33%)	487 (37%)	1,323

3

Track Bias, Part 2: Ins and Outs

Another promise made concerning synthetic tracks was that they would end the sort of biases in which one section or other of the racetrack was faster than another. Guess what? That isn't true, either.

Many synthetic tracks have turned out to be rather uniform, meaning the rail is never better than the outside or the outside is never better than a deep rail.

But biases do exist with synthetic tracks, and not just ones that favor closers. At Keeneland and Presque Isle Downs, there have definitely been occasions when the outside path was the place to be and horses racing along the inside have been at a disadvantage.

I have yet to see a synthetic surface that favored the rail horses—and certainly nothing like what we saw at the 2006 Breeders' Cup at Churchill Downs. That card was run over an extremely biased track, where one winner after another flew down the highway that was the rail path. Four of the five Breeders' Cup races run on the dirt were won by horses breaking from post position 1. Those sorts of situations happen far less often on synthetic tracks.

Depending upon your point of view, that isn't necessarily a plus. Savvy handicappers who pick up on rail or dead-rail biases before their parimutuel competitors can find themselves in the middle of some of the most lucrative gambling situations ever. Betting a speed horse from an inside post on a gold-rail day can seem like stealing. With the advent of synthetic surfaces, some people worried that a bias-free track would produce boring, predictable racing.

In the early days of synthetic surfaces, it looked like the tracks were going to deliver on their promises. At Turfway, which has held far more synthetic-surface races than any other track, Polytrack got off to a great start in providing a uniform racing surface.

From the first 2,232 races run over the synthetic surface at Turfway Park, post 4 produced the highest percentage of winners at 12.9 percent. The lowest percentage was post 11, which produced 8.9 percent winners. Even that slight drop-off is understandable, since outside posts are at a disadvantage at Turfway in two-turn races because horses breaking from those positions lose ground on the first turn.

In the early part of the Polytrack era at Keeneland, there was not any particular bias when it came to gold rails or dead rails. During the first two Polytrack meets, horses breaking from post 1 won 9.9 percent of the time, just a hair better than horses breaking from post 11, which won 9.8 percent of the time.

The idea that synthetic tracks might not normally produce biases where one part of the racetrack is better or less deep than another made perfect sense. With conventional dirt tracks, water typically drains toward the inside after it rains. These tracks have a crown or a slope that causes the water to flow downhill and toward the rail. Because the drainage process can take time, and because it can be uneven, the inside portion of the track can end up being deeper or, perhaps, less deep than the outer portion. Horses racing on an uneven track and running in the lanes that are deeper than others will have virtually no chance.

Synthetic tracks drain differently; they are made so that water, rather than flowing toward the inside, drains straight down. With this system, no area of the track should be any different from any other.

"Take a track like today here at Churchill Downs," Polytrack inventor Martin Collins said on Kentucky Derby Day 2007, when the Churchill Downs track was still drying out from rain the day before. "Yesterday, it was sloppy. Then it gets muddy. That's not good for horses. This track is not consistent and it never will be. It doesn't drain laterally," he explained, meaning that it doesn't drain evenly all the way across its width. "It has to drain from the outside to the inside and what do you get? On the rail, you get a flood. And you can't do anything about it. It's dangerous and you will get a lot of injuries with tracks like these."

The track at Churchill Downs on Kentucky Derby Day was, despite the previous day's inclement weather, bias free. More often than not, that's the case with conventional dirt surfaces. But it didn't take long for Churchill Downs to return to its old tricks. On the first day racing was held at Churchill after the 2007 Derby, the rail was golden. Horses getting the lead on the inside won the first three races of the day on the dirt, a trend that continued throughout the afternoon.

I had all but come to the conclusion that no synthetic surface would ever produce a gold or dead rail, and then Presque Isle Downs came along. The inaugural meet there ran for just 25 days and consisted of only 200 races. That may not be enough data to arrive at firm conclusions about how the Tapeta surface played, but, based on the evidence available, it looked as if horses racing on the inside were at a disadvantage at Presque Isle.

Below is a breakdown of winning post positions, first in sprints and then in routes.

Presque Isle Sprints

Post	No. of Winners	No. of Starters	Winning Percentage
1	9	134	6.7
2	9	134	6.7
3	22	134	16.4
4	15	134	11.1
5	15	132	11.4
6	16	127	12.6
7	16	115	13.9
8	15	103	14.6
9	8	76	14.6
10	4	49	8.2
11	2	27	7.4
12	1	12	8.3

Presque Isle Routes

Post	No. of Winners	No. of Starters	Winning Percentage
1	9	66	13.6
2	7	66	10.6
3	9	66	13.6
4	10	66	10.6
5	4	66	6.0
6	8	64	12.5
7	8	57	14.0
8	5	45	11.1
9	4	34	11.8
10	2	23	8.7
11	0	12	0.0
12	4	2	50.0

Particularly in sprint races, it appears that horses breaking from post 3 or higher had an advantage. A study of the chart footnotes tells a similar story. The vast majority of winners raced on the outside portion of the track.

The second race on September 12, 2007, at Presque Isle pretty much tells what went on there for much of the meet. Stepperupper was a huge class dropper with inside speed breaking from the rail. It wasn't to be her day. She got out front and then tired in the stretch to finish fourth. While she sat on the fence, the first- and second-place finishers got outside trips. (See result chart, next page.)

SECOND RACE **Presque Isle Downs** **SEPTEMBER 12, 2007**

5½ FURLONGS. (1.02^{2}) CLAIMING. Purse $15,000 FOR FILLIES AND MARES THREE YEARS OLD AND UPWARD WHICH HAVE NOT WON TWO RACES SINCE MARCH 12, 2007. Three Year Olds, 118 lbs.; Older, 122 lbs. Non-winners of a race since August 12 Allowed 3 lbs. A race since July 12 Allowed 6 lbs. Claiming Price $5,000.

Value of Race: $26,250 Winner $11,250; second $6,750; third $3,000; fourth $2,250; fifth $1,500; sixth $600; sixth $600; eighth $300. Mutuel Pool $17,146.00 Exacta Pool $13,876.00 Trifecta Pool $11,171.00

Last Raced	Horse	M/Eqt.	A.	Wt	PP	St	¼	⅜	Str	Fin	Jockey	Cl'g Pr	Odds $1
10Aug07 ^{7}Mnr^{2}	Ms. Bluebird	L b	7	116	8	3	3^{1}	2½	1^{1}	1no	Vargas O	5000	11.00
3Sep07 ^{1}PID^{2}	Gem's Wager	L bf	8	118	5	7	5^{hd}	4½	3^{hd}	2$1\frac{1}{2}$	Madrigal R Jr	5000	3.80
3Sep07 ^{1}PID^{4}	Ride Now	L bf	6	116	3	2	2^{1}	3½	4^{3}	3^{2}	Villa-Gomez H	5000	14.20
4Jly07 ^{7}AP^{12}	Stepperupper	L b	4	116	1	1	1^{1}	1^{1}	2½	4$4\frac{3}{4}$	Whitney D G	5000	0.80
26Aug07 ^{10}Mnr^{1}	Outside the Lines	L	5	122	7	4	4^{1}	5$2\frac{1}{2}$	5$2\frac{1}{2}$	5$1\frac{1}{2}$	Feliciano R	5000	6.10
31Aug07 ^{7}Mnr^{8}	DH Fatouma	L	6	116	2	5	6^{3}	6^{1}	6½	6	Winnett B G Jr	5000	37.30
17Aug07 ^{7}Mnr^{1}	DH Misty Sabin	L	5	122	4	6	8	8	8	6^{hd}	Spieth S	5000	37.70
15Aug07 ^{9}Pen^{4}	Muttface Alison	L	8	116	6	8	7^{2}	7^{3}	7^{2}	8	Hampshire J F Jr	5000	7.00

DH–Dead Heat.

OFF AT 5:55 Start Good. Won driving. Track fast.
TIME :22^{1}, :46, :58^{3}, 1:05^{1} (:22.26, :46.01, :58.63, 1:05.26)

$2 Mutuel Prices:				
	8 – MS. BLUEBIRD	24.00	9.20	6.80
	5 – GEM'S WAGER		3.60	3.60
	3 – RIDE NOW			4.60

$2 EXACTA 8–5 PAID $92.00 $2 TRIFECTA 8–5–3 PAID $787.20

B. m, (Feb), by Never Wavering – Billie's Grin, by Smile. Trainer Walker Charles A. Bred by Diable Stable (Fla).

MS. BLUEBIRD stalked the pace while never far back, rallied into the stretch and drew clear, was fully extended to hold on late. GEM'S WAGER was well placed early on the inside, was angled out and rallied into the stretch, was gaining late and just missed. RIDE NOW stalked the pace from the inside, rallied into the stretch, flattened out and ran evenly late. STEPPERUPPER set the pace and dueled for the lead from the inside, weakened in the stretch and began to fade. OUTSIDE THE LINES was in a good stalking position in mid pack, ran evenly and had no rally. FATOUMA was well placed on the inside, had no rally. MISTY SABIN failed to menace. MUTTFACE ALISON was no threat.

Owners– 1, Shady Lady Stable LLC; 2, Home Team Stables; 3, Murtough Stephen B; 4, Elite Stables LLC (Van Dyke); 5, Cox Loren G; 6, Swihart Charles F; 7, Four Valls Thoroughbreds LLC; 8, Schmeltz Joe

Trainers– 1, Walker Charles A; 2, Lake Scott A; 3, Murtough Stephen B; 4, Canani Nick; 5, Cox Loren G; 6, Heinrich Darren; 7, Magrell Jack L Jr; 8, Martinez Jose

$2 Daily Double (2–8) Paid $34.20; Daily Double Pool $10,124.

Stepperupper shipped to Delta Downs for her next start, and someone must have been paying attention. She was sent off at odds of 7–10 and won by 9¼ lengths. At those odds, no one got rich following Stepperupper, but there was some serious money to be made by following another horse out of that Presque Isle race.

Look at the footnote comments for the third-place finisher, Ride Now. She spent much of her trip on the rail and ran a sneaky-good race. She returned eight days later and won at the same level, paying $30.20.

9 **Ride Now**
Turqse **Own: Stephen B Murtough**
Maroon And White Diagonal Quarters
PEREIRA O M (37 5 4 3 .14) 2007: (830 121 .15)

B. m. 6 (Mar)
Sire: Crafty Friend (Crafty Prospector) $6,000
Dam: Legafino (Two's a Plenty)
Br: James D Haley (Ky)
Tr: Murtough Stephen B (11 1 0 2 .09) 2007:(55 8 .15)

L 116

Life	**33**	**8**	**4**	**2**	**$97,435**	**68**
2007	**4**	**2**	**0**	**1**	**$22,996**	**68**
2006	**7**	**2**	**0**	**0**	**$18,352**	**55**
PID	**3**	**1**	**0**	**1**	**$16,500**	**68**

D.Fst	**19**	**4**	**2**	**1**	**$46,081**	**68**
Wet(327)	**11**	**3**	**2**	**0**	**$34,854**	**67**
Synth	**3**	**1**	**0**	**1**	**$16,500**	**68**
Turf(225)	**0**	**0**	**0**	**0**	**$0**	**–**
Dst(333)	**17**	**5**	**2**	**2**	**$52,183**	**65**

20Sep07–3PID	fst	6f	◈	:22^{3}	:46^{2}	:58^{3}	1:11^{2}	3↑ⒻClm 5000N2Y	**68**	6	1	1½	1^{2}	1^{hd}	1^{hd}	Pereira O M	L116 fb	14.10	–	–	RideNow116^{hd} SaharanSunrise116^{2} SilenceIsGolden119$2\frac{1}{2}$	Lasted, driving	12
12Sep07–2PID	fst	5½f	◈	:22^{1}	:46	:58^{3}	1:05^{1}	3↑ⒻClm 5000N2Y	**56**	3	2	2^{1}	3$1\frac{1}{2}$	4$1\frac{1}{2}$	3$1\frac{1}{2}$	Villa-Gomez H	L116 fb	14.20	–	–	Ms. Bluebird116^{no} Gem's Wager118$1\frac{1}{2}$ *Ride Now*116^{2}	Evenly late	8
3Sep07–1PID	fst	6f	◈	:22^{3}	:46^{3}	:59^{1}	1:12	3↑ⒻClm 5000N2Y	**56**	6	1	1^{1}	2^{hd}	3$2\frac{1}{2}$	4$6\frac{1}{4}$	Beech C T	L116 fb	7.30	–	–	Taupo116^{3} Gem's Wager118$1\frac{3}{4}$ **Blue Bay**116$1\frac{1}{2}$	Faltered	9
26Jun07–10Mnr	fst	5f		:22^{3}	:47^{2}		1:01^{4}	3↑ⒻClm 5000N2Y	**42**	8	1	1^{1}	1^{1}	2^{hd}	1^{nk}	Brinkley D W	L118 b	6.50	71–	23	Ride Now118^{nk} U Da Gal118½ Bombay Dreams118^{hd}	Headed, came again	10
9Dec06–5Mnr	fst	6f		:22^{3}	:46^{2}	1:00	1:13^{4}	3↑ⒻAlw 27800N1X	**20**	8	1	2^{hd}	4$1\frac{1}{2}$	10^{13}	10$21\frac{3}{4}$	Rivera L R	L115 b	38.20	53–	28	*Dont Lie*117$1\frac{1}{4}$ Rice Pudding115$2\frac{3}{4}$ Beech Corner121¾	Duel btw,bore out1/4	10
7Oct06–9Mnr	fst	6f		:21^{4}	:45^{1}	:58^{1}	1:10^{3}	3↑ⒻAlw 27800N1X	**47**	6	1	1½	2^{hd}	5^{4}	5$13\frac{3}{4}$	Rivera L R	L115 b	42.00	77–	18	WrightSeeker115^{6} LunaSe115¾ OneOThreeWest115^{3}	Alert,ins duel,tire1/8	9
7Aug06–6Mnr	my	6f		:22^{1}	:46	:59^{1}	1:12^{3}	3↑ⒻClm 7500(7.5-6.5)	**53**	8	1	1^{1}	1^{2}	1½	1$1\frac{1}{4}$	Rivera L R	L115 b	33.60	81–	16	RideNow115$1\frac{1}{4}$ StormtotheTop115^{hd} AlpinSingr115$3\frac{1}{2}$	Drifted out, held on	9
23Jun06–10Mnr	my	5½f		:22^{2}	:46^{2}	:59	1:05^{3}	3↑ⒻClm 5000N1Y	**55**	4	1	1^{2}	1½	1^{hd}	1$1\frac{3}{4}$	Barria J	L121 b	4.90	85–	12	*Ride Now*121$1\frac{3}{4}$ Expectant121^{nk} Our Lilly121$1\frac{3}{4}$	Drifted out driving	10
19May06–2Mnr	sly	5f		:22^{3}	:47		1:00^{2}	3↑ⒻClm 5000N1Y	**37**	8	3	3^{1}	2^{2}	3^{5}	4$3\frac{3}{4}$	Quinones L M	121 b	6.40	73–	17	PicturPls121^{hd} OnthDfnsv121$3\frac{1}{2}$ CrtsMybSo121^{nk}	Hard pursuit, weakened	9
5May06–3Mnr	fst	5f		:22^{2}	:47^{2}		1:01^{1}	3↑ⒻClm 5000N1Y	**29**	1	1	1^{hd}	2½	4$1\frac{1}{4}$	5^{4}	Rivera L R	121 fb	2.60	69–	23	GemmKyle121$1\frac{1}{4}$ OntheDfnsiv121^{nk} AShorttTour121$2\frac{1}{4}$	Hard duel,ins,short	9
14Apr06–9FL	wf^{S}	4½f		:22	:46		:52^{4}	3↑ Clm 4000N1Y	**2**	5	2	3^{5}		8^{16}	9$15\frac{1}{2}$	Beech C T	119 fb	26.50	75–	09	Bond Arbitrage124¾ For Cash Only124$3\frac{1}{4}$ Mugee124¾	Done early	9
14Nov05–8FL	fst	6f		:22^{1}	:45^{2}	:58	1:10^{4}	3↑ Clm 10000(12-8)	**8**	7	3	10$7\frac{3}{4}$	10^{17}	10^{15}	10$24\frac{1}{4}$	Beech C T	L115 fb	58.50	67–	15	Imrlfncydhr121$1\frac{1}{2}$ AnglsWsdm120^{1} MnshdGld120½	Bore out,chkd hard 5/8	10

WORKS: **Aug23 Mnr 3f fst :40^{1} B** *6/6*

TRAINER: Synth(11 .09 $2.75) WonLastStart(18 .06 $3.84) Sprint(83 .14 $5.76)

J/T 2006-07 PID(2 .50 $15.10) J/T 2006-07(5 .20 $6.04)

A couple of jockeys who rode at Presque Isle agreed that the rail was not good.

"You couldn't tell by looking at it, but it seemed like the rail was not the place to be," said Corey Lanerie, who finished second in the Presque Isle standings with 18 wins. "I don't know why that was. You always seemed to need to be in the middle of the track to win."

Here's what Rosemary Homeister Jr., who was the eighth-leading rider, had to say about how Presque Isle played:

"I thought it was more a case of the track being inconsistent," she said. "Some days, you'd see horses winning up the rail and other days every winner would come wide and close. After the first week, everything started to speed up. They started going 21⅘, 44, things like that. Most of the time, I tried to stay around the three path. That seemed to be the best place to be. I don't know why."

About six weeks after Presque Isle closed, Tapeta was unveiled at Golden Gate Fields in northern California. Would Michael Dickinson's track at Golden Gate turn out to be just like his track at Presque Isle? The answer was no. Golden Gate played fair throughout the meet.

What is it about Keeneland? Whether it's the old gold rail, the new track that swallowed up front-runners, or something entirely different, it always seems to have some sort of problem when it comes to a track bias.

There were plenty of days at the spring 2008 meet, especially in the early going, when the rail was dead and the track was definitely biased. Take a look at the third race on April 6. There were dozens of races just like this one at the meet.

THIRD RACE
Keeneland
APRIL 6, 2008

6 FURLONGS. (1.08^{1}) CLAIMING . Purse $26,000 FOR FOUR YEAR OLDS AND UPWARD. Weight, 123 lbs. Non-winners of two races since February 6 Allowed 3 lbs. A Race Since Then Allowed 5 lbs. Claiming Price $20,000 (Races Where Entered For $16,000 Or Less Not Considered).

Value of Race: $26,000 Winner $16,120; second $5,200; third $2,600; fourth $1,300; fifth $780. Mutuel Pool $239,895.00 Exacta Pool $171,745.00 Trifecta Pool $121,086.00 Superfecta Pool $62,001.00

Last Raced	Horse	M/Eqt.	A.	Wt	PP	St	¼	½	Str	Fin	Jockey	Cl'g Pr	Odds $1
6Oct07 ^{10}Beu^{11}	Crack the Cognac	L f	4	118	7	2	$3\frac{1}{2}$	2^{hd}	$1\frac{1}{2}$	$1^{1\frac{1}{4}}$	Velazquez J R	20000	4.90
26Mar08 ^{8}TP^{4}	Eroberer	L	7	118	8	1	$7^{1\frac{1}{2}}$	4^{hd}	3^{hd}	$2\frac{3}{4}$	Castanon J L	20000	10.80
9Mar08 ^{7}Lrl^{8}	Lycurgus	L b	5	118	5	6	8	8	4^{hd}	3^{nk}	Hebert T J	20000	4.70
1Mar08 ^{5}FG^{6}	Warrior Within	L	5	118	1	8	$6\frac{1}{2}$	$1\frac{1}{2}$	2^{1}	4^{nk}	Theriot H J II	20000	2.80
22Mar08 ^{3}TP^{1}	Speak of Kings	L b	6	118	4	5	2^{hd}	6^{hd}	6^{hd}	$5^{2\frac{1}{4}}$	Lanerie C J	20000	4.10
22Mar08 ^{3}TP^{3}	Running Play	L	5	118	6	3	$4\frac{1}{2}$	5^{hd}	8	$6\frac{1}{2}$	Lebron V	20000	38.30
15Mar08 ^{8}FG^{7}	Boots Are Walking	L b	7	118	3	4	5^{hd}	7^{2}	5^{hd}	7^{1}	Mena M	20000	4.50
26Mar08 ^{8}TP^{2}	Deputy G	L	5	118	2	7	1^{1}	3^{hd}	7^{hd}	8	Pompell T L	20000	8.80

OFF AT 2:16 Start Good. Won driving. Track fast.
TIME :22^{3}, :46^{1}, :58^{1}, 1:10^{2} (:22.71, :46.25, :58.25, 1:10.57)

$2 Mutuel Prices:				
	8 – CRACK THE COGNAC	11.80	7.20	5.80
	9 – EROBERER		10.00	6.80
	6 – LYCURGUS			5.20

$2 EXACTA 8–9 PAID $135.00 50 CENT TRIFECTA 8–9–6 PAID $242.60
$2 SUPERFECTA 8–9–6–1 PAID $3,611.00

Ch. g, (Apr), by Hennessy – Crack the Code , by Lost Code . Trainer Nihei Michelle. Bred by Mrs Elisabeth H Alexander (Ohio).

CRACK THE COGNAC, briefly in front after the start, allowed the advantage to DEPUTY G, forced the pace to the stretch while three abreast, took over, then edged clear late under strong handling. EROBERER, first to show from the gate, settled five wide, came seven or eight wide when straightened into the lane and earned the place. LYCURGUS, outsprinted early, raced near the inside, split foes two or three wide in the final furlong and couldn't make up the difference. WARRIOR WITHIN was sent up inside on the turn to duel for the lead, gained a slight edge, continued in a pace battle into the final furlong and weakened. SPEAK OF KINGS, between rivals, weakened in the drive. RUNNING PLAY, between horses in a striking position for a half, lacked a further account. BOOTS ARE WALKING, well placed in behind the dueling leaders to the stretch, angled to the rail for the drive and was empty. DEPUTY G moved to the front three wide early, battled up close to the stretch and tired gradually.

Owners– 1, Alexander Elisabeth H; 2, Williams Eric; 3, Roth Toby; 4, Hunter Kent and Kordsmeier Kevin; 5, Rogers Sam Postoian Ralph and Vanovich Steve; 6, Haas Racing Stable; 7, Papiese Richard and Karen; 8, Spade Stable

Trainers– 1, Nihei Michelle; 2, Williams Robert L; 3, Reed Eric R; 4, Autrey Cody; 5, Foley Gregory D; 6, Cook Joanie M; 7, Magana Hector; 8, Pate David E

Deputy G was claimed by Ricatto Michael C; trainer, Cox Brad H,
Warrior Within was claimed by Calabrese Frank C; trainer, Catalano Wayne M,
Speak of Kings was claimed by Reed William T; trainer, Calhoun William Bret.
Scratched– He's a Dixie Boy (28Jan08 ^{9}FG ^{5})

$2 Pick Three (2–4–8) Paid $947.40 ; Pick Three Pool $50,159 .

Horses breaking from the two outside posts finished one-two, had wide trips, and accounted for a $135 exacta. Warrior Within, the 5–2 favorite, broke from the rail, contested the pace inside, and tired to finish fourth. At 9–2, Boots Are Walking darted to the rail and stopped cold, finishing seventh.

The fifth race on April 10 at Keeneland provided still another example. The public liked two horses. Breaking from post 5, 2–1 shot Delta Storm got the perfect wide trip and won by 1 ¾ lengths. Also sent off at 2–1, Reverential broke from post 1, stayed on the rail throughout, and finished last. When both horses ran back, it was a different story. Back on an unbiased track at Prairie Meadows, Reverential won. Delta Storm returned at Keeneland, didn't have the bias in his favor, and ran a poor fifth.

everential
n: Stiritz William

Gr/ro. g. 5 (Mar)
Sire: Holy Bull (Great Above) $15,000
Dam: Joan L. (Greinton*GB)
Br: Steve Riech (Ky)
Tr: Gestes Terry

Life	25	5	0	2	$126,169	93	D.Fst	12	3	0	0	$74,269 93
							Wet(391)	1	0	0	0	$0 69
2008	5	2	0	0	$46,500	88	Synth	3	0	0	1	$6,200 82
2007	9	1	0	1	$37,689	93	Turf(260)	9	2	0	1	$45,700 83

ay08–8PrM	fst	6f	:221 :452 :5731:101	3↑OC 35k/N3x-N	88	5	3	41½	1hd	11	12¼	Quinonez B	LB120 b	2.60	89–15	Rvrntl1202¼ Tmlysuprm120no SmokSmokSmok1202¾	Edged clear, driving	5
pr08–5Kee	fst	5½f ◈	:222 :453 :5711:031	4↑Clm c-32000	71	1	5	52	3½	4¾	86	Albarado R J	L118 b	2.20	96–08	Delta Storm1181¾ County Clerk120no EssenceofGold118nk	Inside,faltered	8

Claimed from Maier Kenneth for $32,000, Amoss Thomas Trainer 2008(as of 4/10): (160 46 31 15 0.29)

eb08–1FG	fst	6f	:221 :451 :5721:102	4↑Clm 50000(50-45)	76	2	5	32	32	44	43	Albarado R J	L119 b	*2.00	89–18	Edgerrin119hd Watchem Smokey121¾ CieloSong1192¼	Inside trip, no avail	6
an08–5FG	fst	6f	:231 :472 :5911:114	4↑Clm 50000(50-45)	75	2	5	31½	2hd	31½	43½	Mena M	L121 b	*.60	81–17	WtchmSmoky119¾ Edgrrin1191¾ SmlltownSlw1191	Bid turn,flattened out	5
an08–3FG	fst	6f	:211 :451 :5821:12	4↑Clm 50000(50-45)	80	1	6	65¼	67¾	46½	12	Martin E M Jr	L119 b	4.00	84–20	Reverentil1192 SmokeMountin1191 IronRogue119nk	Awaited room, clear	8
ec07–10FG	fst	6f	:22 :452 :5721:101	3↑OC 50k/N3x-N	74	7	3	42	21	32½	58¼	Martin E M Jr	L119	17.50	85–17	[D]MrNightlinger119½ Dmrction1171½ Trulyonbrodwy1213¼	Speed, gave way	8
ec07–8FG	fm	*5½f Ⓣ	:221 :463 :5811:042	3↑Alw 42750N3X	82	6	6	74¼	64	31½	51¾	Mena M	L119	14.30	90–08	Zetetic119hd No Fault119½ Matzoh Toga1191	4w, flattened late	8
un07–9Mnr	fst	5½f	:223 :461 :5831:051	3↑Alw 35300N4L	57	1	4	4¾	61¾	67	611½	Whitney D G	L115	*.80	75–22	BairdsVillage1153 SunRiser1212¾ LikelyCndidte1111	Hustle,ins,chase,tired	6
May07–8AP	fst	6½f ◈	:214 :441 1:0831:15	3↑OC 50k/N$Y-N	78	7	5	52¾	22	44½	76¼	Theriot H J II	L118	3.30	- -	LstGrnStnding1181½ MgnusOne1181 ByeByeCrfty118no	Bid 4wd, faltered	9
ay07–9CD	fst	6f	:213 :442 :5621:091	3↑OC 80k/N3x-N	80	8	9	74½	73¼	43½	52¾	Leparoux J R	L120	5.70	88–08	Mr. Meso1201¼ True Course120¾ Edgerrin120¾	Slow start,7w bid	9
Apr07–7Kee	fst	7f ◈	:241 :492 1:1231:241	4↑OC 80k/N3x-N	82	2	6	73¼	83¼	62¼	3¾	Graham J	L118	4.40	85–09	Carnera118no Clootie's Croft118¾ Reverential118nk	Closed well,7w lane	9
Mar07–9OP	fst	6f	:22 :453 :5821:104	4↑OC 40k/N2x-N	93	5	6	51¾	53¼	1hd	12¼	Albarado R J	L118	9.00	89–19	Rvrntil1182¼ NoTrmLimt1181 CrownngVctory1182¼	Asked turn, 5-w, clear	8

)RKS: Apr28 PrM 4f fst :482 B *2/21* Mar31 CD 5f fst 1:001 B *5/13* Feb7 FG 5f fst 1:01 B *4/16*

elta Storm
vn: Campbell A G Jr

B. g. 7 (Mar)
Sire: Storm Boot (Storm Cat) $12,500
Dam: Talkin to Delta (Diesis*GB)
Br: Alex G. Campbell, Jr. (Ky)
Tr: Reinacher R J Jr

Life	19	6	4	1	$150,784	95	D.Fst	9	2	2	1	$42,660 95
							Wet(296)	0	0	0	0	$0 -
2008	2	1	0	0	$22,523	88	Synth	4	2	1	0	$56,263 88
2007	7	3	2	0	$78,596	95	Turf(315)	6	2	1	0	$51,861 95

Apr08–4Kee	fst	6f ◈	:222 :452 :5711:093	4↑Alw 58000N2X	75	5	2	32	32½	53½	56¾	Gomez G K	L118 b	2.50	86–11	RllyingCry118nk JohnsRod118nk ChmbrlinBrdg1184	Close up 3wide, faded	5
Apr08–5Kee	fst	5½f ◈	:222 :453 :5711:031	4↑Clm 32000	88	5	3	42	41	3nk	11¾	Gomez G K	L118 b	*2.10	102–08	DeltStorm1181¾ CountyClerk120no EssncofGold118nk	4-5w,steady urging	8
Oct07–4Kee	fst	5½f ◈	:224 :46 :5721:033	3↑Clm 40000	87	4	2	31	31	11	11	Leparoux J R	L120 b	*2.70	- -	Delta Storm1201 Power Jeans122hd Pimm's O'Clock120nk	4w,hard ridden	8
1Sep07–1Sar	fm	5½f Ⓣ	:212 :44 :5531:013	3↑OC 50k/N2x-N	63	6	5	31	31½	66	1011	Desormeaux K J	L121 b	7.50	86–07	EverFriend1212¼ SouthrnPrinc1231¾ CountOnPl121nk	Chased 3 wide, tired	10
Jly07–7Bel	fm	6f [T]	:214 :442 :56 1:072	3↑OC 50k/N2x-N	88	8	4	52	52¼	62¼	73½	Bejarano R	L121 b	6.10	94–05	SilverTimber1211½ Redefined121nk Mathematicin121¾	4 wide trip, no rally	8
May07–7Bel	fm	6f [T]	:221 :45 :5641:083	3↑Alw 45000N1X	95	8	3	2½	2hd	1½	11¼	Gomez G K	L122 b	1.85	92–10	DeltaStorm1221¼ ChiefOperator1171 BrzenlyBold117hd	When roused, clear	10
Apr07–6Kee	fst	6f ◈	:222 :444 :5621:081	4↑Alw 49450N1X	88	2	6	2hd	2hd	1hd	21	Velazquez J R	L118 b	9.40	101–05	He LovesMeNot1181 DeltaStorm1182¼ Markum118¾	Duel,inside,outfinishd	11
Mar07–8GP	fst	6f	:22 :444 :5641:092	4↑Alw 46000N1X	92	6	4	42	1hd	1hd	22¼	Decarlo C P	L120 b	11.30	93–11	BondNotbook1202¼ DltStrm120nk GrndChmpn1249½	Str duel, outfinished	6
Feb07–1GP	fst	6f	:224 :453 :5731:103	4↑Clm 20000N3L	95	5	2	12	13	14	15	Decarlo C P	L124 b	2.50	89–11	Delta Storm1245 Riggins124hd Holy Intentions124¾	Inside, widened	7
Nov06–5Crc	fm	5f Ⓣ	:213 :441 :554	3↑OC 16k/N1x-N	71	2	4	1hd	2hd	3nk	64½	Decarlo C P	L120 b	*2.20	89–06	Heros Reward120½ Little Genius115nk Miners Bid115¾	Vied, tired	8
Oct06–7Bel	gd	6f [T]	:223 :46 :5821:112	3↑Alw 45000N1X	84	1	8	65½	56½	44½	21	Smith M E	L121 b	9.30	86–13	Macklenin1231 Delta Storm121¾ Bogota Bill121½	Altered course stretch	8
Aug06–5Sar	fm	5½f Ⓣ	:214 :442 :56 1:02	3↑Clm 35000N2L	81	7	2	11	11	13½	1½	Gomez G K	L120 b	5.10	97–04	Delta Storm120½ Erdiston1222 Polished Arrow118hd	Pace, clear, held on	10

ORKS: Apr4 Pay 4f fst :52 B *7/8* Mar30 Pay 4f fst :51 B *7/16* Mar25 Pay 4f fst :504 B *12/22* Mar9 Pay 4f fst :513 B *13/22* Mar2 Pay 4f fst :522 B *11/14* ●Feb24 Pay 3f fst :372 B *1/4*

Keeneland riders didn't seem to have much of a problem figuring out what was going on. On the second day of the meet, Jamie Theriot had the assignment on Lil Tree, a horse with speed who was breaking from post 1. Theriot knew what he needed to do. He blasted out of the gate, opened up on the field, and got as far away from the rail as he could. By the middle of the stretch, he was a good six paths off the rail.

Theriot, who did not ride regularly at Keeneland until 2007, said he patterned his riding style there after the most successful jockeys at the meet. He noticed upon his arrival that most avoided the rail, so he followed suit.

"The majority of the winners at Keeneland do seem to come from four to nine wide," he said. "It was unreal how wide horses would go there and still win. Your top five, six riders there would just follow each other. Everybody else was going wide and winning, so you figured that's what you had to do too. It did seem that the inside was a little boggier, especially after it rains. Why that is, I don't know."

Former jockey Gary Stevens, who is now a television analyst and student of the game, has been playing close attention to the synthetic-surface revolution, and here's what the Hall of Famer had to say about what was going on at Keeneland.

"A lot of horses were winning with wide trips at Keeneland and some people started to say the outside part of the track was better," he said. "I don't agree with that at all. It was more a case of the speed horses were stopping and riders had no choice but to go around them. That's usually easier to do on the outside than the inside."

In any case, as the following example shows, it didn't hurt that Theriot's mount, Lil Tree, loves Keeneland and, apparently, synthetic surfaces.

```
Lil Tree                                  Ch. g. 6 (Mar)                                  Life  18 8 0 4 $98,620 97 | D.Fst      11 3 0 4 $34,700 82
Own: Heflin Driver Racing LLC             Sire: Lil Honcho (Chief Honcho) $500            2008   3 3 0 0 $36,900 85 | Wet(354)    1 1 0 0 $17,400 97
                                          Dam: Marked Cow (Marked Tree)                   2007   7 2 0 0 $18,870 87 | Synth       4 4 0 0 $46,520 87
                                          Br: Ray Shumake (Tex)                                                     | Turf(204*)  2 0 0 0      $0 71
                                          Tr: Autrey Cody

11Apr08-1Kee fst 6f ◈ :224 :461 :5741:10 4↑Alw 10000s        84 4 3 11 11½ 12½ 1no Theriot H J II   L118 b *2.20e 91-10 Lil Tree118no Laudable1234¾ Road Ruler120nk            All out,drvg,lasted 8
5Apr08-2Kee fst 7f ◈ :223 :452 1:1021:232 4↑Clm 16000        85 1 2 12 12 14 13½ Theriot H J II     L118 b *2.10 88-11 Lil Tree1183½ Por Favor1184¼ Tux n' Tales118nk          Off inside,driving 8
1Mar08-4FG fst 6f :214 :452 :5721:102 4↑Clm 10000(10-9)        82 4 4 11½ 11 1hd 1no Theriot H J II   L119 b 2.20 92-14 Lil Tree119no Tea Tax1193¾ Timeaftertimeafter1193½   Collared, gained nod 7
28Dec07-2FG fst 5½f :221 :453 :58 1:043 3↑Clm c-(12.5-10.5)    62 7 7 77 77¼ 78½ 66½ Campbell J M     L119 b 3.60 86-11 Timeftertimefter119¾ MlcolmDCt1191¾ HomeMinistr119½   Veered out break7
  Claimed from Easy Money 2006 LLC for $12,500, Campbell Michael B Trainer 2007(as of 12/28): ( 153 18 17 15 0.12 )
26Oct07-3Kee fst 6f ◈ :224 :453 :5731:10 3↑Clm 7500           86 10 5 13 15 13½ 14¼ Campbell J M     L122 b 2.60 93-10 Lil Tree1224¼ Steelyeyed1202 Ticklish Will1152½       In command,4w,drvg 12
26Sep07-7Haw fst 6f :221 :462 :5911:124 3↑Clm 25000(25-20)     46 4 3 2½ 2½ 54½ 710¾ Campbell Joel    L122 fb 5.90 66-23 Proper Carson122¾ Stars of the Sea122nk MyCalabrese1224 Flattened out 8
2Sep07-4AP fst 6f ◈ :223 :451 :5711:094 3↑Clm 10000(10-9)     87 7 1 12 13 13 1½ Campbell J M        L120 fb 7.70 - - Lil Tree120½ Iron Rogue1201½ Spruce Lake1202¾           Held off rival7
4Jly07-9PrM fst 2f :21 3↑Alw 35632nc                           - 5 7 83¼ 63 ♦Corbett G W              LB121 fb 3.90 103-13 Seadrift1161 Rising Thunder1241¾ Robyn's Sharkey121no Never menaced10
28Jun07-6AP fm *5f Ⓣ :222 :454 :58 3↑Clm 35000(35-30)          69 6 6 53 74¼ 77½ 77 Campbell J M      L121 fb 16.00 85-08 Boots Are Walking121¾ Mighty Beau1211 Rapid Raj124nk  Through early7
7Jun07-7AP yl *5f Ⓣ :213 :443 :564 3↑Clm 30000(35-30)          71 1 1 1hd 2hd 2hd 85 Campbell J M     L119 fb 9.30 93-02 RapidRj119¾ BootsAreWlking121no ChoticAchiever121no  Vied, inside, tired12
11Sep06-6AP sly 5½f ⊗ :22 :441 :56 1:022 3↑Alw 29000n1x        97 4 1 1½ 13 11½ 12¼ Campbell J M      L118 b 3.60 104-10 Lil Tree1182¼ Mysterious Legend1186 Erdiston1184       Not menaced late 8
20Aug06-4AP fst 6f :214 :443 :5721:111 3↑Clm 25000n2l          79 1 1 14 16 13 11¼ Campbell J M       L121 b 3.70 86-14 Lil Tree1211¼ Wicked Facts1181¼ Sir Spencer1182¾        Inside, not menaced10

18Jun05-5AP fst 6f :222 :453 :58 1:111 OC 50k/n1x              74 1 2 1hd 2½ 3½ 34½ Campbell J M      L120 b 3.40 82-09 Quiet Style1202 Be a Halo1202½ Lil Tree1202            Inside, outfinished 5
26May05-7AP fst 7f :222 :444 1:1021:24 OC 50k/n1x              81 7 1 1hd 3nk 2½ 31 Campbell J M        120 b 15.00 88-10 Dangerous Guy120¾ Quiet Style122nk Lil Tree1203¾     4wd-held on well-bled 8
15Apr05-5OP fst 6f :22 :46 :5841:113 Clm c-(25-20)n2l          59 3 3 53½ 41½ 41½ 33¼ Barria J           119 3.10 82-13 ProperCrson1192½ DimondsforDixie114¾ LilTr1191½       Nice move 5-w, hung 7
  Claimed from Shumake Ray for $25,000, Shumake Ray Trainer 2005(as of 4/15): ( 44 3 12 9 0.07 )
31Mar05-8OP fst 6f :22 :454 :5841:121 Clm 35000(40-35)n2l      56 7 3 64½ 76¼ 54½ 31¼ Barria J           116 17.40 81-15 Dj's Choice119½ Half Splendor122¾ Lil Tree1161         5-w rally, willingly 9
12Mar05-7OP fst 6f :213 :454 :5841:12 Clm 25000(25-20)n2l      65 9 2 11 2½ 2½ 41½ Shepherd J          119 7.30 81-14 FstEddChrls119nk ComnndPly1191 GrgLBrwn119nk          Pressed,couldn't last 9
14Oct04-5LaD fst 6f :232 :482 1:0031:142 Md 25000(25-20)       49 2 3 21½ 21½ 12 17 Stanley M K        120 6.00 73-21 Lil Tree1207 Extra Exclusive120½ Better Dancer1204¼     Stalked, well clear 9
WORKS: Mar29 Kee ◈4f fst :501 B 30/39 Mar22 FG 4f fst :522 B 60/62 Mar15 FG 4f fst :544 B 76/77 Feb24 FG 4f fst :521 B 116/122 Feb16 FG 4f gd :534 B 50/56
```

In the same race, it looks like Jesus Castanon wasn't clued in. Riding second choice Smalltown Slew, he never left the rail, and he paid the price.

SECOND RACE **7 FURLONGS. (1.21) CLAIMING. Purse $22,000 FOR FOUR YEAR OLDS AND UPWARD. Weight, 123 lbs. Non–winners Of Two Races Since February 5 Allowed 3 lbs. A Race Since Then Allowed 5 lbs. Claiming Price $16,000 (Races where entered for $12,500 or less not considered).**

Keeneland

APRIL 5, 2008

Value of Race: $22,000 Winner $13,640; second $4,400; third $2,200; fourth $1,100; fifth $660. Mutuel Pool $251,891.00 Exacta Pool $186,573.00 Trifecta Pool $134,372.00 Superfecta Pool $56,714.00

Last Raced	Horse	M/Eqt.	A.	Wt	PP	St	¼	½	Str	Fin	Jockey	Cl'g Pr	Odds $1
1Mar08 ^{4}FG^{1}	Lil Tree	L b	6	118	1	2	1^{2}	1^{2}	1^{4}	$1^{3\frac{1}{2}}$	Theriot H J II	16000	2.10
21Mar08 ^{4}FG^{10}	Por Favor	L b	7	118	7	3	$6^{\frac{1}{2}}$	$6^{1\frac{1}{2}}$	4^{2}	$2^{4\frac{1}{4}}$	Lebron V	16000	34.00
2Feb08 ^{7}FG^{5}	Tux n' Tales	L f	5	118	6	1	$2^{\frac{1}{2}}$	2^{1}	$2^{1\frac{1}{2}}$	3^{nk}	Albarado R J	16000	3.00
16Mar08 ^{5}OP^{5}	IndependentBanker	L	4	118	3	8	8	8	$6^{1\frac{1}{2}}$	$4^{2\frac{3}{4}}$	Lopez J	16000	13.80
16Feb08 ^{1}FG^{6}	Smalltown Slew	L	7	118	2	5	3^{hd}	$4^{\frac{1}{2}}$	3^{2}	$5^{2\frac{3}{4}}$	Castanon J L	16000	2.40
15Mar08 ^{4}TP^{2}	Prince Kong	L f	5	118	4	6	$7^{3\frac{1}{2}}$	7^{2}	$7^{2\frac{1}{2}}$	$6^{\frac{1}{2}}$	Mena M	16000	26.80
22Mar08 ^{3}TP^{4}	Cab	L	5	118	8	4	5^{2}	3^{hd}	5^{1}	$7^{4\frac{1}{4}}$	Felix J E	16000	9.00
14Mar08 ^{7}Mnr^{2}	Bobby Jack	L b	5	118	5	7	4^{hd}	5^{2}	8	8	McKee J	16000	8.80

OFF AT 1:51 Start Good. Won driving. Track fast.

TIME :22^{3}, :45^{2}, 1:10^{2}, 1:23^{2} (:22.75, :45.48, 1:10.45, 1:23.51)

$2 Mutuel Prices:

1 – LIL TREE	**6.20**	**4.40**	**3.20**
7 – POR FAVOR		**21.60**	**7.60**
6 – TUX N' TALES			**2.80**

$2 EXACTA 1–7 PAID $138.80 50 CENT TRIFECTA 1–7–6 PAID $151.30
$2 SUPERFECTA 1–7–6–3 PAID $5,541.20

Ch. g, (Mar), by Lil Honcho – Marked Cow, by Marked Tree. Trainer Autrey Cody. Bred by Ray Shumake (Tex).

LIL TREE moved to the front three wide early, edged clear before going a furlong, floated wider into the lane, made the balance of the pace and was under pressure late. POR FAVOR, five or six wide early, moved wider into the stretch and was clearly second best. TUX N' TALES, briefly in front after the break, surrendered the advantage to the winner from the inside, chased LIL TREE four wide the remainder and weakened. INDEPENDENT BANKER, outrun to the stretch, maneuvered eight wide into the stretch and improved position. SMALLTOWN SLEW raced forwardly inside, was asked for more leaving the three furlong marker and came up empty. PRINCE KONG, bumped at the start by BOBBY JACK and shuffled back, moved six wide on the backstretch, edged in around the turn but never threatened. CAB followed the pace four wide for a half, came out seven abreast leaving the turn and weakened. BOBBY JACK hopped while breaking awkwardly, came over bumping with PRINCE KONG soon after, rushed to contention between foes and was finished upon going a half.

Owners– 1, Heflin Driver Racing LLC; 2, Englander Richard A; 3, Heppermann Ken; 4, Gerald Dixon Revocable Trust; 5, Cardinal Stables; 6, Pegasus Equine Performance Center; 7, Zapp Billy and Kinmon Keith; 8, Kerr Richard T

Trainers– 1, Autrey Cody; 2, Fahey John III; 3, Bindner Walter M Jr; 4, Danner Mark; 5, Amoss Thomas; 6, Zeis Kevin; 7, Kinmon Keith; 8, Connelly William R

Tux n' Tales was claimed by Ross David A; trainer, Smithwick Daniel M Jr,
Independent Banker was claimed by Zeoli Joseph; trainer, Mathieson R Glen,
Smalltown Slew was claimed by L T B Inc; trainer, Flint Bernard S.

$2 Daily Double (5–1) Paid $39.80; Daily Double Pool $141,110.

There were also days at the 2007 Keeneland fall meet where the rail was not the place to be. What about 2008 fall, 2009 spring, etc.? With Keeneland, it's always a guessing game.

4

Turf to Synthetic: Is the Grass Greener?

I'm not sure who first said it, or why he said it, but someone once made the statement that grass horses love synthetic surfaces. This person said that there would be grass runners romping over synthetic surfaces all over the country, and these turf monsters that couldn't run on the dirt would be flocking to places like Keeneland and Turfway to run over Polytrack. That was supposed to be a great benefit for Turfway Park, which doesn't have a turf course but would, with Polytrack, have dozens of turf horses filling entries every night.

Someone picked up on this and repeated it. Then someone else said it, and then someone else, and then someone else. Trainers said it. Racing writers said it. TV commentators said it. Track executives said it. It was said enough times that it became conventional wisdom that grass horses love synthetic surfaces and would duplicate their turf form over them.

The truth? Horses that can only run on turf and are proven failures on conventional dirt tracks usually won't handle synthetic surfaces, either. It's not a good idea to bet a "turf-only" horse on synthetic surfaces.

"Whenever we breezed one of our good dirt horses against one of our best grass horses on our [Tapeta] track, the dirt horses always beat them," said Michael Dickinson. "Whatever horse it was, the dirt horse always beat the grass horse on the synthetic surface."

Before we get too far, what is a grass horse? It's not that easy a question to answer, and it probably depends upon your point of view. For the sake of simplicity and in order to answer the questions posed by the turf-to-synthetic angle, let's consider a "grass horse" to be any horse who has won a race on the turf in his or her career. While that may seem to be an unsophisticated method, most horses have not and never will win on the grass. That's how dirt-oriented the sport is. Many never try it and only a small percentage of horses will become grass winners.

Not surprisingly, trainers were eager to try their grass horses on the Polytrack surface at the 2006 Keeneland fall meet. Not only are the purses spectacular at Keeneland, but also, horsemen had been told that their grass runners were going to love Polytrack. Even Keeneland management got into the act. Races that never would have come off the turf in the pre-Polytrack days were shifted to the main track after only moderate amounts of rain. Perhaps knowing that many grass horses would stay in the race rather than scratch, management seemed to jump at opportunities to get off the grass course.

It didn't take long before Keeneland handicappers were asked to deal with the mysteries of how grass horses would perform over Polytrack. In the sixth race on opening day of the fall meet, a horse named Black Jack Attack was entered in a seven-furlong allowance race on the main track. Though Black Jack Attack was no star, his form on the grass was not half bad. He broke his maiden on the grass at Del Mar and was coming off a second-place finish in a $40,000 claimer on the turf, also at Del Mar. If he ran back to his last race or any of his better turf efforts, he figured to have a chance and, at the very least, needed to be used in the exacta, trifecta, and superfecta.

However, Black Jack Attack's form on the dirt was dismal. He had run on the surface four times and had finished last every time, while losing by a combined 99½ lengths. His lone start over the old Keeneland main track turned out to be the worst race of his life. Making his career debut there in a 2003 maiden race, he finished 10th, beaten 31¾ lengths.

The bettors didn't seem to know what to do with Black Jack Attack. Based on his previous main-track form, he was a sure throw-out, not worth considering at any price. On his grass form, though, he was a contender, and perhaps a potential overlay. The crowd neither loved him nor hated him, sending him off at 10–1.

Actually, Black Jack Attack didn't run too badly. This time, he actually beat a couple of horses. But his grass form did not hold up and, in hindsight, he should not have been used in any wagers.

In the very next race on the Keeneland card, a horse named Pyramid Love presented another conundrum for handicappers. Though she was bred for the dirt (by Fusaichi Pegasus out of a Broad Brush mare), her best races had clearly come on the turf. She won twice on the grass in France before coming to the United States, and her turf debut in the U.S. wasn't that bad. She ran sixth, beaten six lengths, in the Grade 3 Lake George at Saratoga. Then trainer Patrick Biancone, one of the biggest advocates of Polytrack in the country, tried her on the dirt in the Grade 1 Alabama, and the results were disastrous. She was eased in the stretch. Which Pyramid Love would show up in this race, a mile-and-a-sixteenth allowance event over Polytrack?

Pyramid Love
Own: Farish William S. and Mooney, Steve

Dk. b or b. f. 4 (Mar)
Sire: Fusaichi Pegasus (Mr. Prospector) $75,000
Dam: Pyramid Lake (Broad Brush)
Br: Jean Pierre Dubois (Ky)
Tr: Biancone Patrick L

Life	9	4	1	0	$140,121	87	D.Fst	1	0	0	0	$3,000
2007	2	0	1	0	$28,158	84	Wet(417)	0	0	0	0	$0
2006	4	2	0	0	$73,697	87	Synth	4	2	1	0	$98,102
							Turf(286)	4	2	0	0	$39,019

6May07–3Hol fst 1 1/16 :232 :463 1:111 1:44 3↑ⒻHawthrnH-G3 81 1 1hd 1hd 1hd 31½ 45¼ Leparoux J R LB117 3.60 83–10 RiverSavage1142 Cantabri1161 BlldosThunder1162¼ Inside duel,weakened
18Apr07–8Kee fst 1 1/16 :27 :52 1:164 1:462 4↑ⒻDbldgdre-G3 84 1 11 17 12½ 11 21 Leparoux J R L117 2.60 75–19 Asi Siempre1211 Pyramid Love117¾ Warrior Girl1171 Rank, drift 1st trn
27Oct06–7Kee fst 1 1/16 :241 :483 1:133 1:442 3↑ⒻOC 100k/c-N 86 4 2½ 2½ 2hd 12½ 11½ Leparoux J R L117 *1.90 - - PyrmdLov1171½ EysOnEddy124¾ ClssyChrm1241¼ Reluctant gate,4w,drvg
6Oct06–7Kee fst 1 1/16 :231 :47 1:12 1:443 3↑ⒻAlw 54000N2x 87 2 21½ 2½ 11 11½ 11¼ Leparoux J R L117 6.10 - - PyrmidLove1171¼ LeosPegsus119no MyChickde1172¾ Forced pace,4w,drvg
19Aug06–9Sar fst 1¼ :471 1:114 1:37 2:024 ⒻAlabama-G1 – 8 2hd 913 920 - - Leparoux J R L121 b 12.00 - 11 Pine Island1211¼ Teammate1218½ Lemons Forever1211¾ Eased stretch
28Jly06–8Sar yl 1 1/16 Ⓣ :241 :493 1:142 1:454 ⒻLkGeorge-G3 80 4 67 63½ 55½ 75¼ 66 Leparoux J R L116 *2.30 64–24 MgnifcntSong120¾ Somthnboutbtty1161¼ QutBrd1222¼ Off slowly, no rally
Previously trained by Yves de Nicolay
10Nov05♦Fontainebleau (Fr) sf *1⅛ Ⓣ LH 2:003 ⒻPrix Hula Dancer Alw 36500 1no Soumillon C 126 *.70 Pyramid Love126no Alix Road1221 Sureyya1221½ *Tracked leaders,led 1f out,dueled,just he*
18Oct05♦Deauville (Fr) gs *1 Ⓣ RH 1:451 ⒻPrix des Reservoirs-G3 Stk 90200 43 Mendizabal I 121 7.00 Emily Bronte1211 Sanaya121no Souvenance1212 *Rated in 6th,drifted right,up for 4th.Zaynab 5th,Alix Road 8t*
Racing Post Rating: 94
16Sep05♦Chantilly (Fr) gs *1 Ⓣ RH 1:412 ⒻPrix de Toutevoie-EBF Maiden (FT) 22000 1nk Mendizabal I 126 7.30 Pyramid Love126nk Going Day1262½ Mary Louhana1262½ *Tracked leaders,led over 1f out,quickly clear,handil*
Racing Post Rating: 82

Score one for a grass horse. Pyramid Love won and paid $14.20 under Julien Leparoux and came back three weeks later to win again over Keeneland's Polytrack. Was Pyramid Love a prime example of a turf horse loving Polytrack?

Not necessarily.

In her case, there were still questions that needed to be answered: Was her recent success due to a drop in class rather than a surface switch? And how would she perform the next time she showed up on a conventional dirt track? After all, it was hard to gauge her dirt ability when her lone start on the surface had come in a Grade 1 stakes race where she was hopelessly overmatched.

Unfortunately, those questions remain unanswered. In the early part of 2007, Biancone stayed with the synthetic tracks; Pyramid Love ran second in a Grade 3 stakes at Keeneland and fourth in a Grade 3 at Hollywood Park. As of May 2008 she hadn't started in a year.

Biancone, who is on record saying he believes turf horses will thrive on synthetic surfaces, tried another grass runner on the Polytrack surface two days later. Asi Siempre had never run on anything but grass when she went into the Grade 1 Spinster. She began her career in France and then turned in several strong efforts in grass stakes in the U.S.

How would she handle Polytrack? It was anybody's guess, but the bettors respected her chances, sending her off at 9–2. Those who had predicted she could run on something other than grass were right. In what turned out to be the most important victory of her career, she won the Spinster by 2¼ lengths under Leparoux.

Did this prove that grass horses like Polytrack? Not necessarily. Given the choice of running his filly on the grass or on the dirt in the Breeders' Cup at Churchill Downs, Biancone chose the dirt, entering Asi Siempre in the Distaff, run at a mile and an eighth over the main track. It was her first career start on conventional dirt.

Asi Siempre ran a strong race, rallying to finish second before being disqualified to fourth place. Her Beyer Speed Figure was a 91, just one point slower than she had run when winning the Spinster. It turned out that Asi Siempre was not a Polytrack-turf horse but the type of filly that can run over grass, dirt, Polytrack, or the New Jersey Turnpike.

Asi Siempre
Own: Schwartz Martin S

Gr/ro. m. 5 (Mar)
Sire: El Prado*Ire (Sadler's Wells) $125,000
Dam: Siempre Asi (Silver Hawk)
Br: Almagro de Actividades Commerciales (Ky)
Tr: Biancone Patrick L

Life	19	7	5	2	$938,000	101	D.Fst	2	0	1	0	$179,469	98
2007	3	1	2	0	$176,724	98	Wet(317)	1	0	1	0	$45,183	97
2006	7	2	1	1	$544,210	101	Synth	2	2	0	0	$377,332	92
							Turf(340)	14	5	3	2	$336,016	101

16Jun07-9CD	fst	1⅛	:471 1:11 1:361 1:49	3↑ⒻFlrDLisH-G2	98	3	65½	65¼	54½	31½	21½	Gomez G K	L122 b	2.40	89-10	Indian Vale1191½ Asi Siempre122nk Kettleoneup1171¾	4w bid,second best	7
4May07-8CD	slyS	1 1/16	:233 :474 1:12 1:44	3↑ⒻLouvlBC-G2	97	1	57½	55½	43	21½	2hd	Gomez G K	L122 b	2.50	90-14	Fiery Pursuit118hd Asi Siempre122¾ Baghdaria1181¾	Bmp start,4w,missed	6
18Apr07-8Kee	fst	1 1/16 ◈	:27 :52 1:164 1:462	4↑ⒻDbldgdre-G3	86	4	42	510	44½	21	11	Gomez G K	L121 b	*.40	76-19	Asi Siempre1211 PyramidLove117¾ WarriorGirl1171	Gathered up very late	5
4Nov06-8CD	fst	1⅛	:463 1:112 1:372 1:502	3↑ⒻBCDistaf-G1	91	12	108¾	108½	95¼	53	25½	Leparoux J R	L123 b	11.30	79-07	Round Pond1235½ ⒹAsi Siempre123½ Happy Ticket1231	Rough trip	14
Disqualified and placed 4th																		
8Oct06-8Kee	fst	1⅛ ◈	:502 1:161 1:40 1:514	3↑ⒻSpinster-G1	92	6	64¼	63¼	52	1hd	12¼	Leparoux J R	L123 b	4.50	- -	AsiSiempre1232¼ SoulSearch123nk PromendeGirl123nk	6w lane,drvg,clear	9
26Aug06-8Sar	fm	1 1/16 Ⓣ	:243 :484 1:124 1:413	3↑ⒻBlstSpaH-G2	101	1	66½	54½	63¾	45	32¼	Leparoux J R	L117 b	5.00	89-14	My Typhoon118¾ Karen's Caper1151½ Asi Siempre117nk	Good finish outside	7
9Aug06-9Sar	fm	1 Ⓣ	:233 :464 1:103 1:342	4↑ⒻⓇDeLaRose73k	101	3	65	64½	31	2½	1nk	Leparoux J R	L117 b	*1.80	95-06	AsiSimpr117nk BrightAbundnc1194¾ ConniBll1173¼	Saved ground, gamely	7
24Jun06-8Bel	sf	1¼ Ⓣ	:523 1:182 1:433 2:081	3↑ⒻNYBCH-G2	97	4	45	41	41½	3½	43¼	Desormeaux K J	L116 b	3.75	52-45	Noble Stella116nk Angara1181¼ Argentina1161¾	Inside run, faded late	7
27May06-8Bel	fm	1⅜ Ⓣ	:50 1:142 1:382 2:124	3↑ⒻShpshdBH-G2	94	4	74¼	73¾	64¼	46½	45½	Leparoux J R	L116	2.05	90-14	Honey Ryder1211 Noble Stella116nk Angara1194¼	Came wide, no rally	7
15Apr06-7Kee	fm	1 1/16 ⓣ	:24 :48 1:114 1:411	4↑ⒻJenyWily-G2	95	5	75	74½	62¼	41	21½	Leparoux J R	L117 b	3.70	94-06	Wend1171½ Asi Siempre1171 Mirabilis118hd	Reared start	8
21Oct05-9Kee	yl	1 1/16 ⓣ	:24 :481 1:132 1:451	ⒻVllyView-G3	95	1	910	78	63	31½	1no	Stevens G L	L120 b	*.40	81-25	AsiSiempre120no DynamiteLss1161¾ VictoryLp120½	Drift start,9w,driving	9
7Oct05-10Kee	fm	1 3/16 ⓣ	:502 1:161 1:423 2:014	3↑ⒻAlw 48735N2x	95	6	610	57	53½	21½	11¼	Stevens G L	L119 b	*.20	70-31	AsiSiempre1191¼ SunnyDisposition1211 YesBth117¾	Hop start,hand urging	9

WORKS: ●Jly4 Kee ◈ 5f fst :593 B *1/9* Jun12 Kee ◈ 5f fst 1:01 B *6/30* Jun5 Kee ◈ 6f fst 1:122 H *1/2* May29 Kee ◈ 5f fst 1:004 B *6/29* May25 TTC 3f fst :372 Bg *5/9* Apr30 Kee ◈ 5f fst :593 B *3/12*

Another example is the wonderful old pro Lava Man. Entering the 2007 Hollywood Gold Cup, which marked his first career start on a synthetic surface, bettors should not have had any reservations about how he would handle the surface. Few racehorses are more versatile than Lava Man, who had already won several times on dirt and grass. He handled Cushion Track just fine and won the Gold Cup, becoming the first horse in history to win a Grade 1 race on turf, dirt, and synthetic courses.

It's true that many horses have made a successful transition from turf to synthetic, but I believe that's because most of them are the kinds of runners that can handle just about any type of track. There have not been many examples of horses that are good on the grass and horrible on the dirt, but good on a synthetic surface.

Bettors didn't appear to know what to do with a horse named Swan Creek when she showed up in a starter-allowance race at Hollywood Park on November 18, 2006. The filly's form on conventional dirt surfaces was abysmal. In three dirt starts, she had been beaten a combined 70½ lengths and her career-best Beyer figure was an 11. She was a totally different horse when trying the grass in a $32,000 maiden claimer at Golden Gate Fields, which she won by four lengths while earning a 75 Beyer.

She needed to duplicate her turf form on the Cushion Track to have any chance in this race. Enough people thought she would, which was why she was sent off at a ridiculously low 5–1. Predictably, she was trounced, losing by more than 30 lengths. Trainer Craig Dollase put her back on the turf, where her Beyers immediately improved.

Swan Creek
Own: Final Furlong Farm

Dk. b or b. f. 4 (Apr) CALAUG04 $25,000
Sire: Game Plan (Danzig) $3,500
Dam: Marsh Grass (Slewpy)
Br: Tom Clark & Nancy Clark (Cal)
Tr: Dollase Craig(0 0 0 0 .00) 2006:(170 34 .20)

Life	7	1	0	0	$11,850	75	D.Fst	3	0	0	0	$1,200	11
2007	1	0	0	0	$400	52	Wet(397)	0	0	0	0	$0	-
							Synth	1	0	0	0	$500	24
2006	5	1	0	0	$11,050	75	Turf(316)	3	1	0	0	$10,150	75
	0	0	0	0	$0	-	Dst(0)	0	0	0	0	$0	-

11Jan07–4SA	fm	1	Ⓣ	:23	:462	1:11	1:363	4↑ⒻAlw 40000s	52	8	11	11½	1½	76½	911¾	Baze T C	LB120 b	12.50	69– 15	MadmeBlckfoot113½ SeDriver120hd JkSieMcz1201¼	Speed,inside,wkened	10
13Dec06–5Hol	fm	1 1/16	Ⓣ	:23	:47	1:111	1:423	3↑ⒻAlw 40000s	63	5	11	1½	11	21½	86½	Flores D R	LB121	4.70	72– 21	MarkSetGo117nk *MdmeBlckfoot*1121¼ SmoothSis120nk	Pulled,rail,wkened	9
18Nov06–3Hol	fst	1 1/16	◈	:231	:462	1:11	1:451	3↑ⒻAlw 40000s	24	6	11½	1½	22	513	530¼	Valenzuela P A	LB121	5.00	- -	LdyLeBelle1212½ SeDriver1129½ RomnceIsFly117¾	Speed,gave way,eased	6
3Sep06–1GG	fm	1	Ⓣ	:241	:474	1:12	1:374	3↑ⒻMd 30000(32-30)	75	3	11½	11	12	13	14	Flores P10	LB107	9.30	87– 11	Swan Creek1074 Wise Step1133½ Mina Girl1224	Set pace, driving	7
27Jly06–8Dmr	fst	6½f		:221	:453	1:111	1:18	3↑ⒻMd 25000(25-22.5)	8	1	10	2½	42	1217	1225	Baze T C	LB120	8.70	58– 12	*Key Lime Time*120¾ *Rebellious*1191 Racy Ack120¾	Off bit slow,inside	12
12Jan06–8SA	fst	6f		:213	:452	:584	1:123	Ⓕ[S]Md 40000	9	13	2	63½	58	1016	1120¾	Valdivia J Jr	LB121	29.60	55– 18	StripinWger1212¾ TrickyVivin1212 BriteButWild1213½	4wd,3wd,weakened	13
11Dec05–6Hol	fst	6f		:214	:453	:581	1:11	Ⓕ[S]Md Sp Wt 44k	11	11	10	97	129¾	1212	1224¾	Valdivia J Jr	LB120	11.00	57– 15	UnchngdMlody1202¼ Wlkonkydvn1203¼ MnkyFc120½	Off bit slow,wkened	12

WORKS: Feb27 Hol ◈5f fst 1:031 H *20/22* Feb21 Hol ◈5f fst 1:001 H *5/39* Feb15 Hol ◈4f fst :48 H *2/23* Feb2 Hol ◈6f fst 1:144 H *15/19* Jan26 Hol ◈5f fst 1:004 H *15/55* Jan4 Hol ◈6f fst 1:122 Hg *3/26*

Players betting the California circuit continued to have a tough time grasping the fact that most true grass horses won't run their best on the

Cushion Track. That's good news for those who get it and can throw out these underlayed horses. Take Music and Magic, for example.

When she showed up in the second race at Hollywood Park on April 25, 2007, there were a lot of people out there who thought she would duplicate her recent grass form on the Cushion Track and sent her off at 3–1. Predictably, Music and Magic was awful. She returned to the grass in her next start and ran much better.

Music and Magic was the third choice in the April 25 race. By throwing her out, the race came down to only two legitimate contenders. They ran one-two, for a $14.80 exacta. You're not going to get rich hitting $14.80 exactas, but when they make it this easy, take it.

It's harder to figure out what to do with a horse like Dashes N Dots. The filly did, in fact, win on Polytrack, romping in a Turfway maiden race by 14¾ lengths. But it soon became evident that she was far better on turf than on a dirt or synthetic track.

Dashes N Dots
Own: Kaster Richard S., Wieting, Frederick

Dk. b or b. f. 3 (Feb)
Sire: Aptitude (A.P. Indy) $20,000
Dam: Mystery Code (Lost Code)
Br: Scott E. Ricker & Richard S. Kaster (Ky)
Tr: Fox Gregory(0 0 0 0 .00) 2007:(92 14 .15)

Life	10	2	1	4	$93,351	93	D.Fst	0	0	0	0	$0	-
2007	9	2	0	4	$83,351	93	Wet(334)	1	0	0	0	$250	51
							Synth	4	1	1	1	$28,930	74
2006	1	M	1	0	$10,000	65	Turf(278)	5	1	0	3	$64,171	93
	0	0	0	0	$0	-	Dst(0)	0	0	0	0	$0	-

20Oct07-8Kee	fm	1	Ⓣ	:23^{3}	:49	1:13^{4}	1:37^{1}	3↑ⒻAlw 47695N2x	84	7	3^{1½}	3^{1}	3^{nk}	5^{2½}	3^{4¼}	Mena M	L117	10.60	77-17	YoGWstGrl117^{1¼} KssWthTwst117^{3} DshsNDts117¼	Forced pace,4w,empty	9
22Sep07-12TP	fst	1$\frac{1}{16}$	◈	:24	:48^{1}	1:13^{2}	1:46	3↑ⒻOC 40k/N2x-N	69	1	1^{3}	1^{1½}	1½	3^{1½}	3^{8½}	Sterling L J Jr	L117	*1.20	73-28	Rayona117^{nk} Hoochie Glide115^{8¼} Dashes N Dots117^{6¼}	3 path, tired	5
19Aug07-9AP	fst	1$\frac{1}{16}$	⊗	:23^{4}	:47^{2}	1:11^{3}	1:41^{2}	ⒻHatoof47k	59	6	5^{2½}	4^{1½}	5^{2¾}	6^{6¾}	6^{16¼}	Albarado R J	L119	3.10	- -	Pitamakan116^{1} YouGoWestGirl118^{4¼} ClltheKitty119^{7¼}	Stumbled stretch	7
27Jly07-8Sar	fm	1$\frac{1}{16}$	Ⓣ	:23	:46^{4}	1:10^{3}	1:40^{1}	ⒻLkGeorge-G3	75	3	1^{2½}	1^{1}	1^{1½}	4^{2}	9^{8½}	Albarado R J	L117	12.80	87-04	*Rutherienne*122^{nk} Lady Attack117^{nk} *Sharp Susan*122^{1}	Set pace inside, tired	11
16Jun07-11CD	fm	1⅛	Ⓣ	:47	1:10^{4}	1:34^{3}	1:47^{2}	ⒻRegret-G3	93	6	1^{1½}	1^{2}	1^{1}	1^{2}	3^{2}	Gomez G K	L116	4.70	94-04	GoodMood116^{1¾} YouGoWestGirl118^{nk} DshsNDots116^{2¾}	3w,could not last	10
20May07-9CD	fm	1$\frac{1}{16}$	Ⓣ	:22^{3}	:46^{1}	1:10^{4}	1:41^{1}	3↑ⒻAlw 48200N1x	91	4	1^{1½}	1^{2½}	1^{1}	1^{3}	1^{3¾}	Albarado R J	L117	13.80	100-05	Dashes N Dots117^{3¾} Arosa120^{1} Lordly120½	Clear,inside,driving	10
26Apr07-4Kee	fm	1⅛	Ⓣ	:49^{2}	1:14^{3}	1:39^{1}	1:51^{3}	ⒻAlw 54000N1x	80	2	2^{2}	2^{1}	2^{1}	1^{hd}	3^{4}	Bridgmohan S X	L118	18.50	73-23	WhsprtoM118^{3½} KssWthTwst118½ *DshsNDts*118½	Chased,led,weakened,4w	10
31Mar07-9TP	fst	1	◈	:24^{1}	:47^{3}	1:12^{3}	1:38^{3}	ⒻMd Sp Wt 26k	74	6	1^{1}	1^{1}	1^{4}	1^{12}	1^{14¾}	Graham J	L122	*1.10	85-18	DshsNDots122^{14¾} BrkFstTffny117^{1} WhsprLdr122½	Rated on pace, driving	8
15Mar07-5FG	sly^{S}	5½f	⊗	:22^{2}	:46	:58^{2}	1:05^{1}	ⒻMd Sp Wt 58k	51	7	9	9^{6½}	6^{7}	6^{8}	6^{11¾}	Campbell J M	L122	4.30	78-16	Molly by Golly122^{2} *You Go West Girl*122^{1¼} *Hidden Grove*122¾	No real threat	11
Previously trained by Werner Ronny 2006(as of 10/15): (215 47 49 21 0.22)																						
15Oct06-5Kee	fst	6f	◈	:22^{2}	:46	:57^{4}	1:09^{4}	ⒻMd Sp Wt 50k	65	3	2	4^{1}	3^{1½}	3^{2}	2^{2¾}	Graham J	L118	6.60	- -	*Zofzig*118^{2¾} Dashes N Dots118½ Simply Divine118½	Between,no match late	12

WORKS: Oct11 KeeⓉ 4f fm :52^{4} B(d) *2/2* **Sep15 TTC 4f fst :50 B** *2/29* **Sep8 TTC 5f fst 1:02^{3} B** *2/21*

She hit a peak when running third in the Grade 3 Regret on the turf at Churchill, earning a career-best 93 Beyer, far better than anything she had ever done on synthetic tracks. Trainer Gregory Fox decided to go back to the synthetics and ran her at Arlington and then at Turfway again. Both times, the bettors seemed mesmerized by her figures on the grass and pounded her down to low odds. Big mistake.

At the 2006 Keeneland fall meet, no one did themselves any favors by blindly betting on grass horses running on the Polytrack. A total of 221 horses that had won a race on the turf started on the Polytrack, a sign that trainers were eager to try their turf runners on the new surface. Twenty-eight of them, or 12.67 percent, won.

Anyone wagering $2 to win on every one of these grass horses would have lost $66.20, meaning the return on investment was $1.70. Considering that Keeneland's takeout rate is 16 percent on straight wagers, grass horses, basically, fared no better or no worse than all other horses that ran on the Polytrack surface.

During its first test, the Woodbine Polytrack was even less kind to grass horses, which, again, means any horse who had won at least one race on the grass. From Polytrack's inception at Woodbine through the end of the 2006 racing season there, 124 grass horses raced over Polytrack. A mere 14 of them won. The return on investment was just $1.13.

Perhaps the most interesting stat to come out of the Woodbine meet was how few grass horses actually tried Polytrack as compared to Keeneland. For whatever reason, Canadian trainers were less inclined to experiment with the new surface.

"The track has been too loose," top Canadian trainer Robert Tiller said in mid-May 2007. "It's not quite like some of the other Polytracks. They are trying to correct it. It gets deep and it gets cuppy and the kickback is severe. It's always sandy and beachy. It's not like the Polytrack at Keeneland and that might be why you aren't seeing so many grass horses win here."

At the inaugural Hollywood Park meet run over Cushion Track, 84 horses fitting the grass-horse definition started over Cushion Track. Thirteen, or 15.48 percent, won. The ROI was $1.75. Again, the numbers show that grass horses didn't necessarily move up over Hollywood's synthetic surface.

There was an inordinate amount of rain during October 2006 in Kentucky, which caused management to take some races off the turf, something that rarely used to happen at Keeneland. When the races were moved to Polytrack, few trainers scratched their horses, no doubt believing the turf form would hold up on the new surface. That gave handicappers a crash course in how to handicap synthetic-surface races filled with grass horses.

The October 20 Valley View, a Grade 3 race that had been scheduled for the Keeneland turf course, was a real handicapping challenge. All 13 horses entered stayed in, and 12 of the 13 had won on the grass at some point in their careers.

9

Keeneland *1 1/16 MILES* **(Turf). (1:401) ⒻVllyView-G3 16th Running of THE VALLEY VIEW. Grade III. Purse $125,000 For Fillies, Three Years Old. Bysubscription of $125 each which should accompany the nomination or by Supplementary Nomination of $6,250 by time of entry $625 to enter and an additional $625 to start, with $125,000 guaranteed, of which $77,500 to the owner of the winner, $25,000 to second, $12,500 to third, $6,250 to fourth and $3,750 to fifth. Weight: 123 lbs. Non-winners of a graded or group stakes on the turf in 2006 allowed 2 lbs.; $45,000 twice on the turf in 2006, 4 lbs.; three races other than maiden or claiming, 6 lbs. The maximum number of starters for the Valley View will be limited to twelve. In the event that more than twelve fillies pass the entry box, the twelve starters will be determined at that timewith preference by condition eligibility, beginning with graded or group stakes winners. Starters to be named through the entry box by the usual time of closing. A gold julep cup will be presented to the owner of the winner. Closed Wednesday, October 11, 2006 with 32 nominations.**

'ransmit
wn: Adele B Dilschneider
lver, Blue Cross Sashes, Blue Stripe
CON L (21 1 2 1 .05) 2006: (250 41 .16)

Ch. f. 3 (Mar)
Sire: Horse Chestnut*SAf (Fort Wood) $10,000
Dam: Broadcast (Broad Brush)
Br: Adele B Dilschneider (Ky)
Tr: Penrod Steven C(4 0 1 0 .00) 2006:(42 8 .19)

L 117

Life	5	2	0	0	$32,665	86	D.Fst	1	0	0	0	$1,200 51
2006	5	2	0	0	$32,665	86	Wet(373)	0	0	0	0	$0 -
2005	0	M	0	0	$0	-	Turf(375)	4	2	0	0	$31,465 86
KeeⓉ	0	0	0	0	$0	-	DstⓉ(362)	0	0	0	0	$0 -

6KD gd 1 Ⓣ :261 :48 1:12 1:373 3↑ⒻAlw 27000N1x 85 3 55½ 45 21 11 13½ Melancon L L114 fb *2.60 94- 06 Transmit1143½ BabyNeedsShoes118½ Blue'sFirstBaby1131 4w,hand urging 11
9EIP fm 1 Ⓣ :23 :454 1:101 1:343 3↑ⒻMd Sp Wt 20k 86 1 63½ 65 62¼ 11½ 15¼ Melancon L L118 fb 3.40 91- 14 *Transmit*1185¼ Pay the Toll1182¼ Supple1181¼ 5w,mild urging lane 9
CD fm 1⅛ Ⓣ :48 1:13 1:381 1:503 3↑ⒻMd Sp Wt 50k 62 3 33 42¼ 21 42½ 49 Melancon L L118 fb 5.10 71- 19 MaryCt1132¾ *EsthersBigBnd*1183½ *HeyGorgeous*1183 Bmp,rank,drift 1st trn 8
CD fm 1 Ⓣ :234 :474 1:124 1:371 3↑ⒻMd Sp Wt 43k 60 6 85¾ 84¾ 75 78 76¾ Melancon L L117 9.70 76- 16 What Will Be112nk Ambling117¾ Hey Gorgeous117¾ No rally 10
6CD fst 1 1/16 ⊗ :25 :50 1:142 1:453 3↑ⒻMd Sp Wt 48k 51 6 64 65 64½ 57½ 515 Melancon L L117 6.90 67- 18 **Precious Kitten**1171 Earth to Nina1242¾ Mary Cat1179¼ Split foes,bmp 1/8p 6
Oct16 CD 3f fst :371 B *2/8* **Oct11 CD 5f fst 1:014 B** *5/31* **Sep8 CD 5f fst 1:022 B** *7/13* **Aug27 CD 3f fst :372 B** *4/12* **Jly28 CD 4f fst :482 B** *5/28* **Jly22 CD 3f my :361 B** *2/3*
R: 2Off45-180(8 .12 $1.45) 31-60Days(26 .23 $2.04) WonLastStart(12 .25 $2.92) Turf(52 .19 $1.62) Routes(47 .17 $1.39) J/T 2005-06 KEE(6 .00 $0.00) J/T 2005-06(55 .18 $1.84)

Meribel
wn: Arthur B Hancock III and Catesby W Cl
rey, Yellow Sash, Yellow Sleeves
G K (29 8 3 7 .28) 2006: (1025 204 .20)

Dk. b or br f. 3 (Apr)
Sire: Peaks and Valleys (Mt. Livermore) $8,000
Dam: Count to Six (Saratoga Six)
Br: Arthur B Hancock III & Catesby W Clay (Ky)
Tr: Clement Christophe(3 3 0 0 1.00) 2006:(330 65 .20)

L 117

Life	9	3	2	2	$150,950	96	D.Fst	2	0	0	2	$8,700 61
2006	8	3	2	1	$146,650	96	Wet(361)	0	0	0	0	$0 -
2005	1	M	0	1	$4,300	56	Turf(212)	7	3	2	0	$142,250 96
KeeⓉ	0	0	0	0	$0	-	DstⓉ(347)	5	2	2	0	$109,350 96

0Lrl fm 1 1/16 Ⓣ :234 :472 1:112 1:411 ⒻMWashtonBC200k 93 3 87¾ 87 75 31 2nk Dominguez R A L122 2.40 94- 06 **Precious Kitten**116nk Meribel1222½ Gasia122hd Swung 5-6w,bid,floated 10
6Sar gd 1 1/16 Ⓣ :233 :472 1:121 1:422 ⒻⓇDynasty72k 96 5 913 910 95¼ 3nk 1no Gomez G K L118 *1.60 84- 22 Meribel118no Amansara1184½ Better Now120½ Fast finish, got nod 9
0Sar gd 1 [T] :234 :48 1:122 1:362 3↑ⒻAlw 51000N1x 94 10 1021 1013 88¼ 5¾ 12¼ Gomez G K L116 *2.65 85- 19 *Meribel*1162¼ Calla Lily1183½ *Forest Code*116no Rolled home outside 10
4Bel fm 1 Ⓣ :24 :48 1:114 1:344 3↑ⒻAlw 46000N1x 84 6 84¼ 95½ 86¼ 63¾ 4nk Gomez G K L116 6.70 86- 13 **SouthernProtocol**116hd Ohbeegewhyn121no ForstCod116no Traffic stretch 11
5Med gd 1 1/16 Ⓣ :242 :481 1:113 1:414 ⒻTrenton60k 77 7 73¾ 64¼ 53¼ 65 56 Bravo J L117 5.80 91- 03 *QuiteBride*1192¾ KittyHwk121¾ ***SouthrnProtocol***1172 Checked btwn near 1/8 8
0GP fm 1 1/16 Ⓣ :25 :491 1:124 1:421 ⒻMd Sp Wt 32k 71 7 64 56 54 42½ 1nk Cruz M R L121 *.70 80- 14 Meribel121nk **Precious Kitten**121¾ Ghost Tapping1211¼ 4 wide, up late 9
8GP fm 1 1/16 Ⓣ :224 :454 1:092 1:394 ⒻMd Sp Wt 32k 81 3 55 58 55 35 2½ Castellano J J L121 7.40 91- 14 Miracle Moment121½ *Meribel*1213¾ St. Hildegard121nk Gaining quickly 12
3Aqu fst 1 1/16 [•] :243 :49 1:132 1:451 ⒻMd Sp Wt 44k 61 7 32½ 31½ 21½ 37½ 311 Luzzi M J L119 2.50 73- 18 *Regal Engagement*1197 *Red Damask*1194 Meribel1192 Chased 3 wide, tired 7
7Aqu fst 6f [•] :223 :462 :59 1:112 ⒻMd Sp Wt 43k 56 11 7 72¾ 52½ 42¾ 35½ Luzzi M J 120 2.50 76- 16 MississippiMadam1204¾ Southfield1201¼ Meribel120no 3 wide trip, got 3rd 12
Oct13 Bel 4f fst :491 B *18/29* **Sep24 Bel 4f fst :50 B** *22/50* **Sep18 Bel[T] 4f yl :50 B(d)** *2/9* **Aug23 Sar tr.t 4f fst :501 B** *6/16* **Aug11 Sar tr.tⓉ 4f gd :49 B(d)** *7/14* **Jly23 BelⓉ 4f sf :511 B** *5/11*
R: Turf(514 .22 $1.61) Routes(545 .20 $1.45) GrdStk(59 .20 $2.15) J/T 2005-06 KEE(3 1.00 $7.13) J/T 2005-06(40 .28 $2.15)

Idle Quest
wn: Stonerside Stable LLC
White, Forest Green Inverted Chevron
C H (33 3 3 3 .09) 2006: (805 113..14)

Ch. f. 3 (Feb)
Sire: Coronado's Quest (Forty Niner) $23,741
Dam: Idle Rich (Sky Classic)
Br: Stonerside Stable (Ky)
Tr: Flint Bernard S(6 0 0 0 .00) 2006:(339 65 .19)

L 117

Life	8	3	1	0	$81,120	95	D.Fst	3	1	1	0	$26,760 65
2006	4	2	0	0	$52,710	95	Wet(386)	2	1	0	0	$20,550 74
2005	4	1	1	0	$28,410	65	Turf(307)	3	1	0	0	$33,810 95
KeeⓉ	0	0	0	0	$0	-	DstⓉ(364)	1	0	0	0	$0 68

4Mnr sly 1 ⊗ :232 :471 1:13 1:403 3↑ⒻAlw 31500N2x 74 6 32½ 42 2½ 15 18¾ Whitney D G L111 *1.10 73- 25 IdlQust1118¾ FstndFluid1152¼ TouchofSplndor1151¼ Fired turn, drove off 6
0CD fm 1 Ⓣ :23 :46 1:11 1:344 ⒻHvnlyCausH71k 45 3 1½ 1½ 2hd 914 923½ Toups R L115 9.30 71- 09 TkethRibbon1154 **PrciousKittn**1182¾ KickinthClouds114½ Gave way readily 10
8CD yl 1 Ⓣ :234 :481 1:133 1:384 ⒻAlw 50150N1x 95 5 12½ 12 12½ 13 17 Toups R7 L111 10.50 75- 25 IdleQuest1117 *FantasticShirl*118¾ DaylightDncer118¾ Kept to task,widened 10
9CD gd 1 1/16 Ⓣ :232 :472 1:113 1:421 ⒻAlw 51800N1x 68 6 11½ 11 2½ 32½ 66¼ Borel C H L118 12.60 89- 09 SaltyResponse111½ FantasticShirl1181½ SssySkipper1182 Pace,weakened 9
7EIP wfS 7f :214 :45 1:101 1:234 ⒻAMFsherDeb62k 34 2 4 2½ 21 59½ 519½ Nakatani C S L116 6.50 67- 12 She Says It Best1187 Claremont1162¾ Swept Gold116½ Pressed,4w,tired 5
3AP fst 1 :24 :481 1:132 1:374 ⒻMd Sp Wt 27k 65 2 11 11 1½ 12½ 13 Bridgmohan S X L118 2.10 79- 07 Idle Quest1183 Candy Ma'am1185¾ Swain Lake118no Pace, rail, ridden out 5
0CD fst 5½f :221 :452 :581 1:042 ⒻMd Sp Wt 45k 42 4 1 21½ 21 46 57½ Martin E M Jr L119 3.20 85- 07 LucyMkesEight1193 EverythingGood1191½ Moppl1191 Chased,4-5w,tired 7
3CD fst 5f :223 :453 :574 ⒻMd Sp Wt 47k 65 6 6 3nk 1½ 1½ 23¼ Martin E M Jr L119 2.80 91- 09 Artemus Runner1193¼ IdleQuest1196 SlewMarker119¾ Sluggish,drft, start 6
Oct14 CD 5f fst 1:002 B *2/27* **Oct7 CD 5f fst 1:004 B** *4/24* **Sep17 CD 4f fst :481 B** *9/48* **Aug13 CD 5f fst :594 B** *2/10* **Aug4 CD 5f fst 1:003 B** *3/15*
R: Dirt/Turf(50 .10 $3.10) 31-60Days(181 .18 $1.25) WonLastStart(157 .18 $1.94) Turf(72 .08 $2.47) Routes(273 .21 $1.49) GrdStk(28 .00 $0.00) J/T 2005-06(29 .14 $4.61)

May Night
Own: Harvey A Clarke and Frederick J Seitz
Grey, Green Sash, Green Chevrons On
ADO R J (37 5 7 6 .14) 2006: (788 130 .16)

Ch. f. 3 (Apr) OBSMAR05 $210,000
Sire: Gulch (Mr. Prospector) $40,000
Dam: Riverjinsky (Riverman)
Br: Luis de Hechavarria (Fla)
Tr: Seitz Fred(3 0 2 0 .00) 2006:(65 7 .11)

Ⓛ 117

Life	11	1	4	1	$137,422	92	D.Fst	3	0	2	0	$15,340 79
2006	8	0	3	1	$92,662	92	Wet(337)	0	0	0	0	$0 -
2005	3	1	1	0	$44,760	78	Turf(305)	8	1	2	1	$122,082 92
KeeⓉ	1	0	1	0	$21,820	84	DstⓉ(338)	2	1	0	1	$51,650 85

7Bel gd 1⅛ [T] :47 1:114 1:362 1:482 ⒻGrdnCyBC-G1 40 2 108 83½ 108¼ 1020 1027½ Luzzi M J 116 18.20 55- 17 MagnificentSong1182 TaketheRibbon116½ JdeQueen116¾ Rank gate, tired 11
8Dmr fm 1⅛ Ⓣ :48 1:123 1:362 1:48 ⒻDMrOaks-G1 92 6 106¾ 96¾ 84½ 83½ 62½ Gryder A T 122 14.20 86- 13 Arravale1221½ [D]Take the Ribbon122hd Foxysox122¾ Split foes,outkicked 10
8Cnl fm 1⅛ Ⓣ :47 1:101 1:342 1:47 ⒻVaOaks200k 91 6 107½ 107 89¾ 67 2no Albarado R J 118 5.10 110 - Aunt Henny120no May Night1181 Art Show118¾ Settld,angld 7w,w/rush 10
8CD fm 1⅛ Ⓣ :461 1:103 1:351 1:471 ⒻRegret-G3 89 10 79 89 84¼ 76½ 55¼ Albarado R J 120 18.40 92- 04 LdyofVenice1204 *MgnificentSong*120nk **PreciousKitten**116½ Fanned 8w lane 11
8CD fst 1 1/16 ⊗ :242 :481 1:123 1:45 ⒻAlw 67200NC 79 2 42½ 42 41½ 32½ 21¼ Albarado R J 122 2.80 84- 18 Fiery Dancer1201¼ May Night1224¾ Red CherriesSpin1173½ 6w bid,2ndbest 5
5CD fm 1 1/16 Ⓣ :234 :474 1:114 1:42 ⒻEdgewood114k 85 6 67¼ 74 73¾ 52½ 31¼ Albarado R J 122 4.00 95- 04 MagnificentSong116½ *FieryDncer*116¾ MyNight122no Failed to sustain bid 9
8Kee fm 1 Ⓣ :243 :481 1:123 1:354 ⒻApplachian109k 84 1 53 53½ 52½ 42½ 22¼ Albarado R J 117 8.00 86- 14 *Lady of Venice*1172¼ May Night117¾ **J'ray**1211¾ 5-6w bid,2ndbest 5
8GP fm 1 Ⓣ :232 :471 1:103 1:332 ⒻAlw 33000N1x 77 7 105¾ 115¾ 116¼ 62¾ 42¾ Castro E 117 16.70 87- 12 *Ebony Rose*1171¼ Nice Nelly117nk **Southern Protocol**1171¼ No late gain 12
8Sar yl 1 1/16 Ⓣ :242 :491 1:133 1:443 ⒻⓇPGJohnson67k 78 2 75 78¾ 63¼ 41 11 Albarado R J 117 14.90 72- 22 MyNight1171 MyInterprtion118½ DrssdtoKill1142¾ Bumped start, gamely 10
6EIP fst 6f :222 :462 1:00 1:132 ⒻMd Sp Wt 19k 60 1 11 85 87¾ 31½ 2½ Mojica O 120 4.30 78- 18 High Heritage120½ *May Night*1202½ Thunder Bayou120¾ 7w lane,gaining 11
6CD fst 6f :214 :461 :582 1:113 ⒻMd Sp Wt 41k 40 2 12 1213 1218 915 59 Day P 120 4.40 74- 13 RrElgnc120¾ Suchprttygirl120nk JillIndyPulpit1205 Swerve in bad start,ck 12
S: Oct16 KeeⓉ 4f fm :522 B(d) *1/1* **Oct9 KeeⓉ 5f fm 1:01 H(d)** *1/2* **Oct2 Kee ◈ 4f fst :522 B** *55/60* **Sep2 TTC 5f gd 1:024 B** *2/15* **Aug10 TTC 5f fst 1:021 B** *2/12* **Jly31 TTC 4f fst :503 B** *2/6*
ER: 1stLasix(2 .00 $0.00) 31-60Days(11 .27 $14.33) Turf(56 .11 $1.44) Routes(60 .12 $3.40) GrdStk(5 .00 $0.00) J/T 2005-06 KEE(1 .00 $0.00) J/T 2005-06(9 .11 $3.53)

Continued on Following Page

5 Rasta Farian

Own: Helen K Groves
Lavender, Rust Cross Sashes, Rust Cap
GUIDRY M (35 2 5 6 .06) 2006: (749 110 .15)

Dk. b or br f. 3 (Mar)
Sire: Holy Bull (Great Above) $15,000
Dam: Chic Corine (Nureyev)
Br: Helen K Groves Revokable Trust (Ky)
Tr: Matz Michael R(1 0 0 1 .00) 2006:(203 37 .18)

L 117

Life	11	2	3	1	$92,653	94	D.Fst	2	0	0	0	$48
2006	6	1	2	0	$49,373	94	Wet(382)	1	0	0	0	$30
2005	5	1	1	1	$43,280	77	Turf(271)	8	2	3	1	$91,87
Kee Ⓣ	2	0	1	0	$13,500	75	DstⓉ(349)	3	0	1	1	$23,97

31Aug06-6Sar gd 1 1/16 Ⓣ :233 :472 1:121 1:422 ⒻⓇDynasty72k 85 9 54½ 53½ 31½ 41¾ 55 Castellano J J L118 8.60 79-22 **Meribel**118no Amansara1184½ Better Now120½ Wide, no resp
19Aug06-9Sar fm 1 3/16 Ⓣ :472 1:112 1:353 1:533 3↑ⒻAlw 53000n2x 94 10 11½ 12½ 11½ 1hd 2½ Castellano J J L117 8.50 96-15 Jade Queen119½ Rasta Farian1172¼ Wait It Out121¾ Dug in gamely ins
15Jly06-9Del gd 1⅛ Ⓣ :51 1:153 1:40 1:521 3↑ⒻAlw 38900n1x 92 5 1½ 11 11 15 16¼ Dominguez R A L114 2.30 75-25 Rasta Farian1146¼ *Palmilla*1182¾ Le Cordon Bleu1143¾ Ridden
27May06-8Del fst 1 1/16 :233 :472 1:114 1:432 ⒻGoForWand100k 48 3 1½ 1½ 52 614 625 Caraballo J C L116 19.70 71-13 UnbridledBelle118hd Amandtude1203¾ DimondSpirit1168¾ Rail, weaken
23Apr06-6Kee fm 1 1/16 Ⓣ :24 :483 1:124 1:431 ⒻAlw 53190n1x 75 12 21 2½ 2½ 1½ 22¼ Castellano J J L120 8.80 84-14 *Nottawasaga*1182¼ RastaFarian120hd FantsticShirl1201¼ 4w,led,outfinish
7Apr06-9Kee fm 1⅛ Ⓣ :47 1:122 1:372 1:494 ⒻAlw 54000n1x 67 4 1hd 2hd 2½ 22½ 45¼ Castellano J J L120 6.30 81-16 *Magnificent Song*1203¾ My Tale1181¼ My Way123nk Bmp foe start,weak
19Nov05-4Lrl fm 1 1/16 Ⓣ :231 :473 1:12 1:414 ⒻSelima100k 76 7 11 2hd 11 21 34 Pino M G L121 12.30 91-04 *J'ray*1213¾ Nice Nelly121nk Rasta Farian121nk Duel 4-1/2, held w
22Oct05-8Del slyS 1 1/16 :23 :474 1:133 1:471 ⒻBlueHen100k 3 8 51½ 62¾ 711 727 743 Pino M G L116f 6.20 34-26 Love Locket1203¾ Stylish Yankee116no *She's Indy Money*1164¾ Ti
3Oct05-6Del fm 1 Ⓣ :24 :48 1:121 1:354 ⒻMd Sp Wt 41k 74 7 1½ 11 13 16 16½ Pino M G L120 *1.70 94-08 RastaFarian1206½ *ItsJustaDrem*1202¾ RisePrtner1131¾ Got in start, hand
3Sep05-9Del fm 1 Ⓣ :233 :483 1:133 1:363 ⒻMd Sp Wt 41k 77 3 11½ 11½ 1½ 11½ 2nk Pino M G L120 2.40 90-06 *Art Show*120nk *Rasta Farian*12012½ Proud of Rosie120no Clear, failed to l
4Aug05-4Sar fst 5f :212 :451 :584 ⒻMd Sp Wt 45k 49 8 7 45¾ 46 46½ 69¼ Castellano J J L118 19.40 81-11 Unobstructed View1181 *Fast Deal*1183¾ SkyIsland1181 Chased inside, ti
WORKS: Oct16 Kee ◇3f fst :353 H 2/8 Oct10 Fai 5f fst 1:032 B 2/5 ●Sep23 Fai 5f fst (W) 1:022 B 1/8 Aug25 Sar tr.t Ⓣ 3f gd :362 B(d) 1/2 Aug5 Sar tr.t 5f fst 1:021 B 4/7

6 Southern Protocol

Own: G Watts Humphrey Jr
Green, White Diamonds, White Stripes On
GRAHAM J (27 1 4 1 .04) 2006: (779 95 .12)

B. f. 3 (Jan)
Sire: Dixieland Band (Northern Dancer) $50,000
Dam: Proper Protocol (Deputy Minister)
Br: G Watts Humphrey Jr (Ky)
Tr: Arnold George R II(6 1 1 0 .17) 2006:(132 21 .16)

L 117

Life	8	2	0	2	$58,030	85	D.Fst	0	0	0	0	$0
2006	6	1	0	2	$41,595	85	Wet(393)	0	0	0	0	$0
2005	2	1	0	0	$16,435	80	Turf(314)	8	2	0	2	$58,030
Kee Ⓣ	0	0	0	0	$0	-	DstⓉ(371)	5	0	0	1	$14,410

31Aug06-6Sar gd 1 1/16 Ⓣ :233 :472 1:121 1:422 ⒻⓇDynasty72k 68 8 79½ 75 62½ 75¾ 712¾ Migliore R L118 29.75 71-22 **Meribel**118no Amansara1184½ Better Now120½ Wide throughout, tired
28Jly06-8Sar yl 1 1/16 🅃 :241 :493 1:142 1:454 ⒻLkGeorge-G3 79 2 34 32½ 43 54¼ 76¼ Castellano J J L116 17.30 64-24 *MgnfcntSong*120¾ Somthnboutbtty1161¼ QutBrd1222¼ Came wide, no rally
3Jly06-4Bel fm 1 Ⓣ :24 :48 1:114 1:344 3↑ⒻAlw 46000n1x 84 1 3½ 31½ 41½ 4¾ 1hd Castellano J J L116 5.30 86-13 SothrnProtocl116hd Ohbgwhyn121no FrstCd116no Altered course stretch
12Jun06-5Med gd 1 1/16 Ⓣ :242 :481 1:113 1:414 ⒻTrenton60k 82 6 42 41¾ 41¾ 22 33½ Castellano J J L117 4.00 93-03 *QuiteaBride*1192¾ KittyHawk121¾ *SouthernProtocol*1172 4-wide,not enough
5May06-5CD fm 1 1/16 Ⓣ :234 :474 1:114 1:42 ⒻEdgewood114k 85 9 42¼ 42½ 31½ 31½ 51¼ Bejarano R L116 10.20 95-04 MagnificentSong116½ *FieryDncer*116¾ **MyNight**122no Tracked,4-5w,weaken
25Mar06-8GP fm 1 Ⓣ :232 :471 1:103 1:332 ⒻAlw 33000n1x 80 6 21 22 2hd 1hd 31½ Trujillo E L117 12.20e 88-12 *EbonyRose*1171¼ NicNlly117nk SouthrnProtocol1171¼ Slim lead, weakened
2Sep05-8Sar yl 1 1/16 Ⓣ :242 :491 1:133 1:443 ⒻⓇPGJohnson67k 69 6 32 31½ 41¾ 3½ 44¼ Prado E S L118 *2.75 68-22 **MyNight**1171 MyInterprettion118½ DrssdtoKill1142¾ Buried inside stretch
22Jly05-5EIP gd 5½f Ⓣ :222 :463 :584 1:051 ⒻMd Sp Wt 20k 80 2 2 32 42 1½ 13¼ Lanerie C J L120 17.00 76-24 SothrnPrtcl1203¼ CtsEyWtnss1205¾ SymphnyfMtn1202 3-4w,driving,clear
WORKS: Oct12 Kee ◇5f fst 1:033 B 24/25 Aug24 Sar tr.t Ⓣ 4f fm :514 B(d) 17/18 Jly22 Bel 🅃 4f sf :513 B(d) 3/10
TRAINER: 31-60Days(122 .15 $1.59) Turf(155 .17 $2.34) Routes(189 .14 $1.90) GrdStk(19 .16 $1.51)
J/T 2005-06 KEE(1 .00 $0.00) J/T 2005-06(1 .00 $0.

7 Tiz a Fantasy

Own: Gary L and Mary E West
Fluorescent Pink, Black Diamond Belt
DECARLO C P (5 0 0 0 .00) 2006: (371 67 .18)

B. f. 3 (May) KEESEP04 $225,000
Sire: Tiznow (Cee's Tizzy) $40,000
Dam: Fantasy Angel (Saint Ballado)
Br: Twin Hopes Farm (Ky)
Tr: Frankel Robert(9 2 1 1 .22) 2006:(474 116 .24)

L 117

Life	3	2	0	0	$39,380	83	D.Fst	2	1	0	0	$14,780
2006	2	1	0	0	$24,980	83	Wet(403)	0	0	0	0	$0
2005	1	1	0	0	$14,400	54	Turf(251)	1	1	0	0	$24,600
Kee Ⓣ	0	0	0	0	$0	-	DstⓉ(335)	1	1	0	0	$24,600

18Aug06-7Mth fm 1 1/16 Ⓣ :222 :462 1:101 1:404 3↑ⒻAlw 41000n1x 83 1 21½ 23 2hd 13 14¼ Decarlo C P L116 5.90 95-05 Tiz a Fantasy1164¼ Sanserif1202¼ Daylight Dancer116nk Tracked,bid,clear
30Jly06-5Mth fst 6f :22 :452 :573 1:11 3↑ⒻAlw 38000n1x 47 6 2 52¼ 65 69 510¾ Decarlo C P L115b 3.50 74-16 Carryanun1151¼ Aerocat1171½ Memorable Night120no Bobbled start,wknd
Previously trained by Norman Cole 2005(as of 9/4): (683 198 104 84 0.29)
4Sep05-4LaD fst 6f :222 :461 :584 1:13 ⒻMd Sp Wt 24k 54 6 3 32½ 3½ 11 13¼ Jacinto J L120b *1.60 80-16 Tiz a Fantasy1203¼ Lively1202½ Zeras120½ Took over, driving
WORKS: Oct16 Kee ◇4f fst :471 H 2/29 Oct10 Kee ◇4f fst :482 B 10/22 Oct3 Kee ◇4f fst :502 B 38/46 Sep25 Mth 5f gd 1:013 B 2/21 ●Sep18 Mth 4f fst :48 B 1/53 Sep7 Mth 4f fst :49 B 8/41
TRAINER: 61-180Days(194 .25 $1.60) WonLastStart(239 .27 $1.62) Turf(590 .21 $1.42) Routes(713 .24 $1.60) GrdStk(226 .18 $1.26)
J/T 2005-06(7 .43 $4.

8 Soothsay (Ire)

Own: Deron Pearson and Rachel and Bruno De
Yellow, Blue Diamonds, Blue Band On
BLANC B (14 0 3 0 .00) 2006: (264 18 .07)

B. f. 3 (Mar)
Sire: Mujadil (Storm Bird) $11,840
Dam: Second Omen*GB (Rainbow Quest)
Br: Maurice Burns (Ire)
Tr: Cassidy James(1 0 0 0 .00) 2006:(134 21 .16)

L 117

Life	12	3	3	2	$141,233	93	D.Fst	2	1	0	0	$6,505
2006	7	1	2	2	$126,700	93	Wet(282*)	0	0	0	0	$0
2005	5	2	1	0	$14,533	-	Turf(359)	10	2	3	2	$134,728
Kee Ⓣ	0	0	0	0	$0	-	DstⓉ(267)	2	1	1	0	$37,700

9Sep06-8AP fm 1⅛ Ⓣ :491 1:141 1:381 1:493 ⒻPuckerUp-G3 75 4 42½ 43 32 64½ 88¼ Smith M E L118 *1.60 87-05 *Vacare*1164 Walklikeanegyptian116hd BalletPacific1182 Off rail, gave way
19Aug06-8Dmr fm 1⅛ Ⓣ :48 1:123 1:362 1:48 ⒻDMrOaks-G1 93 8 85¾ 85¾ 94¼ 73¼ 42¼ Smith M E LB122 15.80 87-13 Arravale1221½ 🄳Take the Ribbon122hd Foxysox122¾ Pulled,stdied late
Placed third through disqualification
23Jly06-5Dmr fm 1 Ⓣ :222 :47 1:11 1:343 ⒻSnClmntH-G2 89 4 76 76¼ 64½ 63½ 31¼ Nakatani C S LB119 5.40 87-11 Attima1201¼ Sol Mi Fa116hd Soothsay119no Late 3wd for 3rd
2Jly06-10Hol fm 1 Ⓣ :23 :47 1:104 1:343 ⒻFlawlessly100k 87 5 77 74¾ 64 43 21½ Flores D R LB117 5.80 89-07 ChrmingNLovble1191½ Soothsy1172¼ TshsDlight115½ Came out str,rallied
29May06-8BM fm 1 1/16 Ⓣ :241 :483 1:124 1:441 ⒻBMBCOaks81k 82 3 32 31½ 42 21½ 2¾ Martinez L V LB122 3.40 85-17 Sol Mi Fa117¾ Soothsay1223½ Make a Pass1172½ Rail trip, steady bid
29Apr06-1GG fm 1 1/16 Ⓣ :233 :483 1:13 1:44 +ⒻMontclair43k 71 4 63¼ 53¾ 61¾ 32½ 1¾ Flores D R LB117 *1.60 88-03 Soothsay117¾ Royal Cheer1172½ Helmsgold1181¼ Chckd 5/16s,strong run
25Mar06-5SA fm *6½f Ⓣ :213 :434 1:071 1:133 ⒻOC 80k/n1x-N 74 6 8 66 55 42½ 43½ Desormeaux K J LB118 6.40 83-12 NoGreterLove1202½ Tonnerre113¾ HillofGrc118nk Came out str,missed 3d
Previously trained by John Hills
11Nov05 Wolverhampton (GB) ft 7f LH 1:293 Betdirect.co.uk Nursery Hcp(dirt) Hcp 10000 12 Ahern E 125 8.00 Soothsay1252 Moi Aussi1243 Ballybeg122no
Timeform rating: 73 *Close up,2nd 2f out,led 1f o*
20Oct05 Brighton (GB) gs 7f Ⓣ LH 1:271 Sporting Index Nursery Hcp Hcp 10200 22 Ahern E 125 14.00 Sands of Barra1232 *Soothsay*125no Earl Kraul1311¼
Timeform rating: 64 *Rank tracking leaders,2nd 200y out,saved 2r*
12Oct05 Lingfield (GB) ft 6f LH 1:122 Dawson News Cndtns Stks(dirt) Alw 13000 54½ Hills M 121 33.00 Cape of Luck128¾ Brandywell Boy1301¼ Cavewarrior128½
Timeform rating: 66 *Rated wide at rear,roused over 1f out,one-paced la*
WORKS: Oct9 SA 5f fst 1:022 H 25/35 Oct1 SA Ⓣ 5f fm 1:014 H(d) 2/4 Sep2 Dmr Ⓣ 4f fm :512 B(d) 1/2 ●Aug12 Dmr Ⓣ 5f fm 1:00 H(d) 1/10 Jly22 Dmr Ⓣ 5f fm 1:033 H(d) 4/4
TRAINER: 31-60Days(75 .17 $1.69) Turf(188 .12 $1.15) Routes(189 .14 $1.26) GrdStk(53 .04 $0.68)

9 Precious Kitten

Own: Kenneth L and Sarah K Ramsey
White, Red 'R', White Band On Red
BEJARANO R (55 17 7 7 .31) 2006: (1149 219 .19)

Dk. b or br f. 3 (Jan)
Sire: Catienus (Storm Cat) $6,500
Dam: Kitten's First (Lear Fan)
Br: Kenneth L Ramsey & Sarah K Ramsey (Ky)
Tr: Romans Dale(16 4 3 2 .25) 2006:(657 117 .18)

L 117

Life	8	2	3	1	$205,286	94	D.Fst	2	1	0	0	$31,620
2006	8	2	3	1	$205,286	94	Wet(328)	0	0	0	0	$0
2005	0	M	0	0	$0	-	Turf(276)	6	1	3	1	$173,666
Kee Ⓣ	0	0	0	0	$0	-	DstⓉ(342)	3	1	1	0	$127,900

Previously trained by Fox William I 2006(as of 9/30): (2 1 0 0 0.50)
30Sep06-10Lrl fm 1 1/16 Ⓣ :234 :472 1:112 1:411 ⒻMWashtonBC200k 94 10 65½ 75 42 1hd 1nk Rodriguez E D L116 9.20e 94-06 Precious Kitten116nk **Meribel**1222½ Gasia122hd 4wd run,drifted,dug in
Previously trained by Romans Dale 2006(as of 8/12): (540 97 79 80 0.18)
12Aug06-10EIP gd 1 1/16 Ⓣ :243 :49 1:143 1:454 ⒻAudubonOak50k 81 4 46 56½ 62¾ 63¼ 54 Jacinto J L116 *1.20 62-37 PalaceRumor118nk BeauDre1162¾ ClssiclRyder120½ Lost position far turn
16Jly06-10CD fm 1 Ⓣ :23 :46 1:11 1:344 ⒻHvnlyCausH71k 88 10 810 59½ 44½ 22½ 24 Bejarano R L118 *2.70 91-09 TkthRbbon1154 PrcosKttn1182¾ KcknthClods114½ 7w much of way,2nbst
17Jun06-8CD fm 1⅛ Ⓣ :461 1:103 1:351 1:471 ⒻRegret-G3 92 7 67½ 68 73¾ 42 34¼ Valdivia J Jr L116 60.40 93-04 LdyofVnic1204 *MgnifcntSong*120nk PrcousKttn116½ 2-3w,not good enough
25May06-6CD fst 1 1/16 ⊗ :25 :50 1:142 1:453 3↑ⒻMd Sp Wt 48k 77 3 11 1½ 11 11 11 Douglas R R L117 2.10 82-18 PreciousKitten1171 EarthtoNin1242¾ MryCt1179¼ Lost whp,used goggles
10May06-6CD fm 1 Ⓣ :241 :482 1:132 1:364 3↑ⒻMd Sp Wt 50k 70 8 43 32½ 21 1hd 21¾ Douglas R R L117 2.70 83-11 KintotheWind1171¾ *PrciousKittn*117¾ MryCt1171¾ Between,led,outgamed
8Apr06-10GP fm 1 1/16 Ⓣ :25 :491 1:124 1:421 ⒻMd Sp Wt 32k 70 5 42½ 45 42½ 32½ 2nk Madrid S O L121 13.80 80-14 **Meribel**121nk Precious Kitten121¾ Ghost Tapping1211¼ 3 wide rally, edged
19Mar06-6GP fst 6f :221 :451 :571 1:094 ⒻMd Sp Wt 32k 50 7 2 94½ 97 77¾ 712¼ Guidry M L121 32.70 83-04 *HowTrueItIs*1217 Swetsothrnbrz121¾ Profumo121hd In traffic backstretch
WORKS: Sep26 CD 4f fst :474 B 2/41 Sep18 CD 5f fst 1:03 B 30/45 Sep4 CD 4f fst :501 B 23/45
TRAINER: 2OffA5-180(158 .15 $1.39) Turf(324 .15 $1.45) Routes(610 .17 $1.64) GrdStk(69 .10 $2.03)
J/T 2005-06 KEE(1 1.00 $14.20) J/T 2005-06(52 .17 $1.18

0 Mysterious Lina (Fr)
Own: Dream With Me Stable Inc
Navy, Yellow Epaulets, Yellow Seams On
QUIER S (—) (—)

Gr/ro. f. 3 (Mar)
Sire: Linamix*Fr (Mendez*Fr) $41,440
Dam: Mysterious Guest*Fr (Barathea*Ire)
Br: Jean-Pierre-Joseph Dubois (Fr)
Tr: Demercastel Philippe(—) (—)

L 117

Life	13	2	6	1	$115,614	-	D.Fst	0	0	0	0	$0	-
2006	8	1	4	0	$98,986	-	Wet(192*)	0	0	0	0	$0	-
2005	5	1	2	1	$16,628	-	Turf(260)	13	2	6	1	$115,614	-
Kee(T)	0	0	0	0	$0	-	Dst(T)(303)	0	0	0	0	$0	-

06 Longchamp (Fr) gd *1½ (T) RH 2:291 3↑ (F)Prix Vermeille-G1 Stk 380000 — 96¼ Pasquier S 119 15.00 — Mandesha119½ Montare128½ Royal Highness128½ 11 — Trckd ldr,bid 1-1/2f out,weakened late.Freedonia4th,AlixRoad5th
imeform rating: 104

06 Deauville (Fr) sf *1¼ (T) RH 2:111 (F)Prix de la Nonette-G3 Stk 102000 — 23 Spanu F 126 6.20 — Germance1263 Mysterious Lina126nk Ballet Pacifica1262 5 — Tracked in 3rd,bid 1f out,prevailed in duel for 2nd.Alix Road4th
imeform rating: 105

06 Deauville (Fr) sf *1 (T) RH 1:404 (F)Prix de la Calonne (Listed) Stk 63700 — 21½ Spanu F 128 4.00 — Heaven's Cause1231½ Mysterious Lina128½ Travel Team1231 8 — Tracked leader,led 1f to 100y out,second best
imeform rating: 102

06 La Teste de Buch (Fr) gd *1 (T) RH 1:372 (F)Prix La Sorellina (Listed) Stk 63200 — 12½ Spanu F 123 4.20 — Mysterious Lina1232½ Kezia123nk Viapervita123nk 9 — Tracked in 3rd,led 1f out,handily
meform rating: 102

06 Longchamp (Fr) gd *1¼ (T) RH 2:062 (F)Prix des Belles Filles Hcp 73300 — 2hd Pasquier S 130 6.00 — Snake Dancer121hd Mysterious Lina1301½ Tizina1271½ 18 — Never far away,bid over 1f out,dueled,just missed
meform rating: 94

6 Longchamp (Fr) sf *1 (T) RH 1:422 Prix du Bel Air Hcp 72500 — 2½ Pasquier S 123 11.00 — Indianski123½ Mysterious Lina1231 La Demoiselle121½ 17 — Led to 1f out,gave ground grudgingly
imeform rating: 92

06 Chantilly (Fr) sf *1¼ (T) RH 2:071 (F)Prix Brunehaut Alw 32100 — 44 Peslier O 128 15.00 — Grande Melody1211 Tonic Star1211½ Heaven's Cause1281½ 15 — Rated in 7th,mild bid 2f out,held by leaders
imeform rating: 88

06 Maisons-Laffitte (Fr) gd *1 (T) LH 1:43 (F)Prix Nubienne Alw 31600 — 43 Pasquier S 125 7.50 — Impressionnante1212½ Koanga124nk Foret d'Or121nk 7 — Tracked in 3rd,outpaced late
imeform rating: 88

reviously trained by Jean-Pierre Dubois

5 Lyon-Parilly (Fr) hy *1 (T) LH 1:422 (F)Prix des Orchidees Alw 14400 — 13½ Dal Balcon T 128 4.60 — Mysterious Lina1283½ La Valliere1208 Baratineuse1182 15 — Tracked leaders,led 1-1/2f out,drew clear in hand

5 Saint-Cloud (Fr) gd *1 (T) LH 1:42 (F)Prix Barquette Maiden 21800 — 610 Mendizabal I 126 2.50 — Sendnowar126no Sweet Shop1264 Nibbana1261½ 11 — Mid-pack,ridden without response 2f out
imeform rating: 64

RKS: Oct18 Kee ◇6f fst 1:151 B 6/7

---

1 Delmarva
Own: Robert S Evans
Blue, Red Triangle, Blue And Red Halved
AROUX J R (61 13 4 6 .21) 2006: (1472 359 .24)

B. f. 3 (Apr)
Sire: Unbridled's Song (Unbridled) $150,000
Dam: Precipice (Gulch)
Br: R S Evans (Ky)
Tr: Kimmel John C(—) 2006:(173 35 .20)

L 117

Life	7	2	2	1	$81,165	92	D.Fst	0	0	0	0	$0	-
2006	5	1	2	0	$50,365	92	Wet(395)	0	0	0	0	$0	-
2005	2	1	0	1	$30,800	80	Turf(311)	7	2	2	1	$81,165	92
Kee(T)	0	0	0	0	$0	-	Dst(T)(373)	4	1	2	0	$49,530	92

06-10Lrl fm 1 1/16 (T) :234 :472 1:112 1:411 (F)MWashtonBC200k 79 5 22 22 31 84¾ 86¾ Velez J A Jr L116 6.10 87-06 Precious Kitten116nk Meribel1222½ Gasia122hd Stalked 2wd, weakened 10
06-7Bel gd 1⅛ [T] :47 1:114 1:362 1:482 (F)GrdnCyBC-G1 89 3 64½ 62½ 54 84½ 95¼ Castellano J J L116 16.20 78-17 MgnificentSong1182 TketheRibbon116½ JdeQuen116¾ Inside, no response 11
06-6Sar fm 1 1/16 [T] :234 :472 1:11 1:404 3↑(F)Alw 51000N1x 92 1 12 12½ 1½ 14½ 13 Castellano J J L117 *2.05 95-06 Delmarva1173 Captiva Bay1212¼ Dean's List1191¼ Speed in hand, clear 9
06-8GP fm 1 1/16 (T) :224 :461 1:094 1:393 (F)GailyGaily60k 88 1 64 53 2hd 1hd 2¾ Castellano J J L119 5.10 92-13 Dyna's Destiny123¾ Delmarva1192 Diamond Spirit117nk Gamely, edged late 10
06-4GP fm 1 1/16 (T) :241 :484 1:122 1:414 (F)Alw 33000N1x 80 1 11 11½ 11 12½ 2no Castellano J J L117 2.60 82-17 Sprightly117no Delmarva1171 Diamond Spirit117½ Hit rail str,bmpd late 8
v05-6Aqu gd 1 (T) :232 :482 1:131 1:383 (F)Md Sp Wt 44k 80 8 57 53½ 35½ 33½ 11¾ Castellano J J L119 *2.35 83-17 Delmarva1191¾ Cuaba1192¾ Miracle Moment119nk Came wide, clear late 10
05-6Bel fm 1 (T) :233 :471 1:114 1:352 (F)Md Sp Wt 44k 71 8 74 74¼ 52½ 43½ 31½ Migliore R L119 21.70 82-12 Holiday Tune1191 Omi Princess119½ Delmarva119nk Altered course stretch 10
KS: Oct13 Kee ◇5f fst 1:002 B 9/35 Sep1 Sar 4f fst :502 B 50/62 Aug5 Sar 4f fst :502 B 42/54 Jly28 Sar 4f fst :50 B 36/56 Jly21 Sar 4f fst :502 B 16/26
INER: Turf(191 .21 $2.56) Routes(307 .20 $2.32) GrdStk(35 .11 $4.53)

---

2 J'ray
Own: Lawrence Goichman
Red, Purple Diamonds, Red And Purple Cap
AZQUEZ J R (4 0 1 0 .00) 2006: (781 184 .24)

Ch. f. 3 (Mar)
Sire: Distant View (Mr. Prospector) $15,000
Dam: Bubbling Heights*Fr (Darshaan*GB)
Br: Lawerence Goichman (NY)
Tr: Pletcher Todd A(23 2 3 3 .09) 2006:(991 257 .26)

L 119

Life	6	4	0	1	$228,155	86	D.Fst	1	0	0	0	$205	49
2006	2	1	0	1	$70,910	85	Wet(331)	0	0	0	0	$0	-
2005	4	3	0	0	$157,245	86	Turf(336)	5	4	0	1	$227,950	86
Kee(T)	2	1	0	1	$80,350	86	Dst(T)(359)	4	4	0	0	$217,040	86

r06-8Kee fm 1 (T) :243 :481 1:123 1:354 (F)Applachian109k 82 2 31 31½ 41 32½ 33 Bejarano R L121 *1.20 85-14 Lady of Venice1172¼ May Night117¾ J'ray1211¾ Split foes,bmp 3/16s 5
n06-9Crc fm 1 1/16 (T) :231 :471 1:111 1:404 (F)TrPOaks100k 85 2 41½ 31½ 31½ 21 11 Velazquez J R L121 *.50 92-09 J'ray1211 Stolen Prayer118nk Nice Nelly1162 Wore down rival late 9
v05-4Lrl fm 1 1/16 (T) :231 :473 1:12 1:414 (F)Selima100k 85 11 84¼ 85 42 11 13¾ Bailey J D L121 *1.20 95-04 J'ray1213¾ Nice Nelly121nk Rasta Farian121nk 4-5wd,quick mv,drvng 11
ct05-8Kee gd 1 1/16 (T) :224 :471 1:131 1:452 (F)Jessamine112k 86 7 68 711 59 44 1¾ Blanc B L116 11.40 80-24 J'ray116¾ Beau Dare1221 Dyna's Destiny1163¾ 6w lane,steady drive 8
g05-4Sar fm 1 1/16 (T) :233 :481 1:132 1:434 (F)[S]Md Sp Wt 46k 70 5 64 56 62¼ 2hd 12¼ Bailey J D L118 *.60e 76-11 Jray1182¼ FairytleStory1183½ ToweringEscpe1184½ Stumbled start, 3 wide 9
y05-2Bel fst 5½f :23 :464 :591 1:053 (F)[S]Md Sp Wt 41k 49 7 7 811 99 75 65 Bailey J D L118 14.10 78-20 Doll Baby1182½ Point Me to It1181¼ Curtana118¾ Altered course stretch 9
RKS: Oct15 CD 5f fst 1:02 B 7/23 Oct8 CD 5f fst 1:023 B 10/18 Oct2 CD 5f fst 1:012 B 15/40 Sep25 CD 4f fst :483 B 6/77 Sep18 CD 4f fst :51 B 50/58 Sep11 CD 4f sly :484 B 6/42
INER: 61-180Days(200 .24 $1.78) Turf(683 .21 $1.73) Routes(1277 .26 $1.91) GrdStk(398 .23 $1.91) J/T 2005-06 KEE(72 .35 $1.94) J/T 2005-06(802 .28 $1.87)

Also Eligible:

13 Pure Incentive
Own: Lewis Lakin and James Kintz
Forest Green, Red Diamond Frame, Gold
PAROUX J R (61 13 4 6 .21) 2006: (1472 359 .24)

B. f. 3 (Mar) KEEAPR05 $65,000
Sire: Fusaichi Pegasus (Mr. Prospector) $125,000
Dam: Freshwater Pearl*Ire (Alzao)
Br: Becky Thomas & Ashford Stud (Ky)
Tr: Biancone Patrick L(25 7 3 3 .28) 2006:(262 58 .22)

L 117

Life	9	2	3	1	$106,284	97	D.Fst	4	2	0	0	$60,154	85
2006	6	1	3	1	$78,604	97	Wet(350)	0	0	0	0	$0	-
2005	3	1	0	0	$27,680	85	Turf(289)	5	0	3	1	$46,130	97
Kee(T)	0	0	0	0	$0	-	Dst(T)(364)	2	0	1	1	$20,320	90

ct06-9Kee fst 1⅛ ◇ :52 1:172 1:411 1:523 3↑(F)Alw 50830N1x 73 3 62¼ 84¼ 84¼ 41½ 11¾ Leparoux J R L117 *.40 - - PureIncentive1171¾ [DH]Bootry117 [DH]WhtWillB1191¼ Lack room 1/4p,drvg 9
p06-8Sar gd 1⅛ (T) :513 1:161 1:401 1:524 3↑(F)Alw 51000N1x 83 6 65¼ 65 65 32 21 Leparoux J R5 L113 *.95 66-32 Moya1181 Pure Incentive1132 Ocean Beauty118nk Four wide move turn 9
g06-7Sar fm 1 [T] :24 :473 1:114 1:352 AinSocilgy73k 97 7 710 714 55 4¾ 21 Leparoux J R L111 6.40 89-13 Carnera1161 PureIncentive1111½ YnkeeMster123hd Hit gate start, gamely 7
ly06-8Bel fm 1 1/16 (T) :232 :462 1:101 1:40 (F)CstleRoyle67k 90 2 43½ 43½ 42 21½ 32 Leparoux J R L116 3.70 91-13 MssShop1201¼ Somthnboutbtty118¾ PrIncntv116no Inside run, weakened 8
un06-7Bel gd 1 1/16 (T) :244 :484 1:132 1:432 (F)LateBlmr67k 87 7 63¼ 64 63¼ 42¼ 22¾ Gomez G K L118 13.20 73-24 PerilousPursuit1182¾ PureIncentive118½ Zaynab120½ Game finish outside 9
Previously trained by McAnally Ronald 2005: (323 39 48 35 0.12)
b06-5SA fm *6½f (T) :214 :441 1:071 1:132 (F)OC 80k/N1x-N 72 8 7 84¾ 86½ 76¾ 53¼ Espinoza V LB118 7.70 85-11 HrriettLne120¾ RunwyCozzn120¾ HorsBWithYou1181½ 4 wide into stretch 11
c05-2SA fst 6½f :212 :444 1:103 1:172 (F)OC 80k/N1x-N 60 7 2 43 31 22 45½ Valdivia J Jr LB118 *1.60 79-13 TricksPic1185¼ Imaladytak118nk StrletofSettle118hd Loomed btwn, tired 8
c05-2Hol fst 6½f :222 :444 1:093 1:16 (F)Md Sp Wt 40k 85 3 2 21½ 2½ 11 12¾ Valdivia J Jr LB120 4.50 91-10 Pure Incentive1202¾ Toppisme1205 A. P. Surprise1205¾ Led into lane,clear 5
v05-6OSA fst 6f :211 :441 :563 1:10 (F)Md Sp Wt 41k 64 7 6 85¼ 75¾ 54 55½ Valdivia J Jr LB120 46.00 82-11 Talullah Lula120no Tonnerre1202 Texas Kitty120no 4wd,3wd,no late bid 9
RKS: ●Oct12 Kee ◇5f fst :593 H 1/25 Oct5 Kee ◇4f fst :491 B 24/39 Sep27 Sar tr.t(T) 4f gd :50 B(d) 14/22 Aug25 Sar tr.t(T) 4f gd :482 H(d) 3/26 Aug2 Sar 4f fst :493 B 22/34 Jly26 Sar tr.t(T) 4f fm :481 B(d) 8/24
INER: 1-7Days(7 .14 $1.51) WonLastStart(87 .22 $1.40) Turf(172 .23 $2.51) Routes(278 .20 $2.12) GrdStk(130 .16 $1.75) J/T 2005-06 KEE(55 .24 $1.60) J/T 2005-06(221 .23 $1.54)

Among the 13, five were taking serious action at the betting windows. The 2–1 favorite was Meribel, who was deserving of the role. She had run third in two dirt starts before moving to the grass, an indication she was versatile enough to win on Polytrack.

Precious Kitten and J'Ray were both 5–1. Precious Kitten had won on the dirt, but J'Ray was another story. In her lone dirt try, she was sixth against New York-breds and earned a paltry Beyer figure of 49. At 5–1, and considering her dirt form, she was the type of horse you had to throw out.

Fourth choice Pure Incentive had already won over Keeneland's Polytrack, so she was another obvious contender. Fifth choice Mysterious Lina, who was shipping in from France and had never run on anything but turf, was another easy elimination.

By tossing out J'Ray and Mysterious Lina, the race became playable, and anyone concentrating on horses with proven dirt form probably had the exacta and, maybe, the superfecta.

NINTH RACE
Keeneland
OCTOBER 20, 2006

1 1/16 MILES. (1.41^{3}) 16TH RUNNING OF THE VALLEY VIEW. Grade III. Purse $125,000 FOR FILLIES, THREE YEARS OLD. By subscription of $125 each which should accompany the nomination or by Supplementary Nomination of $6,250 by time of entry (Includes entry and starting fees). $625 to enter and an additional $625 to start, with $125,000 guaranteed, of which $77,500 to the owner of the winner, $25,000 to second, $12,500 to third, $6,250 to fourth and $3,750 to fifth. Weight: 123 lbs. Non-winners of a graded or group stakes on the turf in 2006 allowed 2 lbs.; $45,000 twice on the turf in 2006, 4 lbs.; three races other than maiden or claiming, 6 lbs. The maximum number of starters for the Valley View will be limited to twelve. In the event that more than twelve fillies pass the entry box, the twelve starters will be determined at that timewith preference by condition eligibility, beginning with graded or group stakes winners. Starters to be named through the entry box by the usual time of closing. A gold julep cup will be presented to the owner of the winner. Closed Wednesday, October 11, 2006 with 32 nominations. In the event that this race is taken off the turf it will be contested at Eight and One Half Furlongs on the main track.(ORIGINALLY SCHEDULED FOR TURF).

Value of Race: $125,000 Winner $77,500; second $25,000; third $12,500; fourth $6,250; fifth $3,750. Mutuel Pool $366,962.00 Exacta Pool $208,615.00 Trifecta Pool $162,059.00 Superfecta Pool $95,009.00

Last Raced	Horse	M/Eqt.	A.	Wt	PP	St	¼	½	¾	Str	Fin	Jockey	Odds $1
30Sep06 ^{10}Lrl^{2}	Meribel	L	3	117	2	12	1^{3}	1^{3}	12^{hd}	5½	1½	Gomez G K	2.10
30Sep06 ^{10}Lrl^{1}	Precious Kitten	L	3	117	9	5	7^{1}	6^{hd}	8^{1}	3^{hd}	2½	Bejarano R	5.70
9Sep06 ^{7}Bel^{10}	May Night	L	3	117	4	3	3½	3½	3½	1½	3½	Albarado R J	10.90
15Oct06 ^{9}Kee^{1}	Pure Incentive	L	3	117	13	11	11½	12^{2}	11½	71½	4no	Leparoux J R	6.30
31Aug06 ^{6}Sar^{5}	Rasta Farian	L	3	117	5	2	2^{hd}	2^{1}	2½	21½	5¾	Guidry M	29.10
23Apr06 ^{8}Kee^{3}	J'ray	L	3	119	12	9	9½	10^{hd}	9^{hd}	81½	6^{hd}	Velazquez J R	5.50
10Sep06 LCH^{9}	Mysterious Lina-FR	L	3	117	10	8	6^{hd}	7^{hd}	6^{1}	4½	7^{nk}	Pasquier S	8.90
30Sep06 ^{10}Lrl^{8}	Delmarva	L	3	117	11	7	8½	9^{hd}	10½	9^{2}	8^{2}	Jacinto J	36.40
31Aug06 ^{6}Sar^{7}	Southern Protocol	L f	3	117	6	6	5½	5^{hd}	4^{hd}	6½	91½	Graham J	77.40
9Sep06 ^{8}AP^{8}	Soothsay-Ire	L	3	117	8	13	12^{1}	11^{1}	13	11^{1}	10½	Blanc B	14.40
18Sep06 ^{6}KD^{1}	Transmit	L bf	3	117	1	10	10^{1}	81½	7^{hd}	10^{2}	11¾	Melancon L	33.90
18Aug06 ^{7}Mth^{1}	Tiz a Fantasy	L	3	117	7	4	4½	4^{1}	5^{hd}	12^{1}	121½	Decarlo C P	14.70
28Aug06 ^{4}Mnr^{1}	Idle Quest	L	3	117	3	1	11½	1^{1}	1½	1^{3}	1^{3}	Borel C H	41.20

OFF AT 5:16 Start Good. Won driving. Track fast.

TIME :23^{4}, :48, 1:13^{1}, 1:37^{1}, 1:42^{4} (:23.85, :48.19, 1:13.35, 1:37.27, 1:42.95)

$2 Mutuel Prices:

2 – MERIBEL	6.20	3.80	3.00
9 – PRECIOUS KITTEN		5.20	3.60
4 – MAY NIGHT			6.20

$2 EXACTA 2–9 PAID $25.20 $2 TRIFECTA 2–9–4 PAID $229.80
$2 SUPERFECTA 2–9–4–13 PAID $1,714.40

None of this is meant to convince you to throw out all grass horses on synthetic tracks. Horses who have proven to be versatile and have good dirt, as well as good turf, lines in their form are exactly the type of horses you should be using when handicapping synthetic-surface races.

Take Cheroot, a starter in the 2006 On Trust Handicap at Hollywood Park. He came into the race with four wins on the grass from 11 tries and just one win in 11 career dirt starts. Upon further examination, the case could be made that he was actually better on the dirt than on the turf. Among his last 12 starts, his two best Beyer figures were run on the dirt, even though they came in defeat. At the very least, he was the type of horse who could carry his form from track to track, surface to surface. Anyone having faith in his ability to handle the Cushion Track was rewarded as he paid $8.40 to win.

Just when I thought I had it all figured out—that the ability of grass horses to translate their form to synthetic surfaces was highly overrated—a funny thing happened at the 2007 Keeneland spring meet. A handful of grass horses—the type who had no ability on conventional dirt—started winning. Oddly, the best two examples of this phenomenon occurred on the same day, April 14.

In the first race, Tiger Woodman looked like a sure throw-out, since his three races on conventional dirt had been abysmal.

7 Tiger Woodman
Own: Devil Eleven Stable
nge White, Blue Yoke, Blue Blocks On
MEZ G K (16 5 2 1 .31) 2007: (334 84 .25)

$50,000

Dk. b or br h. 5 (Mar)
Sire: Woodman (Mr. Prospector) $20,000
Dam: Bangkok (Riverman)
Br: Gainesway Thoroughbreds Ltd (Ky)
Tr: Arnold George R II(1 0 0 1 .00) 2007:(45 6 .13)

L 118

Life	11	2	1	1	$32,147	88	D.Fst	2	0	0	0	$642	47
2007	3	0	0	1	$4,565	88	Wet(298)	1	0	0	0	$340	38
							Synth	0	0	0	0	$0	-
2006	2	2	0	0	$21,300	88	Turf(296)	8	2	1	1	$31,165	88
Kee	0	0	0	0	$0	-	Dst(306)	1	0	0	0	$340	38

Previously trained by Hills Timothy A 2006: (512 72 76 63 0.14)
Mar07-7GP fm 1 1/16 Ⓣ :224 :463 1:10 1:391 4↑ Alw 41500N2X 85 6 42½ 42 31 32½ 53 Trujillo E L120 b 29.00 91-12 MysticRulr120½ BrodwyProducr120½ ObiWnKnobi1201½ 3 wide, weakened 12
Feb07-8GP fm 1 1/16 Ⓣ :232 :47 1:11 1:404 4↑ Alw 41500N2X 80 11 910 77½ 83¼ 106¾ 106 Trujillo E L120 b 22.70 80-22 LastBestPlace120½ Mangircin1202¼ ForeignRuckus120nk 3 wide, no factor 12
Jan07-7GP fm 1⅛ Ⓣ :48 1:114 1:352 1:464 4↑ Alw 41500N2X 88 5 11 11 11½ 1½ 31¼ Trujillo E L122 b 16.30 88-19 BeeCharmer1201 Mangircin120nk TigerWoodmn122hd Inside, outfinished 12
Nov06-4Crc fm 1 Ⓣ :221 :471 1:103 1:371 3↑ Alw 20500N2L 88 2 31 41¼ 3nk 1hd 11¼ Trujillo E L123 b *2.40 83-13 TigerWoodmn1231¼ SirSilverFox1184½ TlntScout118½ 3 wide, edged away 8
Oct06-3Crc fm 1 1/16 Ⓣ :222 :462 1:103 1:412 3↑ Md 32000 86 5 33 44 41½ 2½ 13¼ Trujillo E L123 b 4.60 89-15 *Tiger Woodman*1233¼ Sonic Cat1185¾ *Never Absent*1181¼ Waited far turn 8
Previously trained by Breen Kelly J 2005(as of 10/20): (232 55 34 28 0.24)
Oct05-3Med fm 170 Ⓣ :23 :47 1:121 1:422 3↑ Md 30000 -0 6 54 32 79¾ 716 733¼ Winants R L138 fb *2.50 48-19 Encased1383½ Execution1384 Solar Surprise1381½ 3 wide, faded 9
Jly05-4Mth fm 1⅛ Ⓣ :511 1:152 1:402 1:522 3↑ Md Sp Wt 40k 68 1 56½ 52½ 41½ 41¾ 94 Gryder A T L117 b 3.90 65-31 Revivl117¾ *LittleDovefether*123nk DelryDilmm1231½ Steadied leaving chute 9
Jly05-2Mth sly[s] 1 1/16 ⊗ :242 :494 1:142 1:471 3↑ Md Sp Wt 34k 38 3 41¾ 31 31 55½ 513½ Bravo J L118 b 2.60 55-27 GracieTerrce123½ CherokeeBreeze1181¼ Orison1183 4wd,chased,gave way 6
May05-4Atl fm 1 1/16 Ⓣ :231 :48 1:123 1:444 3↑ Md Sp Wt 24k 62 4 22½ 44½ 21½ 41¼ 24 Molina V H L117 b *1.90 89-10 AKingsSml1234 TgrWoodmn117no MkrsRock1161¼ Rallied between rivals 8
Apr05-5Aqu fst 6f :214 :45 :571 1:101 3↑ Md Sp Wt 41k 13 2 2 22½ 88 819 824 Elliott S L118 b 13.10 63-08 Lively Up Yourself113¾ Heretic1182 Illustrious Kiss118nk Finished early 8
Previously trained by Dowd John F 2004(as of 6/19): (67 10 11 4 0.15)
Jun04-3Mth fst 5f :224 :463 :584 Md Sp Wt 37k 47 4 3 41½ 42 53½ 510 Elliott S L118 2.80 78-18 Smokescreen1181½ AllnsKt1183¼ *DoctorVoodoo*1184¼ Inside,no stretch bid 8
ORKS: Apr9 GP 5f fst 1:022 B *5/5* Mar31 GP 3f fst :38 B *4/5* Mar5 GP 3f fst :371 B *4/6* Feb9 GP 5f fst 1:03 B *14/18* Jan29 GP 5f fst 1:014 B *6/19*
RAINER: 1stW/Tm(7 .14 $0.89) Synth(54 .15 $1.49) Turf/Synth(16 .06 $0.58) 31-60Days(84 .13 $1.12) Routes(154 .16 $1.67) Claim(4 .00 $0.00)

He took to the Polytrack, however, and won by a half-length at odds of 5–1. It happened again in the seventh race. Carnera had failed to hit the board in three starts on conventional dirt before becoming a minor stakes winner on the turf.

```
3    Carnera                                                Dk.b or br c. 4 (Feb) KEESEP04 $550,000
     Own: Darley Stable                                     Sire: Old Trieste (A.P.Indy) $25,000
Blue Maroon, White Sleeves, White Star On                   Dam: Beyond the Sun (Kingmambo)
LEPAROUX J R (17 5 2 1 .29) 2007: (375 86 .23)              Br: Edward Seltzer & Marilyn Seltzer (Ky)
                                                            Tr: McLaughlin Kiaran P(5 2 0 0 .40) 2007:(153 41 .27)

       Life  13  3  2  1  $231,927  99 | D.Fst      3  0  0  0    $3,616  64
       2007   2  0  0  0      $860  80 | Wet(384)   0  0  0  0        $0  -
L 118                                  | Synth      0  0  0  0        $0  -
       2006  10  3  2  1  $228,917  99 | Turf(321) 10  3  2  1  $228,311  99
       Kee    0  0  0  0        $0   - | Dst(285)   0  0  0  0        $0  -

23Feb07-8GP  fm  1 1/16 Ⓣ :241 :48  1:1141:404 4↑Alw 43000N3x  74 8 5¹¾ 4¹¼ 3¹½ 8⁸¼ 8⁸ Jara F  L120 4.20 78-18 Yankee Master124¾ Salinja120² Rock Lobster120¹  Ducked out start 8
14Jan07-8GP  fm  1 1/16 Ⓣ :231 :47  1:1011:391 4↑Alw 43000N3x  80 8 8⁴¼ 8²¾ 5²¼ 5⁵½ 7⁸¼ Jara F  L120 *2.20 86-16 Heat of theNight120nk Defer120³ WoodBeWilling120¹½  4 wide move, tired 12
14Oct06-8Bel gd  1⅛ 🅃 :4931:124 1:3621:474  JmacaBCH-G2  75 2 2hd 2hd 2hd 5⁶½ 7¹⁴½ Coa E M  L116 6.80 71-24 ShowingUp124³½ Outperformance115² SpiderPower115¹½  Vied inside, tired 8
9Sep06-10Del sf  1⅛ Ⓣ :5121:161 1:4241:563  KentBC-G3  95 5 5⁷ 5⁵ 4⁴½ 2³½ 2⁶½ Coa E M  L116 7.90 46-51 Brilliant120⁶½ Carnera116²¾ Sea of Trees116¾  Bid, no match stretch 10
5Aug06-7Sar  fm  1 🅃 :24 :473 1:1141:352  AinSocilgy73k  99 5 3⁵½ 3⁷½ 3¹½ 1hd 1¹ Coa E M  L116 - 90-13 Carnera116¹ Pure Incentive111¹½ Yankee Master123hd  Ran for purse only 7
  Raced for purse money only
9Jly06-8Bel  fm  1⅛ 🅃 :4641:11 1:36 1:484  Lexingtn-G3  98 1 2¹½ 2½ 2hd 1½ 2¹½ Coa E M  L117 3.05 79-19 After Market117¹½ Carnera117hd Crossword117⁸  Dug in gamely inside 5
9Jun06-10Bel sf  1 Ⓣ :24 :48 1:1221:363  HillPrnc-G3  89 6 4⁵½ 4⁵½ 3¹ 1½ 3²¼ Coa E M  L116 16.30 75-23 Outperformance116¹½ SpiderPower118¾ Crner116²  Stumbled start, inside 10
30Apr06-4Aqu fm  1 1/16 Ⓣ :233 :484 1:1341:424  Alw 46000N1x  87 7 1³ 1²½ 1¹½ 1³½ 1³½ Coa E M  L122 8.20 93-11 Carnera122³½ Church Service118no Galantas118⁶½  Soon clear, kept busy 8
24Mar06-8GP  fm  1 1/16 Ⓣ :241 :49 1:1321:42  Md Sp Wt 32k  71 9 2¹ 2¹½ 2¹½ 2hd 1½ Guidry M  L122 2.90 81-16 Carnera122½ Letter Perfect122nk Union Avenue122½  All out, prevailed 10
23Feb06-6GP  fm  1 Ⓣ :231 :464 1:10 1:341  Md Sp Wt 32k  71 3 9⁷¼ 9⁸½ 8⁹½ 5⁶½ 4²¾ Guidry M  L122 9.70 83-08 Noble Deeds122¹½ Flight West122nk Coburn122¹  Rough trip, rallied 10
28Jan06-6Aqu fst 1 1/16 ⊡ :23 :464 1:12 1:453  Md Sp Wt 44k  32 10 5³ 5¹½ 6⁵¼ 9²⁰ 9³²¼ Arroyo N Jr  L120 8.40 50-21 Scanlon's Song120²¾ Marco's Tale120⁵ Tasteyville120³¼  Wide trip, tired 10
7Jan06-6Aqu  fst 6f ⊡ :223 :453 :5711:09  Md Sp Wt 43k  56 6 5 2¹½ 2²½ 5⁹ 5¹⁷½ Arroyo N Jr  L120 3.40 76-14 Sweetnorthernsint120⁷¾ TheirHGos115⁵¼ ClrthWy120hd  Saved ground turn 9
WORKS: Apr8 Kee ◈3f fst :37 B 7/8 Mar31 PmM 5f fst 1:032 B 15/16 Mar24 PmM 4f fst :51 B 28/31 Mar17 PmM 5f fst 1:012 H 11/30 Mar9 PmM 5f fst 1:01 H 5/14 Feb16 PmM 4f fst :48 H 3/17
TRAINER: Synth(5 .40 $5.52) Turf/Synth(2 .50 $8.00) Route/Sprint(35 .34 $3.21) 31-60Days(210 .24 $2.91) Sprint(272 .25 $2.63) Alw(182 .19 $1.91)
                                                                     J/T 2006-07 KEE(1 .00 $0.00) J/T 2006-07(1 .00 $0.00)
```

At odds of 9–2, he seemed to be ridiculously overbet. Yet he, too, ran to the best of his abilities to win by a nose. Had I been betting the race, I would have based my entire wagering strategy around trying to profit from throwing out a 9–2 shot that, in my opinion, should have been 25–1 or 30–1.

What happened? The only answer is that synthetic surfaces often don't provide any easy answers. Still, it appears that the best strategy is to be wary of grass runners on synthetic surfaces; that is, unless they have proven to be versatile types that can win on something besides the turf.

There is at least one aspect about racing on synthetic surfaces, particularly at Keeneland, that does indeed resemble grass racing, which is the way races seem to unfold. Speed has long been a dominant factor on conventional dirt surfaces, particularly in sprints. Horses racing in the back early rarely loop the field in the stretch and win with one powerful late move. Rather, front-runners and stalkers dominate.

Turf races are different. The early pace is often slow and plenty of winners charge from well off the pace. That same sort of style works far better on synthetic tracks than it does on conventional ones.

Retired jockey Gary Stevens analyzed it this way. "On synthetic tracks, the style is a lot more like it is on the turf. That's a key," he said. "You have to save something in your horse for the final quarter-mile or else you are putting yourself at a risk.

"Typically, a turf horse can accelerate much faster than a dirt horse. A dirt horse that goes along and clicks off a 12-second pace one furlong after another is going to have a good chance of winning. But you'll see a turf horse click off that last eighth of a mile in 11 seconds, and that's how they'll win. We've seen a lot of that on the Polytrack at Keeneland."

And Keeneland jockeys have adjusted their style on the main track.

"You ride it like a grass course," Kentucky-based jockey Dean Butler agreed. "It's very rare that you see horses running off early and winning on this kind of track unless they're tons the best. On the old tracks, you had speed horses running off and winning by six, seven, eight lengths. You get a lot more close finishes and photo finishes, like you get on grass. You rarely see horses win by 10 or 12 on the grass and there's usually something running at the winner at the end."

Whatever the reason, races on synthetic surfaces produce closer finishes and fewer strung-out fields. My guess is that has something to do with eliminating races on sloppy tracks, where the horses who can handle the off going tend to open up and win by double-digit lengths while the others stagger home.

Having had a full meet of Polytrack racing under its belt in 2007, Arlington presents a good case study of how tightly bunched fields are at the finish.

Average Lengths Separating Winner from Last-Place Finisher

2006 (Conventional Dirt)	19.21
2007 (Polytrack)	17.98

Average Winning Margin

2006 (Conventional Dirt)	2.60
2007 (Polytrack)	2.04

The differences between old-fashioned dirt and Polytrack were even more striking at Keeneland. At the final Keeneland dirt meet, the number of average lengths separating the field was 29.71. For the first Polytrack meet, the number dipped to 17.15. The average winning margin went from 4.33 lengths on dirt to 1.63 on the Polytrack.

Every track that has switched to synthetic surfaces has seen the same phenomenon occur. That is among the reasons people often compare synthetic-surface racing to grass racing, which also tends to produce fields that are tightly packed at the wire.

The 2007 Blue Grass was a prime example of a Polytrack contest that unfolded as if it were a turf race. With no one wanting the lead, Teuflesburg was able to get to the front in fractions of 26.12, 51.46, and 1:16.65, the type of pace that is unheard of when it comes to conventional dirt surfaces. Despite the slow pace, Dominican, who was fifth in midstretch, was able to close in time for the win. He was part of a blanket finish that featured four horses, including Teuflesburg, within a length of one another at the wire.

Read on. There's more on this subject to come.

5

Synthetic-Surface Sires: Who's Who

Everyone has seen them—horses who turn into dynamos the minute they try the grass. These same horses frequently can't run a step on the dirt and they usually are by one of the many sires known for throwing grass runners. There was a time when you couldn't bet enough on horses by Northern Dancer when they were making their turf debuts. Stage Door Johnnys were terrific on the grass. In more recent years, handicappers started to jump on the bandwagons of sires such as Dynaformer, Red Ransom, Diesis, and More Than Ready when it came to grass racing.

Anyone trying to handicap races in which most of the starters were making their turf debuts had to have a knowledge of breeding and an inkling as to which horses were likely to improve on the grass and which ones were not. Otherwise, you didn't stand a chance.

The same is true of mudders, horses that suddenly become killers when they run in the slop or goo. As with turf horses, the best mudders often share the same bloodlines. Sons of Conquistador Cielo always loved the wet going. I spent the better part of my youth playing sons and grandsons of Double Hitch when they ran in the mud at Suffolk Downs.

It stands to reason that there will now be "synthetic sires"—stallions whose offspring improve on synthetic surfaces and are automatic bets the first time they race on the stuff. Admittedly, it's a little early to tell who is about to become the Stage Door Johnny, Northern Dancer, Conquistador Cielo, or Double Hitch of synthetic sires, but some patterns are already starting to emerge.

In my opinion, most of the lists tracking synthetic sires that have emerged thus far have not gotten it right. It doesn't do the handicapper any good to know that Bold Executive is the leading synthetic-surface sire in North America. He's a Canadian stallion with dozens of offspring racing at Woodbine. He's had almost 300 more starters over synthetic surfaces than any other sire, so of course he's the leader. His horses have been fine on Woodbine's Polytrack, but there's no evidence to suggest that they move up on the surface.

To figure out which sires are producing the best synthetic-surface runners, you need to look at other numbers, such as how a stallion's progeny fare "first-time synthetic," as well as their ROI when they run on synthetic tracks. That's where you'll find which sires are truly producing horses that move up, and which ones throw runners that can't run a lick on the synthetics.

I contacted Thoro-Graph, a racing-data and speed-figure service, and asked them to run a comprehensive computer study of how sires were faring on synthetic surfaces in this country. The information runs through April 30, 2007, and, courtesy of Thoro-Graph, is reprinted later in this chapter.

There were 17 sires on the list that met all of the criteria listed below. They are my Super 17 synthetic sires.

1. They have produced at least five winners on synthetic tracks.
2. Their offspring have won at least 18 percent of their starts on synthetic tracks.
3. Their offspring have produced a positive ROI on synthetic tracks.
4. Their offspring have produced a positive ROI when making their first starts on synthetic tracks.
5. They have had at least 10 different horses start over synthetic surfaces.

The sires are: Belong to Me, Tribal Rule, Pembroke, Montbrook, E Dubai, Wild Event, Tour d'Or, Distant View, Put

It Back, Danzig, Decarchy, The Name's Jimmy, Unbridled, Cat's Career, Ghazi, Tribunal, and Unbridled Jet.

It's going to take time for the breeding industry to fully sort itself out when it comes to synthetic sires. At this writing, there simply isn't enough data available to answer all the questions. The smart horseplayer is going to have to stay on top of pedigrees when it comes to handicapping races on synthetic surfaces.

Everyone knows that Gary Stevens was a great jockey, but he's also a sharp handicapper and, now that he is retired, he doesn't mind backing up his opinions at the betting windows.

"On the synthetic tracks, I've been betting on a lot of horses who have good turf pedigrees," he said. "Those are the kinds of horses who seem to fit the winning style on the synthetic tracks.

"The kickback is a big part of this. You'll see a lot of turf horses who will work great on the dirt and you start to think they'll run just as well on the dirt, then they get out there and it doesn't happen. The reason is because there is no kickback on the turf. They're used to that and then they get out there in a dirt race and things are completely different. Nobody likes to get hit in the face with 60-mile-per-hour fastballs, not horses or riders."

Anyone who was ahead of the curve on synthetic sires should have made a couple of scores on a filly named Happy Celyna. She is by Tour d'Or, who is off to a great start as a synthetic-track sire.

py Celyna
James K. and Tan, Mary

B. f. 4 (Feb) KEEJAN04 $16,000
Sire: Tour d'Or (Medaille d'Or) $5,000
Dam: Lauren's Buck (Buchman)
Br: John Martin Silvertand (Fla)
Tr: Baltas Richard

Life	12	2	2	2	$40,310	73	D.Fst	6 0 2 1 $13,060 62
2007	4	1	0	0	$16,300	73	Wet(335)	0 0 0 0 $0 –
2006	8	1	2	2	$24,010	62	Synth	2 2 0 0 $23,400 73
							Turf(255)	4 0 0 1 $3,850 72

-5Hol	fst	6½f ⊕	:21⁴ :44⁴ 1:11¹ 1:18¹	3↑ⒻAlw 40000s	73	3	8	86½	77¾	34	12	Delgadillo A	LB122	8.80	82-16	HppyCelyn1222 DixieDixieDixie111no ChnlMyBll118½	4wd into lane,rallied	8
-4SA	fm	*6½f Ⓣ	:21⁴ :44¹ 1:06³ 1:12³	4↑ⒻAlw 40000s	65	3	6	65¼	54	66½	67½	Arias S	LB119	32.70	84-06	PttheCoolCt1194¾ PromisofSpring119hd LuckyStb1191	Bit tight hill,inside	8
-3SA	fm	*6½f Ⓣ	:21³ :44 1:07 1:13²	4↑ⒻAlw 40000s	65	9	4	77¾	87	74¼	54½	Baze M C	LB122	8.10	83-12	GoldnPlygrl1222 LckyStb119¾ PromsofSprng122¾	3wd into str,outkicked	9
-4SA	fm	1 Ⓣ	:23 :46² 1:11 1:36³	4↑ⒻAlw 40000s	72	10	76½	76	75½	65½	62½	Baze M C	LB123	47.20	78-15	MdmeBlckfoot113½ SeDriver120hd JkSieMcz1201¼	4wd into str,outkicked	10
-8Hol	fst	6f ⊕	:22¹ :45⁴ :58³ 1:11²	3↑ⒻMd 25000(25-22.5)	62	6	8	118¼	74¾	21	11	Baze M C	LB122	15.30	- -	HppyClyn1221 TrickyVivin120½ Twightlightspirit1224¾	4wd into lane,rallied	3
-5OSA	fst	7f	:22¹ :45¹ 1:11⁴ 1:26¹	3↑ⒻMd 25000(25-22.5)	47	5	2	56½	48½	45½	43½	Espinoza V	LB121	3.00	65-23	RomnclsFly121½ ItsAnothrStory121hd DDsPrincss1243	Off rail,no late bid	9
-1GG	gd	1 1/16 Ⓣ	:22⁴ :47⁴ 1:12⁴ 1:44¹	+3↑ⒻMd 32000(32-30)	53	3	43½	62¾	85¾	49	310½	Ochoa J	LB120	7.90	76-13	Devon's Queen1207 Mina Girl1223½ Happy Celyna1202	Shuffled back 1/2p	9
-13Fpx	fst	6½f	:22² :46³ 1:11⁴ 1:19	3↑ⒻMd 32000	62	1	2	65¼	52¼	31½	33¾	Flores D R	LB121	2.80	76-18	GirlyGirl117nk ForestSprite1163½ HappyCelyna1215	3wd bid,forced out3/16	8
-5Dmr	fst	6f	:22¹ :45¹ :57⁴ 1:11	3↑ⒻMd 32000(32-28)	56	6	8	87	79¼	58¼	26½	Baze M C	LB120	4.00	77-14	Ella Ella1206½ Happy Celyna1203 Have At It120½	4wd into str,2nd best	10
-2Hol	fst	1 1/16	:23³ :47 1:11⁴ 1:46²	3↑ⒻMd 40000(40-32)	43	7	53	45½	46½	47½	412½	Enriquez I D	LB117	17.50	56-24	NancysRose1121¼ BritneyHet1188 SenoritSeson1243¼	4wd 1st turn,no rally	7
-4Hol	fst	6f	:21⁴ :44³ :58² 1:12¹	3↑ⒻMd 32000(32-28)	50	3	4	43	56½	44½	28¾	Enriquez I D	LB118	26.00	67-18	NstyMood1138¾ HppyClyn118¾ MissNorthrnDwn1193	Came out ,stdied late	8
-10SA	fst	6f	:21³ :45¹ :58³ 1:12²	ⒻMd 32000(32-28)	38	9	10	910	912	98¼	57¼	Figueroa O	LB121	75.70	70-13	Isabella Monique1212½ Denaell121½ Wickersham121nk	Off rail,no rally	14

S: Apr22 Hol ⊕4f fst :49² H *40/59* Apr17 Hol ⊕5f fst 1:04² H *46/48* Apr11 Hol ⊕4f fst :48 H *10/42* Mar9 Hol ⊕4f fst :50¹ H *26/32* Mar3 Hol ⊕4f fst :49² H *29/48* Feb24 Hol ⊕5f fst 1:01⁴ H *42/64*

Bettors who were on to the Tour d'Or angle should have had her on top when she made her Cushion Track debut December 14, 2006, at Hollywood Park. A first-time-synthetic horse, she won by one length and paid $32.60.

EIGHTH RACE **Hollywood** **DECEMBER 14, 2006**

6 FURLONGS. (1.07^{2}) MAIDEN CLAIMING . Purse $14,000 (plus $3,320 Other Sources) FOR MAIDENS, FILLIES AND MARES THREE YEARS OLD AND UPWARD. Three Year Olds, 122 lbs.; Older, 124 lbs. Claiming Price $25,000, if for $22,500, allowed 2 lbs.

Value of Race: $17,320 Winner $8,400; second $2,800; third $1,680; fourth $840; fifth $400; sixth $400; seventh $400; eighth $400; ninth $400; tenth $400; eleventh $400; twelfth $400; thirteenth $400. Mutuel Pool $304,555.00 Exacta Pool $212,185.00 Quinella Pool $14,307.00 Trifecta Pool $193,018.00 Superfecta Pool $174,272.00

Last Raced	Horse	M/Eqt.	A.	Wt	PP	St	¼	½	Str	Fin	Jockey	Cl'g Pr	Odds $1
25Oct06 ^{5}OSA^{4}	Happy Celyna	LB	3	122	6	8	11^{5}	7^{hd}	2^{2}	1^{1}	Baze M C	25000	15.30
23Nov06 ^{8}Hol^{5}	Tricky Viviana	LB f	3	120	8	11	13	11^{4}	4^{1}	$2^{\frac{1}{2}}$	Espinoza V	22500	9.80
	Twightlightspirit	LB	3	122	11	3	$3^{\frac{1}{2}}$	$3^{1\frac{1}{2}}$	1^{1}	$3^{4\frac{3}{4}}$	Potts C L	25000	7.80
17Nov06 ^{8}Hol^{5}	Teddy Bear Tuff	LB	3	113	1	7	$10^{\frac{1}{2}}$	10^{1}	$7^{\frac{1}{2}}$	$4^{2\frac{1}{4}}$	Antongrgi III W^{7}	22500	23.30
22Nov06 ^{3}Hol^{5}	Dancin Music	LB	4	124	7	9	8^{hd}	8^{hd}	$5^{1\frac{1}{2}}$	$5^{2\frac{1}{2}}$	Chavez J F	25000	13.90
1Dec06 ^{3}Hol^{8}	Gold Coin	LB	3	120	12	2	$6^{2\frac{1}{2}}$	6^{1}	6^{hd}	6^{2}	Bisono A	22500	85.80
1Dec06 ^{5}Hol^{12}	Cat's Rene	LB	3	122	2	13	$9^{1\frac{1}{2}}$	9^{2}	11^{2}	7^{1}	Alferez J O	25000	84.00
1Dec06 ^{3}Hol^{3}	Acts Like Reign	LB f	4	124	13	1	4^{1}	4^{hd}	$8^{1\frac{1}{2}}$	$8^{2\frac{1}{4}}$	Gryder A T	25000	1.00
1Dec06 ^{5}Hol^{11}	Razi's Star	LB b	3	122	10	4	$5^{1\frac{1}{2}}$	$5^{1\frac{1}{2}}$	10^{hd}	$9^{3\frac{1}{2}}$	Portillo D A	25000	26.30
	Timeless Wager	B bf	3	122	4	12	12^{hd}	$12^{1\frac{1}{2}}$	12^{6}	$10^{2\frac{1}{4}}$	Castanon A L	25000	128.60
22Nov06 ^{3}Hol^{3}	Love My Rose	LB b	3	122	3	6	1^{hd}	1^{hd}	3^{hd}	$11^{1\frac{1}{2}}$	Valdivia J Jr	25000	4.60
	Unladylikebehavior	LB b	3	122	5	5	2^{hd}	$2^{\frac{1}{2}}$	9^{1}	$12^{14\frac{3}{4}}$	Delgadillo A	25000	19.80
	Copperjet	B f	3	122	9	10	$7^{\frac{1}{2}}$	13	13	13	Olivera J M	25000	34.80

OFF AT 4:05 Start Good. Won driving. Track fast.

TIME :22^{1}, :45^{4}, :58^{3}, 1:11^{2} (:22.33, :45.91, :58.71, 1:11.48)

$2 Mutuel Prices:				
	6 – HAPPY CELYNA	32.60	12.20	6.40
	9 – TRICKY VIVIANA		10.60	6.00
	12 – TWIGHTLIGHTSPIRIT			6.60

$1 EXACTA 6–9 PAID $80.00 $2 QUINELLA 6–9 PAID $80.20

$1 TRIFECTA 6–9–12 PAID $614.80 $1 SUPERFECTA 6–9–12–1 PAID $5,984.10

B. f, (Feb), by Tour d'Or – Lauren's Buck, by Buchman. Trainer Baltas Richard. Bred by John Martin Silvertand (Fla).

HAPPY CELYNA chased between horses then a bit off the rail, came out leaving the turn and four wide into the stretch and rallied under some left handed urging and a strong hand ride to prove best. TRICKY VIVIANA squeezed at the start, settled off the rail, came out on the turn and four wide into the stretch and gained the place late. TWIGHTLIGHTSPIRIT dueled between horses on the backstretch and three deep on the turn, took the lead into the stretch, inched clear, could not hold off the winner and lost second late. TEDDY BEAR TUFF saved ground off the pace, came out into the stretch and bested the others. DANCIN MUSIC squeezed at the start, chased between horses then outside a rival, came out three deep into the stretch and lacked the needed rally. GOLD COIN angled in and chased off the rail, came outside a rival into the stretch and lacked a further response. CAT'S RENE broke out and steadied, settled a bit off the rail then inside, was in tight in midstretch and was not a threat. ACTS LIKE REIGN prompted the pace four wide then stalked outside on the turn, came three deep into the stretch and weakened. RAZI'S STAR broke in and bumped foes, angled in and stalked a bit off the rail then inside on the turn and weakened in the stretch. TIMELESS WAGER broke a bit slowly, settled outside a rival then inside, came out into the stretch and failed to menace. LOVE MY ROSE dueled inside, fought back on the turn and weakened in the stretch. UNLADYLIKEBEHAVIOR sped to the early lead off the rail, dueled between horses on the backstretch and turn and had little left for the stretch. COPPERJET bumped at the start, chased outside and three deep into the turn, dropped back off the rail and gave way.

Owners– 1, Li James K and Tan Mary; 2, Miller Michael J; 3, Shen Peter Tsujimoto Stuart Uragami Stan et al; 4, Harrington Mike; 5, Madera Thoroughbreds LLC; 6, Sun Stables; 7, Vargas Toribio; 8, Gerson Racing Smith Burton H VanBurger Carl F et al; 9, Girvin Russell R and Shirley; 10, Olivarez Teresa and Turnowski Loretta; 11, Campbell Stephen and Periban Jorge; 12, Gunderson William and Lynn and Shefa Fabira; 13, Urvana Thomas

Trainers– 1, Baltas Richard; 2, Knapp Steve; 3, Matlow Richard P; 4, Harrington Mike; 5, Stute Glen; 6, Harrington Mike; 7, Soto Antonio; 8, Mitchell Mike; 9, Rosales Richard; 10, Olivarez Mario; 11, Periban Jorge; 12, Garcia Juan; 13, Martinez Rafael A

Scratched– Slew's Prayer (23Nov06 ^{8}Hol^{3}), Mystifing Miss (14Sep06 ^{11}Fpx^{3}), Mimithemidget (01Dec06 ^{3}Hol^{5})

$2 Daily Double (6–6) Paid $131.40 ; Daily Double Pool $89,815 .

$1 Pick Three (7–6–6) Paid $233.30 ; Pick Three Pool $94,446 .

$1 Pick Four (4/5–4/7–6–6) Paid $771.90 ; Pick Four Pool $320,167 .

$2 Pick Six (8–3–4/5–4/7–6–6) 6 Correct Paid $38,978.20 ; Pick Six Pool $541,126 .

$2 Pick Six (8–3–4/5–4/7–6–6) 5 Correct Paid $376.40 .

$1 Place Pick All (8–OF–8 CORRECT) Paid $2,142.20 ; Place Pick All Pool $18,905 .

Hollywood Park Attendance: 3,555 Mutuel Pool: $799,018.00 ITW Mutuel Pool: $2,478,848.00 ISW Mutuel Pool: $3,785,601.00

Shortly after Happy Celyna's Cushion Track debut, racing in southern California shifted to Santa Anita, which, at the time, still had a conventional dirt track. Now that she was jumping up in class and was back on turf, where she had lost before, Happy Celyna struggled, failing to hit the board in three starts at Santa Anita. It was a different story the minute she got back to Hollywood Park. Running in the same class of races that had given her fits at Santa Anita, she won an April 27, 2007, race on the Cushion Track and paid $19.60. Considering how well she ran in her only other start on a synthetic surface, Happy Celyna was an obvious bet when she returned to Hollywood Park.

"I knew she kind of liked the Cushion Track at Hollywood, but I didn't know just how much she liked it," trainer Rich Baltas said. "She trains all along at Hollywood on Cushion Track. I thought that helped her. She has feet issues and this track at Hollywood is easier on her. It doesn't sting her like dirt tracks do. She runs okay on the grass, but not like she does on the Cushion Track.

"When she won that second race on the Cushion Track I didn't think she was going to win that day. I thought the race was a little too tough for her. But she won again and she was impressive. She was impressive both times she ran on the Cushion Track."

Paying attention to the Super 17 synthetic sires—and any others that begin to catch on as more horses run on the new surfaces—is sure to present you with some mouthwatering opportunities to cash in. For instance, My Tune was coming off a win in a maiden claimer in which he got a mere 43 Beyer Speed Figure and might have looked like a throw-out when he showed up at Arlington on June 29, 2007, facing far classier.

Based on his breeding, though, My Tune was the type of horse who was worth a play at 24–1. His sire, Belong to Me, looks like one of the best synthetic sires in the country. The dam's sire, Robyn Dancer, also shows some good numbers on synthetic surfaces.

y Tune
n: Montesano Racing LLC

B. g. 3 (May) KEESEP05 $25,000
Sire: Belong to Me (Danzig) $12,500
Dam: Robyns Tune (Robyn Dancer)
Br: Ivy Dell Stud (Pa)
Tr: Hinsley David H

Life	2	2	0	0	$18,300	77	D.Fst	1	1	0	0	$6,900	43
							Wet(377)	0	0	0	0	$0	-
2007	2	2	0	0	$18,300	77	Synth	1	1	0	0	$11,400	77
2006	0	M	0	0	$0	-	Turf(310)	0	0	0	0	$0	-

un07–5AP fst 6f ◈ :224 :454 :58 1:104 3↑ Clm 32500N2L 77 6 6 55½ 56 33½ 1nk Thornton T L117 24.20 - - My Tune117nk Seventysevenstreet1211½ Deploy121hd Off rail, just up 8
an07–11Tam fst 7f :231 :463 1:131 1:27 Md 25000(25-20) 43 9 1 33½ 44 2½ 12¼ Hole T M L120 17.70 76– 13 My Tune1202¼ Lambeth120nk Coyote Trust1204¼ Split h, pulled away10
RKS: Jun24 AP ◈4f fst :50 B *50/81* Jun16 AP ◈7f fst 1:284 Hg *1/1* Jun9 AP ◈6f fst 1:15 B *7/8* Jun4 AP ◈5f fst 1:023 B *23/34* May30 AP ◈5f fst 1:03 B *18/27* May24 AP ◈5f fst 1:064 B *28/28*

Sure enough, My Tune took to the Polytrack surface at Arlington and rewarded his few backers.

FIFTH RACE
Arlington
JUNE 29, 2007

6 FURLONGS. (1.08²) CLAIMING . Purse $19,000 (plus $10,374 IOA – Illinois Registered Owner Award) FOR THREE YEAR OLDS AND UPWARD WHICH HAVE NEVER WON TWO RACES. Three Year Olds, 120 lbs.; Older, 124 lbs. Non-winners Of A Race Since May 29 Allowed 3 lbs. Claiming Price $32,500.

Value of Race: $19,000 Winner $11,400; second $3,800; third $2,090; fourth $1,140; fifth $570. Mutuel Pool $189,357.00 Exacta Pool $157,364.00 Trifecta Pool $125,280.00 Superfecta Pool $55,530.00

Last Raced	Horse	M/Eqt.	A.	Wt	PP	St	¼	½	Str	Fin	Jockey	Cl'g Pr	Odds $1
27Jan07 11Tam1	My Tune	L	3	117	6	6	5¹	5²	3²½	1nk	Thornton T	32500	24.20
20May07 9AP5	Seventysevenstreet	L	5	121	3	1	2¹½	1½	1²	2¹½	Graham J	32500	1.40
15Jun07 9AP8	Deploy	L	6	121	1	5	7²	7¹½	4½	3hd	Perez E E	32500	9.50
10May07 8AP8	Zoran	L	3	117	2	4	3¹½	3¹½	2¹½	4nk	Emigh C A	32500	8.30
10May07 8AP10	Frankie R.	L	3	117	7	3	4²½	4²	5¹	5¹½	Baird E T	32500	7.60
3Jun07 8AP3	Win Ticket	L f	4	121	8	7	6hd	6½	6⁵	6⁷	Douglas R R	32500	1.90
13Jun07 8CD6	Martins Point	L	4	121	5	8	8	8	7hd	7⁷¾	Fires E	32500	9.50
3Jun07 8AP9	American Racer	L b	6	121	4	2	1hd	2²	8	8	Sanchez D	32500	77.70

OFF AT 4:42 Start Good For All But MARTINS POINT. Won driving. Track fast.

TIME :22⁴, :45⁴, :58, 1:10⁴ (:22.82, :45.98, :58.02, 1:10.84)

$2 Mutuel Prices:				
	6 – MY TUNE	50.40	12.40	5.20
	3 – SEVENTYSEVENSTREET		3.20	2.80
	1 – DEPLOY			5.00

$2 EXACTA 6–3 PAID $209.20 $2 TRIFECTA 6–3–1 PAID $1,660.40
$2 SUPERFECTA 6–3–1–2 PAID $7,026.40

B. g, (May), by Belong to Me – Robyns Tune , by Robyn Dancer . Trainer Hinsley David H. Bred by Ivy Dell Stud (Pa).

MY TUNE raced off the rail near the middle of the field, rallied and was up at the wire. SEVENTYSEVENSTREET vied for the lead inside and just failed to last. DEPLOY lacked speed inside, angled out and rallied belatedly. ZORAN raced close up inside but failed to rally. FRANKIE R. raced off the rail and also failed to rally. WIN TICKET was not a factor. MARTINS POINT was fractious in the gate and broke in the air. AMERICAN RACER vied for the lead off the rail and gave way.

Owners– 1, Montesano Racing LLC; 2, Fulton Stan E; 3, Inman Barr H; 4, Iron County Farms Inc; 5, Cherrywood Racing Stables II; 6, WinStar Farm LLC; 7, Ernie T Poulos Racing Stable Counts J and Schafer H; 8, Lazuka Margaret and Law Dog Stables Inc and Maril Steven

Trainers– 1, Hinsley David H; 2, Maker Rebecca; 3, Livesay Charlie; 4, Kirby Frank J; 5, Boyce Michele; 6, Ritter Shannon; 7, Poulos Dee; 8, Lazuka William E

Zoran was claimed by Ralls and Foster LLC and Smith Ridge Stables; trainer, McGee Paul J.

$1 Pick Three (1–4–6) Paid $931.40 ; Pick Three Pool $11,257 .
$1 Pick Four (1–1–4–6) Paid $5,298.10 ; Pick Four Pool $31,712 .
$2 Daily Double (4–6) Paid $98.80 ; Daily Double Pool $8,624 .

He continued to reward anyone who stayed on his bandwagon whenever he ran on a synthetic surface. Note what happened when he shipped into Presque Isle Downs after a poor showing on the dirt at Philadelphia Park.

My Tune
Own: Sobczak Adam

B. g. 4 (May) KEESEP05 $25,000
Sire: Belong to Me (Danzig) $12,500
Dam: Robyns Tune (Robyn Dancer)
Br: Ivy Dell Stud (Pa)
Tr: Lake Scott A

Life	10	5	1	0	$69,502	84	D.Fst	3	1	0	0	$7,230
							Wet(375)	0	0	0	0	$0
2008	5	3	0	0	$49,202	84	Synth	7	4	1	0	$62,272
2007	5	2	1	0	$20,300	77	Turf(305)	0	0	0	0	$0

10May08–6PID fst 6f ◈ :22 :45² :57² 1:10² 3↑ [S]Alw 54600n2x 83 4 3 1hd 1¹ 1² 1¹¼ Fogelsonger R L116 f 2.30 89– 13 My Tune116¹¼ Sunshine Bo116⁴¾ Pass the Punch116nk Steady urging
29Apr08–7Pha fst 6f :22⁴ :46² :59 1:11⁴ 3↑ Alw 25000s 60 5 4 6³¼ 5⁴¼ 5⁵½ 5⁸¼ Vega H L121 3.80 72– 21 AimtoVictory114¾ PrimeChilly119¹¼ ClmndCollectd121²¾ Wide, no factor
26Mar08–8TP fst 6f ◈ :22² :46¹ :58² 1:11 3↑ Clm c-(25-20) 84 5 7 8⁴½ 4³½ 2² 1¾ Mojica O L118 4.00 87– 22 My Tune118¾ Deputy G118¹¼ Friendsturnedfoes118²½ 5 wide run turn
Claimed from Scarlet Stable for $25,000, Maker Michael J Trainer 2007: (332 95 52 35 0.29)
22Feb08–11TP fst 5½f ◈ :21³ :45¹ :58² 1:05² 4↑ OC 40k/n2x 49 2 6 5⁷¾ 6⁹¾ 6¹⁰ 6⁹¼ Lebron V L118 3.60 80– 20 National Day118no Markum118½ Southern Island118³ No menace
4Jan08–7TP fst 6½f ◈ :22⁴ :45⁴ 1:11 1:17⁴ 4↑ Clm c-(15-10)n3l 74 6 2 5² 4¹¾ 1² 1³½ Martinez L J Jr L118 4.60 87– 16 My Tune118³½ Cherokee Legacy120²¾ Starry Knight118¾ 4 wide 1/4 pl
Claimed from Montesano Racing LLC for $15,000, Salazar Marco P Trainer 2007: (175 21 22 17 0.12)
20Dec07–4TP fst 6f ◈ :22 :44⁴ :57 1:09⁴ 3↑ Clm 15000(15-10)n3l 67 5 6 4nk 1¹ 2¹ 2⁵¾ Martinez L J Jr L119 10.10 87– 10 Forest Attack123⁵¾ My Tune119³¼ Katzmetic115nk Fast pace, used up
Previously trained by Hinsley David H 2007(as of 10/8): (192 18 19 19 0.09)
8Oct07–8Haw fst 6f :22¹ :45¹ :57³ 1:10³ 3↑ Clm 17500n3l 51 3 7 8⁴¾ 8⁸¾ 8¹³ 8¹⁰ Thornton T L119 3.60 78– 15 Play Thru119¹ Bearific122hd Cockadoodle119no No speed, no facto
4Aug07–6AP fst 6½f ◈ :22² :45² 1:10² 1:16³ OC 50k/n1x -N 63 6 2 2¹½ 2½ 7⁴½ 8⁷¾ Emigh C A L117 7.80 - - Greeley'sAngel116hd GallantAgain118½ StandTall116¹¾ Through after half
29Jun07–5AP fst 6f ◈ :22⁴ :45⁴ :58 1:10⁴ 3↑ Clm 32500n2l 77 6 6 5⁵½ 5⁶ 3³½ 1nk Thornton T L117 24.20 - - My Tune117nk Seventysevenstreet121¹½ Deploy121hd Off rail, just up
27Jan07–11Tam fst 7f :23¹ :46³ 1:13¹ 1:27 Md 25000(25-20) 43 9 1 3³½ 4⁴ 2½ 1²¼ Hole T M L120 17.70 76– 13 My Tune120²¼ Lambeth120nk Coyote Trust120⁴¼ Split h, pulled away

WORKS: Apr26 Pha 3f fst :36⁴ B *9/32* ●Mar21 CDT 5f fst :59¹ B *1/10* Mar13 CDT 4f fst :48⁴ B *5/12* Feb17 CDT 4f sly :48² B *1/1*

Handicapping grass races has also taught us that some horses hate that surface. Again, the reason often has something to do with their pedigrees. In general, horses from the Mr. Prospector line are much better on the dirt than they are on the turf. Will there be sires that produce nothing but synthetic flops? The answer is . . . probably.

Here is a list of sires you might want to avoid in synthetic races: Cryptoclearance, Deputy Minister, Buddha, Afternoon Deelites, Ecton Park, Flying Continental, Theatrical, Cartwright, Randy Regent, Unreal Zeal, Silver Deputy, Thunder Gulch, and Royal Academy.

The betting public was fooled when Peaceful Flight showed up at Hollywood to race over Cushion Track in a $25,000 maiden claimer on June 21, 2007. He didn't show much of anything in his one other start on the artificial track at Hollywood, but had since prospered on the dirt and turf elsewhere. How would he fare now that he was back on Cushion Track? Anyone who knew about the record of futility by the offspring of Buddha (they would be 0 for 47 first-time synthetic by December, making him one of the worst synthetic sires there is) on synthetic tracks surely would have tossed this horse out. They would have been right.

A look at sires and pedigrees might also help shed some light on the question of whether or not grass horses will also run well on synthetic surfaces. With more evidence needed before this question can be answered conclusively, it appears that some turf sires will do fine with synthetic horses while some others may not. At the very least, it's apparent that good grass sires don't necessarily make good synthetic sires.

The top 10 turf sires of 2007 according to the earnings of their progeny on grass during that year were Smart Strike, Giant's Causeway, Dynaformer, Lemon Drop Kid, Langfuhr, Royal Academy, Rahy, Stormy Atlantic, Theatrical, and Distorted Humor.

Stormy Atlantic and Smart Strike are good synthetic sires. Royal Academy and Theatrical are lousy synthetic sires. The rest fall somewhere in between.

Gary Stevens offered this prediction: "The synthetic tracks will even change the breed, and change it for the better. I think you're going to see the breeding industry forced to shift back to the old days, when the great Thoroughbreds had not just speed but stamina. People who breed just for speed are going to put themselves at a disadvantage."

Thoro-Graph's data on synthetic sires follows. The charts include the overall records for stallions' progeny on synthetic surfaces and the records for those progeny when making their first starts on synthetic surfaces. I believe the most relevant number is the ROI when a horse makes its first start on these new tracks. Large ROIs could be signs that these horses improve on synthetic tracks and that money can be made from betting blindly on horses by certain sires when they debut on synthetic surfaces. All sires that had at least 10 starters on synthetic tracks through December 18, 2007, are included.

Overall Records through Dec. 18, 2007								First Time on Synthetic					
Name	**Horses**	**Strts**	**Wins**	**Win %**	**ITM**	**ITM %**	**ROI**	**Strts**	**Wins**	**Win %**	**ITM**	**ITM %**	**ROI**
Grand Slam	140	406	64	15.76	169	41.63	1.82	140	23	16.43	62	44.29	2.05
Tale of the Cat	138	443	67	15.12	174	39.28	1.80	138	28	20.29	56	40.58	2.80
Distorted Humor	128	411	50	12.17	148	36.00	1.81	128	21	16.41	49	38.28	2.09
Bold Executive	120	760	103	13.55	271	35.66	2.00	120	13	10.83	39	32.50	1.86
Langfuhr	118	486	56	11.52	160	32.92	1.73	118	12	10.17	37	31.36	2.63
Swiss Yodeler	115	451	43	9.53	157	34.81	1.01	115	16	13.91	41	35.65	1.87
Mutakddim	113	489	66	13.50	217	44.38	1.75	113	13	11.50	42	37.17	1.98
Bertrando	109	385	55	14.29	143	37.14	1.90	109	10	9.17	30	27.52	1.18
Touch Gold	105	329	28	8.51	100	30.40	0.87	105	12	11.43	31	29.52	1.29
Honour and Glory	104	331	42	12.69	124	37.46	1.40	104	11	10.58	38	36.54	0.93
Silver Deputy	104	333	28	8.41	107	32.13	0.83	104	7	6.73	27	25.96	0.63
Cherokee Run	104	283	32	11.31	100	35.34	1.05	104	7	6.73	28	26.92	0.83
A.P. Indy	102	231	37	16.02	92	39.83	1.81	102	20	19.61	46	45.01	2.70
Unusual Heat	101	328	41	12.50	123	37.50	1.80	101	7	6.93	24	23.76	1.08
Smart Strike	100	314	50	15.92	130	41.40	2.59	100	15	15.00	40	40.00	3.00
More Than Ready	99	295	41	13.90	108	36.61	1.63	99	14	14.14	39	39.39	2.20
Stormy Atlantic	97	339	58	17.11	142	41.89	1.77	97	14	14.43	38	39.18	2.24
Thunder Gulch	94	291	24	8.25	104	35.74	1.05	94	4	4.26	25	26.60	0.67
Maria's Mon	94	362	58	16.02	141	38.95	2.34	94	11	11.70	30	31.91	1.44
Deputy Commander	92	333	47	14.11	119	35.74	2.15	92	10	10.87	26	28.26	1.08

Name	Horses	Strts	Wins	Win %	ITM	ITM %	ROI	Strts	Wins	Win %	ITM	ITM %	ROI
Forest Wildcat	92	260	39	15.00	106	40.77	1.89	92	11	11.96	34	36.96	1.33
Giant's Causeway	91	289	45	15.57	127	43.94	1.95	91	12	13.19	35	38.46	1.75
El Corredor	91	323	48	14.86	135	41.80	1.57	91	13	14.29	33	36.26	1.65
Tiznow	90	298	50	16.78	137	45.97	2.00	90	12	13.33	33	36.67	1.28
Royal Academy	90	258	28	10.85	89	34.50	1.13	90	5	5.56	24	26.67	0.53
Victory Gallop	90	300	30	10.00	103	34.33	1.38	90	9	10.00	32	35.56	1.91
Elusive Quality	89	244	24	9.84	85	34.84	1.59	89	10	11.24	30	33.71	1.81
Unbridled's Song	87	205	29	14.15	82	40.00	1.18	87	9	10.34	35	40.23	0.78
Benchmark	86	304	40	13.16	122	40.13	1.87	86	12	13.95	29	33.72	1.51
Bold n' Flashy	85	538	54	10.04	159	29.55	1.78	85	9	10.59	21	24.71	2.07
Storm Boot	85	310	37	11.94	101	32.58	1.89	85	11	12.94	28	32.94	1.98
Catienus	85	441	72	16.33	189	42.86	1.85	85	11	12.94	33	38.82	1.93
Petionville	84	282	33	11.70	98	34.75	2.54	84	8	9.52	24	28.57	4.30
Devil His Due	83	424	41	9.67	144	33.96	1.25	83	5	6.02	22	26.51	1.11
Fusaichi Pegasus	83	219	28	12.79	85	38.81	1.25	83	10	12.05	30	36.14	1.45
Doneraile Court	83	338	39	11.54	120	35.50	1.77	83	6	7.23	20	24.01	1.12
Mr. Greeley	82	261	46	17.62	114	43.68	1.91	82	14	17.07	29	35.37	2.32
Storm Cat	82	183	25	13.66	75	40.98	1.36	82	9	10.98	32	39.02	0.86
In Excess (IRE)	82	287	40	13.94	127	44.25	1.55	82	7	8.54	32	39.02	1.76
Pulpit	80	251	29	11.55	89	35.46	1.18	80	7	8.75	24	30.00	1.12
Carson City	80	214	32	14.95	88	41.12	1.80	80	5	6.25	24	30.00	0.36
Awesome Again	79	263	27	10.27	92	34.98	0.90	79	10	12.66	33	41.77	1.50
Stephen Got Even	78	315	43	13.65	119	37.78	2.01	78	8	10.26	17	21.79	1.62
Broken Vow	77	232	25	10.78	88	37.93	1.77	77	8	10.39	25	32.47	1.25
Gilded Time	76	273	38	13.92	114	41.76	2.14	76	14	18.42	35	46.05	3.21
Dixie Union	76	228	28	12.28	74	32.46	1.49	76	8	10.53	24	31.58	1.40
Chief Seattle	75	293	43	14.68	109	37.20	1.80	75	11	14.67	25	33.33	2.06
Golden Missile	75	256	22	8.59	86	33.59	1.17	75	4	5.33	22	29.33	0.35
One Way Love	75	358	41	11.45	107	29.89	1.77	75	8	10.67	22	29.33	2.40
Indian Charlie	74	215	39	18.14	98	45.58	1.75	74	16	21.62	32	43.24	2.89
Yes It's True	74	270	24	8.89	83	30.74	1.12	74	4	5.41	18	24.32	0.91
Stormin Fever	73	259	31	11.97	85	32.82	1.29	73	8	10.96	23	31.51	0.92
Ascot Knight	72	400	43	10.75	121	30.25	2.22	72	6	8.33	18	25.00	2.40
Richter Scale	72	262	31	11.83	93	35.50	1.71	72	8	11.11	24	33.33	1.62
Forest Camp	72	183	19	10.38	57	31.15	1.17	72	7	9.72	22	30.56	0.73
Holy Bull	72	253	25	9.88	73	28.85	1.90	72	7	9.72	20	27.78	1.95
Cat Thief	71	248	34	13.71	92	37.01	1.97	71	7	9.86	24	33.80	1.75
Tactical Cat	71	244	38	15.57	92	37.70	1.46	71	9	12.68	26	36.62	1.25

Name	Horses	Strts	Wins	Win %	ITM	ITM %	ROI	Strts	Wins	Win %	ITM	ITM %	ROI
Out of Place	71	256	24	9.38	87	33.98	1.17	71	4	5.63	19	26.76	0.50
Lemon Drop Kid	71	210	29	13.81	84	40.00	2.37	71	9	12.68	20	28.17	3.23
Lord Carson	71	291	37	12.71	107	36.77	2.10	71	12	16.90	29	40.85	4.38
El Prado (IRE)	71	186	23	12.37	68	36.56	1.52	71	8	11.27	21	29.58	2.29
Tethra	70	405	30	7.41	112	27.65	1.40	70	2	2.86	17	24.29	0.52
Silver Charm	70	262	30	11.45	97	37.02	1.27	70	11	15.71	26	37.14	1.65
High Yield	70	243	20	8.23	82	33.74	1.29	70	8	11.43	16	22.86	2.22
Trajectory	69	344	35	10.17	112	32.56	1.48	69	7	10.14	18	26.09	1.96
Salt Lake	69	269	33	12.27	109	40.52	1.32	69	9	13.04	23	33.33	1.35
Beau Genius	69	230	23	10.00	69	30.00	1.58	69	6	8.70	19	27.54	0.95
Smoke Glacken	69	186	17	9.14	57	30.65	1.26	69	5	7.25	20	28.99	0.77
Cryptoclearance	68	282	15	5.32	68	24.11	0.75	68	6	8.82	18	26.47	1.23
Gold Case	67	254	47	18.50	95	37.40	2.59	67	6	8.96	13	19.40	1.79
Dynaformer	67	153	23	15.03	67	43.79	1.60	67	9	13.43	29	43.28	1.35
Forestry	66	172	28	16.28	71	41.28	1.78	66	10	15.15	22	33.33	1.83
Aptitude	66	195	24	12.31	60	30.77	1.23	66	3	4.55	15	22.73	0.51
Valid Wager	65	189	20	10.58	68	35.98	0.88	65	7	10.77	23	35.38	1.11
Belong to Me	65	193	37	19.17	84	43.52	2.59	65	13	20.00	28	43.08	3.55
Old Topper	65	236	37	15.68	86	36.44	1.96	65	9	13.85	23	35.38	2.25
Cee's Tizzy	65	185	20	10.81	55	29.73	1.70	65	4	6.15	18	27.69	0.41
Menifee	64	223	33	14.80	105	47.09	1.51	64	7	10.94	31	48.44	1.41
High Brite	64	230	24	10.43	78	33.91	1.27	64	5	7.81	17	26.56	1.34
Hennessy	63	174	32	18.39	66	37.93	1.64	63	9	14.29	17	26.98	1.81
Pioneering	63	229	20	8.73	79	34.50	1.21	63	9	14.29	19	30.16	1.62
Perigee Moon	63	280	22	7.86	74	26.43	1.78	63	4	6.35	14	22.22	1.93
Dance Brightly	62	341	34	9.97	106	31.09	1.49	62	4	6.45	21	33.87	0.46
Slew City Slew	61	282	47	16.67	119	42.20	2.41	61	10	16.39	24	39.34	3.30
Sky Classic	61	263	36	13.69	104	39.54	1.80	61	5	8.20	27	44.26	0.94
Peaks and Valleys	61	322	37	11.49	116	36.02	1.55	61	5	8.20	19	31.15	1.08
Alphabet Soup	61	233	23	9.87	80	34.33	2.01	61	5	8.20	16	26.23	1.58
Gone West	60	119	15	12.61	39	32.77	1.23	60	8	13.33	17	28.33	1.43
Deputy Minister	60	180	11	6.11	48	26.67	0.68	60	4	6.67	12	20.00	0.56
Storm Creek	59	182	21	11.54	54	29.67	1.40	59	7	11.86	16	27.12	1.11
Chester House	59	186	31	16.67	83	44.62	1.86	59	7	11.86	29	49.15	2.50
Yonaguska	59	223	21	9.42	56	25.11	1.11	59	2	3.39	12	20.34	0.52
Point Given	59	185	25	13.51	61	32.97	2.36	59	4	6.78	17	28.81	1.94
Sea of Secrets	58	236	19	8.05	65	27.54	0.96	58	5	8.62	17	29.31	0.67
Running Stag	58	270	37	13.70	105	38.89	1.73	58	10	17.24	21	36.21	3.26

Name	Horses	Strts	Wins	Win %	ITM	ITM %	ROI	Strts	Wins	Win %	ITM	ITM %	ROI
Louis Quatorze	57	274	29	10.58	97	35.40	1.24	57	7	12.28	19	33.33	2.25
Glitterman	57	216	23	10.65	73	33.80	1.66	57	8	14.04	16	28.07	3.49
Brahms	57	215	28	13.02	81	37.67	2.19	57	7	12.28	24	42.11	1.95
Stravinsky	56	204	27	13.24	78	38.24	2.13	56	6	10.71	20	35.71	1.53
Mizzen Mast	56	166	18	10.84	61	36.75	1.47	56	4	7.14	16	28.57	1.01
Orientate	56	191	22	11.52	80	41.88	1.70	56	6	10.71	15	26.79	2.88
Quiet American	56	200	16	8.00	50	25.00	1.44	56	3	5.36	13	23.21	0.56
Whiskey Wisdom	56	398	40	10.05	133	33.42	1.61	56	3	5.36	18	32.14	1.20
Matty G	55	224	17	7.59	67	29.91	1.00	55	6	10.91	15	27.27	1.77
Compadre	55	339	40	11.80	107	31.56	1.92	55	4	7.27	13	23.64	1.37
Roar	54	194	22	11.34	74	38.14	1.36	54	7	12.96	18	33.33	1.32
Mt. Livermore	54	192	15	7.81	57	29.69	0.85	54	2	3.70	12	22.22	0.40
Cape Town	54	156	18	11.54	60	38.46	1.36	54	3	5.56	17	31.48	1.31
Wild Rush	53	208	28	13.46	84	40.38	1.49	53	6	11.32	22	41.51	0.69
Dixieland Band	52	133	19	14.29	50	37.59	1.31	52	5	9.62	14	26.92	0.82
Gulch	52	195	25	12.82	73	37.44	1.20	52	6	11.54	15	28.85	0.85
Siphon (BRZ)	52	166	12	7.23	47	28.31	0.60	52	2	3.85	14	26.92	0.31
Real Quiet	52	204	27	13.24	69	33.82	1.53	52	4	7.69	14	26.92	0.95
Lit de Justice	52	232	32	13.79	88	37.93	2.17	52	4	7.69	12	23.08	2.15
Johannesburg	52	145	17	11.72	47	32.41	1.77	52	9	17.31	23	44.23	2.56
Black Minnaloushe	51	185	15	8.11	47	25.41	1.21	51	3	5.88	8	15.69	1.30
Pleasant Tap	51	173	28	16.18	78	45.09	1.72	51	10	19.61	22	43.14	2.15
Northern Afleet	51	170	28	16.47	68	40.00	1.87	51	6	11.76	16	31.37	2.07
Skip Away	50	258	39	15.12	110	42.64	2.50	50	8	16.00	20	40.00	4.63
Grindstone	50	168	15	8.93	48	28.57	1.52	50	5	10.00	11	22.00	2.18
Crafty Prospector	50	193	19	9.84	67	34.72	1.57	50	4	8.00	14	28.00	2.30
Banker's Gold	50	219	21	9.59	74	33.79	1.01	50	3	6.00	14	28.00	1.21
Marquetry	50	203	26	12.81	80	39.41	1.04	50	5	10.00	14	28.00	0.85
Cat's At Home	50	224	15	6.70	43	19.20	0.81	50	4	8.00	8	16.00	1.53
Bernstein	50	191	26	13.61	68	35.60	2.49	50	5	10.00	18	36.00	4.06
Jump Start	50	140	18	12.86	36	25.71	1.74	50	3	6.00	9	18.00	1.34
Exploit	49	220	31	14.09	89	40.45	2.03	49	8	16.33	15	30.61	1.47
Monarchos	48	148	21	14.19	55	37.16	2.14	48	7	14.58	14	29.17	3.76
Came Home	47	136	15	11.03	50	36.76	1.33	47	6	12.77	13	27.66	1.28
Buddha	47	136	9	6.62	30	22.06	0.89	47	0	0.00	5	10.64	0.00
Street Cry (IRE)	47	148	23	15.54	65	43.92	2.61	47	8	17.02	18	38.30	2.33
Souvenir Copy	46	167	23	13.77	70	41.92	1.89	46	6	13.04	20	43.48	0.85
Rahy	46	141	21	14.89	56	39.72	1.76	46	9	19.57	17	36.96	3.23

Name	Horses	Strts	Wins	Win %	ITM	ITM %	ROI	Strts	Wins	Win %	ITM	ITM %	ROI
Seeking the Gold	46	127	17	13.39	53	41.73	1.24	46	7	15.22	20	43.48	1.35
Coronado's Quest	46	161	21	13.04	59	36.65	1.28	46	6	13.04	15	32.61	1.41
Arch	46	176	22	12.50	68	38.64	2.36	46	5	10.87	15	32.61	1.46
Officer	46	133	21	15.79	47	35.34	1.60	46	7	15.22	14	30.43	1.69
Alydeed	46	200	16	8.00	44	22.00	0.93	46	2	4.35	9	19.57	1.05
You and I	46	190	16	8.42	54	28.42	1.35	46	3	6.52	14	30.43	0.85
Service Stripe	46	238	26	10.92	84	35.29	2.80	46	4	8.70	12	26.09	1.80
Include	45	140	19	13.57	55	39.29	1.06	45	6	13.33	19	42.22	1.01
War Chant	45	133	20	15.04	56	42.11	2.01	45	6	13.33	17	37.78	2.76
Comic Strip	45	126	15	11.90	43	34.13	1.70	45	6	13.33	20	44.44	2.46
With Approval	45	178	18	10.11	57	32.02	1.30	45	2	4.44	11	24.44	0.51
Mazel Trick	45	208	26	12.50	84	40.38	1.18	45	2	4.44	15	33.33	0.92
Five Star Day	45	133	15	11.28	53	39.85	1.26	45	4	8.89	13	28.89	0.90
Vicar	45	166	19	11.45	58	34.94	1.37	45	4	8.89	15	33.33	1.01
Meadowlake	45	171	21	12.28	69	40.35	1.11	45	4	8.89	15	33.33	0.85
Runaway Groom	45	145	20	13.79	60	41.38	1.55	45	5	11.11	15	33.33	1.06
Horse Chestnut (SAF)	44	110	11	10.00	33	30.00	3.02	44	5	11.36	13	29.55	1.16
Artax	44	142	14	9.86	51	35.92	0.89	44	1	2.27	9	20.45	0.44
Charismatic	43	176	19	10.80	66	37.50	1.19	43	2	4.65	13	30.23	0.21
Foxtrail	43	211	18	8.53	58	27.49	1.77	43	2	4.65	5	11.63	0.37
Kiridashi	43	268	38	14.18	105	39.18	2.51	43	9	20.93	13	30.23	5.53
Lite the Fuse	43	146	20	13.70	54	36.99	2.21	43	4	9.30	10	23.26	2.02
Formal Gold	42	167	13	7.78	60	35.93	0.82	42	1	2.38	13	30.95	0.38
Evansville Slew	41	177	28	15.82	68	38.42	2.21	41	5	12.20	9	21.95	2.06
Skimming	41	143	19	13.29	49	34.27	1.63	41	2	4.88	8	19.51	0.67
Commendable	41	143	15	10.49	44	30.77	0.62	41	1	2.44	9	21.95	0.15
Malibu Moon	40	134	19	14.18	51	38.06	1.43	40	6	15.00	11	27.50	2.20
Cape Canaveral	40	127	20	15.75	47	37.01	1.87	40	5	12.50	14	35.00	2.17
Albert the Great	40	144	17	11.81	47	32.64	2.77	40	4	10.00	8	20.00	1.02
Capote	40	111	14	12.61	35	31.53	1.52	40	3	7.50	8	20.00	0.72
Yankee Victor	40	148	18	12.16	69	46.62	1.40	40	4	10.00	15	37.50	1.35
Archers Bay	40	220	36	16.36	88	40.00	2.53	40	6	15.00	17	42.50	3.06
Hold That Tiger	40	118	13	11.02	39	33.05	0.98	40	5	12.50	10	25.00	1.16
Bartok (IRE)	39	155	13	8.39	51	32.90	1.15	39	3	7.69	8	20.51	1.74
General Meeting	39	139	21	15.11	59	42.45	2.33	39	7	17.95	14	35.90	5.76
Count the Time	39	169	24	14.20	60	35.50	1.82	39	5	12.82	17	43.59	2.08
Songandaprayer	38	98	12	12.24	31	31.63	1.29	38	1	2.63	7	18.42	0.24
Afternoon Deelites	38	141	12	8.51	50	35.46	1.03	38	2	5.26	13	34.21	0.33

Name	Horses	Strts	Wins	Win %	ITM	ITM %	ROI	Strts	Wins	Win %	ITM	ITM %	ROI
Trippi	38	136	18	13.24	56	41.18	2.79	38	6	15.79	18	47.37	5.16
Sir Cat	38	155	25	16.13	64	41.29	1.75	38	6	15.79	17	44.74	1.92
Silver Ghost	38	121	18	14.88	46	38.02	1.19	38	5	13.16	11	28.95	1.42
Woodman	37	104	12	11.54	27	25.96	1.53	37	6	16.22	10	27.03	2.26
Cozzene	37	113	17	15.04	45	39.82	1.83	37	5	13.51	11	29.73	1.96
Scatmandu	37	158	17	10.76	63	39.87	1.26	37	5	13.51	13	35.14	1.72
Regal Classic	37	179	27	15.08	60	33.52	2.11	37	6	16.22	11	29.73	5.42
Tribal Rule	37	128	28	21.88	58	45.31	2.86	37	8	21.62	19	51.35	4.28
Ecton Park	37	130	8	6.15	42	32.31	0.74	37	1	2.70	10	27.03	0.34
Pure Prize	37	106	20	18.87	49	46.23	2.70	37	7	18.92	16	43.24	1.70
Pembroke	37	154	29	18.83	65	42.21	2.26	37	7	18.92	20	54.05	2.30
Montbrook	36	124	24	19.35	63	50.81	2.02	36	8	22.22	17	47.22	2.14
Sefapiano	36	246	23	9.35	89	36.18	1.22	36	7	19.44	16	44.44	3.83
Boundary	36	148	20	13.51	54	36.49	1.32	36	5	13.89	13	36.11	1.75
Theatrical (IRE)	36	71	6	8.45	19	26.76	0.79	36	1	2.78	6	16.67	0.31
Favorite Trick	36	176	23	13.07	74	42.05	1.52	36	7	19.44	13	36.11	2.13
Game Plan	36	144	25	17.36	67	46.53	2.08	36	4	11.11	12	33.33	1.22
Sahm	36	132	16	12.12	54	40.91	2.90	36	4	11.11	14	38.89	4.86
Crown Attorney	36	205	20	9.76	56	27.32	2.62	36	2	5.56	5	13.89	2.67
Western Fame	36	109	19	17.43	45	41.28	2.44	36	6	16.67	13	36.11	4.12
Tejano Run	35	164	18	10.98	57	34.76	2.52	35	3	8.57	10	28.57	3.17
Royal Anthem	35	153	20	13.07	68	44.44	2.00	35	4	11.43	13	37.14	1.22
Flying Continental	35	121	8	6.61	37	30.58	0.90	35	1	2.86	7	20.00	0.21
Harlan's Holiday	35	77	15	19.48	33	42.86	1.89	35	4	11.43	10	28.57	1.47
Cartwright	35	110	6	5.45	30	27.27	0.99	35	1	2.86	6	17.14	0.39
E Dubai	35	90	18	20.00	37	41.11	2.48	35	9	25.71	13	37.14	2.59
Saint Ballado	34	98	11	11.22	41	41.84	1.44	34	5	14.71	13	38.24	2.35
Tiger Ridge	34	106	15	14.15	43	40.57	1.71	34	6	17.65	13	38.24	1.48
Crafty Friend	34	122	8	6.56	39	31.97	1.41	34	1	2.94	11	32.35	2.36
Lear Fan	34	104	11	10.58	32	30.77	2.74	34	6	17.65	11	32.35	7.45
The Deputy (IRE)	34	160	19	11.88	44	27.50	1.80	34	5	14.71	9	26.47	2.07
Helmsman	33	87	8	9.20	26	29.89	2.46	33	3	9.09	10	30.30	4.47
General Royal	33	121	13	10.74	29	23.97	2.84	33	1	3.03	5	15.15	0.57
Old Trieste	33	109	10	9.17	32	29.36	1.62	33	4	12.12	11	33.33	2.12
Free House	33	136	17	12.50	57	41.91	1.71	33	1	3.03	8	24.24	0.22
Pine Bluff	33	136	10	7.35	49	36.03	0.84	33	3	9.09	8	24.24	1.64
Siberian Summer	33	94	13	13.83	29	30.85	1.86	33	1	3.03	3	9.09	1.25
Our Emblem	32	85	7	8.24	19	22.35	2.68	32	3	9.38	6	18.75	1.12

Name	Horses	Strts	Wins	Win %	ITM	ITM %	ROI	Strts	Wins	Win %	ITM	ITM %	ROI
Luhuk	32	123	10	8.13	36	29.27	1.07	32	2	6.25	10	31.25	0.89
Bianconi	32	96	13	13.54	30	31.25	1.65	32	3	9.38	5	15.63	0.77
Double Honor	31	91	10	10.99	34	37.36	1.51	31	4	12.90	13	41.94	2.96
Rubiano	31	152	23	15.13	56	36.84	1.39	31	2	6.45	9	29.03	0.75
Red Ransom	31	118	12	10.17	47	39.83	0.81	31	3	9.68	10	32.26	0.99
Perfect Mandate	31	107	8	7.48	27	25.23	1.56	31	3	9.68	7	22.58	1.77
Randy Regent	31	140	5	3.57	33	23.57	0.91	31	0	0.00	2	6.45	0.00
Vindication	31	60	11	18.33	22	36.67	1.55	31	4	12.90	11	35.48	1.41
Lac Ouimet	31	143	21	14.69	55	38.46	2.34	31	1	3.23	5	16.13	1.10
King of Kings (IRE)	31	135	12	8.89	50	37.04	0.65	31	2	6.45	11	35.48	0.36
Labeeb (GB)	31	171	13	7.60	60	35.09	1.57	31	3	9.68	14	45.16	1.51
Kissin Kris	31	120	11	9.17	41	34.17	1.18	31	4	12.90	9	29.03	1.77
Kingmambo	31	83	9	10.84	25	30.12	1.43	31	3	9.68	11	35.48	0.55
Lost Soldier	30	89	7	7.87	22	24.72	1.18	30	2	6.67	7	23.33	0.80
Halo's Image	30	94	6	6.38	38	40.43	0.89	30	3	10.00	12	40.00	1.30
Not For Love	30	115	17	14.78	56	48.70	2.18	30	4	13.33	14	46.67	1.14
Twining	30	131	17	12.98	51	38.93	1.67	30	8	26.67	11	36.67	3.37
Malabar Gold	30	83	7	8.43	25	30.12	0.93	30	1	3.33	7	23.33	0.30
Sandpit (BRZ)	30	141	16	11.35	48	34.04	1.84	30	2	6.67	10	33.33	0.53
Canyon Creek (IRE)	30	165	8	4.85	41	24.85	0.78	30	2	6.67	8	26.67	0.40
Jade Hunter	30	81	10	12.35	21	25.93	2.34	30	6	20.00	9	30.00	2.67
Unreal Zeal	30	87	3	3.45	22	25.29	0.49	30	0	0.00	5	16.67	0.00
Smokester	30	96	11	11.46	31	32.29	1.00	30	1	3.33	7	23.33	0.28
Fit to Fight	29	120	13	10.83	37	30.83	1.02	29	3	10.34	7	24.14	0.96
Sky Mesa	29	52	9	17.31	20	38.46	3.77	29	5	17.24	12	41.38	2.18
Behrens	29	92	10	10.87	20	21.74	1.85	29	2	6.90	5	17.24	2.26
Mercer Mill	29	92	5	5.43	16	17.39	0.57	29	2	6.90	6	20.69	0.68
Southern Halo	29	112	15	13.39	40	35.71	2.00	29	2	6.90	10	34.48	1.13
Graeme Hall	29	110	11	10.00	51	46.36	1.00	29	7	24.14	14	48.28	2.76
Kinshasa	29	124	7	5.65	26	20.97	0.52	29	1	3.45	5	17.24	0.38
King Cugat	28	94	15	15.96	34	36.17	2.17	28	6	21.43	9	32.14	2.77
Editor's Note	28	122	13	10.66	31	25.41	1.64	28	2	7.14	7	25.00	0.48
Military	28	90	12	13.33	33	36.67	1.68	28	2	7.14	5	17.86	1.68
Van Nistelrooy	28	62	9	14.52	24	38.71	1.86	28	4	14.29	9	32.14	2.20
Sultry Song	28	165	20	12.12	58	35.15	1.61	28	2	7.14	7	25.00	2.13
Mud Route	28	91	15	16.48	38	41.76	3.31	28	2	7.14	6	21.43	4.69
Vision and Verse	28	102	15	14.71	38	37.25	2.49	28	4	14.29	10	35.71	3.61
Successful Appeal	28	71	10	14.08	34	47.89	1.21	28	1	3.57	9	32.14	0.74

Name	Horses	Strts	Wins	Win %	ITM	ITM %	ROI	Strts	Wins	Win %	ITM	ITM %	ROI
Prized	28	127	17	13.39	48	37.80	2.29	28	3	10.71	10	35.71	2.90
Event of the Year	27	99	17	17.17	47	47.47	2.05	27	7	25.93	14	51.85	4.95
A Fleets Dancer	27	131	8	6.11	28	21.37	1.63	27	1	3.70	4	14.81	3.51
Honor Grades	27	111	10	9.01	38	34.23	1.61	27	1	3.70	4	14.81	0.28
Two Punch	27	77	8	10.39	18	23.38	1.23	27	3	11.11	6	22.22	1.63
Anees	27	113	12	10.62	50	44.25	0.81	27	2	7.41	13	48.15	0.57
Lion Cavern	27	121	8	6.61	35	28.93	1.43	27	1	3.70	12	44.44	0.46
Demidoff	26	125	12	9.60	43	34.40	0.85	26	1	3.85	6	23.08	0.35
War Deputy	26	163	14	8.59	41	25.15	1.34	26	1	3.85	6	23.08	0.40
Millennium Wind	26	68	10	14.71	19	27.94	2.21	26	3	11.54	6	23.08	2.66
Pyramid Peak	26	104	9	8.65	35	33.65	2.33	26	2	7.69	7	26.92	0.60
Larry the Legend	26	106	12	11.32	43	40.57	1.38	26	0	0.00	8	30.77	0.00
Gentlemen (ARG)	26	136	16	11.76	53	38.97	1.55	26	2	7.69	6	23.08	1.05
Classified Facts	26	76	8	10.53	33	43.42	1.57	26	1	3.85	9	34.62	0.12
Notebook	26	71	6	8.45	20	28.17	1.05	26	1	3.85	6	23.08	0.69
Muqtarib	25	79	8	10.13	21	26.58	1.06	25	3	12.00	7	28.00	1.46
Pikepass	25	98	16	16.33	42	42.86	2.38	25	3	12.00	9	36.00	3.42
Outflanker	25	126	23	18.25	54	42.86	2.72	25	3	12.00	9	36.00	0.75
Memo (CHI)	25	82	9	10.98	30	36.59	1.95	25	4	16.00	10	40.00	3.10
Suave Prospect	25	94	8	8.51	28	29.79	0.93	25	0	0.00	5	20.00	0.00
Broad Brush	25	73	8	10.96	28	38.36	0.88	25	3	12.00	10	40.00	1.10
Proud Citizen	25	62	6	9.68	17	27.42	1.59	25	1	4.00	3	12.00	1.42
Lil E. Tee	25	99	10	10.10	28	28.28	1.08	25	1	4.00	6	24.00	1.28
Greenwood Lake	24	109	17	15.60	45	41.28	2.32	24	5	20.83	8	33.33	4.75
Atticus	24	93	10	10.75	32	34.41	1.32	24	1	4.17	4	16.67	0.26
Go for Gin	24	99	9	9.09	32	32.32	1.42	24	3	12.50	6	25.00	1.25
Golden Gear	24	99	12	12.12	39	39.39	1.21	24	1	4.17	4	16.67	0.60
Thunderello	24	107	12	11.21	39	36.45	1.16	24	0	0.00	5	20.83	0.00
Slewdledo	24	89	14	15.73	41	46.07	2.87	24	3	12.50	10	41.67	5.44
Down the Aisle	24	99	4	4.04	22	22.22	1.99	24	2	8.33	7	29.17	7.13
Subordination	24	78	10	12.82	26	33.33	2.18	24	1	4.17	5	20.83	1.84
Alaskan Frost	24	74	10	13.51	27	36.49	1.92	24	2	8.33	6	25.00	1.39
Best of Luck	24	131	8	6.11	41	31.30	0.73	24	1	4.17	3	12.50	0.78
Dayjur	24	83	9	10.84	30	36.14	3.19	24	2	8.33	9	37.50	3.80
Acceptable	23	127	11	8.66	38	29.92	1.02	23	2	8.70	6	26.09	1.11
Devon Lane	23	77	4	5.19	26	33.77	1.50	23	2	8.70	8	34.78	1.37
Posse	23	53	9	16.98	18	33.96	2.02	23	1	4.35	7	30.43	0.39
Boston Harbor	23	64	5	7.81	17	26.56	1.43	23	4	17.39	7	30.43	3.47

Name	Horses	Strts	Wins	Win %	ITM	ITM %	ROI	Strts	Wins	Win %	ITM	ITM %	ROI
Devil's Bag	23	73	8	10.96	20	27.40	1.62	23	1	4.35	5	21.74	0.45
Straight Man	23	70	13	18.57	32	45.71	2.08	23	1	4.35	7	30.43	0.51
D'wildcat	23	78	9	11.54	33	42.31	1.70	23	2	8.70	7	30.43	1.01
Wheaton	22	77	8	10.39	38	49.35	0.74	22	2	9.09	11	50.00	0.53
Dixieland Heat	22	146	19	13.01	62	42.47	2.01	22	5	22.73	12	54.55	4.05
Future Storm	22	59	4	6.78	13	22.03	1.90	22	1	4.55	4	18.18	3.73
Three Wonders	22	80	12	15.00	30	37.50	2.41	22	2	9.09	9	40.91	1.82
Exchange Rate	22	52	8	15.38	18	34.62	1.95	22	3	13.64	7	31.82	1.91
Yankee Gentleman	22	63	11	17.46	29	46.03	2.55	22	5	22.73	11	50.00	4.02
Flatter	22	76	8	10.53	24	31.58	1.46	22	1	4.55	5	22.73	0.94
Lil Tyler	22	104	8	7.69	39	37.50	0.99	22	2	9.09	7	31.82	0.51
Ide	22	102	12	11.76	29	28.43	2.31	22	1	4.55	6	27.27	0.53
Wild Event	22	81	17	20.99	31	38.27	2.16	22	6	27.27	10	45.45	2.99
Illinois Storm	22	61	3	4.92	10	16.39	3.29	22	1	4.55	3	13.64	1.17
Kafwain	22	51	4	7.84	19	37.25	0.41	22	1	4.55	8	36.36	0.30
Wavering Monarch	22	93	7	7.53	22	23.66	1.96	22	3	13.64	5	22.73	2.99
Proud Irish	22	69	7	10.14	21	30.43	0.66	22	2	9.09	4	18.18	0.87
Crown Ambassador	22	75	6	8.00	21	28.00	1.12	22	1	4.55	4	18.18	0.63
Lil's Lad	22	64	7	10.94	22	34.38	2.00	22	4	18.18	8	36.36	1.84
Hold for Gold	21	85	13	15.29	36	42.35	1.84	21	1	4.76	8	38.01	0.28
K. O. Punch	21	61	1	1.64	8	13.11	0.46	21	0	0.00	2	9.52	0.00
Wagon Limit	21	70	4	5.71	18	25.71	0.30	21	2	9.52	7	33.33	0.50
Olympio	21	64	5	7.81	15	23.44	1.13	21	2	9.52	5	23.81	1.62
Captain Bodgit	21	119	9	7.56	37	31.09	1.23	21	2	9.52	8	38.01	0.90
Latin American	21	62	3	4.84	14	22.58	0.95	21	1	4.76	5	23.81	0.24
Highland Ruckus	21	104	5	4.81	30	28.85	0.58	21	1	4.76	7	33.33	0.59
Ciano Cat	21	80	9	11.25	24	30.00	2.09	21	1	4.76	4	19.05	1.20
Porto Foricos	21	88	7	7.95	22	25.00	1.57	21	1	4.76	6	28.57	0.88
Aljabr	21	64	6	9.38	21	32.81	0.66	21	1	4.76	6	28.57	0.20
Ordway	21	87	10	11.49	29	33.33	1.97	21	1	4.76	4	19.05	0.59
Lucky Lionel	21	98	16	16.33	39	39.80	2.03	21	2	9.52	10	47.62	0.56
Sunday Break (JPN)	21	54	3	5.56	12	22.22	1.17	21	0	0.00	6	28.57	0.00
Jambalaya Jazz	21	72	9	12.50	25	34.72	2.10	21	4	19.05	8	38.01	2.48
Tour d'Or	21	94	18	19.15	38	40.43	3.58	21	6	28.57	9	42.86	9.00
Unbridled Time	21	66	12	18.18	26	39.39	1.82	21	6	28.57	7	33.33	3.27
Announce	21	108	14	12.96	42	38.89	1.45	21	1	4.76	5	23.81	0.65
Distant View	21	59	11	18.64	20	33.90	3.54	21	4	19.05	8	38.01	2.35
Red Bullet	21	56	8	14.29	20	35.71	1.90	21	3	14.29	8	38.01	3.03

Name	Horses	Strts	Wins	Win %	ITM	ITM %	ROI	Strts	Wins	Win %	ITM	ITM %	ROI
Outofthebox	21	48	1	2.08	12	25.00	0.23	21	0	0.00	5	23.81	0.00
Put It Back	20	61	18	29.51	33	54.01	3.38	20	5	25.00	8	40.00	4.15
Rio Verde	20	69	8	11.59	19	27.54	2.39	20	3	15.00	6	30.00	2.05
Phone Trick	20	64	3	4.69	15	23.44	0.32	20	1	5.00	7	35.00	0.60
Turkoman	20	55	4	7.27	7	12.73	3.96	20	2	10.00	2	10.00	1.19
Bright Launch	20	63	5	7.94	18	28.57	4.06	20	1	5.00	3	15.00	0.29
Silic (FR)	20	76	9	11.84	22	28.95	2.00	20	2	10.00	4	20.00	2.33
Joyeux Danseur	20	62	12	19.35	31	50.00	2.26	20	3	15.00	8	40.00	1.44
Madraar	20	61	2	3.28	17	27.87	1.04	20	0	0.00	2	10.00	0.00
Wild Wonder	20	75	11	14.67	33	44.00	2.80	20	2	10.00	4	20.00	0.73
Is It True	20	107	9	8.41	29	27.10	2.22	20	1	5.00	4	20.00	0.64
Repriced	20	128	18	14.06	48	37.50	1.53	20	3	15.00	5	25.00	1.02
Robyn Dancer	20	65	6	9.23	19	29.23	2.17	20	4	20.00	7	35.00	6.29
Adcat	20	85	9	10.59	27	31.76	1.88	20	1	5.00	4	20.00	1.05
Friendly Lover	20	101	20	19.80	41	40.59	1.79	20	2	10.00	8	40.00	0.46
I Can't Believe	19	136	13	9.56	35	25.74	1.96	19	2	10.53	6	31.58	8.32
Crowning Storm	19	45	2	4.44	11	24.44	0.25	19	1	5.26	3	15.79	0.32
Concerto	19	77	13	16.88	34	44.16	1.26	19	3	15.79	6	31.58	1.33
Wild Again	19	68	8	11.76	30	44.12	1.51	19	2	10.53	6	31.58	2.14
Whywhywhy	19	47	3	6.38	12	25.53	1.47	19	2	10.53	5	26.32	2.84
Danzig	19	48	11	22.92	30	62.50	2.34	19	8	42.11	16	84.21	4.07
Skywalker	19	126	14	11.11	49	38.89	1.73	19	6	31.58	7	36.84	5.57
Slew Gin Fizz	19	68	6	8.82	19	27.94	1.56	19	0	0.00	2	10.53	0.00
Wekiva Springs	19	77	7	9.09	27	35.06	0.91	19	2	10.53	7	36.84	1.17
Geri	19	72	7	9.72	20	27.78	2.05	19	2	10.53	5	26.32	4.72
Storm and a Half	19	56	8	14.29	20	35.71	1.20	19	3	15.79	5	26.32	2.03
Decarchy	19	56	13	23.21	30	53.57	4.48	19	4	21.05	9	47.37	5.45
Snow Ridge	19	75	13	17.33	35	46.67	1.67	19	4	21.05	13	68.42	2.92
Richly Blended	19	41	8	19.51	11	26.83	2.47	19	2	10.53	3	15.79	0.55
Minardi	19	59	1	1.69	20	33.90	0.41	19	1	5.26	5	26.32	1.26
Eltish	18	60	8	13.33	21	35.00	1.91	18	2	11.11	7	38.89	1.03
Composer	18	110	21	19.09	47	42.73	2.70	18	2	11.11	8	44.44	0.61
Judge T C	18	76	3	3.95	19	25.00	0.40	18	0	0.00	5	27.78	0.00
Cobra King	18	65	6	9.23	21	32.31	0.87	18	1	5.56	6	33.33	0.38
Perfect Vision	18	71	4	5.63	19	26.76	0.59	18	0	0.00	0	0.00	0.00
Sweetsouthernsaint	17	77	12	15.58	32	41.56	1.28	17	1	5.88	7	41.18	1.26
Iron Cat	17	45	4	8.89	16	35.56	0.75	17	1	5.88	5	29.41	0.76
Barkerville	17	54	3	5.56	11	20.37	1.04	17	2	11.76	3	17.65	3.04

Name	Horses	Strts	Wins	Win %	ITM	ITM %	ROI	Strts	Wins	Win %	ITM	ITM %	ROI
Truckee	17	52	2	3.85	7	13.46	2.57	17	1	5.88	1	5.88	4.22
Elajjud	17	108	17	15.74	38	35.19	2.67	17	4	23.53	5	29.41	2.54
Clever Trick	17	77	9	11.69	31	40.26	1.74	17	2	11.76	6	35.29	0.72
Confide	17	66	4	6.06	21	31.82	2.34	17	0	0.00	2	11.76	0.00
Canaveral	17	65	3	4.62	11	16.92	1.54	17	1	5.88	2	11.76	0.44
Unaccounted For	17	88	11	12.50	28	31.82	2.35	17	0	0.00	3	17.65	0.00
Comet Shine	17	45	5	11.11	16	35.56	0.88	17	2	11.76	7	41.18	1.34
Proudest Romeo	17	52	10	19.23	20	38.46	1.60	17	1	5.88	6	35.29	0.91
Explicit	17	55	7	12.73	17	30.91	2.29	17	2	11.76	7	41.18	4.27
Line In The Sand	17	78	7	8.97	22	28.21	1.18	17	0	0.00	3	17.65	0.00
Najran	17	58	7	12.07	19	32.76	3.21	17	1	5.88	3	17.65	8.56
Mineshaft	17	38	3	7.89	17	44.74	0.41	17	1	5.88	5	29.41	0.32
Wolf Power (SAF)	17	55	6	10.91	19	34.55	1.42	17	1	5.88	6	35.29	1.78
American Chance	16	75	7	9.33	20	26.67	1.28	16	2	12.50	4	25.00	1.20
City Zip	16	35	7	20.00	15	42.86	4.14	16	3	18.75	4	25.00	1.43
Patton	16	57	4	7.02	12	21.05	1.65	16	1	6.25	4	25.00	1.64
Lasting Approval	16	76	8	10.53	31	40.79	2.52	16	4	25.00	7	43.75	8.83
Empire Maker	16	24	5	20.83	9	37.50	1.88	16	3	18.75	5	31.25	1.55
Miswaki	16	37	5	13.51	15	40.54	2.19	16	2	12.50	9	56.25	1.79
Conquistador Cielo	16	80	6	7.50	27	33.75	1.07	16	0	0.00	5	31.25	0.00
Jules	16	36	2	5.56	10	27.78	1.01	16	2	12.50	5	31.25	2.26
Pentelicus	16	45	10	22.22	17	37.78	1.97	16	4	25.00	7	43.75	2.91
Valid Expectations	16	49	4	8.16	11	22.45	0.98	16	1	6.25	4	25.00	1.03
Way West (FR)	16	41	3	7.32	11	26.83	1.16	16	1	6.25	3	18.75	1.76
Rhythm	16	50	6	12.00	15	30.00	2.55	16	3	18.75	5	31.25	3.13
Lexicon	16	42	0	0.00	11	26.19	0.00	16	0	0.00	5	31.25	0.00
Parade Ground	16	76	8	10.53	26	34.21	1.69	16	1	6.25	1	6.25	0.64
Noble Cat	15	80	8	10.00	27	33.75	1.87	15	0	0.00	1	6.67	0.00
Matter of Honor	15	66	7	10.61	15	22.73	1.39	15	0	0.00	1	6.67	0.00
Private Terms	15	48	1	2.08	10	20.83	0.20	15	1	6.67	3	20.00	0.64
Six Below	15	34	2	5.88	8	23.53	0.92	15	1	6.67	1	6.67	1.85
Eastern Echo	15	58	2	3.45	22	37.93	0.77	15	1	6.67	7	46.67	0.40
Cahill Road	15	39	3	7.69	9	23.08	0.85	15	1	6.67	2	13.33	0.92
Gold Spring (ARG)	15	61	5	8.20	17	27.87	1.00	15	1	6.67	1	6.67	1.96
Not Impossible (IRE)	15	47	4	8.51	9	19.15	0.83	15	1	6.67	1	6.67	1.52
Polish Navy	15	60	9	15.00	18	30.00	4.01	15	1	6.67	3	20.00	0.67
Moscow Ballet	15	53	4	7.55	21	39.62	1.16	15	0	0.00	9	60.00	0.00
Twin Spires	15	42	4	9.52	10	23.81	1.01	15	1	6.67	4	26.67	0.63

Name	Horses	Strts	Wins	Win %	ITM	ITM %	ROI	Strts	Wins	Win %	ITM	ITM %	ROI
Partner's Hero	15	45	4	8.89	19	42.22	0.97	15	1	6.67	5	33.33	1.44
Trail City	15	57	14	24.56	25	43.86	1.90	15	1	6.67	5	33.33	0.47
Parisianprospector	15	46	0	0.00	2	4.35	0.00	15	0	0.00	0	0.00	0.00
Surachai	15	56	4	7.14	12	21.43	1.60	15	0	0.00	3	20.00	0.00
Trust N Luck	15	39	4	10.26	11	28.21	0.75	15	1	6.67	2	13.33	0.88
Cactus Ridge	15	62	12	19.35	27	43.55	2.47	15	2	13.33	6	40.00	2.71
Islefaxyou	15	59	2	3.39	4	6.78	0.66	15	1	6.67	2	13.33	1.69
Talk Is Money	15	46	4	8.70	14	30.43	0.74	15	2	13.33	4	26.67	1.43
Snuck In	15	35	3	8.57	5	14.29	3.56	15	2	13.33	2	13.33	2.00
Syncline	15	43	5	11.63	12	27.91	2.56	15	2	13.33	3	20.00	1.03
The Name's Jimmy	15	57	11	19.30	22	38.60	3.73	15	1	6.67	5	33.33	4.60
Birdonthewire	14	67	8	11.94	21	31.34	2.02	14	3	21.43	4	28.57	2.67
Mecke	14	42	7	16.67	20	47.62	1.22	14	1	7.14	5	35.71	0.39
Rizzi	14	35	2	5.71	8	22.86	0.65	14	0	0.00	1	7.14	0.00
Gold Market	14	42	2	4.76	17	40.48	0.35	14	0	0.00	4	28.57	0.00
Globalize	14	39	3	7.69	11	28.21	0.57	14	0	0.00	1	7.14	0.00
Dance Master	14	39	5	12.82	12	30.77	0.75	14	1	7.14	3	21.43	0.40
Sword Dance (IRE)	14	76	6	7.89	24	31.58	0.99	14	1	7.14	4	28.57	0.94
Great Gladiator	14	70	6	8.57	21	30.00	2.16	14	1	7.14	2	14.29	4.49
Lord Avie	14	73	4	5.48	22	30.14	1.48	14	0	0.00	2	14.29	0.00
Will's Way	14	72	6	8.33	16	22.22	0.84	14	1	7.14	3	21.43	0.50
Accelerator	14	101	14	13.86	44	43.56	2.06	14	3	21.43	7	50.00	5.07
Part the Waters	14	38	4	10.53	14	36.84	3.68	14	1	7.14	2	14.29	0.51
Defrere	14	51	3	5.88	15	29.41	1.09	14	0	0.00	1	7.14	0.00
Prospect Bay	14	70	7	10.00	27	38.57	1.15	14	1	7.14	4	28.57	2.66
Soft Gold (BRZ)	14	75	8	10.67	25	33.33	3.22	14	2	14.29	6	42.86	11.69
Formal Dinner	14	54	5	9.26	15	27.78	1.73	14	1	7.14	4	28.57	0.89
Dixie Dot Com	14	44	3	6.82	22	50.00	0.57	14	2	14.29	5	35.71	0.81
Ole'	14	43	2	4.65	11	25.58	0.44	14	0	0.00	3	21.43	0.00
Unbridled	14	36	9	25.00	17	47.22	3.62	14	4	28.57	6	42.86	2.77
Good and Tough	14	51	5	9.80	20	39.22	1.37	14	1	7.14	5	35.71	0.81
Capsized	13	46	3	6.52	15	32.61	0.44	13	0	0.00	2	15.38	0.00
Mr. Broad Blade	13	49	3	6.12	14	28.57	0.89	13	0	0.00	4	30.77	0.00
Tejabo	13	55	2	3.64	10	18.18	0.49	13	0	0.00	1	7.69	0.00
Quaker Ridge	13	79	7	8.86	26	32.91	1.36	13	1	7.69	4	30.77	1.38
Fly So Free	13	41	4	9.76	11	26.83	1.11	13	1	7.69	3	23.08	1.05
Deerhound	13	50	2	4.00	14	28.00	0.43	13	0	0.00	6	46.15	0.00
Miesque's Son	13	56	7	12.50	19	33.93	1.30	13	1	7.69	3	23.08	0.57

Name	Horses	Strts	Wins	Win %	ITM	ITM %	ROI	Strts	Wins	Win %	ITM	ITM %	ROI
Cat's Career	13	66	15	22.73	31	46.97	2.02	13	2	15.38	4	30.77	2.75
Nineeleven	13	49	2	4.08	12	24.49	0.60	13	1	7.69	2	15.38	1.34
Poteen	13	40	3	7.50	10	25.00	0.50	13	1	7.69	5	38.46	0.60
Littlebitlively	13	57	5	8.77	19	33.33	1.31	13	0	0.00	3	23.08	0.00
Zavata	13	44	3	6.82	15	34.09	0.41	13	1	7.69	5	38.46	0.26
Diesis (GB)	13	30	1	3.33	10	33.33	0.16	13	0	0.00	2	15.38	0.00
Milwaukee Brew	13	42	6	14.29	16	38.01	3.47	13	1	7.69	4	30.77	0.77
Dove Hunt	13	46	4	8.70	16	34.78	0.68	13	3	23.08	6	46.15	1.88
Irgun	13	47	2	4.26	6	12.77	0.28	13	1	7.69	1	7.69	0.45
Sea Wall	13	51	2	3.92	11	21.57	0.59	13	1	7.69	3	23.08	1.02
Laabity	13	47	4	8.51	9	19.15	0.55	13	0	0.00	0	0.00	0.00
Corslew	13	34	3	8.82	13	38.24	0.80	13	1	7.69	6	46.15	0.42
Macho Uno	13	33	5	15.15	12	36.36	2.65	13	1	7.69	4	30.77	0.71
Vying Victor	12	40	6	15.00	11	27.50	1.55	12	1	8.33	2	16.67	1.17
Dare and Go	12	57	9	15.79	24	42.11	2.01	12	1	8.33	4	33.33	3.23
Party Manners	12	61	4	6.56	16	26.23	2.16	12	0	0.00	3	25.00	0.00
Dumaani	12	38	6	15.79	11	28.95	1.12	12	2	16.67	4	33.33	1.38
Lake Austin	12	50	8	16.00	23	46.00	1.69	12	3	25.00	5	41.67	3.52
Royal Cat	12	39	2	5.13	6	15.38	0.54	12	0	0.00	1	8.33	0.00
Full Mandate	12	41	6	14.63	16	39.02	2.22	12	2	16.67	4	33.33	1.80
Flame Thrower	12	45	7	15.56	14	31.11	1.97	12	2	16.67	3	25.00	2.60
Old Kentucky Home	12	54	4	7.41	12	22.22	0.76	12	0	0.00	2	16.67	0.00
Mancini	12	42	3	7.14	18	42.86	0.80	12	2	16.67	3	25.00	1.07
Bates Motel	12	37	1	2.70	9	24.32	0.11	12	0	0.00	1	8.33	0.00
Red	12	39	4	10.26	10	25.64	1.08	12	1	8.33	2	16.67	0.32
Zamindar	12	39	3	7.69	8	20.51	1.25	12	1	8.33	1	8.33	0.40
Anziyan	12	33	2	6.06	5	15.15	1.41	12	0	0.00	2	16.67	0.00
Spinning World	12	56	10	17.86	20	35.71	2.17	12	2	16.67	5	41.67	2.38
Presidential Order	12	75	11	14.67	29	38.67	1.95	12	1	8.33	6	50.00	3.87
Sligo Bay (IRE)	12	22	3	13.64	8	36.36	1.58	12	2	16.67	5	41.67	2.17
Bartlettsunbridled	12	71	5	7.04	15	21.13	1.26	12	0	0.00	2	16.67	0.00
Gold Fever	12	51	4	7.84	16	31.37	1.02	12	0	0.00	2	16.67	0.00
Slewvescent	12	36	1	2.78	9	25.00	0.30	12	1	8.33	4	33.33	0.90
Avenue of Flags	12	36	4	11.11	14	38.89	1.86	12	3	25.00	5	41.67	2.32
Housebuster	12	36	5	13.89	13	36.11	2.26	12	0	0.00	1	8.33	0.00
For Really	12	42	4	9.52	8	19.05	0.69	12	1	8.33	2	16.67	0.43
Anet	12	32	1	3.13	8	25.00	0.42	12	0	0.00	2	16.67	0.00
Worldly Manner	12	44	1	2.27	11	25.00	0.34	12	1	8.33	3	25.00	1.23

Name	Horses	Strts	Wins	Win %	ITM	ITM %	ROI	Strts	Wins	Win %	ITM	ITM %	ROI
Wonneberg	11	60	2	3.33	9	15.00	0.43	11	0	0.00	1	9.09	0.00
Western Playboy	11	46	2	4.35	14	30.43	0.30	11	0	0.00	5	45.45	0.00
Academy Award	11	29	2	6.90	5	17.24	4.64	11	0	0.00	0	0.00	0.00
Tricky Creek	11	31	2	6.45	4	12.90	1.09	11	1	9.09	1	9.09	2.25
Houston	11	43	4	9.30	12	27.91	1.31	11	1	9.09	2	18.18	2.71
Domasca Dan	11	80	6	7.50	24	30.00	0.74	11	0	0.00	3	27.27	0.00
Bold Badgett	11	40	5	12.50	13	32.50	4.24	11	1	9.09	4	36.36	0.82
Prospectors Gamble	11	43	2	4.65	14	32.56	1.90	11	0	0.00	3	27.27	0.00
Delaware Township	11	39	7	17.95	12	30.77	2.27	11	2	18.18	2	18.18	1.45
Texas Glitter	11	36	2	5.56	10	27.78	0.86	11	1	9.09	5	45.45	2.22
Freespool	11	22	0	0.00	4	18.18	0.00	11	0	0.00	0	0.00	0.00
Honor Glide	11	18	0	0.00	1	5.56	0.00	11	0	0.00	0	0.00	0.00
Inspired Prospect	11	49	6	12.24	17	34.69	4.74	11	0	0.00	1	9.09	0.00
Take Me Out	11	26	2	7.69	4	15.38	0.60	11	0	0.00	1	9.09	0.00
Rainbow Blues (IRE)	11	32	7	21.88	18	56.25	1.37	11	2	18.18	4	36.36	0.95
Malek (CHI)	11	33	4	12.12	9	27.27	1.90	11	2	18.18	2	18.18	2.76
Puerto Madero (CHI)	11	25	0	0.00	1	4.00	0.00	11	0	0.00	1	9.09	0.00
Flying Chevron	11	51	8	15.69	20	39.22	1.64	11	0	0.00	3	27.27	0.00
Score Quick	11	34	0	0.00	6	17.65	0.00	11	0	0.00	1	9.09	0.00
Saratoga Six	11	62	3	4.84	12	19.35	0.69	11	1	9.09	3	27.27	2.13
Candy Stripes	11	48	5	10.42	19	39.58	0.71	11	1	9.09	3	27.27	0.45
Roy	11	45	5	11.11	16	35.56	0.75	11	1	9.09	3	27.27	0.36
Sabona	11	35	2	5.71	10	28.57	0.82	11	1	9.09	3	27.27	2.05
Allen's Prospect	11	20	3	15.00	5	25.00	2.37	11	1	9.09	2	18.18	0.33
One Man Army	11	40	4	10.00	13	32.50	0.42	11	0	0.00	1	9.09	0.00
Cozar	11	59	7	11.86	17	28.81	3.67	11	1	9.09	2	18.18	1.36
Rod and Staff	11	57	10	17.54	26	45.61	2.16	11	1	9.09	4	36.36	0.64
Just a Cat	11	58	4	6.90	18	31.03	1.02	11	1	9.09	2	18.18	0.35
Family Calling	11	44	3	6.82	9	20.45	1.02	11	2	18.18	4	36.36	3.55
Bring the Heat	11	29	3	10.34	9	31.03	0.77	11	2	18.18	4	36.36	1.58
Leelanau	11	33	2	6.06	9	27.27	1.48	11	1	9.09	1	9.09	0.38
Bahri	11	54	4	7.41	14	25.93	0.47	11	1	9.09	2	18.18	0.45
High Demand	11	27	3	11.11	5	18.52	1.41	11	2	18.18	3	27.27	3.20
Gulf Storm	11	29	3	10.34	7	24.14	0.62	11	0	0.00	0	0.00	0.00
State Craft	11	29	2	6.90	8	27.59	1.54	11	1	9.09	3	27.27	0.93
Tabasco Cat	11	44	10	22.73	23	52.27	1.82	11	5	45.45	8	72.73	3.22
Numerous	11	41	3	7.32	8	19.51	0.57	11	1	9.09	3	27.27	0.69
Dance Floor	11	49	10	20.41	25	51.02	2.77	11	1	9.09	3	27.27	0.47

Name	Horses	Strts	Wins	Win %	ITM	ITM %	ROI	Strts	Wins	Win %	ITM	ITM %	ROI
Ghazi	11	68	15	22.06	36	52.94	3.08	11	2	18.18	3	27.27	2.24
Mongoose	11	42	3	7.14	10	23.81	1.45	11	1	9.09	2	18.18	1.78
Wild Zone	11	43	5	11.63	13	30.23	0.94	11	1	9.09	2	18.18	0.62
Rocket Cat	10	33	2	6.06	11	33.33	0.46	10	0	0.00	2	20.00	0.00
Paynes Bay	10	26	1	3.85	9	34.62	0.24	10	0	0.00	2	20.00	0.00
Caller I. D.	10	25	3	12.00	9	36.00	1.01	10	2	20.00	4	40.00	1.96
A. P Jet	10	26	1	3.85	7	26.92	0.67	10	1	10.00	3	30.00	1.74
Colony Light	10	34	4	11.76	11	32.35	0.80	10	1	10.00	3	30.00	0.60
Waki Warrior	10	32	1	3.13	6	18.75	0.16	10	0	0.00	2	20.00	0.00
Hussonet	10	31	4	12.90	9	29.03	1.70	10	1	10.00	3	30.00	3.10
Valiant Nature	10	53	7	13.21	18	33.96	2.50	10	2	20.00	2	20.00	1.60
Level Sands	10	37	3	8.11	10	27.03	1.04	10	1	10.00	2	20.00	0.92
Run Softly	10	39	1	2.56	8	20.51	0.43	10	0	0.00	1	10.00	0.00
Tribunal	10	32	6	18.75	20	62.50	2.14	10	3	30.00	6	60.00	3.68
Littleexpectations	10	39	6	15.38	10	25.64	2.69	10	3	30.00	4	40.00	6.20
Lake William	10	30	5	16.67	10	33.33	1.81	10	1	10.00	2	20.00	2.64
Open Forum	10	36	3	8.33	10	27.78	1.72	10	1	10.00	2	20.00	1.64
Gold Tribute	10	45	8	17.78	17	37.78	2.23	10	3	30.00	5	50.00	5.40
Kris S.	10	14	0	0.00	3	21.43	0.00	10	0	0.00	2	20.00	0.00
Fruition	10	37	4	10.81	12	32.43	2.23	10	2	20.00	5	50.00	1.28
Diligence	10	38	3	7.89	9	23.68	0.99	10	0	0.00	1	10.00	0.00
Hesabull	10	36	5	13.89	13	36.11	2.49	10	1	10.00	4	40.00	0.76
Victory Speech	10	64	4	6.25	20	31.25	1.22	10	1	10.00	3	30.00	4.04
Romanov (IRE)	10	50	3	6.00	10	20.00	3.29	10	0	0.00	3	30.00	0.00
Swain (IRE)	10	21	2	9.52	5	23.81	0.86	10	2	20.00	3	30.00	1.80
Northern Spur (IRE)	10	34	2	5.88	12	35.29	0.61	10	1	10.00	4	40.00	1.10
Home At Last	10	30	2	6.67	10	33.33	0.51	10	2	20.00	3	30.00	1.52
Slew of Angels	10	20	2	10.00	8	40.00	0.81	10	1	10.00	4	40.00	0.70
Proud and True	10	24	4	16.67	9	37.50	1.33	10	1	10.00	2	20.00	1.18
Apollo	10	39	3	7.69	13	33.33	0.89	10	1	10.00	3	30.00	1.14
West Acre	10	31	7	22.58	17	54.84	2.35	10	1	10.00	6	60.00	0.46
K One King	10	65	9	13.85	26	40.00	2.46	10	1	10.00	4	40.00	0.84
Unbridled Jet	10	54	19	35.19	30	55.56	3.09	10	2	20.00	5	50.00	5.24
Winthrop	10	26	3	11.54	11	42.31	2.08	10	2	20.00	3	30.00	4.44
Truly Met	10	22	1	4.55	1	4.55	0.49	10	1	10.00	1	10.00	1.08
Fast Play	10	31	3	9.68	9	29.03	0.99	10	2	20.00	3	30.00	2.66
Danehill	10	23	3	13.04	13	56.52	0.78	10	2	20.00	8	80.00	1.14
Hap	10	35	3	8.57	6	17.14	0.86	10	1	10.00	1	10.00	0.66

6
Synthetic Sensations

When a cheap gelding named Step to the Music showed up in a claiming race on December 21, 2006, at Turfway Park, a lot of players were probably convinced he didn't have any chance. In his previous start, he was badly beaten in a $5,000 claimer at Hawthorne and was now stepping up a notch in class. But had handicappers dug a little deeper into his past performances, they might have realized that Step to the Music was a live horse that night.

The last time Step to the Music raced at Turfway, he finished third in a $15,000 claimer, and he had won his two previous starts over the track's Polytrack surface. There was reason to believe that the son of Catienus would improve dramatically now that he was back on a synthetic track. That's exactly what happened. Though Step to the Music didn't win that night, he finished a game third at 18–1, losing by just 1½ lengths. He was the key to unlocking a trifecta that paid $4,976.60.

Trainer Kim Hammond understood that Step to the Music was a different horse at Turfway and kept him there through the long winter. Before he was claimed away from her for $8,000, Step to the Music would win three times at Turfway. He never finished out of the money in the seven starts he made at the meet.

There was nothing fluky about what Step to the Music accomplished at Turfway or his third-place finish at 22–1 when he tried

Keeneland in 2007. While most horses that handle conventional dirt will handle synthetic tracks just fine, there are more Step to the Musics out there, horses who clearly have an affinity for synthetic tracks.

```
Step to the Music                  Dk. b or b. g. 4 (Feb)                              Life  21 5 5 4  $49,790 72 | D.Fst      8 0 1 0  $
Own: Jennifer B. Tilley            Sire: Catienus (Storm Cat) $7,500                   2007   7 3 2 2  $19,770 72 | Wet(322)   1 0 1 0  $
                                   Dam: Clairvoyance (Siphon*Brz)                      2006   9 2 0 2  $14,930 67 | Synth     12 5 3 4  $3
                                   Br:  Kenneth L Ramsey & Sarah K Ramsey (Ky)                0 0 0 0       $0  - | Turf(245)  0 0 0 0
                                   Tr:  Murphy Carolyn S(0 0 0 0 .00) 2007:(2 0 .00)                                | Dst(0)     0 0 0 0

22Apr07-1Kee fst 6f ◈ :224 :462 :581 1:102 4↑Alw 8000s       71 2 6 63½ 51¾ 52 33 Troilo W D      L118 fb 22.50 88-11 OkieDozer118no RubaDubDub1203 SteptotheMusic118no 5w trip,m
 5Apr07-7TP fst 6½f ◈ :224 :462 1:122 1:19 3↑Clm c-(8-7)     72 8 1 41 3nk 1hd 21¼ Troilo W D     L120 fb 8.90 80-19 PinecrestInn1201¼ SteptotheMusic1201¼ GoldSnekr1201¼ 4w, outf
  Claimed from Hammond Everett for $8,000, Hammond Kim Trainer 2007(as of 4/5): (91 15 24 7 0.16)
15Mar07-9TP fst 6f ◈ :221 :453 :582 1:113 3↑Clm 5000N3Y     65 3 3 25 23½ 11½ 1½ Prescott R      L124 fb *2.40 84-15 SteptotheMusic124½ FlyingChance1201¼ MrPopeye120no Off inside
25Feb07-4TP fst 5½f ◈ :222 :462 :591 1:054 3↑Clm 5000B      70 1 4 3nk 11 14 12¼ Prescott R      L124 fb 5.90 87-16 Step to the Music1242¼ Suleiman1241 Best Prospect1201 Inside,
 2Feb07-6TP fst 6f ◈ :23 :47 :594 1:131 3↑Clm 7500N3L       65 4 2 1hd 11 12 1nk Prescott R      L120 fb *2.00 76-20 SteptotheMusic120nk CinnmonKid1201½ Rvncliff120¾ Jumped objec
18Jan07-2TP fst 5½f ◈ :223 :462 :591 1:053 4↑Clm 5000N3L    58 9 1 4nk 31 22 2½ Mena M          L120 f *.70 87-13 Orville Forest120½ Step to the Music1201¼ Preston T120¾ 4 wide in
11Jan07-3TP fst 6½f ◈ :222 :452 1:102 1:171 4↑Clm 7500N3L   55 6 1 32½ 21½ 24 35 Leparoux J R   L120 *1.90 85-10 Pirate's Bid1204½ Escape Tactics122½ Step to the Music1203¾ 4 wid
21Dec06-10TP fst 6f ◈ :213 :443 :57 1:10 3↑Clm 7500N3L      58 9 1 43½ 3½ 21½ 31½ Butler D P     L119 18.70 96-02 C C Ryder1201¼ Ahnand119nk SteptotheMusic119no 4 wide, bid, wea
30Sep06-3Haw fst 6f :224 :471 1:00 1:13 3↑Clm 5000N3L       36 7 5 53 64¾ 78½ 711 Campbell J M   L119 f 4.70 60-26 BllothWoods1223½ Wvgotchcovrd122no CmptonHlls122¾ 3 wide, ga
16Sep06-1Hoo fst 6f :221 :46 :591 1:132 3↑Clm 5000N3L       49 6 7 43 42¼ 44 42¾ Macias G Jr    L115 f 4.10 78-18 King's Peace123no Fraz120nk Disorderinthecourt1172½ 4 wide turn.
 2Sep06-4EIP fst 5½f :231 :463 :584 1:051 3↑Clm 5000N3L     50 7 1 2hd 21 42 52½ Jacinto J      L117 f *1.60 89-09 FreeLanceCt115no WrnerJzzMn1201½ [D]YodelerLke120½ Bmp,stea
  Placed 4th through disqualification
 6May06-9Ind fst 6f :222 :451 :573 1:104 3↑Alw 12000N1X     61 7 7 51¼ 31½ 32½ 66¼ Zuniga J E     LB115 f 10.80 86-16 Buteo1184 Flank Drive120½ Littlebitaglitter115½ 4wide tur
22Apr06-9Ind fst 5½f :221 :451 :573 1:04 3↑Alw 12000N1X    67 6 2 32 64¾ 75½ 52¼ Lebron V5      LB111 f 9.80 93-12 Scrubbin Speed1231 Hoosierholic115nk Buteo1181 Widest lane,be
26Mar06-4TP fst 6f ◈ :222 :454 :583 1:122 Clm 15000(15-10)  49 1 4 21½ 34 33½ 32¾ Leparoux J R5  L115 1.80 83-10 KndonVlly118nk PostvCshFlow1222½ StptothMsc1152½ Lost footin
 3Mar06-5TP fst 5½f ◈ :224 :464 :592 1:061 Clm 10000(15-10) 61 2 3 2hd 1½ 11½ 13¼ Leparoux J R5  L108 *1.10 92-17 SteptotheMusic1083¼ KendonVlley114½ WeselTim1201½ Off inside,
19Feb06-1TP fst 5½f ◈ :23 :474 1:004 1:072 Md c-7500        53 1 4 32 32 12½ 17 Butler D P      L122 *.30 86-15 Step to the Music1227 Blackenberry1225 Royal Claire117¾ 3 wide,
  Claimed from Ramsey, Kenneth L. and Sarah K. for $7,500, Romans Dale Trainer 2005: (523 95 83 59 0.18)
27Dec05-2TP fst 6f ◈ :224 :47 1:001 1:14 Md 15000(15-10)    56 3 4 2½ 2hd 2hd 2no Troilo W D     L122 *1.10 - - Bobby Jack122no Step to the Music1224¼ Weasel Time1221 Between,
13Nov05-10CD fst 6f :22 :46 :583 1:112 Md 30000(30-25)      51 4 2 51¼ 51¾ 414 57¼ Guidry M       L120 *2.30 77-19 Mark of Success1202 Deputy's Case1204¾ Readily120nk Empty i
 7Oct05-6Bel fst 6f :221 :462 :591 1:123 Md 50000           50 9 4 33½ 31½ 43 58½ Migliore R     L120 *1.90 67-24 Sleek John1201¾ Like Now1203¾ Dixie Whiz1151¼ Chased 3 wid
16Sep05-2Bel gd 5½f :231 :472 1:00 1:064 Md 50000          35 3 2 32 21½ 26 27½ Prado E S      L120 2.90 69-18 FrndlyTorpdo1207½ StptothMsc1201¼ DmdsThndr1201¼ Chased, helc
10Aug05-2Sar fst 5f :222 :461 :59 Md 75000                 36 6 3 33 23 210 210½ Prado E S     L118 4.10 78-13 Archer11810½ Step to the Music118no Teddy Hull1181¼ Bumped afte
WORKS: Mar31 TP ◈3f fst :381 B 3/6 Mar10 TP ◈4f fst :52 B 25/26
```

After he finished third in the April 22, 2007, starter allowance at Keeneland, Step to the Music had won five of 12 starts on Polytrack while never finishing out of the money on the surface. He was winless in nine tries on conventional dirt.

Many "Polytrack freaks" are horses with fairly serious feet or ankle problems. Because synthetic surfaces are softer than regular dirt tracks, they tend to be kinder and less jarring. With the aches and pains being less pronounced, these horses will perform better over synthetic tracks.

According to Hammond, Step to the Music is affected by green osselets, which is a form of arthritis that produces swelling and inflammation in the joint capsule of the ankle. The term "green" refers to the fact that abnormal bone growth has not yet occurred.

"He moves up on that type of surface because he has green osselets and those tracks are much kinder on him," Hammond said. "These racetracks that have a limestone-based bottom, they put the dirt and sand on top of them, but they never get rid of the limestone. That kind of track just kills him."

Racing for trainer Carolyn Murphy, Step to the Music returned to a conventional dirt track on May 11, 2007, to run in a starter allowance at River Downs. The bettors blew it, sending him off at 5–2. He finished a distant fifth, no doubt wondering what had happened to his beloved Polytrack.

A horse named Indy Energy produced a similar story. A cheap claimer with moderate ability, he caught fire shortly after Turfway Park went to Polytrack, at one point winning seven out of eight races.

"He's a little bit of an older horse and he's arthritic, plus he has very tender feet," said Arthur Zeis, who trained Indy Energy during his torrid run at Turfway. "The Polytrack is much softer on his feet and it's much easier to get him back into a race. When I run him on the sand it stings him pretty good and his feet get a little sore. The Polytrack works out good for him. He loves it.

"When I ran Indy Energy on a dirt track, he might have started 12 or 13 times a year. Last year [in 2006], he ran 18 times. All together, training and running both, they hold up better.

"It helps mostly with soreness in their feet," Zeis continued. "Sand tends to sting a horse, especially in the summertime. With this, it's soft. On a regular track, you have a hard limestone bottom and in the slop they'll hit right down to the limestone."

Of course, a handicapper usually isn't going to know anything about a horse's medical history and whether or not he has the kind of aches and pains that are going to cause him to improve on a synthetic surface. Unfortunately, there's no way to know if a horse has ouchy feet or not.

Perhaps the best way to try to figure out if a horse is going to improve over a synthetic surface is to use common sense. Any horse working well on a synthetic track is an obvious candidate to run well on a synthetic track.

Take a look at the past performances of Miss Lombardi on the next page. Coming into her first start on a synthetic track, Miss Lombardi had had a series of sharp workouts over the synthetic Tapeta surface at the Fair Hill Training Center, including two bullet works.

```
2 Miss Lombardi                                  Dk.b or br m. 5 (Mar)                                        Life 14 3 3 3 $76,290 83 | D.Fst     13 3 3 3 $76,290
White Own: Linda and Robert Newton               Sire: Unbridled Jet (Unbridled) $4,000                       2007  3 0 1 2 $15,480 79 | Wet(341)   0 0 0 0      $0
  Black, Yellow Cross Sashes, Grey               Dam: Chemise (Secret Hello)                            L 115 2006  1 0 0 0    $750 56 | Synth      0 0 0 0      $0
PRADO E S (6 3 1 1 .50) 2007: (374 74 .20)       Br: Linda D Newton (Md)                                      Kee   0 0 0 0      $0  - | Turf(250)  1 0 0 0      $0
                                                 Tr: Motion H Graham(4 0 1 1 .00) 2007:(150 25 .17)                                    | Dst(338)   1 0 0 0    $300

21Mar07-6Lrl fst 7f    :231 :462 1:1131:251 4↑ⒻOC 32k/N3x-N        67 3 2  21½ 31½ 37  38¾  Carmouche K    L120  3.30  78-19 UrsulsPssion1174¾ HnlBy1113½ MssLombrd120nk   Pressed pace, weakene
 1Feb07-8Lrl fst 7f    :233 :47  1:12 1:25  4↑ⒻOC 32k/N3x-N        78 5 1  31  33  34½ 35¼  Carmouche K    L120  2.80  82-20 HappyinParis1223½ Tsrmin1201¾ MissLombrdi1202¼   Circled 4wd 1/4,no bi
18Jan07-8Lrl fst 6f    :223 :454  :5821:104 4↑ⒻOC 32k/N3x-N        79 1 3  33  32½ 2½  21½  Carmouche K    L120  3.70  87-18 Homestedr1201½ MissLombrdi1205¾ Fortunistic122¾  Rail,angled,bid,2d bs
19Dec06-9Pha fst 7f    :222 :453 1:1021:234 3↑ⒻAlw 26750N$Y        56 7 1  31  31½ 56  59¼  Carmouche K    L117  7.70  78-18 Baldomera117nk Settimo Cielo1171½ Tazaliya1161         Reluctant to loa
  Previously trained by Delozier Joseph III 2005(as of 12/17): ( 177 30 14 18 0.17 )
17Dec05-8Lrl fst 7f    :23  :47  1:1311:262 3↑ⒻSSquanSong50k       65 1 4  23  31½ 78½ 610½ Clifton T      L116  9.40  67-28 MagicalBroad1163¼ Starleena1161 ExpertsOnly1182   Stalked,3wd 3/8,wkn
10Nov05-8Lrl fst 7f    :23  :463 1:1221:26  3↑ⒻOC 25k/N2x-N        83 4 5  1hd 1hd 15  16¾  Clifton T      L118  4.50  80-24 MssLombrd1186¾ EmtnlStrm124½ MsMrynnN1201¼    Duel 2w,drw off,drvn
20Oct05-6Lrl fst 7f    :233 :473 1:1311:262 3↑ⒻClm 25000(25-20)B   63 1 6  52¾ 43  23  21¾  Napravnik A R5 L112 *1.50e 76-24 ForFun1161¾ MissLombrdi1125½ RidthWldWnd1201¾  Saved ground, rallie
 4Oct05-8Del fst 170   :232 :472 1:1311:441 3↑ⒻAlw 44900N2x        41 6 32 33  77½ 712 826½ Napravnik A R  L116 19.00  48-37 Maid Guinevere1179¾ Della Street1212½ Helen's Startax1191¼       Tire
16Sep05-6Lrl fm 5f Ⓣ  :22  :441       :553 3↑ⒻAlw 30000N2x         - 1 6  98¼ -   -   -    Hamilton S D   L116  6.40   - - Mecke's Queen120nk DelivertheRoses1201 IGotYourNumber1242 Pulled u
19Aug05-6Pim fst 6f    :24  :472  :5931:12  3↑ⒻOC 25k/N2x-N        64 6 6  2½  31  77  88¾  Santana J Z    L117 *1.70  78-17 My Pretty Woman1202¼ Rosa P113½ Sticky1191¼      Forced pace 3w, tire
26May05-7Pim fst 6f    :231 :462  :5921:12  3↑ⒻAlw 28000N1x        75 1 4  33  31½ 21  12   Camacho E      L119 *1.00  87-12 Miss Lombardi1192 Double Covey1201¾ Golden Aura120¾  3wd 1/4, drivin
29Apr05-7Pim fst 6f    :234 :464  :5911:123    ⒻMd Sp Wt 26k        68 6 4  31  1hd 14½ 111¼ Dominguez R A  L122 *1.00  84-13 MissLombrdi12211¼ MysticlTp117½ PrincessAnld122½  Bobbled,3wd,handil
WORKS: ●Apr9 Fai tr.t ◈5f fst 1:011 B 1/4  Mar10 Fai tr.t ◈5f fst 1:01 B 2/22  ●Mar3 Fai tr.t ◈5f fst 1:011 B 1/19  Feb24 Fai tr.t ◈5f fst 1:022 B 6/17  Jan12 Fai tr.t ◈5f fst 1:03 B 3/6
TRAINER: 2Off45-180(91 .20 $1.67) Synth(18 .33 $5.44) Sprint/Route(71 .21 $2.98) Routes(458 .19 $1.92) Alw(237 .18 $1.61)      J/T 2006-07 KEE(6 .00 $0.00) J/T 2006-07(52 .13 $1
```

Anyone who picked up on the workout pattern couldn't have been too surprised when she won an April 13, 2007, race at Keeneland in her Polytrack debut and paid $41.40.

In the early days of synthetic surfaces, the greatest horse for these courses may have been Mary Delaney. She began her career in England, where she was an immediate hit on the Polytrack surface at Lingfield, finishing second at 16–1 in her debut. About a year later, and after she had broken her maiden at Lingfield, she ran at Turfway Park. She showed little in her U.S. debut over Turfway's Polytrack, something that would become a rare occurrence.

Some seven months later, she had won five straight over Polytrack, including a wire-to-wire victory at Keeneland, a rarity at a track notoriously unkind to speed horses. Sandwiched in between her Polytrack wins was an eighth-place finish at Churchill Downs over conventional dirt. Did she, too, have bad feet? Was she bred to be a Polytrack wonder? Was it merely a coincidence that she kept running so well on Polytrack surfaces?

Despite the evidence, her trainer, Eddie Kenneally, believed that Mary Delaney would still have her day on regular dirt.

"I think, more than anything, that she improved," Kenneally said in late May 2007. "She came to hand last fall when we got her and she ran very well on the Polytrack at the time. The one time we ran her on the dirt, it didn't set up at all for her. The distance was too far and we ran her back too soon. That was a mistake. If we gave her the proper time between races and ran her at the right distance, I think she would have run well on the dirt."

Kenneally vowed that someday Mary Delaney would prove to be as good on dirt as she was on synthetic surfaces. By late June 2007, he was still waiting. Mary Delaney returned to normal dirt for the

2007 Vagrancy at Belmont Park and it was a disaster. She finished last in the field of six, losing by more than 30 lengths.

ry Delaney
Galvin Fergus

B. f. 4 (Feb) KEESEP04 $85,000
Sire: Hennessy (Storm Cat) $60,000
Dam: Crafty Emerald (Crafty Prospector)
Br: Mary Anne Parris & Ashford Stud (Ky)
Tr: Kenneally Eddie

Life	13	6	3	0	$276,129	100	D.Fst	2	0	0	0	$4,702	74
							Wet(371)	2	1	1	0	$8,043	-
2007	5	3	1	0	$215,973	100	Synth	9	6	2	0	$269,275	100
2006	7	3	1	0	$57,778	86	Turf(268)	2	0	1	0	$2,152	-

7-9Bel	fst	6½f		:22 :442 1:093 1:162	3↑ⒻVagrncyH-G2	28	3	5	2½	41¼	621	630¼	Gomez G K	L117	5.40	60-18	Indian Flare116½ Oprah Winney1176¾ Any Limit1181½	Pressed pace, tired 6
7-6WO	fst	6½f	◈	:22 :443 1:093 1:161	4↑ⒻGCHndri-G3	88	8	2	1hd	2hd	1hd	24	Husbands P	L121	*.80	94-06	Strike Softly1174 Mary Delaney121¾ Bosskiri118nk	Vied,no match winner 8
7-8Kee	fst	7f	◈	:232 :463 1:10 1:221	4↑ⒻMadison-G2	97	5	3	11½	13	11½	11½	Prado E S	L117	*2.90	96-10	Mary Delaney1171½ Ginger Punch117½ Leah's Secret123hd	5w,kept to task10
7-11TP	fst	6f	◈	:221 :451 :57 1:091	4↑ⒻQueen50k	100	6	2	1½	11	12½	13¾	Prado E S	L122	2.40	96-11	MaryDelney1223¾ HotStorm1202¼ NewDimension1166	Drifted out final 1/810
7-11TP	fst	6f	◈	:214 :442 :563 1:091	4↑ⒻWishngWell50k	90	10	1	31	21	12	1½	Leparoux J R	L118	*1.30	96-08	Mary Delaney118½ Mocha Queen1181 Asyouwish1182¾	Bid, clear, lasted11
6-10TP	fst	6f	◈	:213 :441 1:092	3↑ⒻAlw 23810N2x	75	1	10	32½	41½	2½	11½	Leparoux J R	L119	*1.10	101 -	Mary Delaney1191½ Lively Classic120¾ Wild as Elle120nk	Waited late turn11
6-9CD	fst	1		:23 :46 1:103 1:363	3↑ⒻChilukki-G2	74	5	11	11½	32½	89¾	813¼	Lanerie C J	L117	37.00	74-21	Sangrita1162 Joint Effort1181¾ Indian Flare1181	Pace,3w,weakened 9
6-5Kee	fst	*7f	◈	:23 :461 1:101 1:254	3↑ⒻAlw 52000N1x	86	9	3	12	12½	11½	12	Leparoux J R	L118	*1.50	- -	Mary Delaney1182 Sanguinity118¾ Cross Channel1186	Drift out lane,drvg10
6-9TP	fst	6f	◈	:213 :441 :562 1:09	3↑ⒻAlw 23400N1x	75	7	2	53½	63¾	66	46	Leparoux J R5	L112	3.70	97-05	Lady Belsara1173¾ Pleasant Hill121¾ Gently1171½	5 wide late turn 7

viously trained by M J Wallace

♦Nottingham (GB)	gf	6f	Ⓣ Str 1:142	visitnottingham.com Handicap	23	Durcan T E	127	*3.50	Charlie Delta1303 Mary Delaney127nk Night In1331½		11
cing Post Rating:	68			Hcp 11100					*Trckd ldrs,drifted left halfway,angled left 1-1/2f out,up for 2nd*		

KS: Jun9 Kee ◈4f fst :484 B *5/33* Jun1 Kee ◈4f fst :481 B *16/43* May5 TP ◈4f fst :51 B *25/28* Apr28 TP ◈4f fst :48 B *8/27*

It looks like Kenneally eventually gave up on running Mary Delaney on conventional dirt. After the Vagrancy debacle, her next three starts were all on synthetic tracks. Halfway through 2008, she had yet to try normal dirt again.

Perhaps the best-known Polytrack wonder was Kentucky Derby starter Dominican. Entering the 2007 Derby, he was the biggest mystery in the field.

ninican
Silverton Hill LLC

Ch. g. 3 (May) OBSMAR06 $150,000
Sire: El Corredor (Mr. Greeley) $30,000
Dam: First Violin (Dixieland Band)
Br: Barak Farm (Ky)
Tr: Miller Darrin

Life	8	3	0	2	$596,259	95	D.Fst	4	0	0	2	$26,034	90
							Wet(341)	1	0	0	0	$12,000	83
2007	3	2	0	0	$527,000	95	Synth	3	3	0	0	$558,225	95
2006	5	1	0	2	$69,259	90	Turf(304)	0	0	0	0	$0	-

7-10CD	fst	1¼		:461 1:11 1:37 2:02	KyDerby-G1	84	19	108	106¼	104½	1413	1117¾	Bejarano R	L126	24.90	78-09	Street Sense1262¼ Hard Spun1265¾ Curlin126½	7w,bmp 7/16s, in tight20
7-9Kee	fst	1⅛	◈	:512 1:163 1:394 1:511	BlueGras-G1	93	2	53½	53½	54	52¼	1no	Bejarano R	L123	8.00	88-15	Dominican123no Street Sense123hd Zanjero123hd	Hop start,7w,all out 7
7-9TP	fst	1 1/16	◈	:234 :473 1:12 1:432	Rushaway100k	95	2	52¾	42	41½	21	15	Bejarano R	L115	3.90	95-07	Dominican1155 Trust Your Luck116½ Reata's Rocket1192½	Waited 2nd turn10
6-11CD	fst	1 1/16		:233 :472 1:114 1:424	KyJC-G2	90	6	52¼	42½	3½	34	36¼	Albarado R J	L122	30.70	90-11	TizWonderful122½ AnyGivenSaturdy1225¾ Dominicn122nk	5w,bid,empty late9
6-7CD	fst	1 1/16		:24 :484 1:14 1:46	Alw 49120N1x	77	9	74½	63¾	52¾	45	44	Albarado R J	L122	7.40	76-21	Zanjero1221 First Defence1182¾ Wham118nk	Loomed,5w,empty11
6-4Kee	fst	1 1/16	◈	:242 :492 1:143 1:45	Md Sp Wt 50k	65	3	2½	3nk	2hd	11½	11¼	Albarado R J	L118	*1.50	- -	Dominican1181¼ Profiteer118½ Gasconade118no	Between,forced,drvg12
6-9AP	sly	1		:231 :463 1:112 1:363	ArWBCFut-G3	83	1	107	51¾	41¼	53¼	42¼	Martin E M Jr	L118	22.00	87-15	DH OffcrRckt119 DH GtthLstLh1171¾ StrtSns117½	Stumbled, jumped track 10
6-11ElP	fst	6f		:221 :443 :563 1:091	Md Sp Wt 20k	82	6	2	32½	32½	32½	32¾	Castanon J L	L120	3.30	97-02	U D Ghetto1202¾ Espoof120no Dominican12011¾	Drift start,steadied 7

S: Jly9 CD 5f fst 1:031 B *25/27* ●Jly2 CD 5f fst :594 B *1/23* Jun26 CD 5f fst 1:022 B *15/26* Jun18 CD 3f fst :362 B *3/11* ●Apr29 CD 5f fst :592 B *1/26*

The horse began his career with two mediocre performances, including a loss in a maiden special weight race at Ellis Park. Racing in Kentucky shifted to Keeneland and Dominican was in heaven, breaking his maiden over Polytrack there. Then, it was back to conventional dirt at Churchill, where his races weren't bad, but certainly weren't good enough to suggest that he would emerge the next year as a Kentucky Derby candidate.

Back on Polytrack, he won the Rushaway Stakes at Turfway and then, in the Grade 1 Blue Grass at Keeneland, upset a field that included 2-year-old champion and leading Derby contender Street Sense. Entering the Derby, he was 3 for 3 on Polytrack and 0 for 4 on regular dirt.

"I know these questions come up a lot when people handicap the Derby, but I don't think it's a factor," trainer Darrin Miller said of the Polytrack factor in the days leading up to the Derby. "Obviously, the synthetic surface allows a lot of these horses to move up and allows a lot of them to spring across it easier. It does enhance his stride, but he has an outstanding stride anyway. The Polytrack has benefited him, but I think all horses benefit on the synthetic surfaces."

To further complicate matters, Dominican was gelded between his 2-year-old and 3-year-old seasons, and that might also have explained why he ran so well in the Rushaway and the Blue Grass. What was a handicapper to do?

Perhaps Dominican wouldn't have run well in the Kentucky Derby even if it had been run on Polytrack. It was, after all, a very difficult race filled with talented horses such as Street Sense, Hard Spun, and Curlin. But his performance lent credence to the belief that he was a Polytrack specialist. He finished 11th, beaten 17¾ lengths. He couldn't even beat his unheralded stablemate Sedgefield, who had never before run on a conventional dirt surface of any kind. He tried dirt one more time in the West Virginia Derby at Mountaineer Park, and again it wasn't pretty, as he finished sixth.

Is Dominican a one-trick pony that can only win on Polytrack? That may not be answered unless he is given a few more chances on regular dirt. But on the morning after the 2007 Kentucky Derby, he was eligible to become the first inductee into the Polytrack Hall of Fame, and little else.

Actually, there don't seem to be that many runners who are merely "synthetic sensations." Most horses that win on synthetic surfaces will do just fine on conventional dirt.

Take a look at Ready Ruler. After he scored in his Polytrack debut at odds of 20–1, bettors appeared ready to dismiss him as a Polytrack wonder when he showed up at Churchill Downs in his next start. Taking a jump in class, he was sent off at 10–1 in a Churchill claimer on regular dirt. It turned out that Ready Ruler was a horse that was hitting peak form. His Churchill race, which resulted in a 2¼-length win, may have been better than his Polytrack performance.

ady Ruler
. Carlesimo John and Scanlon, Pat

Dk. b or b. g. 6 (Mar)
Sire: More Than Ready (Southern Halo) $40,000
Dam: Reina Victoriosa*Arg (Interprete*Arg)
Br: Vinery, LLC (Ky)
Tr: Bennett Gerald S(0 0 0 0 .00) 2007:(491 114 .23)

Life	31	9	6	2	$261,108	88	D.Fst	9	2	2	0	$59,507 84
2007	10	4	1	0	$68,154	87	Wet(354)	4	1	0	1	$13,694 84
							Synth	2	2	0	0	$48,140 85
2006	7	2	0	0	$33,433	84	Turf(294)	16	4	4	1	$139,767 88
	0	0	0	0	$0	-	Dst(0)	0	0	0	0	$0 -

:07-6Tam	wf	1 1/16 ⊗	:23 :462 1:123 1:464	3↑OC 40k/N3x	11	1	33	410	918	921	942½	Mata F	L118 fb	6.30	38-25	Dubai Gold1201 Fire Striker1202 Art of Diplomacy118nk	Stopped	9
)07-7PID	fst	170 ◈	:241 :48 1:131 1:424	3↑Clm 50000(50-40)	85	3	12	12	11½	1½	1nk	Mata F	L116 b	10.50	- -	ReadyRuler116nk *ImWitingforU*1162¼ PlesntCompny119no	Lasted, driving	7
)07-5Tdn	sly	6f	:222 :451 :573 1:104	3↑OC 35k/N2Y-N	55	2	3	32	46½	58	511¼	Ramgeet A R	L118 b	3.70	81-18	Pforperfectspistol1222½ ICantRefuse118¾ PrinceNick1182½	Dropped back	5
r07-7Tam	fm	1 Ⓣ	:233 :473 1:113 1:362	4↑OC c-32k/N2x	65	1	12½	1hd	2½	54	79¼	Clemente A	L122 b	*1.80	85-08	*Ide Rejoice*1181¼ *Jamian*1221 Curry's Honor1181¾	Fast pace, gave way	9
aimed from Jagger Inc. for $32,000, Ness Jamie Trainer 2007(as of 4/21): (88 26 20 9 0.30)																		
r07-7Tam	wf	1 1/16 ⊗	:23 :463 1:113 1:451	4↑Alw ---s	84	6	23½	23	21	11½	1½	Clemente A	L122 b	5.00	89-22	Ready Ruler122½ FloridaJackPot1221¾ Galaxy1181¼	Took over, just lasted	7
r07-6Tam	fm	*1 Ⓣ	:244 :49 1:141 1:391	4↑OC 32k/N2x	87	9	11	11½	12½	11½	1hd	Villa-Gomez H	L118 b	4.80	95-13	*RedyRuler*118hd BnkersHighYield1181½ ApttoBe118¾	Moderate pce, lasted	10
)07-11Tam	fm	1 Ⓣ	:233 :47 1:104 1:361	4↑Clm c-16000	86	5	11½	11½	12½	11½	1¾	Martinez J R Jr	L118 b	7.20	95-09	*Ready Ruler*118¾ Richie theKid118½ JohnnyTornado120hd	Fast pace, lasted	10
aimed from Hays Billy for $16,000, Woodard Joe Trainer 2006: (179 28 32 21 0.16)																		
o07-7Tam	fst	1 1/16	:241 :48 1:123 1:444	4↑Clm 25000(25-20)	45	3	11	1hd	34	515	527	Goberdhan C P	L120 b	4.60	64-12	Sandy's Secret1208 Oh Oleg1187½ D's Dessert1181½	Pace on rail, faded	6
n07-6Tam	fst	1 1/16	:234 :472 1:12 1:451	4↑Clm 25000(25-20)	82	7	12	13	13½	11½	21½	Centeno D E	L120 b	4.10	87-11	*SndysSecret*1181½ RedyRuler1205½ SummerLgcy1182	Solid pace, second b	8
n07-5Tam	fst	1 1/16	:231 :47 1:113 1:444	4↑Clm 25000(25-20)	21	4	11	12	22½	510	637¼	Lezcano J	L122 b	*1.20	54-16	*Demagoguery*118½ Oh Oleg1166¼ Great Plains1207	Faltered suddenly	7
c06-8Tam	fm	1 1/16 Ⓣ	:231 :471 1:121 1:431	3↑OC 32k/N2x	66	5	3nk	31	2hd	2hd	88	Monterrey R	L118 b	6.70	76-18	Bodgiteer1222¼ Lightning Power1182 Gebb's Power115no	Vied, faded	10
eviously trained by Potts Ron G Jr 2006(as of 11/12): (91 11 14 9 0.12)																		
v06-2CD	fst	1 1/16	:241 :48 1:132 1:452	3↑Clm 25000(25-20)	84	3	13	13½	12½	12½	12¼	Hernandez B J Jr	L120 b	10.60	83-23	Ready Ruler1202¼ *Shop Hill*1201¾ Red Soldier118nk	Control pace,driving	6
t06-2Kee	fst	1 1/16 ◈	:244 :50 1:144 1:452	3↑Clm 16000	75	7	12½	12½	1hd	11	1nk	Hernandez B J Jr	L120 b	20.10	- -	*ReadyRuler*120nk *ForthndForever*1152½ CleverDude120½	Driving,lasted,2-3w	11
t06-5Lrl	gd	1⅛ Ⓣ	:474 1:133 1:374 1:493	3↑Clm 14000(14-12)	73	12	47	48	74	54	53½	Soodeen R	L120 b	27.40	79-16	*Dubai Cat*1133 Access Agenda120hd Earnest Storm120hd	No rally	12
p06-9Mnr	fst	6f	:22 :451 :574 1:104	3↑Clm 15000(15-13)N4L	51	4	6	74¼	74¾	69	614½	Whitney D G	L115	14.00	75-21	*Lucky Express*112¾ Punch Bag1153 LegendGlory118nk	Slow,never factored	7
p06-9Mnr	fst	170	:24 :48 1:131 1:434	3↑Alw 35300N4L	42	6	52½	73¼	98¼	919	825¼	Pereira O M	L115	35.70	51-37	At the Knees1183 Huntin Gene1182½ P. R.Victory113¾	Even,wide,gave way	9
g06-4Mnr	fm	1 Ⓣ	:222 :454 1:102 1:35	3↑Alw 35300N3X	59	8	13	15	2½	36	710¼	Ramgeet A R	L115 b	3.00	83-07	Gurdnofthnorth1211¼ Skyy1153½ FrdomConts115no	Quick pace, wore out	9
eviously trained by Asmussen Steven M 2005(as of 11/5): (1892 399 331 260 0.21)																		
v05-8Hou	fm	1 1/16 Ⓣ	:231 :474 1:12 1:442	3↑BufaloBayu40k	71	7	66¼	65	53¾	87¾	109¾	Murphy B G	L115	4.80	85-05	ChrmngSclt118nk Shkthmhtrsff118nk Mddlht1231½	2w 2nd turn, gave way	12
:t05-4LaD	fm	1 Ⓣ	:23 :472 1:113 1:361	DWilhteMmH50k	88	3	64½	63¼	62¼	4¾	2hd	Bridgmohan S X	L118	*1.30	98-06	Drmsndvisons116hd RdyRulr1181¾ *ClssclAffrm*1162¼	Steadid 1/4,led,caught	11
g05-8Ret	fm	7½f Ⓣ	:24 :474 1:112 1:291	JimBowie40k	80	8	5	42	3½	11½	2nk	Ramos A B	L119	*1.70	96-06	WhiskeyforMe122nk RdyRulr119½ JustRdBird1142¼	4w 1st turn,3w 2nd trn	8
y05-8AP	fm	1 1/16 Ⓣ	:24 :481 1:123 1:43	3↑Alw 31000N2x	85	5	11	1½	1hd	1½	11¼	Guidry M	L118	*2.10	94-12	Ready Ruler1181¼ Bellator120½ Cowboy Code1222	Inside, edged clear	11
y05-9AP	fm	1 1/16 Ⓣ	:232 :473 1:121 1:423	ArlClsc-G3	70	9	31½	34½	53½	67	89½	Sterling L J Jr	L119	49.10	86-07	Purim1192½ United1191 Cosmic Kris1191¾	3-4 wide, gave way	9
n05-8AP	yl	1 Ⓣ	:244 :492 1:14 1:373	Awad42k	81	7	22	21	2½	21½	31½	Sterling L J Jr	L118	9.30	85-13	[D]ExceptionlRide118nk RvingRocket1201¼ RedyRuler1181	No winning bid	8
warded second purse money																		
r05-8Kee	fm	*1 Ⓣ	:222 :453 1:094 1:351	Trnsylvn-G3	66	8	58	56	66½	67¼	613¾	Lanerie C J	L121	19.80	77-09	ChtthoocheeWr121no GuillumeTell117nk *ReydCf*1216	Weakened after 5/8s	8
:t04-9Kee	gd	1 1/16 Ⓣ	:232 :474 1:123 1:424	BourbonCo112k	83	1	54	64¾	63¼	32½	34¾	Guidry M	L122	10.10	85-13	Rey de Cafe116nk *Dubleo*1224½ Ready Ruler1224¼	5w 3/16s,no gain late	10
:t04-7LS	fst	1	:234 :482 1:134 1:39	MddlgrndBC97k	73	2	31½	21	1hd	11	21¼	Beasley J A	L121	4.20	77-22	*Leaving On My Mind*1211¼ ReadyRuler121½ Rubialedo1214¼	Drifted out 1/16	8
reviously trained by Mathiasen Tony 2004(as of 9/4): (5 2 1 0 0.40)																		
p04-8Ret	fm	1 Ⓣ	:233 :474 1:121 1:363	KtlOnElJvn100k	73	12	76¼	76¾	53½	1hd	11	Beasley J A	L120	8.00	89-11	Ready Ruler1201 Malanato1201 Reno Bob120nk	Propped near wire	12
eviously trained by Asmussen Steven M 2004(as of 8/14): (1433 357 227 229 0.25)																		
g04-8Ret	fm	7½f Ⓣ	:241 :48 1:131 1:314	Alw 15000NC	70	4	4	31½	32	1hd	2½	Beasley J A	L119	4.00	82-16	Malanato122½ *Ready Ruler*1191 Dwight Polite1171¾	Dueled stretch,denied	9
y04-10LaD	fst	5½f	:214 :452 :58 1:05	Pioneer50k	55	8	1	33	43	36½	411	Lanerie C J	L116	*1.10	80-14	Crawfish King1127½ Secret Tunnel1143 Reno Bob116½	Little left drive	8
n04-3LS	fst	5½f	:224 :453 :58 1:042	Md Sp Wt 25k	71	7	1	1½	1½	1½	12	Sellers S J	L118	2.20	87-11	RedyRulr1182 *CrwfishKing*1182 Coyotshighstcll1182¼	Dictated terms,best	10
n04-3LS	my	5f	:213 :452 :583	Md Sp Wt 25k	45	1	5	43	54	34½	32¾	Beasley J A	118	4.80	85-14	Pronto Dash1181¾ Virgin Run1191 *Ready Ruler*118¾	Saved ground,willingly	11

As with so many other aspects of handicapping synthetic surfaces, Ready Ruler proved that there are no easy answers.

If there are Polytrack wonders, are there also Polytrack bums? Perhaps, though it's hard to understand why any horse wouldn't like synthetic surfaces.

While many horses that handle dirt will handle synthetic surfaces just as well, there is the occasional horse that apparently can't run on synthetic tracks. Why? No one seems to know. But be on the lookout for horses that return to form or even improve once getting off synthetic tracks.

One of the best examples of this was Street Sense, who lost the Breeders' Futurity over Keeneland's Polytrack before bettering his previous top Beyer Speed Figure by 21 points and winning the Breeders' Cup Juvenile on dirt at Churchill, paying $30.40. Was this a case of a young horse showing sudden improvement, getting a dream trip on a gold rail, or a sign that Street Sense was a much better horse on conventional dirt than on Polytrack?

When he repeated the pattern by losing the Blue Grass at Keeneland the next spring, regressing nine points from his previous start, then rebounded to win the Derby with a new career top, it seemed safe to say that Street Sense did his best running on dirt. Or perhaps trainer Carl Nafzger truly had used the Blue Grass as a prep for the big race ahead and did not have Street Sense fully cranked up. It's your job as a handicapper to take all these possibilities into account.

Similar questions will arise in races every day across the country, and the responsible horseplayer must rely on solid handicapping basics to find the answers.

Bettors could have made a small fortune playing a Kentucky-based claimer named Silver Minister.

Silver Minister
Own: Bearden Wayne

Dk. b or b. g. 6 (Feb)
Sire: Silver Deputy (Deputy Minister) $30,000
Dam: Mint Leaf (Capote)
Br: Twin Hopes Farm (Ky)
Tr: Bearden Wayne

Life	38	9	4	4	$212,374	84	D.Fst	23	7	3	3	$144,4
							Wet(376)	5	2	0	1	$65,5
2007	14	2	2	2	$12,023	78	Synth	9	0	1	0	$2,1
2006	9	2	0	1	$17,940	74	Turf(274)	1	0	0	0	$2

2Dec07-3TP	fst	1	◈	:24	:47	1:12	$1:37^{3}$	3↑ Clm 5000N1Y	**28**	8	9^{10}	8^{7}	8^{10}	9^{15}	$8^{23\frac{3}{4}}$	Sarvis D A	L120	5.70	66– 14	Divine Dancer122^{6} Pretty Swanky$124^{2\frac{1}{2}}$ Cupid's Honour$117^{\frac{3}{4}}$	Ou
20Sep07-7TP	fst	1	◈	$:25^{2}$	:49	1:14	$1:40^{1}$	3↑ Clm 5000	**49**	9	$6^{2\frac{3}{4}}$	$7^{6\frac{1}{4}}$	7^{7}	7^{8}	8^{9}	Williams D R^{5}	L115	3.40	68– 20	SouthphillyBarry120^{nk} DoRunRun$120^{4\frac{1}{4}}$ SneakersnJens$124^{2\frac{3}{4}}$	5-6 wide
5Aug07-8RD	gd^{S}	1		$:24^{4}$	$:49^{3}$	$1:14^{4}$	$1:42^{1}$	3↑ Clm 4000N3Y	**52**	9	$9^{5\frac{1}{2}}$	$7^{2\frac{1}{2}}$	$6^{3\frac{3}{4}}$	$6^{5\frac{3}{4}}$	$5^{5\frac{1}{4}}$	Adam M G	L120	*2.00	71– 26	SthphllyBrry$120^{\frac{1}{2}}$ Appyglcky$120^{3\frac{1}{2}}$ UBthJdg$120^{1\frac{1}{4}}$	Lost ground throug
26Jly07-7RD	fst	$1\frac{1}{16}$		$:25^{1}$	$:49^{4}$	$1:15^{1}$	$1:50^{1}$	3↑ Clm 5000	**58**	4	$5^{8\frac{3}{4}}$	5^{9}	4^{5}	$2^{3\frac{1}{2}}$	$2^{3\frac{1}{2}}$	Adam M G	L120	3.70	63– 41	Thenrdier$120^{3\frac{1}{2}}$ SilverMinistr$120^{5\frac{1}{4}}$ DH CrftyCowboy124	Rallied, no ma
21Jun07-9CD	fst	$1\frac{1}{16}$		$:23^{3}$	$:47^{3}$	$1:12^{2}$	$1:44^{3}$	3↑ Clm 5000	**55**	1	5^{7}	$5^{5\frac{3}{4}}$	$6^{5\frac{1}{2}}$	$5^{6\frac{1}{2}}$	7^{9}	Borel C H	L120	7.30	78– 12	Skipacruise$115^{4\frac{1}{2}}$ StillSmoldering120^{3} BeauRocket120^{nk}	Rail,flattene
2Jun07-5RD	fst	$1\frac{1}{16}$		$:24^{3}$	$:48^{3}$	$1:13^{1}$	$1:47^{2}$	3↑ Clm 5000	**57**	1	$6^{6\frac{3}{4}}$	5^{10}	4^{9}	2^{8}	3^{8}	Sarvis D A	L120	*1.00	73– 26	Cinnamon Kid122^{7} Duesenberg120^{1} Silver Minister$120^{\frac{1}{2}}$	Evenly
19May07-4CD	fst	1⅛		:50	$1:14^{2}$	$1:39^{3}$	1:53	3↑ Clm 5000	**50**	7	$4^{3\frac{1}{2}}$	4^{5}	4^{2}	5^{7}	4^{8}	Leparoux J R	L122	2.70	63– 21	Battledar$122^{2\frac{3}{4}}$ Archie B120^{5} Doctor Hi122^{nk}	3-4w,came up er
5May07-3RD	fst	1		:24	:49	$1:14^{2}$	$1:40^{4}$	3↑ Clm 4000	**78**	6	4^{10}	$4^{6\frac{1}{2}}$	$3^{1\frac{1}{2}}$	1^{5}	$1^{8\frac{1}{4}}$	Sarvis D A	L124	3.20	83– 24	SilverMinistr$124^{8\frac{1}{4}}$ KissofTruth$120^{2\frac{1}{2}}$ FortChstnut$120^{6\frac{1}{4}}$	Drew off, dri
22Apr07-3RD	fst	1^{70}		:25	:50	$1:14^{3}$	$1:45^{3}$	3↑ Clm 4000	**56**	7	$4^{3\frac{1}{2}}$	4^{5}	5^{3}	3^{4}	$3^{2\frac{1}{2}}$	Sarvis D A	L124	*2.60	78– 17	Get On Board124^{2} Monarch's Rule$122^{\frac{1}{2}}$ Silver Minister$124^{\frac{3}{4}}$	Best strid
6Apr07-7RD	fst	1^{70}		$:24^{2}$	:49	$1:14^{1}$	1:48	3↑ Clm 4000N1Y	**57**	9	$8^{9\frac{3}{4}}$	$7^{9\frac{1}{2}}$	$7^{6\frac{3}{4}}$	$3^{1\frac{1}{2}}$	$1^{\frac{3}{4}}$	Sarvis D A	L124	*2.80	69– 34	SilverMinister$124^{\frac{3}{4}}$ DontRockMyBoat124^{hd} LuckyBetheName$124^{4\frac{1}{4}}$	D
8Mar07-9TP	fst	6½f	◈	:23	$:46^{4}$	1:12	$1:18^{3}$	3↑ Clm 5000N2Y	**41**	4	8	7^{10}	$7^{5\frac{1}{4}}$	$7^{9\frac{3}{4}}$	$5^{8\frac{3}{4}}$	Adam M G	L120	12.30	74– 21	Clayton's Party$115^{\frac{3}{4}}$ Treat$120^{2\frac{1}{4}}$ King of the Stars$120^{\frac{1}{2}}$	5 path
19Feb07-2TP	fst	1	◈	$:25^{1}$	$:49^{1}$	$1:13^{2}$	$1:37^{3}$	3↑ Clm 5000	**21**	1	3^{2}	$6^{4\frac{1}{4}}$	6^{8}	6^{13}	$6^{23\frac{1}{2}}$	Mojica O	L120	3.80	66– 12	Get On Board124^{1} Lababa$120^{2\frac{1}{4}}$ Rusty Trawler122^{3}	Inside, sto

WORKS: Nov19 TP ◈4f fst $:48^{3}$ B *2/15* Oct15 TP ◈3f fst $:36^{2}$ B *3/3* Sep15 TP ◈3f fst $:36^{2}$ B *3/7*

By early December 2007, he was 0 for 9 on synthetic surfaces and 9 for 28 on conventional dirt. With him, the Polytrack-to-dirt angle was money in the bank. He made his synthetic debut September 14, 2005, at Turfway, finishing fifth in a $25,000 claimer. In his next start, he returned to regular dirt over the old Keeneland surface and won, paying $7.60. By the following fall, he was back at Turfway, where his form was dismal. After six straight losses there, owner-trainer Wayne Bearden shipped the gelding to River Downs, where, back on dirt, he won—again paying $7.60.

Bearden believes that Silver Minister didn't like that particular surface at Turfway because of the wax content, and predicted that the gelding would handle other synthetic tracks just fine.

"There's quite a few of them that don't like the new track at Turfway," Bearden said, referring to the surface that was tweaked in the fall of 2006. In September 2007, Silver Minister returned to Turfway and its Polytrack. Once again, he was awful, losing by a combined 32 ¾ lengths in two starts.

Bearden's worst Polytrack nightmare, however, came with a horse named Bavarian Baron. He lost six straight at Turfway, despite dropping all the way down to the $8,000 claiming level. Because the co-owner wanted to send Bavarian Baron to Mountaineer Park to get him off Polytrack, Bearden sold his share in the horse and reluctantly let him be turned over to a new trainer. The results were dramatic. Off Polytrack, he went on a four-race winning streak, twice winning at the $30,000 claiming level.

"I knew the horse didn't like the track at Turfway," Bearden said. "I just didn't know he hated it as much as he did."

But Bearden still thinks that the new surface at Turfway, which was put down before the fall 2006 meet, is the exception, and that the vast majority of horses who don't run well on it will like synthetic surfaces elsewhere. Still, be on the lookout for the few horses that seem to have an aversion for synthetic tracks, particularly those who have been racing at Turfway.

It wasn't Turfway that bothered Mistical Plan, but something apparently did when she ran on synthetic tracks.

```
stical Plan                         B. f. 3 (Apr)                                  Life 10 4 1 1 $506,850 94 | D.Fst      7 4 1 1 $475,765 94
 Reddam J. P                        Sire: Game Plan (Danzig) $3,500                                          | Wet(385)   1 0 0 0  $16,085 83
                                    Dam: Mistical Bel (Bel Bolide)                 2007  5 2 0 1 $421,569 93 | Synth      2 0 0 0  $15,000 77
                                    Br:  Carol Anderson (Cal)                      2006  5 2 1 0  $85,281 94 | Turf(338)  0 0 0 0       $0  -
                                    Tr:  O'Neill Doug F

07-10CD  myS 1⅛      :474 1:123 1:374 1:494 ⒻKyOaks-G1         83 13 2½  2hd 2½  32½ 513  Flores D R      L121  24.00 74-14 Rags to Riches1214¼ Octave1213½ High Heels1213¼       4w,press,weakened 14
07-9Kee  fst 1 1/16 ◈ :24 :473 1:124 1:424  ⒻAshland-G1        77 2  2hd 11½ 1½  32  54¾  Albarado R J    L121   3.20 89-11 ChristmasKid121hd Octve121¾ DwnAfterDwn1212  Forced,clear,weakened 8
07-8FG   fst 1 1/16   :232 :464 1:112 1:44  ⒻFGOaks-G2         93 1  11  11  1hd 14  13¼  Nakatani C S    L121   7.20 93-07 MisticlPln1213¼ Octve1213¼ Whtdremsrmdof1213¼  Repulsd bid,kpt to tsk 8
07-2SA   fst 6f       :211 :443 :571 1:102  ⒻⓇSunMilOaks250k   88 3  9   83¾ 86¼ 31½ 1no  Flores D R      LB120 *2.10 87-09 Mistical Plan120no TizElemental1203½ DoubleMajor1201¾  Waited 1/4,up late 12
07-7SA   fst 1 1/16   :231 :472 1:114 1:441 ⒻSntYsabl-G3       81 7  2½  2½  2hd 2½  36   Nakatani C S    LB119 *1.20 73-21 BaronessThatcher114½ RunwyRosie1225½ MisticlPln1192½  Dueled,held 3rd 7
06-9Hol  fst 1 1/16 ◈ :222 :452 1:101 1:423 ⒻHolStrlt-G1       68 11 55½ 44½ 42½ 43  89¾  Nakatani C S    LB120 *2.70  - -  Romance Is Diane1201 QuickLittleMiss120½ Down1202½  4wd 1/4,weakened 12
06-10CD  fst 1        :222 :451 1:101 1:354 ⒻPocahnts-G3       92 6  11  2½  1hd 1hd 22   Borel C H       L121   3.10 89-12 Change Up1212 Mistical Plan121nk Lady Joanne1177  Vied in hand,2ndbest 9
06-5OSA  fst 7f       :212 :44 1:09 1:223   ⒻⓈCoverGal72k      94 8  1   2½  1hd 12½ 17¼  Valenzuela P A  LB118 *1.90 87-13 MisticalPln1187¼ KisstheCooke1176 Ktispsublue1182  Dueled,clear,driving 10
06-8Dmr  fst 7f       :211 :44 1:092 1:231  ⒻDMrDeb-G1         45 1  5   13½ 13  79¾ 821¼ Cohen D         LB117 17.70 68-13 PontAshly1172½ UntchdTlnt121no ShsIncldd117no  Speed,inside,gave way 8
eviously trained by Buckridge Gloria 2006(as of 8/6): ( 104 18 13 13 0.17 )
06-6SR   fst 5½f      :22 :451 :564 1:03    ⒻMd Sp Wt 35k      85 7  2   11½ 12  1½  12½  Noguez T        LB120 14.10 93-12 MisticlPln1202½ NoNmeJustGm1199 EvntofSim114¾  Edged clear,game lane 8
KS: Apr27 Kee ◈6f fst 1:132 H 5/10  Apr20 Kee ◈4f fst :474 B 12/43  Mar30 Hol ◈6f fst 1:14 H 9/22  Mar3 Hol ◈6f fst 1:134 H 5/17  Feb24 Hol ◈6f fst 1:134 H 9/31
```

She threw in a clunker when trying a synthetic track for the first time in the Hollywood Starlet. She rebounded, won a couple on conventional dirt, and then ran poorly over Polytrack at Keeneland in the Grade 1 Ashland. Was it the Polytrack? Was it something else? Is she just an inconsistent filly? These are the questions handicappers have to tackle in this new, mysterious world of synthetic tracks.

The bottom line? Again, use common sense. Many horses will run equally well on dirt and on synthetic surfaces. But, just as there are certain horses for courses that might love Saratoga but hate the inner dirt track at Aqueduct, there will be horses that move up on synthetic tracks. When you see a horse like Step to the Music, whose record is so superior on Polytrack, understand that he might not run as well on regular dirt.

7

Synthetic to Dirt, Dirt to Synthetic: Handling the Switches

On certain racing circuits, regular bettors not only face the challenge of learning how to deal with synthetic surfaces, but also how to handle the switch back to a dirt track when the meet ends at Synthetic Downs. That's already the situation in Kentucky, where racing goes from Turfway (Polytrack) to Keeneland (Polytrack) to Churchill (dirt) to Ellis Park (dirt). Chicago-area bettors face the same problem when the action shifts between Arlington Park (Polytrack) and Hawthorne (dirt).

The best way to handle the situation is to use simple common sense. First off, most horses that run well on synthetic tracks will also run well on the dirt, and vice versa. Just because a horse runs a stinker on a synthetic track, don't necessarily throw that race out when he or she returns to regular dirt. The bad race probably didn't have anything to do with the fake dirt.

You should not ignore the basic tools and principles of handicapping—class, speed figures, trips, trainers, etc. Don't panic. Just keep the thought in the back of your mind that synthetic tracks and dirt tracks are not the same. When encountering a horse that clearly has a preference for synthetic tracks, you should obviously downgrade his or her chances on the regular dirt. The same holds true when handicapping cards at synthetic tracks. You certainly don't want to be betting on horses with a clear fondness for old-fashioned dirt or horses that run their best in the slop or mud. Also, be wary of grass horses running on synthetic tracks. If they have never before shown that they can handle regular dirt, they should not be played on synthetic tracks.

Though we are all still learning about synthetic tracks and how they affect betting and handicapping strategies, I cringe when I hear horseplayers who insist that dirt and synthetic tracks bear little resemblance to each other. The horse that ran well at Hawthorne on dirt will normally run well at Arlington on Polytrack. That horse that ran well on Polytrack at Arlington will normally run well on dirt at Hawthorne. Form does transfer from a synthetic to nonsynthetic track and vice versa.

The very first race run over Polytrack at Arlington was a perfect example of this pattern. Do the Wave had 13 lifetime starts under his belt and was still a maiden. He was no star, but he appeared to be the best of a wretched lot in this race, a $10,000 maiden claimer run at one mile. Yet he had never raced over a synthetic surface in his life, and had never worked on one, either.

Do the Wave
Own: Peter Stamas and Crowns Way Farm $10,000
Green, Black Blocks, Black Band On
ZO E JR (—) 2007: (230 38 .17)

B. g. 5 (Mar)
Sire: Dance Brightly (Mr. Prospector) $5,000
Dam: Wave's Way (Roman Diplomat)
Br: Crown's Way Farm (Ill)
Tr: Geier Greg(—) 2007:(50 1 .02)

L 124

Life	13	M	6	3	$29,534	63
2007	3	M	3	0	$11,680	59
2006	8	M	3	2	$14,994	63
AP	1	0	0	0	$0	55

D.Fst	12	0	5	3	$26,654	63
Wet(346)	1	0	1	0	$2,880	55
Synth	0	0	0	0	$0	-
Turf(283)	0	0	0	0	$0	-
Dst(343)	0	0	0	0	$0	-

r07-2Haw fst 6f :223 :471 1:00 1:131 3↑Md 10000 59 1 4 34½ 36 36 28 Houghton T D L124 *1.00 67-30 Pie Face1248 Do the Wave1241½ Milton1246¾ Rallied, up for place 7
r07-3Haw fst 6f :23 :473 1:00 1:122 3↑Md 10000 49 3 3 31½ 42 35½ 216½ Houghton T D L124 *1.10 62-27 PrinceElis12416½ DotheWv1243¼ MorningGold1242¾ No match for winner 7
ar07-1Haw gd 6f :214 :454 :583 1:124 3↑Md 10000 55 1 6 32½ 22½ 24 25½ Houghton T D L124 *1.50 71-18 Real Diligence1245½ Do the Wave1242 *Luck Is Due*124¾ Inside, second best 6
c06-7Haw fst 6½f :223 :462 1:13 1:201 3↑[S]Md 10000 53 5 3 2½ 1hd 11½ 2hd Zimmerman R L124 *2.20 76-24 Thunder Mesa122hd Do the Wave1241¼ *Prince Elias*1243½ Caught on wire 11
c06-2Haw fst 6½f :222 :444 1:084 1:152 3↑Md 10000 57 5 4 68½ 712 47½ 36¾ Zimmerman R L124 *2.60 93-08 *BattingThousnd*1225¾ WestofGlory1221 DotheWve124nk Off rail, belatedly 9
v06-6Haw fst 6f :222 :463 :593 1:133 3↑Md 10000 57 5 7 76 811 48½ 33½ Artieda P J7 L117 *1.40 64-30 Impressed1221¾ Binerak1221¾ Do the Wave1173 Angled out, late bid 12
v06-2Haw fst 6f :22 :46 :583 1:12 3↑Md 25000(25-20) – 7 5 63¾ - - - Fires E L124 4.40 - 22 Alexagogo1248 Sams Fever122½ Purple Jade1221½ Hit rival, lost jockey 9
t06-7Haw fst 6f :214 :451 :58 1:113 3↑Md 25000(25-20) 55 5 5 93¼ 75¾ 55½ 46½ Razo E Jr L124 4.30 71-24 PanamahDancer121nk GatosPirte1213½ *Alexgogo*1242¾ Improved position 11
p06-2Haw fst 6f :222 :463 :592 1:122 3↑Md 25000(25-20) 63 4 1 33 42½ 2½ 22½ Martin E M Jr L124 9.50 71-26 SouthernVision1212½ DotheWve124¾ GtosPirte1211¾ Rail bid, second best 8
y06-2AP fst 7f :222 :462 1:113 1:25 3↑[S]Md Sp Wt 27k 55 8 2 75 74¾ 78½ 65 Razo E Jr L124 3.00 78-12 Coin of Truth1241 B Like a Lion119½ *Alby*1191¼ No speed, no factor 10
r06-9Haw fst 6f :224 :472 1:001 1:132 3↑[S]Md Sp Wt 25k 59 1 5 64½ 64 32 2¾ Razo E Jr L124 4.60 68-29 DontMkeMeWit124¾ DotheWve1241¾ *Hyhyllthewy*124½ Angled out, missed 10
reviously trained by Hansen Andrew M 2004: (144 12 22 22 0.08)
n05-5Haw fst 6f :224 :472 1:003 1:14 [S]Md Sp Wt 26k 45 6 3 63¾ 67 68½ 610¾ Razo E Jr L120 7.20 55-31 Dress for Success1203 McLord1201¾ *JordanCreek*1202¼ Traded bump start 9
RKS: Apr15 Haw 4f fst :504 B *13/45* Apr1 Haw 4f gd :492 B *15/34* ●Mar23 Haw 3f my :37 B *1/9* Mar8 Haw 5f fst 1:021 H *20/42* Mar2 Haw 5f my 1:053 B *5/6* Feb23 Haw 4f fst :502 B *22/37*
INER: Synth(1 .00 $0.00) Sprint/Route(13 .00 $0.00) 2Sprints/Route(3 .00 $0.00) Routes(83 .11 $1.56) MdnClm(19 .21 $2.43) J/T 2006-07 AP(39 .21 $2.55) J/T 2006-07(72 .21 $2.62)

That may have been among the reasons the public wasn't exactly enamored of him and sent him off as the second choice. But Do the Wave was every bit as good on Polytrack as he had been on dirt. He won by 1¼ lengths and paid a fairly generous $7.20.

Horses are inconsistent creatures, which is among the primary reasons there aren't many rich horseplayers. They can run great one week and terrible the next and that can happen for myriad reasons. But the shift from dirt to synthetic tracks is, normally, not one of the primary reasons. The results of the first 14 days of racing over Polytrack at Arlington in 2007 bear that out. The majority of horses running on those days were Hawthorne shippers, most of whom had never run on Polytrack. As expected, in-form Hawthorne horses did just fine at Arlington.

During those 14 days, there were 190 horses coming off first- or second-place finishes on conventional dirt surfaces, an indication they were in good form coming into their Polytrack debuts at Arlington. Twenty-seven of them won, meaning the winning rate was a respectable 14 percent. More impressive was the ROI on these horses. A flat $2 win bet on each of these 190 starters actually produced a flat-bet profit, though an $89.80 winner certainly helped the stats. The ROI was $2.44.

When horses go in the other direction, from the synthetics to the dirt, every sign points to more of the same: Horses will run to their form, and bettors, by and large, can handicap dirt tracks the same way they do synthetic tracks. People fear that synthetic form won't hold up on dirt. That hasn't been the case.

At the beginning of the 2007 Churchill spring meet, many of the horses last started at Keeneland over Polytrack. If the Polytrack form didn't transfer over to Churchill, it would stand to reason that handicappers would have a miserable time deciphering the merits of Keeneland shippers. That didn't happen.

During the first 13 days of the meet, there were 37 favorites in dirt races that last started at Keeneland. No doubt, some of these horses were favored because they had performed well in their previous starts at Keeneland.

Twelve of them won for a winning rate of 31.6 percent, right on par with the typical winning percentage for favorites. The ROI on these horses was $1.63, again right in line with the norms.

Case in point: Take a look at the form of Louderfasterharder coming into the fourth race on May 12, 2007, at Churchill.

derfasterharder
Hebert Janet

B. g. 6 (Mar)
Sire: Conquistador Cielo (Mr. Prospector) $15,000
Dam: Summer Show (Wavering Monarch)
Br: Russell Springs Farm & Gene McLeane (Ky)
Tr: Gregoire Paul E(0 0 0 0 .00) 2007:(22 5 .23)

Life	31	3	6	4	$117,917	91	D.Fst	19	2	6	2	$93,770	91
2007	12	1	1	2	$23,470	77	Wet(350)	4	1	0	0	$16,812	69
							Synth	7	0	0	2	$6,145	77
2006	7	0	2	0	$19,885	89	Turf(261)	1	0	0	0	$1,190	72
	0	0	0	0	$0	-	Dst(0)	0	0	0	0	$0	-

07-8FG	fst	6f		:222 :461 :58 1:101	3↑Clm 16000(16-14)	54	3	2	62¾	75¾	75¾	711½	Patin J W Jr	L119 b	17.40	81-10	Out for a Spin1193½ Danish Dancer1191¼ Preside121nk	Never dangerous	7
07-2FG	fst	6f		:224 :47 :592 1:124	3↑Clm 12500(12.5-10.5)	69	5	1	65¾	68	45½	2½	Patin J W Jr	L119 b	8.10	79-23	ThnksMrG119½ Loudrfstrhrdr1193¾ BrrowngOwl119¾	Late rally mid track	6
07-6FG	fst	6f		:222 :461 :581 1:104	3↑Clm c-(10-9)	68	6	6	54	55	56	41¾	Mena M	L119 b	8.30	88-12	Sanctuary's Omooni116nk Fire Wheel1181 Tidy Up119½	Modest late gin	8
imed from Thomas, Michael J. and Logan, Ralph for $10,000, Habeeb Donald J Trainer 2007(as of 11/29): (47 2 9 7 0.04)																			
07-2CD	myS	6f		:22 :453 :58 1:104	3↑Clm 10000	69	5	3	32½	22½	25	47½	Woods C R Jr	L120 b	5.40	75-18	Canali1205½ Love This Trick120¾ *Aver*1201¼	4w,flattened out	6
07-6CD	fst	6f		:213 :451 :572 1:101	3↑Clm 16000	62	5	8	97½	76¾	68	56¾	Woods C R Jr	L119 b	24.00	79-16	*Summer Man*1191½ Cielo Song1191¾ Communion1191	6w,no late kick	11
07-3Kee	fst	7f	◈	:23 :461 1:11 1:233	3↑Clm 16000	56	5	6	4¾	53½	99¾	911¼	Woods C R Jr	L120 b	12.30	78-12	Erdiston1203¾ Tidy Up120nk Briar Man1201½	4w,tired	10
07-2CD	fst	1		:23 :46 1:104 1:36	3↑Clm 25000	56	5	62¾	78¾	710	712	715	McKee J	L120	17.20	74-15	Cayenne Call120nk *Mama's Lil' Mon*1201 White Buck1201¾	Tired on turn	7
07-2CD	fst	6½f		:231 :462 1:103 1:17	3↑Clm 25000	66	4	5	56	54¼	53¼	55	Mena M	L120	4.30	86-11	Grady O1222¼ Cab1201 Zumi1151	Off slow,hopped,rail	5
07-9CD	fst	6f		:21 :441 :563 1:10	3↑Clm 25000	72	3	10	811	711	68	42¾	Mena M	L120	31.90	84-15	Delta Charlie120nk Mama's Lil' Mon1202 Conjurer122½	5-6w bid, mild gain	11
07-4CD	fst	6½f		:232 :464 1:113 1:18	3↑Clm c-(15-10)N3L	73	11	3	85¼	74¾	44½	1¾	Leparoux J R	L121	*1.60	86-10	Louderfsterhrder121¾ RchorsDvis1211 Blckpool1211	6-7w lane,drv,in time	11
imed from Linkenhoker, Leslie, and Foley, Gregory D. for $15,000, Foley Gregory D Trainer 2007(as of 5/12): (100 15 13 20 0.15)																			
07-6Kee	fst	7f	◈	:224 :453 1:101 1:222	4↑Clm 16000	77	8	5	84¼	85	73¾	33½	Leparoux J R	L118	6.80	91-08	*ProphetJohn*1203½ JgurJoe118hd *Louderfsterhrdr*1181¾	6w lane, best of rest	10
07-4TP	fst	6f	◈	:221 :452 :573 1:094	4↑Clm 25000(30-20)N3L	62	2	3	37	35½	37½	37¾	Mena M	L118	5.20	85-08	FmlrGhost1202¼ GloblCrss1185½ Lodrfstrhrdr118nk	Off inside, lacked bid	7
06-6TP	fst	1	◈	:234 :471 1:12 1:37	3↑Clm 30000(30-20)N3L	62	9	812	911	106¾	77	58¾	Quinonez A7	L110	*2.50	92-04	Secret Woods1204 Gorbash1201 Bold Star119½	No threat	10
06-6CD	slyS	6½f		:23 :463 1:113 1:182	3↑Clm 30000(30-25)N3L	68	4	6	64	65¼	58	59	Leparoux J R	L121 b	4.60	72-25	Burrowing Owl1212½ Liquoreux119hd *Mt. Splendor*1195¼	4-5w trip,empty	9
06-5TP	fst	6f	◈	:214 :451 :572 1:101	3↑Alw 23400N$Y	58	4	4	67½	64	45	45½	Bejarano R	L120	*1.60	91-01	Eecchhoo1202¼ Shark1202¼ Tidy Up1171	3 wide late turn	7
06-10EIP	fst	7f		:23 :461 1:103 1:224	3↑Alw 22000N1X	66	4	1	33½	21	23	26	Mojica O	L120	*1.60	86-09	PrmiumUnldd1196 Loudrfstrhrdr120½ WingdVlor1206½	Mild bid for place	5
06-9CD	fst	7f		:222 :453 1:102 1:223	3↑Alw 54000N1X	75	5	6	76	85½	77	76½	Melancon L	L120	8.30	83-12	Deep Canyon120hd Preside1161¾ Border Cat116¾	No rally	12
06-8CD	fst	1		:231 :453 1:101 1:361	3↑Alw 45750N1X	89	2	46½	46½	33	21½	2¾	Bejarano R	L117	3.30	88-17	*OffDuty*116¾ Louderfasterharder1172¼ *AttheKnees*1194¼	Gaining slowly, 4w	6
06-8CD	fst	6½f		:222 :45 1:093 1:161	3↑Alw 44650N1X	80	6	7	76½	75½	33	42¼	Douglas R R	L120	12.60	90-11	Ingot1201 Friendsturnedfoes1201¼ Respect120no	5w bid,empty late	10
05-7TP	fst	6f	◈	:222 :464 :59 1:114	3↑Alw 25130N$Y	70	8	5	76½	86¼	66½	67¾	Martin E M Jr	L118	*2.00	- -	BllyforYo1181¾ MyUnbrdld1191¼ ShortyKndtson1183½	Nothing left drive	11
05-8CD	fst	1		:231 :463 1:111 1:354	3↑Alw 50600N1X	89	4	1hd	2hd	31	33½	32¾	Bejarano R	L114	3.30	88-18	RodShow1181¼ WstrnTrrtory1201½ Loudrfstrhrdr114½	Vied,inside,weaken	10
05-4Kee	fst	6f		:212 :45 :581 1:121	Clm 50000	79	9	10	108¼	810	44½	11½	Bejarano R	L117	3.30	80-19	Louderfstrhrdr1171½ SwisslStick1171 *BrokShrply*117hd	5w,drove clear late	12
05-11TP	fst	6½f	◈	:23 :454 1:113 1:181	3↑Alw 25930N1X	74	8	3	62¼	63½	43	41½	Sarvis D A	L113	3.30	- -	Treat1111¼ Contributor116nk Runaway Jewel113hd	5 wide turn	11
05-8EIP	fm	5½f	Ⓣ	:214 :442 :562 1:022	3↑Alw 23800N1X	72	3	6	74¾	85¼	73	43	Martin E M Jr	L117	4.60	87-10	War Tempo116nk Take a Shot1161¼ *Honoring*1201½	Bmp start,mild gain	9
05-4CD	fst	6½f		:224 :454 1:102 1:164	Alw 49120N1X	83	5	1	42¾	42¼	53	24	Martin E M Jr	L118	6.40	84-15	SmileandTears1184 Louderfsterhrder118hd CrftyBrutus120nk	4-5w,all out	7
05-9CD	fst	6f		:214 :451 :564 1:091	3↑Alw 49120N1X	91	4	2	43½	33	24	24¼	Martin E M Jr	L114	6.90	91-11	NorthernStag1244¼ Louderfsterhrder1142 Buchrest1144¾	5w, second best	6
05-8CD	fst	7f		:223 :452 1:101 1:232	Alw 49600N1X	71	2	5	4¾	32½	34½	45¾	Martin E M Jr	L118	19.50	83-14	Middle Earth1223¼ Bridesman118no War Tempo1182½	Came out bmp start	11
05-8TP	fst	6f		:221 :444 :57 1:093	3↑Alw 25400N1X	74	4	1	2hd	3nk	3nk	2hd	Martin E M Jr	L116	*1.50	94-07	Royal Warrior116hd Louderfasterharder116¾ Treat1161¼	3 wide, missed	5
05-10TP	fst	6f		:214 :444 :572 1:102	Alw 23400N1X	76	3	2	31½	21½	32½	34¼	Sarvis D A	L119	5.10	86-18	FlconsPek1192½ StormyAfternoon1191¾ Loudrfstrhrdr1199½	Ridden early	8
05-4TP	my	6f		:221 :45 :564 1:09	Alw 25400N1X	56	6	4	21½	42½	58½	510¼	Butler D P	L119	*1.40	87-05	*CalltheLord*1195¾ YankeeTreaty116¾ Mama'sLilMon116no	3 path, gave way	6
05-7TP	gd	6f		:22 :451 :574 1:11	Md Sp Wt 23k	63	12	4	51¾	1hd	11	11¼	Sarvis D A	L122	2.90	87-12	Louderfasterharder1221¼ MinPoint122½ SnowCpped1221¼	5 wide, driving	12

His last three starts had come over Polytrack, including his last out, a solid third-place finish at Keeneland. He was returning to conventional dirt for the first time since running a poor fifth the previous November at Churchill. Would his Polytrack form hold up over dirt? The betting public voted that it would and make Louderfasterharder the 8–5 favorite. It was the right call.

Southern California horseplayers faced the same dilemma when racing shifted late in 2006 from Hollywood Park's Cushion Track to Santa Anita's conventional dirt surface for the last time. Again, there was no evidence that Cushion Track form didn't hold up. During the first 10 days of racing at the Santa Anita meet, there were 44 favorites in dirt races that last raced over Cushion Track at Hollywood. Thirteen of them won for a winning rate of 29.6 percent. The ROI was $1.60.

Again, there may be differences between synthetic and dirt tracks and some horses may prefer one to the other, but I believe that the differences are not as big as you might think. Not everyone agrees with that, however. One theory I have heard is that horses with proven synthetic form should be preferred on synthetic tracks over horses that have yet to show a preference for the surface.

I decided to put that theory to the test at the 2007 Presque Isle Downs meet, where there was a good mix of horses who had been racing over synthetic and conventional dirt tracks.

There were 218 Presque Isle starters that had previously won on a synthetic surface. Thirty-three of them won, for a winning rate of 15.1 percent. Betting all previous synthetic winners produced an ROI of $1.90.

In the 153 non-maiden races at Presque Isle, previous synthetic winners represented 16.6 percent of the starters. They won 21.6 percent of those races.

The Presque Isle figures might lead you to believe that horses that have shown they can handle synthetic strips have a slight edge over their competitors. However, that edge certainly isn't enough to suggest that you concentrate your bets on synthetic winners or throw out horses that have yet to prove they can handle synthetic tracks. Rather, it provides still more evidence that most horses handle both tracks equally well.

The primary factor you need to keep in mind when playing conventional dirt tracks is that some tend to be more speed-favoring than synthetic surfaces, with Keeneland's Polytrack being particularly unkind to front-runners. Speed horses that flounder at Keeneland must be given a second chance when returning to dirt.

Bettors in Kentucky and simulcast players watching Churchill Downs during Derby Week 2007 certainly weren't fooled by the bad race turned in by Thunder and Belle in her most recent start. She flashed some speed before backing up in the stretch run last time out at Keeneland in a race that was typical of the spring meet. The winner, Pure Classy, closed from 10th and the second-place finisher, Fast Actress, came from seventh to complete the all-closer exacta.

Not only was Thunder and Belle returning to a track where speed horses could win, she was taking a sharp drop in class.

Thunder and Belle
Own: Peter Kirwan and Peter W Salmen Jr
Blue, White Panel, Red And Green
LO W D (2 1 0 0 .50) 2007: (211 30 .14)
$30,000
Ch. f. 3 (Feb)
Sire: Thunderello (Montbrook) $5,000
Dam: Crimson Belle (Royal Academy)
Br: Peter Salmen Jr (Ky)
Tr: Thompson Michael R(—) 2007:(9 2 .22)
L 120

Life	10	3	0	0	$35,137	74	D.Fst	3	0	0	0	$1,500 56
2007	3	1	0	0	$8,640	73	Wet(350)	1	1	0	0	$11,780 63
							Synth	6	2	0	0	$21,857 74
2006	7	2	0	0	$26,497	74	Turf(265*)	0	0	0	0	$0 -
CD	4	1	0	0	$13,280	63	Dst(384)	5	3	0	0	$33,637 74

)7–4Kee fst 7f ◈ :224 :452 1:1021:23 ⒻClm 50000 48 2 6 2½ 31 52 108 Castanon J L L118 f 7.40 84–06 Pure Classy1182 Fast Actress1181 Tylan113nk Bmp start,graze rail 11
07–7TP fst 6f ◈ :223 :46 :5821:114 ⒻClm 30000(30-20) 73 5 2 12½ 14 18 15 Troilo W D L122 f 1.50 83–18 Thunder and Belle1225 Luknluv1182½ Bellagar122hd Ridden out 8
)7-11TP fst 6½f ◈ :222 :451 1:10 1:162 ⒻCinTrophy50k 53 5 5 31 21 66 811 Troilo W D L118 f 18.40 83–12 OvertheEdge116½ MissABomb1222¾ ShesImpossibl1161¼ 3 wide, gave way 8
06-10TP fst 6f ◈ :214 :443 :5641:094 ⒻAlw 20525N1x 74 10 1 11½ 12½ 15 14¾ Troilo W D L116 f *2.90 99–01 ThundrndBll1164¾ *CrryinthDrm*116½ Thtsbunchbull1192¼ Inside, ridden out 10
06–4CD fst 6f :211 :443 :57 1:102 ⒻAlw 50000N1x 56 4 3 33½ 31 44½ 68¾ Castanon J L L118 f 54.00 76–15 FlorlPrk122no Mostbutifulstorm1222½ MissHoldyInn1182 4-5w,flatten out 8
06–1CD slyS 6f :22 :463 :5941:132 ⒻMd 30000(30-25) 63 3 1 11 14 14 15¼ Castanon J L L120 f 3.50 70–25 ThunderndBelle1205¼ DistinctivGold120½ GilddHrt120nk 2-3w,hand urging 12
06–9Kee fst 6½f ◈ :22 :461 1:1111:173 ⒻMd Sp Wt 45k – 1 4 14 11½ 1115 - McKee J L118 f 28.80 - - PerfectMotion118½ IronButtrfly118½ SilntStrt118no Lst irons,bore out,dis 11
06–2TP fst 6f ◈ :222 :453 :5811:101 ⒻMd Sp Wt 21k 48 7 3 2½ 3½ 32 78½ McKee J L121 f 7.20 88–01 RunwyQueen1215¾ PerfeckConnect121nk DoroDoll121hd 3 wide, gave way 11
06-11CD fst 5½f :22 :45 :5731:041 ⒻMd Sp Wt 49k 36 7 4 2½ 3nk 54½ 711¾ Borel C H L120 f 8.90 85–05 Cohiba Miss1203½ Sheets1201¾ *Natalicat*1201½ Forced pace,weaken 8
06–1CD fst 5f :221 :45 :57 ⒻMd 80000(80-75) 41 3 4 43 47 46½ 411¼ Castanon J L L119 f 14.20 86–09 ShsRoughinIt1197 FrySunst1192¾ DstnctvGold1191½ Unseat jock prestart 7
(S: Apr27 CDT 4f fst :491 B *3/8* Apr6 CDT 4f fst :49 B *3/7* Mar16 CDT 4f my :494 B *1/2* Mar7 CDT 4f fst :514 B *7/13*
NER: Dirt(30 .20 $2.83) Sprint(38 .16 $1.28) Claim(34 .21 $3.08) J/T 2006-07(4 .50 $3.20)

At odds of 11–10, she wasn't the type of horse you could break the bank with, but she was a stickout among the field, as long as you understood that her last race was a throw-out.

THIRD RACE
Churchill
MAY 3, 2007

6 FURLONGS. (1.072) CLAIMING. Purse $24,000 FOR FILLIES THREE YEARS OLD. Weight, 123 lbs. Non-winners Of Two Races Since March 3 Allowed 3 lbs. A race since then Allowed 5 lbs. Claiming Price $30,000 (Races where entered for $20,000 or less not considered).

Value of Race: $24,000 Winner $14,880; second $4,800; third $2,400; fourth $1,200; fifth $720. Mutuel Pool $264,686.00 Exacta Pool $224,377.00 Trifecta Pool $172,905.00 Superfecta Pool $55,389.00

Last Raced	Horse	M/Eqt.	A.	Wt	PP	St	¼	½	Str	Fin	Jockey	Cl'g Pr	Odds $1
15Apr07 4Kee10	Thunder and Belle	L f	3	120	2	7	32½	21	11½	1hd	Troilo W D	30000	1.10
1Apr07 8TP4	Flapper	L	3	118	5	3	4hd	42	33	22	Bejarano R	30000	2.50
15Mar07 9OP6	Babes	L b	3	118	3	1	1½	1½	21½	33¼	Leparoux J R	30000	5.70
3Apr07 1FP3	Sulic	L bf	3	118	1	6	7	7	65	42½	Borel C H	30000	12.70
1Mar07 4FG8	Lisa's Love	L f	3	118	6	5	66	54½	5hd	51	Sterling L J Jr	30000	16.20
16Apr07 11Tam1	Suzzona	L	3	120	4	2	2½	31	4½	66¾	Bridgmohan S X	30000	10.90
18Feb07 7CT4	Delaware Debutante	L b	3	118	7	4	51½	61½	7	7	Mena M	30000	10.10

OFF AT 1:43 Start Good. Won driving. Track sloppy (Sealed).
TIME :214, :461, :59, 1:13 (:21.90, :46.26, :59.02, 1:13.00)

$2 Mutuel Prices:

2 – THUNDER AND BELLE	4.20	2.80	2.40
5 – FLAPPER		3.20	2.40
3 – BABES			3.20

$2 EXACTA 2–5 PAID $12.60 $2 TRIFECTA 2–5–3 PAID $34.40
$2 SUPERFECTA 2–5–3–1 PAID $146.40

Ch. f, (Feb), by Thunderello – Crimson Belle, by Royal Academy. Trainer Thompson Michael R. Bred by Peter Salmen Jr (Ky).

THUNDER AND BELLE gained a forward position inside early, rallied from rail entering the stretch, gained a clear lead soon after the rider lost his whip at the three-sixteenths pole, then lasted. FLAPPER, never far back three wide, fanned six wide into the lane, had aim at the winner and couldn't get up. BABES gained the advantage early, raced two or three wide, made the pace into the upper stretch and weakened. SULIC, outrun inside for a half, came out seven wide for the drive and improved position. LISA'S LOVE drifted out at the break, moved in three wide soon after but had no closing punch. SUZZONA went up early to press the pace three or four wide, continued prominently to the lane and weakened. DELAWARE DEBUTANTE drifted out at the start, raced off the inside and tired.

Owners– 1, Kirwan Peter and Salmen Jr Peter W; 2, Motley Crew Stables LLC; 3, Chowhan Naveed; 4, Brown Charles W; 5, Olson Andy; 6, Cunningham Larry and Sharon; 7, Charlie Horse Racing

Trainers– 1, Thompson Michael R; 2, McGee Paul J; 3, Flint Bernard S; 4, Hancock John A; 5, Thomas Gary A; 6, O'Connor Robert R II; 7, Matthews Randy

Flapper was claimed by Mahler Ken, Tipton, Patty and Foley, Vickie; trainer, Foley Vickie L,
Suzzona was claimed by Simon Charles; trainer, Simon Charles.

$2 Daily Double (1–2) Paid $330.80 ; Daily Double Pool $14,645 .
$2 Pick Three (1–1–2) Paid $839.40 ; Pick Three Pool $32,621 .

Handicappers might also have noticed that the last time she made the move from Keeneland to Churchill, she won. On that occasion, she again flashed speed before collapsing (albeit because jockey John McKee lost his irons) and then dropped in class when moving to normal dirt.

Four races later, handicappers were faced with another horse coming off a race at Keeneland in which he had flashed speed before tiring. This time, at least, the horse was a price.

Japengo had had only one bad race in this country, and it had come at Keeneland. Mark Guidry, normally one of the most competent riders out there, made the mistake of sending the horse from the inside post. Even though he got to the front after a slow half-mile in 48.60, he had no chance on the track where speed horses go to die in the stretch. Once you understood that the Keeneland race was a throw-out, Japengo made perfect sense. With Kent Desormeaux taking over for Guidry, who is now retired, the gelded son of Theatrical was given a more sensible ride and closed from sixth to win, paying $18.80.

Probably the only people who cashed an exacta ticket, which paid $404.20, after the fifth race at Churchill Downs on November 12 were people who understood how biased the Polytrack had been at Keeneland. On face value, Matty Fine and Echo Location were automatic eliminations. Coming out of the same race at Keeneland, they had finished 11th and 12th. But there was every reason to throw that race out. Take a look at the chart.

TENTH RACE
Keeneland
OCTOBER 13, 2006

$1\frac{1}{16}$ MILES. (1.41^3) CLAIMING . Purse $16,000 FOR FILLIES AND MARES THREE YEARS OLD AND UPWARD. Three Year Olds, 122 lbs.; Older, 124 lbs. Non–winners of two races at a mile or over since August 13 Allowed 2 lbs. One such race since then Allowed 4 lbs. Claiming Price $7,500 (Races where entered for$6,000 or less not considered).

e of Race: $16,000 Winner $9,920; second $3,200; third $1,600; fourth $800; fifth $480. Mutuel Pool $268,942.00 Exacta Pool $191,625.00 cta Pool $165,182.00 Superfecta Pool $107,475.00

Raced	Horse	M/Eqt.	A.	Wt	PP	St	¼	½	¾	Str	Fin	Jockey	Cl'g Pr	Odds $1
06 ^{4}TP^2	Mentow	L	5	115	10	1	$6^{\frac{1}{2}}$	6^{hd}	7^2	$4^{1\frac{1}{2}}$	1^1	Toups R^5	7500	7.30
06 ^{8}Hoo^7	Bridled Honey	L	4	120	2	5	$1^{1\frac{1}{2}}$	1^1	$1^{1\frac{1}{2}}$	$1^{1\frac{1}{2}}$	2^{hd}	Hernandez B J Jr	7500	30.60
p06 ^{7}KD^2	Miss Quackerjack	L	4	115	6	10	9^2	9^4	8^3	5^4	$3^{\frac{1}{2}}$	Lebron V^5	7500	2.50
p06 ^{2}TP^6	Miss Lucky Strike	L bf	8	120	7	3	8^2	7^2	6^{hd}	2^1	4^2	Sarvis D A	7500	17.50
06 ^{3}TP^2	Darn Cool Gal	L b	3	120	8	8	5^2	5^3	$5^{1\frac{1}{2}}$	$3^{1\frac{1}{2}}$	$5^{4\frac{1}{4}}$	Mena M	7500	5.40
p06 ^{7}KD^9	Mystery Flick	L	4	120	12	9	10^3	$11^{2\frac{1}{2}}$	$11^{\frac{1}{2}}$	$9^{\frac{1}{2}}$	$6^{\frac{1}{2}}$	Graham J	7500	54.20
06 ^{2}EIP^4	Chiacchierone	L b	5	120	11	11	11^1	12	12	10^1	$7^{\frac{3}{4}}$	McKee J	7500	7.20
p06 ^{4}TP^4	Lost Composer	L b	6	120	3	12	12	$10^{\frac{1}{2}}$	10^4	$8^{\frac{1}{2}}$	$8^{2\frac{3}{4}}$	Johnson J M	7500	17.60
g06 ^{5}EIP^7	Steps	L	4	120	1	6	7^1	$8^{1\frac{1}{2}}$	9^2	11^5	$9^{1\frac{1}{4}}$	Mojica O	7500	37.70
p06 ^{7}KD^{10}	Naevushka	L b	3	118	9	2	4^1	$4^{2\frac{1}{2}}$	$3^{\frac{1}{2}}$	6^2	10^1	Enriquez J C	7500	47.00
06 ^{4}TP^9	Echo Location	L b	6	120	4	7	$2^{1\frac{1}{2}}$	$2^{\frac{1}{2}}$	2^1	$7^{\frac{1}{2}}$	$11^{13\frac{1}{2}}$	Teator P A	7500	20.70
p06 ^{7}TP^4	Matty Fine	L bf	6	120	5	4	$3^{\frac{1}{2}}$	3^{hd}	4^{hd}	12	12	Woods C R Jr	7500	2.70

OFF AT 5:49 Start Good. Won driving. Track fast.

TIME :23^2, :47^2, 1:12^2, 1:38^3, 1:45 (:23.45, :47.42, 1:12.48, 1:38.63, 1:45.12)

$2 Mutuel Prices:				
	10 – MENTOW	16.60	8.00	5.00
	2 – BRIDLED HONEY		25.00	13.40
	6 – MISS QUACKERJACK			3.40

$2 EXACTA 10–2 PAID $337.80 $2 TRIFECTA 10–2–6 PAID $2,219.60
$2 SUPERFECTA 10–2–6–7 PAID $20,608.40

Dk. b or br. m, (Apr), by Acceptable – Gin and Jazz , by Taylor's Falls . Trainer Cook Jason. Bred by E H Lane III (Ky).

MENTOW settled in behind rivals early, raced three wide around the far turn, came out six wide for the drive and was hard en to prevail. BRIDLED HONEY gained the advantage near the inside early, was well clear entering the stretch but couldn't tain the winner's surge. MISS QUACKERJACK, unhurried early, was put to a drive three furlongs out, angled six wide into stretch and was going well at the end. MISS LUCKY STRIKE, within striking distance always, made a menacing run five e into the upper stretch, loomed prominently but came up empty. DARN COOL GAL, never far back and three or four wide, de a run from between horses into the upper stretch, then failed to sustain the needed momentum. MYSTERY FLICK, outrun he stretch, improved position while not a serious threat. CHIACCHIERONE, void of early speed, passed tired foes six wide. ST COMPOSER never threatened. STEPS was done early. NAEVUSHKA moved in behind front-running BRIDLED HONEY y, stalked the pace for six furlongs and tired. ECHO LOCATION chased front-running BRIDLED HONEY four wide and kened approaching the stretch. MATTY FINE, well placed while tracking the pace four wide for six furlongs, gave way dily soon after and wasn't abused in the late going.

Owners– 1, Cook Jason Hulett Michael and McDonald James; 2, West Joe R; 3, Smith Ted; 4, Tammaro Michael A; 5, Maker Michael , McSorley Joe; 7, Clarke Harvey A; 8, Carmichael Farm; 9, Richland Stable LLC and Hammonds David; 10, Matejka Pavel; 11, Walsh e L; 12, England David P and Wright James

Trainers– 1, Cook Jason; 2, Orm Jerry; 3, Connelly William R; 4, Tammaro Michael A; 5, Maker Michael J; 6, McSorley Joe; 7, Lay ry; 8, Casey Stephen E; 9, Gogel Donald Carl; 10, Matejka Pavel; 11, Walsh Ryan D; 12, England David P

$2 Daily Double (3–10) Paid $160.00 ; Daily Double Pool $75,756 .
$2 Pick Three (2–3–10) Paid $1,187.00 ; Pick Three Pool $70,320 .
$1 Pick Four (10–2–3–10) Paid $4,266.20 ; Pick Four Pool $200,885 .
$2 Pick Six (6–8–10–2–3–10) 4 Correct Paid $143.60 ; Pick Six Pool $8,511 ; Carryover Pool $3,972.

eneland Attendance: 14,971 Mutuel Pool: $1,424,847.00 ITW Mutuel Pool: $257,349.00 ISW Mutuel Pool: $6,779,152.00

Matty Fine and Echo Location had chased a fast early pace. That they both collapsed in the stretch was hardly a surprise. Note that the chart caller also made a point of mentioning that Matty Fine, the 5–2 second choice in that spot, "wasn't abused in the late going." Back on normal dirt, where a speed horse has a chance, these two combined for a ridiculously generous exacta.

FIFTH RACE **Churchill** **NOVEMBER 12, 2006**

1 MILE. (1.33^{2}) CLAIMING . Purse $14,000 FOR FILLIES AND MARES THREE YEARS OLD A UPWARD. Three Year Olds, 121 lbs.; Older, 124 lbs. Non-winners Of Two Races At A Mile Or Over S October 12 Allowed 2 lbs. Such A Race Since September 11 Allowed 4 lbs. Claiming Price $5,000.

Value of Race: $14,000 Winner $8,680; second $2,800; third $1,400; fourth $700; fifth $420. Mutuel Pool $182,570.00 Exacta Pool $171,18 Trifecta Pool $155,849.00 Superfecta Pool $56,243.00

Last Raced	Horse	M/Eqt.	A.	Wt	PP	St	¼	½	¾	Str	Fin	Jockey	Cl'g Pr	Odd
13Oct06 ^{10}Kee^{12}	Matty Fine	L bf	6	115	2	1	$4^{1\frac{1}{2}}$	4^{3}	$3^{1\frac{1}{2}}$	1^{hd}	1^{2}	Lebron V^{5}	5000	1
13Oct06 ^{10}Kee^{11}	Echo Location	L b	6	120	7	3	1^{1}	1^{2}	1^{2}	2^{3}	$2^{4\frac{3}{4}}$	Teator P A	5000	2
28Oct06 ^{2}Kee^{4}	Imbali	L b	4	122	11	11	10^{4}	10^{2}	9^{1}	6^{3}	$3^{1\frac{1}{2}}$	Castro E	5000	
19Oct06 ^{4}Kee^{9}	Black Magic Lady	L	5	120	1	9	7^{hd}	5^{hd}	5^{hd}	$5^{1\frac{1}{2}}$	$4^{\frac{1}{2}}$	Albarado R J	5000	
5Oct06 ^{3}TP^{7}	Holdamearound	L bf	6	120	4	4	3^{hd}	$2^{\frac{1}{2}}$	2^{1}	3^{2}	5^{nk}	Bejarano R	5000	
5Oct06 ^{6}TP^{5}	Probable Payoff	L	5	120	5	8	9^{hd}	8^{1}	6^{2}	4^{2}	6^{5}	McKee J	5000	1
13Oct06 ^{8}Beu^{5}	Lear Dancer	L f	4	110	3	10	11	11	11	$9^{1\frac{1}{2}}$	$7^{1\frac{1}{4}}$	Quinonez A^{10}	5000	5
5Oct06 ^{6}TP^{10}	Mon Cabo	L f	6	120	8	5	$6^{\frac{1}{2}}$	9^{1}	$10^{1\frac{1}{2}}$	$7^{1\frac{1}{2}}$	$8^{4\frac{1}{4}}$	Hernandez B J Jr	5000	3
1Nov06 ^{4}GLD^{5}	Brigadoon	L	6	120	10	6	$5^{\frac{1}{2}}$	7^{1}	7^{hd}	10^{2}	$9^{2\frac{1}{2}}$	Troilo W D	5000	6
5Oct06 ^{7}TP^{7}	Check Ya Later	L bf	4	120	6	7	8^{2}	6^{1}	8^{1}	11	$10^{2\frac{3}{4}}$	Butler D P	5000	6
15Oct06 ^{2}Kee^{5}	Three Mysteries	L bf	5	120	9	2	$2^{\frac{1}{2}}$	3^{hd}	4^{4}	8^{1}	11	Borel C H	5000	

OFF AT 2:36 Start Good. Won driving. Track fast.

TIME :23^{3}, :47^{1}, 1:12^{4}, 1:26^{2}, 1:40 (:23.63, :47.31, 1:12.96, 1:26.42, 1:40.10)

$2 Mutuel Prices:

3 – MATTY FINE	22.20	9.20	5.60
8 – ECHO LOCATION		19.60	13.60
12 – IMBALI			6.00

$2 EXACTA 3–8 PAID $404.20 $2 TRIFECTA 3–8–12 PAID $3,317.40
$2 SUPERFECTA 3–8–12–2 PAID $22,658.20

Gr/ro. m, (May), by Matty G – Valee Ann , by Bucksplasher . Trainer England David P. Bred by Blaine Davidson (Ind).

MATTY FINE, well placed inside from early on, rallied from the rail, took over at the eighth pole and drove clear un urging. ECHO LOCATION moved to the fore early, raced two or three wide, made the pace into the upper stretch and coul handle the winner in the final furlong. IMBALI, outrun for six furlongs, made a mild gain six wide while unable to seriou menace the winner. BLACK MAGIC LADY, within striking distance and near the inside, failed to fire. HOLDAMEAROU tracked the pace three or four wide into the stretch and flattened out. PROBABLE PAYOFF, outrun early, made a mild run reach contention upon entering the stretch but failed to continue. LEAR DANCER, outrun to the stretch, improved posit while not a threat. MON CABO was finished early. BRIGADOON, within striking distance and five or six wide to the stret weakened in the drive. CHECK YA LATER tired on the turn. THREE MYSTERIES tracked the pace four or five wide to stretch and gave way.

Owners– 1, England David P and Wright James; 2, Walsh Anne L; 3, Bearden Wayne; 4, Stony Oak Farm LLC; 5, Ashcraft Donald Nemann III Teresa and Fred; 7, Alfir David J; 8, Polanco Juan; 9, Jackson Laura; 10, Richard E Hughes Racing Stable; 11, Bowman Co Racing LLC

Trainers– 1, England David P; 2, Walsh Ryan D; 3, Bearden Wayne; 4, Booker John A Jr; 5, England David P; 6, Nemann Ryan; 7, A David J; 8, Polanco Juan; 9, Jackson James R; 10, Hughes Richard E Jr; 11, Moquett Ronald E

Holdamearound was claimed by Sanner Daniel E; trainer, Sanner Daniel E,
Three Mysteries was claimed by Sturgeon Robert C; trainer, Sturgeon Robert C.
Scratched– Trieste's Destiny (06Oct06 ^{5}Haw^{8})

$2 Daily Double (2–3) Paid $184.80 ; Daily Double Pool $12,377 .
$2 Pick Three (4–2–3) Paid $973.40 ; Pick Three Pool $50,828 .
$2 Consolation Pick 3 (4–2–1) Paid $99.60 .
$2 Consolation Daily Double (2–1) Paid $13.60 .

You might have noticed that one other horse ran a particularly strong race in the aforementioned Keeneland claimer featuring Matty Fine and Echo Location. Despite setting a fast pace, Bridled Honey held on to finish second at 30–1 in a remarkable effort. When she returned at Churchill three weeks later, she was a must-bet at 31–1, despite the fact she was coming up in class. Unfortunately, for those who played her that day, she was awful, losing by 18 ½ lengths. A drop in class and a trip to Hoosier Park didn't help, either. She was trounced again.

But it was still too early to give up on Bridled Honey. All she needed was a trip back to Polytrack. She showed up in an $8,000 claimer at Turfway Park and went off at 16–1. Back on her favorite surface, she set the pace and held on to win at a nice price.

Bridled Honey
Own: Carrelli Michael M

Dk. b or b. m. 5 (Mar)
Sire: Bartlettsunbridled (Unbridled) $1,500
Dam: Little Addington (Hero's Honor)
Br: Joe R. West (Ky)
Tr: Carrelli Michael M

Life	26	6	3	2	$38,688	73	D.Fst	13	2	1	1	$11,563	56
2007	6	1	1	1	$11,044	69	Wet(365)	1	1	0	0	$3,600	73
2006	15	4	1	0	$21,869	73	Synth	12	3	2	1	$23,525	69
							Turf(283*)	0	0	0	0	$0	-

15Apr07–9Kee fst 1 1/16 ◈ :233 :462 1:104 1:444 4↑Ⓕ Clm c-10000 67 3 12½ 15½ 14 12 31 Laurente G L120 7.50 83–07 EtrnlSunshin1201 RunwyChrissi118hd BrdldHony120nk Well clear,faltered 10
Claimed from West Joe R. for $10,000, Orm Jerry Trainer 2007(as of 4/15): (32 1 3 2 0.03)
22Mar07–5TP fst 1 1/16 ◈ :234 :472 1:122 1:462 3↑Ⓕ Alw 5000s 69 1 11½ 12½ 17 15 13½ Laurente G L120 8.40 80–22 BridledHoney1203½ ShezyouBrwing1205 TriplKiss1151½ Off inside, driving 5
11Mar07–5TP fst 6½f ◈ :224 :461 1:121 1:19 3↑Ⓕ Clm 8000(8–7) 54 5 4 12 12½ 11 42¼ Laurente G L120 4.70 79–15 JudysGem120½ MoonShineTime1201¼ CubbiesGirl122½ Off inside, faltered 7
18Feb07–8TP fst 1 ◈ :24 :48 1:131 1:392 3↑Ⓕ Clm 8000(8–7) 61 4 12½ 14 12 11½ 2nk Molina J F Jr L120 7.80 81–20 Crimson Dancer120nk Bridled Honey1206½ Mentow1201½ Pace, missed 7
17Jan07–4TP fst 1 ◈ :232 :47 1:123 1:401 4↑Ⓕ Clm 8000(8–7) 33 2 21 21½ 21 69 715 Mena M L120 11.80 62–20 GloryndPower1205¼ CrshingSndstorm1203 PssDue120no Off inside, faded 9
4Jan07–4TP fst 6½f ◈ :221 :451 1:11 1:174 4↑Ⓕ Clm 8000(8–7) 39 1 4 11 1½ 54½ 108¾ Molina J F Jr L122 11.20 78–09 MoonShineTime120½ JudysGem120nk SlickRose120¾ Inside, gave way late 12
20Dec06–6TP fst 6f ◈ :22 :451 :58 1:104 3↑Ⓕ Clm 8000(8–7) 55 4 5 11½ 11 1hd 64¼ Mojica R Jr L124 11.00 90–06 Poochies Moccasin1131¾ Judy's Gem120½ So Hot119hd Near rail, faltered 12
2Dec06–5TP fst 6½f ◈ :231 :461 1:112 1:181 3↑Ⓕ Clm 8000(8–7) 59 11 1 12 14 13 1¾ Mojica R Jr L120 16.60 94–03 Bridled Honey120¾ Moon Shine Time120¾ Triple Kiss120½ All pace, lasted 11
24Nov06–8Hoo fst 1 :231 :472 1:142 1:414 3↑Ⓕ Clm 8000(8–7) 7 1 11½ 11 88 816 830¼ Thompson T J L118 10.40 40–28 TcticlFortune1151 OnEydJcki1151½ SwtPprik1194½ Speed, steadied tiring 10
3Nov06–3CD fst 7f :23 :463 1:121 1:253 3↑Ⓕ Alw 5000s 36 3 2 2hd 2½ 610 818½ Mena M L120 31.50 56–25 Boom Baby122no Bid Made1223 Arete1135 Vied,inside,tired 9
13Oct06–10Kee fst 1 1/16 ◈ :232 :472 1:122 1:45 3↑Ⓕ Clm 7500 59 2 11½ 11 11½ 11½ 21 Hernandez B J Jr L120 30.60 - - Mentow1151 Bridled Honey120hd Miss Quackerjack115½ Couldn't last 12
9Sep06–8Hoo fst 6f :223 :463 :594 1:132 3↑Ⓕ Clm 8000(8–7) –0 7 1 22 511 714 727¼ Pompell T L L118 10.30 54–19 TripleKiss1185 MissingJackie1183½ PuddlesPlesure1182 Well placed, faded 7

Though Bridled Honey has won three times on conventional dirt, she is definitely a better horse on Polytrack. It happens.

Sometimes, a horse is so obvious that he jumps off the page and, after he wins, you start to think this game is easy. (It's not.) Check out the ninth race at Churchill on November 19, 2006.

9 Churchill Downs *1 MILE* (1:332) **OC 80k/N$Y** Purse $55,000 (include $9,600 KTDF – KY TB Devt Fund) For Three Year Olds And Upward Which Have Never Won $8,500 Three Times Other Than Maiden, Claiming, Starter, Or State Bred Or Which Have Never Won Four Races Or Claiming Price $80,000. Three Year Olds, 121 lbs.; Older, 124 lbs. Non–winners Of $28,000 Twice At A Mile Or Over Since August 19 Allowed 2 lbs. $22,000 Twice At A Mile Or Over Since Then Allowed 4 lbs.

START — 1 MILE — FINISH

1 Esprit Du Roi (Chi)
Own: Horacio Parisi
Pink And Green Halves, Pink Bars On $80,000
TOUPS R (62 3 6 8 .05) 2006: (832 91 .11)

B. g. 7 (Sep)
Sire: Gran Lung Fung*Chi (Roy)
Dam: Mi Bonita*Chi (Contador*Arg)
Br: Haras Figuron (Chi)
Tr: Parisi Horacio(1 0 0 0 .00) 2006:(27 4 .15)

L 1155

Life	75	15	8	9	$196,736	97	D.Fst	18	4	2	2	$111,980	97
2006	16	3	2	3	$131,715	97	Wet(319*)	17	2	1	1	$37,321	92
2005	15	5	1	1	$37,652	89	Turf(220*)	40	9	5	6	$47,435	89
CD	6	2	1	1	$80,780	92	Dst(322)	12	2	2	1	$81,031	97

9Nov06–9CD fst 6½f :223 :452 1:093 1:161 3↑OC 80k/N$Y-N 77 2 4 56 67½ 69½ 47 Bridgmohan S X L120 10.20 85–15 ReigningCourt1182 **SilverVist**1203¼ ProPrdo1201¾ Improved position,4-5w 7
20Oct06–3Kee fst 7f ◈ :232 :454 1:093 1:212 3↑OC 80k/N1Y 80 5 4 64¾ 77¾ 54 35 Bridgmohan S X L124 3.70 - - *Gin and Sin*1222¾ Joe Six Pack1202¼ Esprit Du Roi1244 3 path, lacked bid 7
4Oct06–3Kee fst 7f ◈ :233 :463 1:10 1:22 3↑OC 100k/N$Y-N 85 3 4 2hd 2hd 41¼ 52 Toups R5 L115 11.30 - - StrghtLn122nk SmlltwnSlw120hd ArchrfldLnks1181¼ Vie,inside,weakened 6
5Sep06–9TP fst 1 ◈ :234 :471 1:113 1:38 3↑TPFallCh-G3 82 6 72 83½ 1114 99¼ 910½ Toups R L120 25.90 85–18 Gouldings Green122½ *It's No Joke*1183 Alumni Hall1181½ Steady fade 12
25Aug06–10EIP fst 1 :233 :462 1:103 1:35 3↑GovernorsH50k 95 1 43 42½ 33 32 2¾ Toups R L117 5.00 100–12 Junior College118¾ EspritDuRoi117¾ HuntinGene1164½ Inside trip,2ndbest 5
6Aug06–9Mnr fm 1 Ⓣ :231 :464 1:101 1:341 3↑WVSpeakrCp85k 82 6 611 55 65 64¾ 63¼ Laurente G L124 18.10 94–03 LeglControl110no *TouchdbyMdnss*114¾ BuckyBuddy118¾ Steady first turn 11
12Jly06–6CD slyS 1⅛ ⊗ :481 1:124 1:374 1:513 3↑OC 80k/N$Y-N 92 1 31½ 32 31 21½ 1no Toups R5 L115 3.10 79–23 EspritDuRoi115no ChifExport12416¼ EvrythingtoGin120nk 4w rally,just up 4
1Jly06–9CD fst 7½f :23 :453 1:093 1:274 3↑OC 100k/c 90 2 2 32 32 44 22¼ Toups R5 L117 22.60 100–07 Greater Good1202¼ *Esprit Du Roi*117hd Go Now120no Rail, angled 3w late 6
4Jun06–8CD fst 1 :224 :453 1:10 1:353 3↑OC 80k/N$Y 81 2 43½ 63¼ 78 57 33¾ Arce J L122 12.00 88–14 *It's No Joke*1201¾ First Word1202 Esprit Du Roi122¾ Near inside,mild gain 8
29May06–8CD fst 1 1/16 :241 :482 1:13 1:434 3↑OC 80k/N$Y 88 3 32½ 31½ 31 5¾ 42 Bridgmohan S X L124 3.00 89–13 *OConnlls*120½ WhopprVctory115no CopyMyNts1221½ Steadied 1/16p,empty 6
13May06–10CD gd 1 Ⓣ :231 :462 1:103 1:34 3↑OC 100k/c 84 6 79 85¾ 56½ 35½ 37¾ Bridgmohan S X L124 19.00 91–07 Free Thinking1157¼ Sgt. Bert120½ Esprit DuRoi1242½ Split foes,no late bid 8
29Apr06–3CD fst 1 :233 :472 1:12 1:364 3↑OC 80k/N$Y 89 6 32½ 33 21 21½ 11 Bridgmohan S X L122 10.40 86–13 EspritDuRoi1221 EndersShdow1204¼ AskthLord115nk Tracked,4w,driving 6
TRAINER: Sprint/Route(7 .29 $7.49) 2Sprints/Route(4 .00 $0.00) Dirt(39 .15 $4.81) Routes(18 .17 $4.18) Claim(23 .13 $4.59) Alw(8 .12 $1.02) J/T 2005-06 CD(2 .50 $4.10) J/T 2005-06(5 .20 $1.64)

2 Prayer Service
Own: Ofer Stable LLC
Purple, Black And White Stripes On
MCKEE J (69 3 6 7 .04) 2006: (911 113 .12)

Dk. b or br g. 4 (Feb) KEESEP03 $40,000
Sire: Stephen Got Even (A.P. Indy) $25,000
Dam: Real Bad Girl (Housebuster)
Br: Jim H Plemmons (Ky)
Tr: Holthus Robert E(24 3 4 3 .12) 2006:(368 49 .13)

L 120

Life	19	3	3	2	$121,076	102	D.Fst	17	3	2	2	$111,976	102
2006	10	2	1	1	$73,756	102	Wet(368)	2	0	1	0	$9,100	85
2005	7	1	2	1	$44,770	83	Turf(263)	0	0	0	0	$0	-
CD	6	1	2	0	$62,926	102	Dst(347)	11	3	0	0	$83,546	102

3Nov06–10CD fst 1 :223 :452 1:103 1:35 3↑Alw 52500N2X 102 6 1213 129½ 97½ 1½ 15¼ Borel C H L120 b 55.90 95–17 PryerServic1205¼ IslndWrrior116no SimonPur1174½ Rail trip,drew off,drv 12
7Oct06–3Kee fst 1 1/16 ◈ :242 :482 1:131 1:44 3↑Alw 53595N2X 69 3 21½ 21½ 41½ 68½ 612 McKee J L120 b 8.10 - - **StudentCouncil**1221¼ ChampSfi119nk Scipion1204¼ Forced pace,weakened 6
27Jly06–8EIP fst 1 :233 :47 1:111 1:361 3↑OC 40k/N2X-N 80 2 64½ 64 44 42 54½ McKee J L120 b 2.40 90–15 SwtGrssCrk115nk Shdowlnd1202¼ AmricnThundr117hd Stumble start,bmp 6
4Jly06–3CD fst 1 1/16 :24 :481 1:124 1:432 3↑Alw 57400N2X 85 1 34½ 32½ 32½ 2½ 32¾ McKee J L120 b 6.30 90–09 CieloGold1171¼ ⒹCurtinBluff1171½ PryerSrvic1202 Steadied,bmp 1/8p,rail 6
Placed second through disqualification
22Jun06–10CD slyS 1 :23 :462 1:112 1:363 3↑Alw 58000N2X 85 2 78½ 77 77¼ 56 44 McKee J L120 b 12.20 83–13 Chief Export1241¼ Rungius1171¼ *Scion*1111½ Between late,mild gain 7
5May06–4CD fst 1 :222 :45 1:093 1:342 3↑Alw 56800N2X 85 9 72¾ 75¼ 75 65¼ 49 McKee J L120 b 20.60 89–06 Venetian Sunset1227¾ *Bank President*1201¼ Nar113hd 6w lane,no real bid 9
8Apr06–12OP fst 1 :231 :472 1:12 1:374 4↑OC 40k/N2X-N 19 7 54 5¾ 68½ 826 837 Thompson T J L118 b 9.50 58–12 ScrenIdol1182 BigJohnDmpsy1223 PssthBiscuits1132¾ Finished after half 8
25Mar06–10OP fst 1 1/16 :234 :474 1:124 1:451 4↑OC 40k/N2X-N 77 1 611 78¾ 54¼ 45½ 32½ McKee J L123 b 6.40 77–23 SummerMn115nk ProperPrdo1232¼ PryerSrvic123nk Moved out, improved 8
26Feb06–11OP fst 1 :231 :472 1:131 1:393 4↑OC 35k/N2X-N 70 8 1112 1114 119½ 77¾ 99¾ McKee J L122 b 4.20 76–30 Slade118nk Commander Pat1185½ *Summer Man*1181¾ Back throughout 12
6Feb06–8OP fst 1 :224 :464 1:133 1:412 4↑Alw 33000N1X 83 5 1115 1112 84¼ 12½ 14½ McKee J L118 b 8.90 77–34 PryerService1184½ LuckyBid118½ WesternTerritory118¾ Kicked well clear 12
21May05–3CD fst 1 :232 :463 1:112 1:36 Alw 48840N1X 83 1 42 2hd 2½ 32 45¼ McKee J L118 b 2.90 85–13 JamicBy1183¼ MrMlprop118nk CrftyBrutus1181¾ Forced,inside,weakened 7
7May05–12CD fst 1 1/16 :234 :464 1:11 1:443 3↑Alw 50800N1X 82 6 78 915 48½ 33 2hd McKee J L115 b 10.50 87–10 GrandViewCliffs124hd PryerService115no ChippewTril120¾ Roughed early 10
WORKS: Oct30 CD 3f fst :353 B *1/3* Oct22 CD 4f fst :533 B *51/53* Oct3 CD 3f fst :363 B *4/21* Sep16 CD 4f fst :483 B *15/38* Sep7 CD 4f fst :483 B *10/35* Aug28 CD 5f my 1:033 B *22/30*
TRAINER: WonLastStart(120 .21 $1.78) Dirt(724 .15 $1.63) Routes(385 .13 $2.05) Alw(260 .15 $2.70) J/T 2005-06 CD(221 .11 $1.57) J/T 2005-06(678 .14 $1.67)

4 Student Council
Own: W S Farish
Yellow — Green, Gold Chevrons, Gold Hoop On Green
ALBARADO R J (83 11 11 14 .13) 2006: (927 151 .16)

B. c. 4 (May)
Sire: Kingmambo (Mr. Prospector) $300,000
Dam: Class Kris (Kris S.)
Br: W S Farish (Ky)
Tr: Howard Neil J(7 1 1 2 .14) 2006:(136 23 .17)

L 120

Life	12	3	1	1	$104,726	94	D.Fst	7	3	0	0	$84,664 94
2006	8	3	1	1	$99,468	94	Wet(370)	2	0	1	0	$13,300 94
2005	1	M	0	0	$2,500	52	Turf(346)	3	0	0	1	$6,762 89
CD	3	1	1	0	$44,600	94	Dst(374)	1	1	0	0	$14,515 93

28Oct06-9Kee fst 1⅛ ◈ :491 1:133 1:372 1:49	3↑Fayette-G3	85 6 41 72¾ 63¼ 83½ 87	Lanerie C J	L119	19.80	- -	Eccentric121¾ Ball Four1231½ Good Reward1191½	4-5w,flattened out	12
7Oct06-3Kee fst 1 1/16 ◈ :242 :482 1:131 1:44	3↑Alw 53595N2x	90 1 42 43 2½ 1½ 11¼	Albarado R J	L122	*1.60	- -	Student Council1221¼ Champ Safi119nk Scipion1204¼	Stalked,3-4w,drvg	6
6Sep06-9TP fst 1 ◈ :233 :472 1:123 1:373	3↑Alw 21500N1x	93 8 31½ 31½ 2hd 11 11½	Borel C H	L122	*1.10	98-16	*StudntCouncil*1221½ *VictoryDsign*1151½ SilvrdoTrl1202½	4 wide early, driving	8
19Aug06-1Sar fm 1 [T] :231 :462 1:102 1:35	3↑Alw 51000N1x	83 5 814 912 88½ 64 54¾	Gomez G K	L119	*2.00	87-12	SdlersTrick1111¼ *ThunderPss*1193 DH Sweetiewheti119	Steadied first turn	10
5Aug06-6Sar fm 1 3/16 Ⓣ :462 1:101 1:351 1:533	3↑Alw 51000N1x	89 10 34 36 35 1hd 33¼	Gomez G K	L121	4.50	94-09	*BigPririe*1162¾ OprtionRdDwn121½ StudntCouncil121½	Led late, weakened	10
13Jly06-8CD wfs 1 1/16 :241 :481 1:124 1:432	3↑Alw 46300N1x	94 3 32 42 32 22½ 23¾	Albarado R J	L124	3.00	89-17	At the Knees1223¾ Student Council12412 BigSlew1171¼	4w bid,secondbest	7
7Jun06-4CD fst 1 1/16 :24 :48 1:124 1:431	3↑Md Sp Wt 48k	94 6 21 21½ 2½ 1hd 1¾	Albarado R J	L124	4.10	94-12	StudntCouncl124¾ RoylTrsry1171¼ *AntrmConty*1175¾	Tracked,3-4w,driving	7
14May06-6CD fst 6½f :222 :452 1:101 1:163	3↑Md Sp Wt 42k	67 6 1 63¾ 65 56 46¼	Albarado R J	L124	11.10	84-08	Off Duty1181 *Brilliant Son*1183½ Djembe1131¾	5w,minor bid	7
22Oct05-10Kee gd *7f :222 :453 1:121 1:28	3↑Md Sp Wt 50k	52 10 10 105½ 53¾ 69 415½	Albarado R J	L118	10.20	69-13	Radetzky1187¾ Darling Trick1183¼ Phil the Brit1184½	Off inside,empty	11
9Oct04-4Kee fst 1 1/16 :232 :483 1:143 1:46	Md Sp Wt 50k	64 9 115½ 82 51¼ 32½ 45¾	Albarado R J	L118	17.70	76-13	Real Dandy1134½ Chekhov118nk Fan of the Cat1181	Lean in bmp start,tire	12
16Sep04-4Bel fm 1 Ⓣ :233 :474 1:123 1:353	Md Sp Wt 46k	48 11 31½ 21 1½ 55 612¼	Albarado R J	L119	5.50	70-14	Drum Major1194¼ Sku119½ *Dynantonia*119hd	Speed outside, tired	12
28Aug04-3Sar fst 6½f :22 :45 1:094 1:162	Md Sp Wt 45k	31 8 11 94½ 1110 1222 1222¾	Albarado R J	118	52.00	70-04	Silver Train1187 Commander Pat118¾ *Malheur*1181¼	Bumped start, wide	12

WORKS: Nov13 CD 5f fst 1:011 B *12/33* Nov6 CD 4f fst :494 B *22/41* Oct22 Kee ◈6f fst 1:151 B *6/7* Oct16 Kee ◈4f fst :49 B *11/29* Oct3 Kee ◈4f fst :48 B *4/46* Sep27 CD 5f fst 1:013 B *6/25*
TRAINER: Dirt(245 .20 $1.39) Routes(226 .21 $1.76) Alw(121 .21 $1.65)
J/T 2005-06 CD(93 .20 $2.00) J/T 2005-06(232 .21 $1.67)

CD PAGE 24 Sunday, November 19, 2006

5 Little Cliff
Own: Robert V LaPenta
Green — Burgundy, Gold Epaulets, Burgundy Cap
LANERIE C J (78 10 7 8 .13) 2006: (797 106 .13)

Dk. b or br c. 3 (Mar) KEESEP04 $250,000
Sire: Gulch (Mr. Prospector) $40,000
Dam: Favorite Feather (Capote)
Br: Hermitage Farm LLC (Ky)
Tr: Zito Nicholas P(15 3 3 2 .20) 2006:(376 61 .16)

L 117

Life	14	3	1	2	$171,297	93	D.Fst	13	3	1	2	$170,935 93
2006	10	1	1	2	$106,862	93	Wet(375)	0	0	0	0	$0 -
2005	4	2	0	0	$64,435	77	Turf(282)	1	0	0	0	$362 64
CD	2	1	1	0	$42,645	86	Dst(336)	2	1	0	0	$24,000 90

2Nov06-3CD fst 1 1/16 :241 :49 1:134 1:44	3↑OC 80k/N$Y-N	86 3 22 21½ 21 22 23½	Bejarano R	L117	5.40	86-21	Bright One1173½ LittleCliff1175¼ I'mWaitingforU1123¼	Bid 1/4pl, no match	6
25Aug06-8Sar fm 1 [T] :242 :48 1:121 1:352	Equalize72k	64 9 74½ 77½ 910 911 914	Luzzi M J	L120	28.50	76-15	*GimmeCredit*118½ StormTresure1182 RiverCityRebl118nk	3 wide trip, tired	9
6Aug06-12Mth fst 1⅛ :472 1:114 1:363 1:484	HsklInvH-G1	43 4 83¼ 89¼ 99¼ 916 938¼	Lezcano J	L118	52.50	56-11	BlugrssCt1187 PryingforCsh1181¼ *StrongContndr*1184¼	Through after half	9
16Jly06-10Del fst 1 1/16 :232 :464 1:112 1:431	LRichrds-G3	80 1 2hd 31 41¼ 35 39¼	Rose J	L116 b	*1.00	88-04	Awfully Smart1165½ Ah Day1183¾ Little Cliff1166	Bobbled, easily 3rd	6
11Jun06-7Del fst 1 :243 :484 1:131 1:384	Alw 40000N2x	90 5 32 32 1hd 1½ 1no	Rose J	L118	*1.30	86-16	Little Cliff118no Vegas Play118nk Kid Lemonade1183¼	Long drive, all out	5
20May06-8Pim fst 1 1/16 :233 :464 1:104 1:424	SirBarton100k	84 5 44 31½ 32 38 310¾	Castellano J J	L118 b	5.90	86-06	*High Cotton*1225½ UltimateGoal1185¼ *LittleCliff*118nk	Std'd 7/8,4-3wd,faded	7
15Apr06-9Kee fst 1⅛ :454 1:094 1:352 1:484	BlueGras-G1	32 1 32 27 514 926 851	Nakatani C S	L123	12.60	38-11	SnstrMnstr12312¾ StormTrsr1234½ StrongCntndr1234	Off inside, stopped	9
18Mar06-11Tam fst 1 1/16 :241 :491 1:132 1:441	TampaDby-G3	93 5 64 53½ 43½ 44 45½	Rose J	L116	8.60e	92-09	DputyGlittrs1162 BlugrssCt1223¼ WinnisTiggrToo116nk	Failed to respond	9
18Feb06-10Tam fst 1 1/16 :234 :474 1:123 1:44	SamFDavis121k	86 10 53¼ 55 42 41½ 45¾	Rose J	L122	18.30	93-07	BluegrssCt1221¼ *DeputyGlitters*1164¼ RLoylMn120nk	Bid 4w, flattened out	10
7Jan06-7GP fst 1 :231 :46 1:112 1:373	Aventura125k	59 12 2hd 2hd 2hd 68½ 814	Bejarano R	L116 b	14.30	69-07	DoctorDchrd116no Itsllbotthchs1165¼ MyGoldnSng1161	Pressed, faltered	12
13Nov05-8CD fst 1 1/16 :24 :481 1:132 1:452	Alw 50600N1x	77 6 2hd 22 1hd 12½ 14	Bejarano R	L122 b	4.90	83-26	Little Cliff1224 High Blues1183½ *Rungius*118¾	Off inside, driving	9
13Oct05-5Kee fst 1 1/16 :232 :484 1:151 1:494	Md Sp Wt 50k	62 6 32 31½ 31½ 1hd 12¼	Bejarano R	L118 b	5.00	63-29	*Little Cliff*1182¼ Well Said1183¼ Save Big Money1185½	Bumped, drifted out	11

WORKS: ●Nov12 CD 4f fst :471 B *1/41* Oct26 Kee ◈4f fst :471 H *2/28* Oct19 Kee ◈5f fst 1:004 B *10/22* Oct12 Kee ◈4f fst :47 H *4/21* Oct3 Kee ◈4f fst :48 B *4/46* Sep26 Sar tr.t 4f fst :512 B *25/35*
TRAINER: 2Off45-180(107 .15 $1.08) Dirt(773 .19 $1.60) Routes(498 .19 $1.51) Alw(236 .24 $1.95)

6 Spotsgone
Own: Robert Yagos
Black — Purple, Gold 'Y', Gold Sleeves, Purple
GUIDRY M (66 6 12 7 .09) 2006: (855 122 .14)

B. c. 3 (Feb)
Sire: Bright Launch (Relaunch) $3,500
Dam: Double's Lass (Mr. Leader)
Br: Hurstland Farm Inc (Ky)
Tr: Fires William H(11 0 1 2 .00) 2006:(154 15 .10)

L 117

Life	15	3	2	1	$135,402	98	D.Fst	14	3	2	1	$132,902 98
2006	10	2	1	1	$96,482	98	Wet(308)	1	0	0	0	$2,500 73
2005	5	1	1	0	$38,920	74	Turf(165)	0	0	0	0	$0 -
CD	4	0	2	0	$41,711	95	Dst(342)	6	2	1	1	$76,571 98

28Oct06-8Kee fst 1 1/16 ⊗ :234 :47 1:104 1:421	3↑Alw 55580N3x	77 8 32 31½ 31 95¼ 97¼	Fires E	L117 b	9.50	- -	Gray Suitor122hd Minister'sJoy120nk ElectricChant117¾	Track,4w,weaken	11
15Jly06-5CD fst 1 :223 :444 1:091 1:352	ForestryH70k	66 3 31½ 42½ 47 410 418	Hernandez B J Jr	L120	5.30	75-15	*Bright One*1167¼ El Nino1176¾ Hallowed Flag1174	4w,tired	5
30Jun06-8PrM fst 1 1/16 :233 :471 1:104 1:423	IowaDerby250k	94 4 32½ 32 32½ 64 65¼	Fires E	LB116	9.00	86-18	MoreThanRegal116½ BlzingSunset1162½ WitinLine114nk	3 wide, weakened	7
10Jun06-9PrM fst 1 :241 :472 1:112 1:353	PrairieMle50k	98 7 32 31½ 3nk 2hd 1½	Fires E	LB119	*.90	99-08	Spotsgone119½ Kingsfield1224 Vanilla Scoop1151½	3 wide, all out	7
29Apr06-9CD fst 1 :23 :46 1:102 1:361	DerbyTrial114k	95 4 2hd 3nk 1½ 1hd 2nk	Fires E	L116	54.60	89-13	Record116nk *Spotsgone*1162¼ Mister Triester1161¾	Bobble start,game try	7
8Apr06-9Haw fst 6f :223 :463 :583 1:111	LostCode109k	73 3 3 31½ 32½ 46½ 47	McKee J	L116	5.00	73-25	CityDweller1172¼ ClluloidHro1182¾ DontTllMommy1162	3 wide, weakened	5
17Mar06-10OP fst 6f :22 :453 :58 1:102	OC 50k/N2L-N	87 1 6 53 31½ 22 1½	McKee J	L116	2.60	91-14	Spotsgone116½ *Okie Time*1228 Anchor Steam116nk	Slight steady 1/4	8
25Feb06-7OP gd 6f :222 :462 :591 1:12	MntnValley50k	73 2 8 94¾ 87¼ 54¾ 47¾	McKee J	L115	13.50	75-19	Urban Guy1195¾ Fidrych1171¼ Catonight119¾	Modest interest late	10
5Feb06-7OP fst 1 :231 :472 1:123 1:39	OC 75k/N1X-N	77 9 42½ 42 31 34½ 46¾	Compton P	L118	6.80	82-19	MusicSchool118¾ ArbucklBndt1223 SoBustd1223	Forward 3-w,hung drive	11
21Jan06-8OP fst 1 :23 :472 1:13 1:40	OC 75k/N1X-N	82 10 22 21½ 2hd 11 31½	Compton P	L118	13.40	82-28	KingsChllenge115½ AdmirlsArch1181 Spotsgone1182¼	Chased, not enough	11
5Sep05-13RD fst 1 1/16 :233 :47 1:104 1:433	MILtCradle200k	53 2 21 21 42½ 510 517	Fires E	L120	3.50	87-01	Laity12011¾ *Dawn of War*1201 Acts Like a King1202	Faltered, faded	8
20Aug05-5AP fst 1 ⊗ :233 :463 1:12 1:373	Md Sp Wt 25k	65 7 31 32 3½ 14 18	Fires E	L119	*1.80	80-16	Spotsgone1198 Chin High119¾ Onotheregostokyo1191¾	3 wide, ridden out	8

WORKS: Nov11 CD 6f fst 1:17 B *1/2* Oct23 CD 4f fst :491 B *9/42* Oct16 CD 6f fst 1:15 B *1/2* Oct9 CD 6f fst 1:182 B *1/2* Oct3 CD 5f fst 1:004 B *3/39* Sep25 CD 4f fst :524 B *77/77*
TRAINER: 2Off45-180(30 .20 $2.65) Dirt(286 .13 $1.69) Routes(141 .14 $1.72) Alw(73 .15 $1.49)
J/T 2005-06 CD(8 .00 $0.00) J/T 2005-06(9 .00 $0.00)

7 Mark of Success
Own: William A Carl
Orange — Beige, Forest Green Diamond Belt, Forest
CASTRO E (58 6 3 6 .10) 2006: (1129 159 .14)

Dk. b or br g. 3 (Mar)
Sire: Mt. Livermore (Blushing Groom*Fr) $25,000
Dam: Silk n' Sapphire (Smart Strike)
Br: William A Carl (Ky)
Tr: Stewart Dallas(19 2 6 1 .11) 2006:(294 45 .15)

L 117

Life	12	3	1	2	$127,785	93	D.Fst	9	3	1	2	$124,725 93
2006	10	1	1	2	$90,785	92	Wet(395)	1	0	0	0	$0 69
2005	2	2	0	0	$37,000	93	Turf(317)	2	0	0	0	$3,060 76
CD	2	1	0	0	$12,400	69	Dst(369)	3	1	0	0	$22,455 84

15Oct06-7Kee fst 6½f ◈ :221 :451 1:082 1:142	3↑OC 80k/N3X-N	84 9 2 88½ 99¼ 84 46	Guidry M	L118	18.10	- -	Connections1203 Evrybodysfvorit1181½ YsYsYs1221½	10w lane,minor gain	9
10Sep06-6TP fst 6f ◈ :221 :453 :574 1:11	Alw 20245NC	81 5 5 52¾ 42¾ 33 32	Mena M	L120	25.60	91-15	Cognac Kisses120nk Likely1191¾ Mark of Success1203½	Best stride late	5
17Aug06-3EIP fst 1 :242 :48 1:121 1:363	3↑Alw 22000N3L	84 1 11 1hd 1hd 1hd 1nk	Mena M	L116	3.70	93-07	MrkofSccss116nk Rcognton1201½ AppontVctory1171¼	Duel,gamely,inside	6
27Jly06-9EIP fm 1 1/16 Ⓣ :251 :484 1:13 1:443	3↑OC 40k/N2X-N	67 3 1½ 2hd 3nk 54½ 55	McKee J	L115	3.10	67-29	Let It Thunder1201¼ Barnard Man1201¾ Turk'sRansom120nk	Duel,3-4,tired	7
23Jun06-10CD slyS 1 :23 :462 1:112 1:363	3↑Alw 58000N2x	69 3 1hd 1hd 53¼ 710 712¼	Guidry M	L116	4.70	75-13	Chief Export1241¼ Rungius1171¼ *Scion*1111½	Pace,2-3w,tired	7
7Jun06-8CD fm 1 1/16 Ⓣ :234 :471 1:123 1:423	3↑Alw 58000N2x	76 4 2hd 23 22 33½ 46¼	Guidry M	L116	5.60	87-15	BuckeyeBuddy1203 Chrlvoix1203 AwytoBoston120nk	Forced pace,weaken	7
20Apr06-3Kee fst 6½f :214 :451 1:11 1:181	Alw 57565N2x	62 2 4 57 57½ 47½ 37¾	Guidry M	L118	3.40	75-11	Chief What It Is1181½ Fabled1186¼ Mark of Success1181¾	4w,no late bid	5
25Mar06-9TP fst 1 1/16 ◈ :232 :472 1:12 1:45	Rushaway100k	44 5 97¼ 109¼ 1213 1119 1124¼	Flores D R	L117	4.20	73-09	HighCotton1152¼ SpecialInterest1151 BearCharcter1192	Took up 1st turn	12
25Feb06-10OP fst 1 :231 :48 1:133 1:40	Southwest250k	77 1 33 22½ 32 42½ 510¼	Borel C H	L117	14.10	74-25	*Lawyer Ron*122¾ Steppenwolfer1173¼ Red Raymond1172½	Empty, inside	10
14Jan06-9LaD fst 1 1/16 :233 :471 1:113 1:43	RisenStr-G3	92 2 11½ 2hd 21 22½ 28¼	Borel C H	L116	3.60	93-06	*Lawyer Ron*1188¼ MarkofSuccess1161¼ HyteRegency1163½	No match drive	7
17Dec05-8LaD fst 1 1/16 :24 :483 1:134 1:452	OC 50k/N1X-N	93 4 11½ 11 1½ 12½ 14¾	Borel C H	L117	12.00	89-20	MrkofSuccss1174¾ TommysTrn119nk *Stppnwolfr*1221	Stayed clear, driving	8
13Nov05-10CD fst 6f :22 :46 :583 1:112	Md 30000(30-25)	69 8 6 62¾ 41¼ 2hd 12	Flores D R	L120	8.70	84-19	*Mark of Success*1202 Deputy's Case1204¾ *Readily*120nk	5w,steady drive	12

WORKS: Nov13 CD 5f fst 1:022 B *26/33* Nov6 CD 4f fst :492 B *17/41* Oct28 Kee ◈4f fst :494 B *49/61* Oct8 CD 4f fst :491 B *15/38* Sep26 CD 4f fst :474 B *2/41*
TRAINER: Sprint/Route(61 .11 $0.89) 31-60Days(171 .18 $1.93) Dirt(475 .17 $1.57) Routes(262 .15 $1.63) Alw(181 .14 $1.35)
J/T 2005-06 CD(2 .00 $0.00) J/T 2005-06(4 .00 $0.00)

8 Deep Canyon
Own: A Stevens Miles Jr
Pink — White, Blue And White Quartered Sleeves
BOREL C H (86 21 10 5 .24) 2006: (937 137 .15)

Dk. b or br c. 3 (Feb) FTKJUL04 $75,000
Sire: Chester House (Mr. Prospector) $20,000
Dam: Strawberry Lady (Strawberry Road*Aus)
Br: William R Parke (Ky)
Tr: Wilkes Ian R(17 3 2 1 .18) 2006:(194 34 .18)

L 114

Life	5	3	1	0	$109,433	90	D.Fst	4	3	0	0	$98,833 89
2006	5	3	1	0	$109,433	90	Wet(368)	0	0	0	0	$0 -
2005	0	M	0	0	$0	-	Turf(377)	1	0	1	0	$10,600 90
CD	2	2	0	0	$65,110	89	Dst(394)	0	0	0	0	$0 -

15Oct06-6Kee fst 7f ◈ :232 :462 1:102 1:221	3↑Alw 52380N2x	86 10 1 71¾ 62¼ 11 1¾	Borel C H	L120	*1.70	- -	Deep Canyon120¾ Murphy'sBay1202¼ Mutate118hd	Brisk urging,held sway	11
19Aug06-6Sar fm 1 1/16 Ⓣ :234 :472 1:112 1:411	3↑Alw 53000N2x	90 1 42 42 32 22½ 23	Bridgmohan S X	L117	5.30	87-13	Baron Von Tap1213 *Deep Canyon*1171¾ SirHalory1213	Steadied inside early	11
16Jly06-9CD fst 7f :222 :453 1:102 1:223	3↑Alw 54000N1x	89 6 9 97¾ 75 3½ 1hd	Borel C H	L120	14.40	89-12	Deep Canyon120hd Preside1161¾ Border Cat116¾	7w lane,stiff drive	12
23Jun06-1CD fst 6½f :224 :46 1:103 1:17	3↑Md Sp Wt 50k	73 6 6 41½ 4¾ 1½ 1½	Borel C H	L118	*1.10	88-13	*DeepCnyon*118½ PrmiumUnldd113nk ColitionPrtnr118½	Stalked,5w,driving	7
13Apr06-6Kee fst 6½f :22 :454 1:103 1:17	Md Sp Wt 49k	63 10 9 85¼ 74½ 87¼ 815	Castellano J J	120	60.20	74-14	*Minister's Bid*1208¾ *Indian Silver*120hd Cognac Kisses1203	No rally	12

WORKS: Nov14 CD 5f fst 1:02 B *11/23* ●Nov8 CD 5f sly 1:011 B *1/4* Oct30 CD 5f fst 1:004 B *6/40* Oct25 CD 4f fst :511 B *32/41* Oct12 CD 4f fst :512 B *14/20* ●Oct5 CD 5f fst :591 B *1/29*
TRAINER: 2Off45-180(31 .19 $2.13) Sprint/Route(27 .11 $2.24) 31-60Days(54 .17 $2.33) WonLastStart(31 .16 $1.74) Dirt(162 .18 $1.91) Routes(83 .17 $1.71)
J/T 2005-06 CD(38 .21 $3.38) J/T 2005-06(61 .18 $2.63)

Throng
Own: Starlight Stable LLC Paul H Saylor a
Royal Blue, Yellow Circled 'JI', Yellow
NO R (98 9 19 12 .09) 2006: (1312 236 .18)

B. c. 3 (Feb) FTSAUG04 $160,000
Sire: Silver Deputy (Deputy Minister) $30,000
Dam: Fun Crowd (Easy Goer)
Br: Mr & Mrs Gerald J Stautberg (Ky)
Tr: Pletcher Todd A(34 2 7 4 .06) 2006:(1084 273 .25)

L 117

Life	11	3	1	1	$115,945	95		
2006	10	3	1	1	$113,795	95		
2005	1	M	0	0	$2,150	68		
CD	0	0	0	0	$0	-		
D.Fst	8	3	0	0	$92,983	95		
Wet(378)	3	0	1	1	$22,962	87		
Turf(275)	0	0	0	0	$0	-		
Dst(350)	3	1	1	0	$28,730	84		

7Kee fst 1 3/16 ⊕	:502 1:15 1:391 1:561	3↑ Alw 53595N2x	87 5 12 11½ 11½ 12½ 13	Velazquez J R	L119	5.70	- -	Throng1193 Tungsten1201 Crossword1193¾	Control slow pace,drv	10
8Mth fst 1 1/16	:224 :461 1:102 1:423	MajesticPr65k	82 4 32½ 32 55 58½ 58¾	Decarlo C P	L119 b	9.00	83- 19	MstrofDsstr1211½ GottchGold1234½ TctclBrsh1191¾	4p,faded near far turn	6
10Del fst 1 1/16	:232 :464 1:112 1:431	LRichrds-G3	69 3 1hd 1½ 1hd 57½ 515½	Santos J A	L116 b	5.70	81- 04	Awfully Smart1165½ Ah Day1183¾ **Little Cliff**1166	Pace, weakened drive	6
7Del sly^s 1 1/16	:244 :491 1:132 1:454	FloorShow47k	87 3 2½ 2hd 1hd 22 31¾	Dominguez R A	L118	*.60	82- 24	Broadway Ridge1161¾ Kid Lemonade116hd Throng118	Dueled, hung late	3
6WO gd 1 1/16	:233 :464 1:11 1:46	Marine-G3	70 3 32 32½ 46 49½ 412¾	Ramsammy E	L115	2.35	67- 28	Mlkoff1157¼ OkNthnksfrskn1182¼ BrChrctr1173¼	Stalked 3w,no response	5
3Aqu fst 1⅛	:463 1:111 1:363 1:494	OC 100k/N1x-N	95 1 1½ 1½ 11½ 14½ 11½	Luzzi M J	L118	3.50	86- 21	Throng1181½ Harborage1184½ Mr. Hamlen122nk	Drew clear when roused	6
3Aqu sly^s 1	:233 :472 1:122 1:372	OC 100k/N1x-N	84 6 32½ 32 31½ 25½ 24	Smith M E	L118 f	7.60	76- 23	Luxembourg1204 *Throng*1183¾ Marsh Side120no	3 wide, second best	6
8GP fst 1	:234 :46 1:094 1:34	Alw 33000N1x	74 2 72¼ 51¾ 63½ 68 613¾	Velazquez J R	L120	8.10	87- 05	*Showing Up*1182¼ *Chatain*1226 Flanders Fields1184½	Rail trip, faltered	8
6GP fst 1⅛	:482 1:122 1:371 1:493	Alw 33000N1x	57 2 11 11 11 56½ 618¼	Velazquez J R	L122	2.70	76- 06	Corinthian118¾ Jazil1203½ High Blues1184¾	Inside, faltered	8
8GP fst 1	:231 :453 1:102 1:371	Md Sp Wt 32k	76 2 72½ 2hd 1hd 11 16¼	Velazquez J R	L122	*2.50	85- 17	Throng1226¼ Stradivinsky1221½ Marrouche1221	Inside, drew off	12
6Aqu fst 6f ⊡	:221 :454 :581 1:11	Md Sp Wt 43k	68 6 8 48 47½ 49 49¼	Garcia Alan	L120	6.50	75- 20	LptopComputr1203¾ HithrLn1203 JohnnySprdsht1203	Bumped after start	9

: ●Nov13 CD 4f fst :461 B 1/41 Oct20 Kee ⊕5f fst 1:003 B 6/22 Oct12 Kee ⊕5f fst 1:022 B 21/25 Sep15 Del 4f sly :494 B 1/1 Sep5 Del 5f sly 1:03 B 7/20 Aug29 Del 5f fst 1:021 B 8/31
R: WonLastStart(499 .29 $1.93) Dirt(1412 .27 $1.80) Routes(1348 .26 $1.88) Alw(558 .27 $1.97) J/T 2005-06 CD(47 .40 $1.92) J/T 2005-06(105 .30 $1.75)

I'm Waiting for U
Own: Sefas Farm
Yellow, Red Diamonds, Red Diamonds On
NCON L (33 1 4 5 .03) 2006: (299 43 .14)

B. g. 3 (Mar)
Sire: Service Stripe (Deputy Minister) $5,000
Dam: Rose Center (Sefapiano)
Br: Sefas Farm Inc (Ky)
Tr: Hill Brenda M(2 0 0 1 .00) 2006:(50 6 .12)

L 117

Life	11	3	0	3	$65,584	84
2006	9	2	0	3	$51,034	84
2005	2	1	0	0	$14,550	71
CD	4	0	0	2	$16,300	84
D.Fst	9	3	0	2	$60,184	84
Wet(338)	1	0	0	1	$5,400	71
Turf(227)	1	0	0	0	$0	64
Dst(364)	5	0	0	2	$10,700	84

6-3CD fst 1 1/16	:241 :49 1:134 1:44	3↑ OC 80k/N$Y-N	77 6 69 68 65 46 38¾	Lebron V5	L112 b	26.10	81- 21	Bright One1173½ **Little Cliff**1175¼ I'm Waiting for U1123¼	Wide both turns	6
6-9TP fst 1 1/16 ⊕	:244 :494 1:142 1:443	3↑ Alw 26000N2x	83 3 31 1hd 11 12 11	Lebron V	L119 b	8.70	99- 06	ImWitingforU1191 AwytoBoston1201 ProvYourslf1202¼	Off inside, lasted	8
6-8Mnr fst 170	:223 :463 1:121 1:442	Alw 27800N2L	82 10 76¼ 64¼ 2½ 1½ 14½	Spieth S	L114 b	5.50	73- 35	*I'm Waiting for U*1144½ *Ghosttrapper*1124¼ Driskoll1124½	Vied turn, drew off	10
6-2CD fst 1	:231 :46 1:101 1:342	Alw 52900N1x	84 1 3nk 11 1½ 31½ 46	Toups R5	L113 b	22.50	92- 11	Irene's Mon1153¼ *Simon Pure*1131 Clear the Way1181¾	Duel,inside,tired	5
6-4CD fst 1 1/16	:241 :483 1:124 1:434	Alw 51800N2L	80 1 913 912 810 68½ 44	Martinez W	L118 b	14.00	87- 08	Irish Majesty118½ Polarity1182¾ Dubai Gold117¾	Imp position,3-4w	9
6-8CD sly^s 1 ⊗	:231 :461 1:112 1:38	Alw 46850N1x	71 6 52¼ 41½ 41 32 32¾	Martinez W	L118 b	17.50	77- 20	Coach Kent1202½ Beaufort122nk I'm Waiting forU1183¼	4-5w,no final gain	6
6-7CD gd 1⅛ ⓣ	:491 1:131 1:372 1:492	Alw 54000N1x	64 3 814 811 89¼ 89¾ 77¼	Martinez W	L118 b	44.90	79- 09	YatesBlackCt1171 Mercurius1181¾ ThreeCities120nk	Came out bmp start	9
6-10TP fst 1 ⊕	:241 :483 1:132 1:384	WEBN50k	40 7 52 31½ 66 616 729¼	Prescott R	L117 b	30.00	63- 19	Warrior Within1175¼ Malameeze1172½ Final Copy1211¾	Inside 2nd turn	8
6-8TP fst 1 ⊕	:234 :48 1:134 1:41	Alw 25065N1x	73 4 64¾ 41¾ 1½ 11 31½	Martinez W	L120 b	6.40	79- 20	TmporrySint120½ TmplrsCup1181 ImWitngforU1202¾	Drifted out 3/16,1/16	10
5-7TP fst 1 1/16 ⊕	:243 :501 1:164 1:521	Md Sp Wt 23k	71 1 21 31 11½ 12½ 11¾	Martinez W	L122 b	4.20e	- -	I'm Waiting for U1221¾ *Bahri and Grill*1224 Han Solo1221¾	Inside, driving	12
5-12TP fst 1 ⊕	:24 :481 1:143 1:42	Md Sp Wt 23k	62 2 89¼ 913 98½ 710 69¾	Bracho R A	L122 b	44.50	- -	*TemporrySint*1222 StrspngldGtor1222¼ Extortion1224	Came over first turn	12

S: Oct23 TTC 5f fst 1:023 B 2/3
NER: Dirt(168 .12 $1.32) Routes(87 .14 $1.67) Alw(31 .16 $2.00)

2 Silver Vista
Own: Eddie Kenneally et al
Navy, Beige 'K', Navy Cap
$80,000
ROUX J R (66 8 7 8 .12) 2006: (1620 384 .24)

Dk. b or br g. 4 (Jan) KEESEP03 $150,000
Sire: Silver Deputy (Deputy Minister) $30,000
Dam: Canadian Vista (St. Jovite)
Br: Dell Ridge Farm (Ky)
Tr: Kenneally Eddie(15 2 2 0 .13) 2006:(126 25 .20)

L 120

Life	18	3	6	2	$143,034	89
2006	10	2	3	2	$103,348	89
2005	3	0	1	0	$7,656	67
CD	5	2	2	1	$96,170	89
D.Fst	14	3	4	2	$125,974	89
Wet(337)	3	0	2	0	$16,730	71
Turf(274)	1	0	0	0	$330	72
Dst(342)	6	0	3	2	$32,762	84

06-9CD fst 6½f	:223 :452 1:093 1:161	3↑ OC 80k/N$Y-N	89 4 3 44 33½ 23 22	Leparoux J R	L120	7.40	90- 15	Reigning Court1182 Silver Vista1203¼ ProPrado1201¾	4w,not good enough	7
06-7Kee fst 6½f ⊕	:221 :451 1:082 1:142	3↑ OC 80k/N3x	80 8 1 76 75¾ 73¾ 57½	Leparoux J R	L124	8.90	- -	Connections1203 Evrybodysfvorite1181½ YesYsYs1221½	8w lane,minor bid	9
06-7AP fst 1	:232 :461 1:11 1:363	3↑ Cigar47k	84 4 42 64¾ 65½ 65½ 55¾	Leparoux J R	L120	12.00	83- 17	SmpsonsSon1203½ *StrightLine*118nk TpDncingMuk1181¾	Came out stretch	8
06-8CD fst 7f	:224 :451 1:091 1:221	3↑ Alw 58000N3L	88 3 3 21 3½ 41¼ 1nk	Leparoux J R5	L119	*2.20	91- 06	SilverVist119nk KingsChllenge116½ *HuntinGene*1202	Lost positin 3/16s,drv	7
06-8CD fst 7f	:231 :464 1:113 1:234	3↑ Alw 51800N1x	83 2 1 41½ 41¾ 5¾ 1nk	Hernandez B J Jr	L120	7.70	83- 11	*SilverVista*120nk PulpitExchnge120no SilverdoTril1202½	Split foes 4w,drvg	7
06-8CD fst 7½f	:23 :453 1:094 1:29	3↑ Alw 53725N1x	83 5 1 3nk 2½ 32½ 34	Leparoux J R5	L115	4.00	92- 16	CircletheWorld1161¾ TwilightTp1202¼ *SilverVist*1154¼	Between,vie,empty	8
06-6GP fst 1	:232 :46 1:102 1:361	4↑ Alw 33000N1x	84 4 53 32½ 2½ 22 23¼	Prado E S	L120	*.80	87- 15	Kansas City Boy1203¼ Silver Vista1206¾ CalltheMarines1202¾	Bid 2nd best	7
06-9Tam fst 1 1/16	:234 :474 1:123 1:452	4↑ Alw 19200N1x	78 5 31 31½ 31½ 3nk 22½	Houghton T D	L118	*2.50	89- 12	Voodoomon1182½ Silver Vista1182¼ Tampa'sBigCity1184¾	Bid, bested rest	8
06-8GP fm 1⅛ ⓣ	:474 1:112 1:35 1:462	4↑ Alw 33000N1x	72 2 21 22 22 74¼ 107¾	Decarlo C P	L120	33.30	83- 14	*Karelian*1201¼ Clevedale1202 Sand Man122¾	Chased, faltered	12
06-9GP fst 1	:23 :453 1:103 1:352	4↑ Alw 33000N1x	72 1 41¼ 31½ 32½ 36 312	Prado E S	L120 b	32.80	82- 13	Monarch Lane1206½ Time Out1205½ SilverVista1202	Poor st, steadied turn	7
Previously trained by Walden W Elliott 2005(as of 6/13): (85 16 15 11 0.19)										
05-9Mnr fst 170	:224 :461 1:12 1:442	3↑ Alw 28700N1x	56 1 1hd 41 77 812 815½	Whitney D G	L110 fb	*1.10	58- 32	ⒹSand Saba115nk Sine Die1187 Carson City Star1151	Sent,vied,gave way	8
05-8Mnr sly^s 1	:232 :462 1:113 1:39	Alw 28700N2L	66 4 56½ 43½ 34 33 22	Whitney D G	L112 fb	1.60	79- 20	Rendies Summer1122 Silver Vista112nk *OntheRiver*115½	Checked first turn	7

KS: Oct29 Kee ⊕4f fst :492 B 22/29 Oct4 Kee ⊕4f fst :472 H 6/40 Sep24 CD 4f fst :484 B 5/14 Sep16 CD 4f fst :512 B 35/38 ●Sep8 CD 4f fst :474 B 1/37 Aug29 CD 5f gd 1:003 B 2/23
NER: Sprint/Route(23 .22 $1.60) Dirt(232 .21 $2.22) Routes(111 .19 $1.85) Claim(36 .22 $1.73) Alw(55 .27 $2.03) J/T 2005-06 CD(17 .18 $1.35) J/T 2005-06(33 .27 $2.15)

The betting public was focused on three horses coming off the Keeneland meet, but it had the wrong favorite in Student Council and the wrong second choice in Deep Canyon. Both had won at Keeneland, but had taken advantage of the closers' bias. Throng, meanwhile, had done something truly exceptional, winning wire to wire. The horse was 5–1, yet should have been the favorite. To those who were paying attention, it came as no surprise when he romped to a 2½-length win and paid $13.60.

NINTH RACE
Churchill
NOVEMBER 19, 2006

1 MILE. (1.33^{2}) ALLOWANCE OPTIONAL CLAIMING . Purse $55,000 (includes $9,600 KTDF Kentucky TB Devt Fund) FOR THREE YEAR OLDS AND UPWARD WHICH HAVE NEVER WC $8,500 THREE TIMES OTHER THAN MAIDEN, CLAIMING, STARTER, OR STATE BRED WHICH HAVE NEVER WON FOUR RACES OR CLAIMING PRICE $80,000. Three Year Olds, 121 lb Older, 124 lbs. Non-winners Of $28,000 Twice At A Mile Or Over Since August 19 Allowed 2 lbs. $22,(Twice At A Mile Or Over Since Then Allowed 4 lbs. (Races Where Entered For $62,500 Or Less N Considered In Allowances).

Value of Race: $55,000 Winner $34,388; second $11,000; third $5,500; fourth $2,750; fifth $1,362. Mutuel Pool $328,962.00 Exacta P $276,779.00 Trifecta Pool $219,991.00 Superfecta Pool $78,023.00

Last Raced	Horse	M/Eqt.	A.	Wt	PP	St	¼	½	¾	Str	Fin	Jockey	Cl'g Pr	Odds
26Oct06 ^{7}Kee^{1}	Throng	L	3	117	8	3	2^{hd}	$2^{\frac{1}{2}}$	1^{hd}	1^{1}	$1^{2\frac{1}{2}}$	Bejarano R		5
15Oct06 ^{6}Kee^{1}	Deep Canyon	L	3	117	7	7	8^{5}	7^{2}	$5^{\frac{1}{2}}$	3^{4}	2^{1}	Borel C H		3.
28Oct06 ^{9}Kee^{8}	Student Council	L	4	120	3	6	$7^{\frac{1}{2}}$	5^{hd}	2^{1}	2^{hd}	$3^{6\frac{1}{4}}$	Albarado R J		3
2Nov06 ^{3}CD^{2}	Little Cliff	L	3	117	4	4	$4^{\frac{1}{2}}$	$6^{1\frac{1}{2}}$	6^{3}	4^{hd}	4^{nk}	Lanerie C J		5.
5Nov06 ^{9}CD^{2}	Silver Vista	L	4	120	10	2	3^{2}	4^{1}	$4^{\frac{1}{2}}$	$6^{1\frac{1}{2}}$	$5^{2\frac{1}{4}}$	Leparoux J R	80000	8.
3Nov06 ^{10}CD^{1}	Prayer Service	L b	4	120	2	9	9^{hd}	9^{2}	$7^{\frac{1}{2}}$	$7^{\frac{1}{2}}$	$6^{\frac{3}{4}}$	McKee J		7.
28Oct06 ^{8}Kee^{9}	Spotsgone	L b	3	117	5	1	$1^{\frac{1}{2}}$	$1^{1\frac{1}{2}}$	$3^{\frac{1}{2}}$	5^{hd}	$7^{\frac{3}{4}}$	Guidry M		12.
2Nov06 ^{3}CD^{3}	I'm Waiting for U	L b	3	117	9	10	10	10	8^{1}	$8^{2\frac{1}{2}}$	8^{nk}	Melancon L		35.
5Nov06 ^{9}CD^{4}	Esprit Du Roi-Chi	L	7	120	1	8	$5^{1\frac{1}{2}}$	$3^{\frac{1}{2}}$	9^{1}	$9^{1\frac{1}{2}}$	$9^{1\frac{3}{4}}$	Bridgmohan S X	80000	16
15Oct06 ^{7}Kee^{4}	Mark of Success	L	3	117	6	5	6^{hd}	$8^{\frac{1}{2}}$	10	10	10	Castro E		27.

OFF AT 4:38 Start Good. Won driving. Track fast.

TIME :22^{4}, :45^{4}, 1:10^{3}, 1:22^{3}, 1:35^{1} (:22.84, :45.87, 1:10.62, 1:22.61, 1:35.23)

$2 Mutuel Prices:				
	10 – THRONG	13.60	7.00	4.40
	8 – DEEP CANYON		4.80	2.80
	4 – STUDENT COUNCIL			2.80

$2 EXACTA 10–8 PAID $67.60 $2 TRIFECTA 10–8–4 PAID $236.20
$2 SUPERFECTA 10–8–4–5 PAID $825.80

B. c, (Feb), by Silver Deputy – Fun Crowd , by Easy Goer . Trainer Pletcher Todd A. Bred by Mr & Mrs Gerald Stautberg (Ky).

THRONG pressed the pace off the inside, challenged in earnest on the turn and edged clear late under pressure. DEE CANYON reserved early, made a quick move between rivals on the turn, angled out for the drive, reached a challenging positi in upper stretch but had no late bid. STUDENT COUNCIL within striking distance, made a good three wide move on the tur challenged approaching the stretch but weakened late. LITTLE CLIFF never far back, made a good five wide middle move b tired in the drive. SILVER VISTA prompted the pace three wide and tired in the stretch. PRAYER SERVICE as no threa SPOTSGONE set the pace near the rail, held on well to the stretch and gave way. I'M WAITING FOR U was no factor. ESPRI DU ROI (CHI) close up along the inside, faded. MARK OF SUCCESS was through early.

Owners– 1, Starlight Lucarelli and Saylor; 2, Miles A Stevens Jr; 3, Farish WS; 4, LaPenta Robert V; 5, Kenneally Eddie et al; 6, OFE Stables LLC; 7, Yagos Robert; 8, Sefa's Farm; 9, Parisi Horacio; 10, Carl William A

Trainers– 1, Pletcher Todd A; 2, Wilkes Ian R; 3, Howard Neil J; 4, Zito Nicholas P; 5, Kenneally Eddie; 6, Holthus Robert E; 7, Fir William H; 8, Hill Brenda M; 9, Parisi Horacio; 10, Stewart Dallas

Scratched– Alpha Capo (03Nov06 ^{12}CD ^{2}) , American Man (02Sep06 ^{5}AP ^{5})

$2 Daily Double (7–10) Paid $429.60 ; Daily Double Pool $19,923 .
$2 Pick Three (7–7–10) Paid $1,551.00 ; Pick Three Pool $35,970 .

And what about the one horse who managed to win wire to wire in the early part of the first ever Keeneland Polytrack meet? His name is Cat and a Half and you can bet that trainer Wayne Catalano, who is normally as shrewd as they come, regrets dropping him in for a measly $16,000. He lost him through the claim box that day, and Cat and a Half went on to prove how remarkable his front-running win was. Two starts later, he won a $50,000 claimer over the Cushion Track at Hollywood Park.

Another warning: Should a horse win over a synthetic surface, don't automatically assume that his form will hold up if he shifts to the grass. I can't repeat this enough: Synthetic surfaces and grass surfaces are not one and the same. Horses that cannot run on the dirt but run well on grass are unlikely to win on Polytrack, Cushion Track, etc.

Generally, though, their synthetic-surface form will hold up, especially when they have been running at tracks like Hollywood where there was not a strong bias of any sort. You'll see a lot of horses like Level Red.

1 Level Red — B. c. 3 (Apr) KEENOV04 $160,000
Own: William K Warren Jr — Sire: Aptitude (A.P. Indy) $20,000
Fuschia, Green Sash, Green Chevrons On — Dam: Sedona Berry (Strawberry Road*Aus)
Br: Dr & Mrs Ronald H Grothaus DVM (Ky)
PINOZA V (100 17 13 15 .17) 2006: (1285 259 .20) — Tr: Hofmans David(15 1 1 3 .07) 2006:(117 19 .16)

L 120

Life	3	1	1	0	$37,600	84	D.Fst	3	1	1	0	$37,600	84
2006	3	1	1	0	$37,600	84	Wet(322)	0	0	0	0	$0	-
2005	0	M	0	0	$0	-	Turf(276)	0	0	0	0	$0	-
SA	2	1	0	0	$29,200	84	Dst(352)	2	1	1	0	$37,200	84

ec06-5SA fst 1 1/16 :23³ :48¹ 1:12¹ 1:44¹ Md Sp Wt 50k 84 4 1½ 1½ 1½ 1 1½ 1nk Espinoza V LB120 3.30 79-26 LevlRd120nk TimSqurd1203¼ SpnkyComHom1201¼ Inside,held on gamely 12
ec06-2Hol fst 1 1/16 ◈ :23¹ :47 1:11² 1:41⁴ Md Sp Wt 42k 78 2 2½ 1hd 1hd 2 1½ 2 3½ Espinoza V LB120 16.40 - - Ravel1203½ *Level Red*1202¼ Got a Question1202¾ Inside duel,held 2nd 7
ct06-6OSA fst 7f :22¹ :45 1:10⁴ 1:24¹ Md Sp Wt 51k 43 3 11 10¹⁰ 11¹¹ 12¹² 9 14½ Solis A LB120 17.50 64-16 Pwnee1202¾ ForwrdCommitment1201 *SilentSoul*120¾ Saved ground to 1/4 13
RKS: ●Jan14 Hol ◈6f fst 1:11¹ H *1/34* Dec26 Hol ◈5f fst 1:00³ H *5/25* Dec20 Hol ◈6f fst 1:14² H *11/19* Dec14 Hol ◈5f fst 1:01² H *14/34* Nov26 Hol ◈6f fst 1:12¹ H *3/32* Nov21 Hol ◈5f fst 1:04¹ H *55/59*
AINER: WonLastStart(18 .17 $1.12) Dirt(89 .15 $1.25) Routes(60 .13 $1.11) Alw(24 .21 $1.30) J/T 2006-07 SA(7 .43 $3.00) J/T 2006-07(16 .25 $1.69)

When he showed up in a December 30, 2006, maiden race at Santa Anita, he probably had a lot of bettors confused. His one race on conventional dirt had been awful. Making his career debut at Santa Anita, he finished ninth and his Beyer Speed Figure was a 43. But just when it looked like he was on his way to $2,000 claimers at the Tillamook County Fair, he turned in a big effort over Cushion Track at Hollywood, finishing second in a maiden special weight race while earning a 78 Beyer.

Was he simply a Cushion Track freak or were his problems in his first race the result of something other than a dislike of synthetic tracks? The smart players knew that very few horses will run well on dirt and not on synthetic tracks and vice versa. They played Level Red right back and collected a nice $8.60 mutuel.

8

A Leg Up: Does Training and Racing over a Synthetic Track Help?

Though the 2006 Breeders' Cup was run over a conventional surface at Churchill Downs, Polytrack very much came into play. The trainers of several Breeders' Cup horses decided to train their horses over the Polytrack at Keeneland. For some, it was a matter of staying in familiar surroundings; they had been stabled at Keeneland for the fall meet and didn't want to move. For others, it was a matter of wanting to train over Polytrack, a surface many believe helps make their horses as fit as possible.

Trainer Doug O'Neill brought his contingent of Breeders' Cup horses in early from California, in part because he wanted to give Lava Man, who was winless outside of California, time to acclimate to his new surroundings. Yet O'Neill chose to do most of his serious training not at Churchill Downs, but at Keeneland. The reason? Polytrack.

Still other Breeders' Cup contenders had made a name for themselves winning races over the Polytrack at Keeneland, which left handicappers wondering what to do with horses like Juvenile Fillies starter Bel Air Beauty. She had had only two lifetime starts and both of them had come over Polytrack, including her win in the Alcibiades at Keeneland.

On normal dirt for the first time in the Breeders' Cup, she was a complete mystery. As it turned out, she was sent off at 11–1, made a mild middle move, and finished eighth of 14.

Most of the Polytrack horses fared well in the Breeders' Cup. Of the five races run on the dirt, four of the winners had had workouts on Polytrack. The list included upset winner Round Pound, who had spent the better part of the summer and fall training first on the synthetic surface at the Fair Hill Training Center in Maryland and then at Keeneland for trainer Michael Matz. The only Breeders' Cup dirt winner who had not trained on a synthetic surface was Invasor, who prepared for the Classic at Belmont Park.

In addition, the first three finishers in the Breeders' Cup Juvenile all came out of the Breeders' Futurity at Keeneland.

"When I saw Street Sense and Great Hunter and Circular Quay [three Breeders' Futurity starters] coming down that stretch, it hit me that the Juvenile was going to be an exact one-two-three of the Breeders' Futurity," Keeneland's Nick Nicholson said. "I thought, 'That settles that.' I knew at that moment that Polytrack form would hold up on dirt tracks. It just carried through all day long. It was an astounding piece of data for an industry that has been the same for 1,000 years. To have something this dramatic be so obvious that key day is one of the reasons things have moved so quickly and people have been so quick to accept Polytrack."

The Breeders' Cup results seemed to suggest that, at the very least, horses that trained over synthetic surfaces were at no disadvantage.

Some six months later, trainers eyeing the Kentucky Derby also seemed to believe that their best interests would be served by training nearby at Keeneland over Polytrack. In some respects, they were right. Because the Polytrack never gets sloppy or muddy, it's easier to train over a synthetic track. You don't have to worry about adverse conditions or missing days of training.

"That's the main thing I like about these surfaces," trainer Bobby Frankel said. "You don't have to miss any days of training because they never get wet."

Todd Pletcher spent a lot of time with his horses at Keeneland leading up to the 2007 Kentucky Derby. Four of his five Derby starters had all of their pre-Kentucky Derby workouts over the Polytrack at Keeneland. The exception was Sam P., arguably the worst of the five.

"Even though I did make the decision to train four of the five Derby horses at Keeneland, I still consider myself a traditionalist and I like seeing the Kentucky Derby run on a traditional dirt track," Pletcher said. "I think the synthetic surfaces are great to train on, though. I think we're all still learning about them and that there's going to be some fine tuning on everyone's end, including track maintenance and management."

In hindsight, Pletcher, whose record of Derby failures stretched to 0 for 21 in 2008, might have made a mistake. None of his Kentucky Derby starters managed to hit the board. Meanwhile, Derby winner Street Sense had had four works at Churchill, and runner-up Hard Spun put in his final Derby work at Churchill, a fast five furlongs in 57.30. Old-time horsemen will tell you that horses have to have a work over Churchill Downs in order to be successful in the Kentucky Derby.

Yet synthetic surfaces may have played an important role in the 2007 Kentucky Derby in another way. The Derby trail in 2007 was an unusual one in that relatively few horses were injured. In fact, most of the best 2-year-olds of the fall of 2006 were the best 3-year-olds in the spring of 2007, something that rarely seems to happen anymore. Not only did Street Sense become the first Breeders' Cup Juvenile winner to win the Derby, as well as the first 2-year-old champion to do so since Spectacular Bid in 1979, but the first five finishers from the Juvenile also returned six months later for the Kentucky Derby. I believe that it can't be a coincidence that so many top 3-year-olds did a significant amount of their training on synthetic surfaces in 2007.

In 2008, even more horses completed their major Derby preps and training over synthetics, but the first five finishers came out of conventional-dirt races.

Obviously, you can't judge the merits of training over Polytrack on just two or three races or events. But some trainers insist that conditioning a horse over Polytrack or any of the other synthetic surfaces is the way to go. Not only are they conducive to better training conditions but, some trainers say, they have the ability to get a horse fitter.

For handicappers, the question is this: Do horses that train and race over synthetic tracks have an advantage over their peers?

Equibase has put out some interesting statistics on the subject and they indicate that all horses are pretty much created equal when it comes to where they have been training and racing. According to Equibase's data, horses who last raced on dirt won 10.3 percent of the time on all-weather tracks, while horses that last raced on the all-weathers won 11.9 percent of the time. The difference is not enough to get excited about. Horses that last raced on the grass won 12.3 percent of the time when shifting to a synthetic surface. Again, not a big difference.

Racing in southern California provided a perfect opportunity to judge the merits of training over a synthetic surface, in this instance the Cushion Track at Hollywood. Santa Anita still held all of its racing over dirt tracks in 2006 and during its winter and early spring meet of 2007, meaning some horses racing in California would be training over a synthetic track and others over a dirt track.

The Cushion Track horses held a slight advantage at the fall 2006 meet at Hollywood. They accounted for 822 of the 1,307 starters, or 62.9 percent of total runners for races listed on the main track. Yet, they won 98 of the 126 races, or 77.8 percent of them. That was not, however, an angle that did anyone any good at the betting windows. The return on investment when playing every horse that had trained over Cushion Track was $1.69.

Oddly enough, horses who trained over Polytrack for the 2006 fall meet at Keeneland seemed to be at a disadvantage. A total of 630 of Keeneland's 1,366 starters at the meet trained over a synthetic track, which is 46 percent of the total runners. Most of the other starters were training on the dirt at Churchill Downs. Yet the Polytrack trainees accounted for only 43 percent of the winners. Worse yet, the return on investment on these horses was a sorry $1.16. Anyone following this angle must have had a rough meet.

That's not to suggest that horses training over synthetic surfaces were somehow at a disadvantage at Keeneland. With the fall meet at Keeneland being so short, there is not a lot of data available and the numbers are probably a statistical aberration. Nonetheless, they're a strong indicator that horses training over synthetic tracks are probably no better or worse off than horses training over regular tracks.

This has been another case where perception has trumped reality. Before synthetics were introduced in this country, people assumed they would be deep, tiring surfaces that would help the horses that trained over them get in peak condition—similar to the Oklahoma training track at Saratoga, a longtime favorite of horsemen there.

As it turns out, most synthetic surfaces are anything but slow, deep, and tiring. In fact, Keeneland's new main track has turned out to be substantially faster than the old dirt track there.

There are horses, however, that seem to thrive once they begin training over synthetic surfaces. There is something about training over a consistent and forgiving surface that makes them more comfortable and, possibly, more willing to exert themselves in the afternoons. Perhaps the best example of this is Jacsonzac. Training over conventional dirt tracks in New York, he was in the midst of a 45-race losing streak when the My Samsara Stable decided to try something different. They sent Jacsonzac to Michael Dickinson, who began to train him over his synthetic Tapeta surface. Two and a half months after his 45th straight loss, he made his debut for Dickinson and ran second. He then won two of his next three starts. (He started only once more and was retired.)

"He was a lovely old horse but he'd lost his confidence," Dickinson said. "He came to the farm, started three times, and he won two of them."

The next big test for some of these theories could come in the 2008 Breeders' Cup at Santa Anita, which will be the first Breeders' Cup ever run over a synthetic surface. It might just behoove a trainer to familiarize his horses with the track if they have never set foot on it before.

We shall see.

9

To Bounce or Not to Bounce?

Every handicapper has encountered situations like this one: A horse who normally runs six furlongs in 1:11 or so pops up one day and runs the same distance in 1:09, while winning by 10 lengths. After running Beyer Speed Figures in the 70s, he gets a 90 for his last performance. He's coming back in 10 days and running at the same class level. The betting public, seeing how he dominated similar competition last time out, is convinced the horse will do the same thing again and sends him off at 6–5.

Good bet or not? Those who believe in something called the bounce theory couldn't throw this horse out fast enough. To bounce means that after a horse turns in an extraordinarily fast effort, he or she will regress. The theory is that the unusually fast race has taken so much out of the horse that he will have a hard time recovering and may not be the same for a while. Horses that come back on particularly short rest after a big effort are most susceptible to bouncing.

The bounce theory's main advocates have been the "sheet guys," notably Len Ragozin's The Sheets and the producers of Thoro-Graph. Both companies calculate performance figures that take into account factors such as the time of the race, beaten lengths, ground lost, weight, etc. The numbers were originally laid out on sheets of graph paper and are arranged in a format that enables users to quickly spot patterns, or "form cycles."

The bounce believers who handicapped the 2004 Florida Derby might have made a score. Read the Footnotes was coming off a smashing 3-year-old debut in the Fountain of Youth and was the even-money favorite, which was a surprise to no one.

Read the Footnotes
Own: Klaravich Stables Inc

B. h. 6 (Apr)
Sire: Smoke Glacken (Two Punch) $25,000
Dam: Baydon Belle (Al Nasr*Fr)
Br: Lawrence Goichman (NY)
Tr: Violette R A Jr

Life	8	5	0	0	$450,660	113	D.Fst	7	5	0	0	$450,660
2004	3	1	0	0	$210,000	113	Wet(377)	1	0	0	0	$0
2003	5	4	0	0	$240,660	105	Synth	0	0	0	0	$0
							Turf(239)	0	0	0	0	$0

1May04-10CD	sly	1¼	:463	1:114	1:371	2:04	KyDerby-G1	86	12	64¼	42	34	45½	714¾	Albarado R J	L126	22.50	64-21	SmartyJones1262¾ LionHeart1263¼ Imperilism1262	Stdied 1st turn,wkene
13Mar04-9GP	fst	1⅛	:47	1:112	1:373	1:511	FlaDerby-G1	86	3	33	34½	2hd	2½	44	Bailey J D	L122	*1.00	79-15	Friends Lake122¾ Value Plus122¾ The Cliff's Edge1222½	Rail trip, gave wa
14Feb04-11GP	fst	1$\frac{1}{16}$	:234	:473	1:111	1:423	FntnOYth-G2	113	8	32½	31	21	2½	1nk	Bailey J D	L122	2.10	96-14	RdthFootnots122nk ScondofJun1207½ SilvrWgon1205½	Long drive, just up
29Nov03-8Aqu	fst	1⅛	:481	1:121	1:373	1:503	Remsen-G2	105	9	21	2½	1hd	16	13¾	Bailey J D	L122	*2.00	83-19	RdthFootnots1223¾ MstrDvid11610¾ WstVirgn116¾	When roused, kept bu
2Nov03-8Aqu	fst	1	:232	:461	1:102	1:362	Nashua-G3	92	1	1½	1½	1hd	12	12¼	Bailey J D	L118	2.90	83-20	RedthFootnots1182¼ Pddington1206½ WhoIsChrisG1163¼	Pace inside, clea
4Oct03-7Bel	fst	1$\frac{1}{16}$	:234	:481	1:133	1:44	Champagn-G1	68	6	2hd	2½	32½	512	615	Santos J A	L122	4.10	65-26	Birdstone1222½ ChpelRoyl1226¾ DshbordDrummr1222	Pressed inside, tire
7Sep03-6Bel	fst	7f	:223	:453	1:103	1:232	Alw 47000N1x	89	2	4	42	42¼	2½	12½	Bailey J D	116	*.45	83-20	Read the Footnotes1162½ Adage119nk Artie Schiller1194½	Rallied 4 wic
17Aug03-2Sar	fst	5f	:22	:451		:572	[S]Md Sp Wt 41k	93	4	6	1hd	1½	15½	19¼	Velazquez J R	119	*1.05	102-08	RedtheFootnotes1199¼ RodneyBy1197¼ Sptso119¾	Drew away when rouse

But was his performance in the Fountain of Youth too good? Not only did he turn in a career-best Beyer of 113, but he also engaged in a gut-wrenching duel with Second of June in which the two horses battled for nearly three-eighths of a mile. By every definition, his Fountain of Youth win was the result of a very strenuous effort.

Even though he had four weeks off after the Fountain of Youth, Read the Footnotes was a suspect horse in the Florida Derby. As it turned out, he bounced and he bounced hard. Read the Footnotes finished fourth, and his Beyer number dropped to 86, lousy for a Kentucky Derby contender. It can be argued that the horse was never again the same after the Fountain of Youth and that his strenuous race was the reason why. He ran just one more time, finishing seventh in the Kentucky Derby.

Initially, many otherwise savvy and sharp handicappers and horsemen dismissed the bounce theory, but it is now widely accepted. Top trainers such as Todd Pletcher, Kiaran McLaughlin, and Bobby Frankel have become believers and will often give their horses a month or more off after big efforts, hoping that will diminish the bounce factor. They are also among the big-name trainers who look at either The Sheets or Thoro-Graph.

Of course, not every horse bounces, and the likelihood of a bounce depends greatly on the situation. A veteran claimer who merely runs a few Beyer points better than his previous races may not bounce or bounce by much. It also helps to have substantial time off between races. A cheap horse that runs 20 Beyer points better than any previous start and comes back in a week is all but guaranteed to bounce and is a terrible bet. Horses running big numbers on the grass are less likely to bounce than horses running on the dirt. Fillies seem to be more likely to bounce than colts or geldings.

What about synthetic surfaces? When these new tracks were being introduced, the belief was that they would be kinder on horses' legs and less jarring. That, some experts said, would help horses recover faster and more smoothly after running hard races. If that turned out to be true, horses would be less likely to bounce after racing on synthetic tracks than after racing on conventional dirt tracks. Would it work out that way? That question is just one more reason why handicapping races run on synthetic tracks can be intimidating.

"What I can tell you is that it's made handicapping a whole lot more complicated," said Thoro-Graph's Jerry Brown when asked if horses were less inclined to bounce after synthetic-surface races.

Like so many other things when it comes to synthetic surfaces, in this area, the answers are not perfectly clear and may not be until tens of thousands of races have been run over the new surfaces. Nonetheless, the evidence suggests that the claims are true: Horses are less likely to bounce after racing over synthetic surfaces.

Let's examine the case of a horse named Knocker:

2 Knocker
Own: The Very Dry Stable
me Blue, White And Yellow Emblem, Yellow
RK D (58 8 10 6 .14) 2007: (58 8 .14)

B. f. 4 (Apr) FTKOCT04 $9,000
Sire: Evansville Slew (Slew City Slew) $2,500
Dam: Hard Knockin Lady (Hard Work)
Br: Billy Hay (Ky)
Tr: Tiller Robert P(46 10 9 5 .22) 2007:(46 10 .22)

L 121

Life	19	7	1	2	$170,183	85	D.Fst	11	2	1	2	$35,595	72
2007	2	1	0	0	$36,305	85	Wet(345)	1	0	0	0	$1,274	57
2006	13	5	1	0	$119,543	76	Synth	7	5	0	0	$133,314	85
WO	7	5	0	0	$133,314	85	Turf(271)	0	0	0	0	$0	-
							Dst(351)	8	2	0	2	$35,245	73

r07-10WO fst 7f ◈ :22^2 :45^2 1:09^4 1:23 3↑ Ⓕ OC 62k/N2x-N 85 4 7 3^1 2^1 2^2 4$^{1\frac{3}{4}}$ Wilson E L121 b 1.65 85- 07 ShesIndyMoney121$\frac{1}{2}$ ClssyFlower119$^{1\frac{1}{4}}$ FeistDr121^{no} Pressed outfinished 10
r07- 3WO fst 6$\frac{1}{2}$f ◈ :22^4 :45^3 1:11^3 1:18^1 3↑ Ⓕ Alw 62800N1x 80 5 2 3^{nk} 2$\frac{1}{2}$ 1^{hd} 1$^{5\frac{1}{2}}$ Wilson E L119 b *1.25 88- 13 Knocker119$^{5\frac{1}{2}}$ To the Brim119$\frac{3}{4}$ Anna'sBallerina120^2 Forced pace,bid,drvg 5
c06- 8WO fst 7f ◈ :22 :45 1:10^4 1:24^2 Ⓕ Clm c-(50-47.5) 76 8 7 6$^{2\frac{1}{4}}$ 4^{nk} 1^{hd} 1^{nk} Wilson E L119 b *1.85 - - *Knocker*119^{nk} Parrsboro Gold121^2 One Quiet Cat119^{nk} Bid 5w,vied,driving 10
aimed from Ye Weila for $47,500, Carey Julia Trainer 2006(as of 12/1): (49 11 5 7 0.22)
v06-10WO fst 7f ◈ :22^3 :45^2 1:10^4 1:24^3 Ⓕ Clm 37500(40-37.5) 74 3 10 5$^{1\frac{1}{4}}$ 3^2 2^1 1$^{1\frac{1}{4}}$ Wilson E L119 b *3.20 - - *Knocker*119$^{1\frac{1}{4}}$ You and Me Baby118$^{1\frac{3}{4}}$ Norbrook121$\frac{3}{4}$ Bid str,drove clr late 11
t06- 5WO fst 7f ◈ :22^3 :45^1 1:10^4 1:24^3 Ⓕ Clm 30000(32-30) 74 10 3 7$^{3\frac{1}{4}}$ 6$^{4\frac{3}{4}}$ 3$^{5\frac{1}{2}}$ 1$\frac{1}{2}$ Wilson E L119 b 6.55 - - *Knocker*119$\frac{1}{2}$ YouandMeBaby118^2 WgersTresure119$^{2\frac{1}{4}}$ Rallied,up late drvg 12
t06- 7WO fst 6f ◈ :23^2 :46^3 :59 1:11^4 Ⓕ Clm 25000(25-23.5) 73 4 5 3^1 4$^{2\frac{3}{4}}$ 3$^{2\frac{1}{2}}$ 1^{nk} Wilson E L121 b 4.00 - - *Knockr*121^{nk} NoCompromisng121$^{1\frac{1}{2}}$ *SnDgoNghts*118$^{1\frac{1}{2}}$ Rallied,up late drvg 6
p06- 2WO fst 6f ◈ :23 :46^2 :58^3 1:11^2 Ⓕ Clm 37500(40-37.5) 68 3 6 7$^{1\frac{3}{4}}$ 7$^{5\frac{3}{4}}$ 7^5 5$^{2\frac{1}{4}}$ Ramsammy E L119 b 4.35 - - Norbrook119^{hd} Undercover Lover116^{hd} NoCompromising114$\frac{1}{2}$ 3wd,all out 8
g06- 8WO fst 5f ⊡ :22^1 :46^4 :59^1 Ⓕ Clm 32000(32-30) 65 8 1 5$\frac{3}{4}$ 4$^{1\frac{1}{2}}$ 4^{nk} 2$^{1\frac{1}{4}}$ Ramsammy E L121 b *1.35e - - Whirly Carol121$^{1\frac{1}{4}}$ Knocker121$^{2\frac{1}{4}}$ Santa FeStar119$\frac{3}{4}$ 4wd,rallied,outgunned 8
y06- 8WO gd 7$\frac{1}{2}$f ⊡ :22^4 :45^4 1:11^3 1:32^3 Ⓕ Clm 37500(40-37.5) 57 2 4 1$^{1\frac{1}{2}}$ 1^2 2^1 5$^{3\frac{3}{4}}$ McAleney J S L119 b 6.45 - - Untouched113^{nk} PulMcCrtney116$^{1\frac{3}{4}}$ MostTresured118^{nk} Yielded str,tired 8
reviously trained by Von Hemel Don 2006(as of 6/7): (80 10 10 13 0.13)
n06- 6AP fst 6$\frac{1}{2}$f :22^3 :45^4 1:11^1 1:18 Ⓕ Clm 30000(30-25) 63 3 6 4^3 4^4 5^4 4$\frac{3}{4}$ Laviolette B S L122 b 5.50 84- 17 Special Fan119$\frac{1}{2}$ Heavenly Oil122^{hd} Lil Dove110^{hd} Angled out, late bid 7
y06- 7PrM fst 6f :22^1 :45^2 :58^1 1:11 3↑ Ⓕ Alw 25000N1x 63 5 6 6$^{6\frac{1}{4}}$ 5$^{3\frac{1}{2}}$ 5^6 4$^{5\frac{1}{2}}$ Thompson T J LB114 b 3.10 78- 20 ShowUstheCheck123^{nk} TrufflHony120$^{2\frac{1}{2}}$ *Nottgry*120$^{2\frac{3}{4}}$ Passed tiring rivals 8
y06- 7AP fst 1 :22^4 :45^4 1:11^2 1:37^2 Ⓕ OC 50k/N1x 52 1 4$^{2\frac{3}{4}}$ 4$^{1\frac{1}{2}}$ 4$^{1\frac{1}{2}}$ 5^7 5$^{12\frac{1}{4}}$ Laviolette B S L117 b 14.10 72- 15 Meadow Skippin116$\frac{1}{2}$ *Rolling Sea*121$^{4\frac{3}{4}}$ Hey Hey Hey115^5 Inside, weakened 7
KS: Mar31 WO tr.t 5f fst 1:01^3 B *2/4* **Mar22 WO ◈ 4f fst :48^4 B** *17/53* **Mar13 WO tr.t 4f fst :49^2 B** *9/22* **Mar4 WO ◈ 3f fst :38^2 B** *22/37*
INER: Synth(156 .18 $1.52) Sprint(282 .21 $1.63) Alw(69 .22 $1.72) J/T 2006-07 WO(82 .22 $1.59) J/T 2006-07(82 .22 $1.59)

The first time she raced over the Polytrack surface at Woodbine, which she clearly has an affinity for, she improved from a 65 Beyer to a 68. Yet, she didn't bounce.

The pattern kept repeating itself. On October 20, 2006, she ran what was then a career-best Beyer number of 74. Typically, after a horse runs a lifetime best number or, as the sheet guys say, a new lifetime top, he or she is very likely to bounce. But Knocker kept on getting better.

After taking the winter off, she returned in an allowance at Woodbine on April 8, 2007, and again ran a lifetime-best Beyer figure. Running back in just 14 days off a big number like that, she appeared a certainty to bounce in her next start. Even though she was beaten at odds of 8–5, she improved yet again, running an 85 Beyer. Still, she had won five straight and seemed to improve every step of the way. That's something you don't see too often on conventional dirt.

I did a random study of 400 horses that had run career-best Beyer figures on conventional dirt tracks and 400 that ran career-best numbers on synthetic surfaces. The idea was to see whether or not they bounced in their next race and, if so, how much they were affected by the big effort. In order to qualify, they had to run back within two months of their last race and could not switch to a grass surface for the next start.

I used a cross-section of horses, some from middle- and lower-tier tracks (Turfway, River Downs, Philadelphia Park), and some from top-tier tracks (Hollywood, Keeneland, and Belmont). I made every attempt to make the two sets of horses as similar as possible.

The bottom line: While horses are likely to regress after running big efforts on synthetic surfaces, the bounce factor is definitely less pronounced on synthetic tracks. Below are the results of the study of 400 horses coming back off career-best Beyer figures after racing on synthetic surfaces. The numbers reflect the change in their Beyer figures in their next race.

Faster Beyer	Slower Beyer	Same Beyer	Average Change
69	311	20	- 8.56

That 69 horses actually ran faster numbers after running what were career-best races is rather remarkable. Normally, you wouldn't expect a horse to improve after running the best race of his life, especially older horses who have already established their form.

Say a horse has run 20 times and ran the best race of his life, Beyer figure-wise, in his last start. If he could only run that number once in 20 starts, what are the odds he can do it again, or even improve on it? They're not good. When handicapping, it always pays to judge a horse off a lot more than just the last race.

Now, let's take a look at how 400 different horses fared after running career-best numbers on conventional-dirt surfaces.

Faster Beyer	Slower Beyer	Same Beyer	Average Change
20	366	14	- 11.94

Clearly, there's a difference, and it shows that hard races on conventional dirt tracks have more of an effect on horses than hard races on the softer, kinder synthetic tracks.

"The Polytrack is kinder to horses," said David England, one of the top trainers at Turfway. "Horses with minor problems—feet, ankle, knee problems—they just have an easier trip over the Polytrack. It's not just that they run well over it, but they come back well off it. They can come back much quicker to the next race. When you take them and run them on a hard dirt surface, they kind of jar themselves. It might take them three or four weeks to bounce back to where they're 100 percent for the next race. On Polytrack, they tend to come back a little quicker."

Though horses can't tell us in words that synthetic surfaces take less of a toll on their bodies, perhaps ex-jockey Gary Stevens can speak for them on this topic.

"I was one of the first riders to jump on the synthetic-surface bandwagon," he said. "With my history of knee problems, if I rode five races in a day my knee would swell up and I'd be in a lot of pain. My last couple of years of riding, there was no way I could ride in a lot of races in one day.

"I rode on the Kentucky Cup Day card at Turfway the first year they had Polytrack. I rode seven races that day and I could have ridden in seven more. I had no swelling in my knee. The difference was that the track wasn't jarring, so I wasn't hurting. If it made that big a difference to me, think of the difference it makes to the horse."

When the England-trained Beautiful Becke won a claiming race at Turfway on February 15, 2006, she was a prime bounce candidate in her next start. She hadn't run a 66 Beyer figure in nearly three years and she was coming back in just 15 days. On top of that, she was a cheap and inconsistent filly; they are prime bounce candidates.

Beautiful Becke
Own: Peach Melissa L

B. m. 8 (Mar)
Sire: Mecke (Maudlin) $3,500
Dam: Beautifully Bare (Naked Sky)
Br: Emerald Pastures Corp., Inc. (Fla)
Tr: Peach Melissa L(0 0 0 0 .00) 2007:(0 0 .00)

Life	56	8	13	10	$107,467	72	D.Fst	38	5	6	8	$68,98
2006	5	2	2	1	$11,980	68	Wet(302)	11	1	4	2	$24,97
2005	17	3	4	1	$39,145	63	Synth	6	2	3	0	$13,51
	0	0	0	0	$0	-	Turf(282)	1	0	0	0	$
							Dst(0)	0	0	0	0	$

29Jly06-5Far	fst	5f	1:031	3↑ⒻAlw 3000NC	–	1	4	51½	53½	44	3½	Benjamin C	LB131 fb	3.80	81- 22	ElusivWolf125no DonutsTomorrow124½ ButifulBck1311¾	Rallied well l
Previously trained by England David P 2005: (132 10 19 15 0.08)																	
2Mar06-2TP	fst	6f ◈	:231 :474 1:002 1:131	3↑ⒻClm 5000N2Y	68	8	5	51½	31	11½	13½	Leparoux J R5	L118 fb	*1.30	82- 17	Beautiful Becke1183½ *Babbling Girl*1231 Sassy Trisha1191	4 wide, driv
15Feb06-3TP	fst	6f ◈	:231 :472 1:003 1:144	3↑ⒻClm 5000N1Y	66	2	3	1hd	1hd	13	17½	Leparoux J R5	L114 fb	*1.10	74- 19	*Beautiful Becke*1147½ Of LegalAge1192¾ LazySahana112¾	Between, driv
28Jan06-1TP	fst	6f ◈	:232 :483 1:021 1:162	3↑ⒻClm 5000N1Y	45	5	8	85	86¾	63¼	21½	Felix J E	L123 fb	*2.30	64- 23	Bannerstone1211½ *Beautiful Becke*123no *Knotty Knows*121nk	Closed w
12Jan06-1TP	fst	6½f ◈	:231 :472 1:142 1:213	4↑ⒻClm 5000N1Y	46	8	3	41½	1hd	12	2½	Felix J E	L122 fb	3.10	76- 18	Derby Doll122½ Beautiful Becke1225¾ Miss Sandy113hd	6 path into t
29Dec05-7TP	fst	6f ◈	:223 :464 :593 1:132	3↑ⒻClm 7500(7.5-6.5)	42	4	8	65	57	88	77	Ouzts P W	L119 fb	3.50	- -	Marquet First119hd Kissinleaf119½ Mistress in Red119½	Gave w
11Dec05-4TP	fst	6½f ◈	:234 :484 1:144 1:212	3↑ⒻClm 7500(7.5-6.5)	60	6	6	41½	41¼	21½	22½	Ouzts P W	L119 fb	15.10	- -	SilverSilence1192½ BeautifulBecke1193¼ *Ghazd*1193¼	Inside run, no ma
18Nov05-4CD	fst	6½f	:23 :462 1:114 1:182	3↑ⒻClm 10000(10-9)	49	5	10	108½	109¼	67½	55½	Borel C H	L120 fb	46.90	74- 11	*Quick Advice*1132 Hay Daisy1202 Good as Silver120¾	8-9w lane,minor g
19Oct05-9Kee	fst	7f	:23 :471 1:134 1:28	3↑ⒻClm c-7500	34	7	3	43	43	45	68¼	Sarvis D A	L119 fb	*2.20	59- 24	SassyTrisha1192 MigratingZel1193 KnottyKnickles119½	Drift in bmp st
Claimed from Botty Kathleen for $7,500, Botty John T Trainer 2005(as of 10/19): (51 9 6 7 0.18)																	
7Oct05-4Kee	fst	6½f	:223 :47 1:132 1:202	3↑ⒻClm 15000	45	5	7	72¾	74¼	710	711¾	Sarvis D A	L120 fb	18.70	60- 25	Susan's Song120no Rose Fever1182¾ Gold Run Type1201¼	No ra
14Sep05-7Suf	fst	6f	:221 :453 :583 1:124	3↑ⒻAlw 17640N2X	59	4	7	77¾	68½	57½	46½	Bush W V	LB119 fb	5.40	75- 19	Funny Woman114hd Beautiful Lassie1196¼ Family Outing117nk	No fac
31Aug05-8Suf	slyS	6f	:212 :443 :574 1:121	3↑ⒻAlw 17640N2X	62	1	6	68¼	69½	69	55¼	Hole T M	LB119 fb	5.40	80- 18	NonefortheRod117hd Shmplicus1191¾ ShyAlon1193¼	Slow st, late spd 3
17Aug05-9Suf	fst	6f	:22 :451 :582 1:122	3↑ⒻAlw 17640N2X	49	3	6	69½	610	410	48¾	Hole T M	LB119 fb	4.60	75- 16	Ravidashinal1196¾ Caged Glory118¾ *None for the Road*1181¼	No thr
22Jun05-8Suf	fst	1	:232 :481 1:144 1:433	3↑ⒻAlw 17640N2X	34	4	713	87¼	76½	88¼	812¼	Arroyo E N	LB119 fb	3.60	58- 27	FamilyFavorite1191¾ *Unthinkble*1232¾ GoldenCoin119¾	2-path trns, no s
8Jun05-9Suf	fst	6f	:221 :453 :584 1:131	3↑ⒻAlw 17640N2X	59	7	7	811	610	37	2½	Hole T M	LB119 fb	3.80	79- 24	CpeCodRos116½ ButifulBck1195 Dncwithdolly1191¼	4wd top str,strong
25May05-6Suf	slyS	6f	:23 :474 1:003 1:132	3↑ⒻAlw 17640N2X	56	6	4	67½	64½	33½	21½	Hole T M	LB119 fb	8.20	77- 24	Killer App1231½ BeautifulBecke1195½ GoldenHair123hd	Rail turn, willir
11May05-5Suf	fst	6f	:222 :461 :591 1:122	3↑ⒻAlw 5000s	59	2	7	65½	54¾	31½	1nk	Hole T M	LB121 fb	2.60	84- 13	Beautiful Becke121nk Big Wolf1192¼ *Don't TellPapa*1216¾	Angled out, d
20Apr05-1Kee	fst	7f	:23 :474 1:143 1:283	4↑ⒻClm 10000	63	6	4	41½	3½	13	111¾	Sarvis D A	L118 fb	4.30	64- 20	*BeautifulBecke*11811¾ FuzzEDelight118no LeeGge1183	Drew off,stiff dr
8Apr05-4Kee	fst	6½f	:221 :452 1:123 1:201	4↑ⒻClm 10000	60	7	1	53¾	33½	34	28¼	Sarvis D A	L118 fb	14.60	65- 23	Nachen1188¼ *Beautiful Becke*118½ Lee Gage118½	5w,no bid,all
17Mar05-6OP	fst	1	:231 :472 1:14 1:423	4↑ⒻClm 5000	50	7	53	43	43	1½	12	Clemente A V	L118 fb	9.20	71- 27	BeautifulBecke1182 Wtchsusnrun1181¾ *KissforJulie*118½	Outside bid, cl
11Feb05-1OP	fst	6f	:222 :47 :594 1:123	4↑ⒻClm 5000N1Y	50	10	7	87¾	87	76¾	56½	Clemente A V	L122 fb	21.70	73- 16	Chocolate Rose1144 Whosoeverbelieveth1131½ Sallyhooks122½	Outs
28Jan05-1OP	wf	6f	:222 :471 1:002 1:132	4↑ⒻClm 5000N1Y	49	3	2	65	75¼	53½	34½	Clemente A V	L122 fb	20.80	71- 21	Texas Tree1223½ Biangood1181 Beautiful Becke122¾	Traffic, mild ra
23Nov04-7Suf	fst	6f	:22 :453 :583 1:113	3↑ⒻClm 12500(12.5-10.5)	44	8	2	811	810	89½	610¾	Lanci H L	LB123 b	42.00	79- 12	Ice Carnival1192¾ Laced Up1191½ *Knock Out Prospect*1213	W
25Oct04-7Suf	fst	6f	:223 :462 :592 1:13	3↑ⒻClm 10500(12.5-10.5)	39	9	9	96¼	98¾	611	613½	Hampshire J F Jr	LB119 b	10.40	69- 21	KnckOtPrspct1195¾ *AnswrthStrm*1192¾ LcdUp1191	Frct, unprepared st
9Oct04-7Suf	fst	6f	:221 :454 :591 1:134	3↑ⒻClm 12500(12.5-10.5)N3L	51	10	1	2½	2hd	2hd	11¼	Hampshire J F Jr	LB119 b	4.20	79- 19	Beautiful Becke1191¼ Shaye Alone118½ Cynthus1192	2wd duel, stiff dr
25Sep04-5Suf	fst	1	:244 :49 1:143 1:43	3↑ⒻClm 10500(12.5-10.5)N3L	46	4	21	21	21	21	34½	Hampshire J F Jr	LB117 b	4.60	72- 28	WithmomsImge1153¼ NncysSpirit1191¼ *BeutifulBecke*1175¾	Stalked, ti
14Sep04-8Suf	fst	170	:234 :484 1:151 1:464	3↑ⒻClm 12500(12.5-10.5)	43	2	1½	1½	2hd	45½	417¼	Hampshire J F Jr	LB119 b	6.10	55- 33	PrettyGlore1191¼ *ETPhonLur*1194¼ NncysSpirit11911¾	Rail duel, empty
20Jly04-6Suf	fst	6f	:222 :46 :591 1:133	3↑ⒻClm 12500(12.5-10.5)N3L	43	2	4	21	33½	22½	45	Hampshire J F Jr	LB119	*1.50	75- 18	Mountain Miss1191½ MezmerEyes119¾ Smarty'sMoney1192¾	Inside, wk
14Jun04-5Suf	fst	6f	:221 :461 :594 1:15	3↑ⒻClm 12500(12.5-10.5)N3L	39	5	3	21	22	22½	22	Hampshire J F Jr	LB119	3.50	71- 22	*Term's Love*1172 Beautiful Becke1192¼ Bare Beware119no	2nd b
15Nov03-1FL	sly	5½f	:223 :463 :593 1:062	3↑ⒻClm 8000(10-8)N3L	56	4	4	2½	21½	21	2¾	Frates D	L116	*1.30e	82- 20	My Girl Nessa120¾ Beautiful Becke1163¾ Hello Judy118hd	Second b
31Oct03-7FL	gd	6f	:222 :461 :59 1:13	3↑ⒻAlw 9800N3L	25	7	7	63¼	43	68	710¾	Frates D	L120 f	5.40	67- 19	AvaMris1202¼ CooColdBird116no *Thectbelongstome*1203	5 wide turn, ti
16Oct03-3Kee	fst	6½f	:223 :462 1:121 1:19	3↑ⒻClm 10000	57	1	1	2hd	21	21½	32¾	D'Amico A J	L118	7.20	75- 17	LexisMoon1161¼ QuietChrm1201½ BeutifulBck1181	Vied,inside,weake
23Sep03-7Suf	gd	*5f Ⓣ	:593	3↑ⒻAlw 17640N2X	47	5	7	77¾	79	78	66¾	Hampshire J F Jr	LB119	6.80	83- 10	BrnnnD1191¾ StrofCollnL123no Missstormytlntic1172¾	Inside, no mena
11Jun03-7Suf	wf	1	:234 :472 1:132 1:414	3↑ⒻAlw 17640N2X	46	5	21½	32½	32	33½	59¾	Hampshire J F Jr	LB119 f	3.70	74- 22	MissImgintion119½ TrnquilityBse1194½ AyresHll119nk	Loomed 3wd, fa
31May03-3Suf	fst	1	:241 :49 1:143 1:422	3↑ⒻAlw 17640N2X	66	6	1½	11	1½	11½	32¾	Hampshire J F Jr	LB119	4.30	78- 21	*Megan's Halo*1162½ Lyd's a Winnah114nk Beautiful Becke1192½	Weaker
14May03-4Suf	fst	6f	:23 :474 1:002 1:131	3↑ⒻAlw 17640N2X	52	7	2	52½	51¾	45½	411¾	Bermudez J E	LB121 f	3.40	69- 30	PentUpFantsy12111¼ *GloryBeGood*114no PrincessAttitude119½	5 wide tu
19Apr03-7Suf	fst	6f	:222 :47 1:00 1:131	3↑ⒻAlw 17640N2X	71	7	2	64½	54½	44	35½	Bermudez J E	LB121 f	7.70	75- 29	*SilvrtonBy*1235½ FortuntCitln119hd ButfulBck1213½	Rail trip, needed m
2Apr03-8Suf	gd	6f	:223 :463 :592 1:123	3↑ⒻAlw 17640N2X	62	2	4	54½	35	35½	37½	Bermudez J E	LB123 f	4.10	76- 25	*OuttLuck*1197¼ KnockOtProspct119nk BtflBck1231¾	Rail-3w turn, outfi
15Mar03-8Suf	gd	6f	:214 :454 :583 1:111	4↑ⒻAlw 16660N1X	72	8	1	76¼	64	41½	22	Bermudez J E	LB119 f	18.60	89- 11	[D]LydsWinnh1192 BeutifulBck119½ *SilvrtonBy*1211¼	Came wd 1/4, game
Placed first through disqualification																	
1Mar03-8Suf	fst	6f	:222 :47 1:001 1:14	4↑ⒻAlw 16660N1X	55	3	2	64	64¾	63¼	45¼	Bermudez J E	LB119 f	25.40	72- 24	Gem's Flora1194¼ Firing1191 Beautiful Lassie121no	Wide t
11Jan03-6Suf	fst	6f	:231 :47 1:00 1:13	4↑ⒻAlw 16660N1X	44	7	1	41¼	55	69	614	Parenti J Jr	LB119	9.60	68- 22	Silent Academy1236 Firing1192¼ Grotto119hd	Off rail, ti
30Dec02-5Suf	fst	6f	:23 :464 :593 1:131	3↑ⒻAlw 16660N2X	56	12	2	74¼	45½	33½	44¾	Phillips M5	LB112 f	18.50	76- 21	Seattle Ash1173 Locust Moon1191¼ Firing117½	Wide t
14Dec02-6Suf	sly	6f	:224 :481 1:013 1:153	3↑ⒻAlw 16660N1X	51	9	4	84¾	85¾	74½	63	Molinari E	LB117	19.70	66- 27	Key Water119hd *Seattle Ash*118½ Firing117nk	Wide tu
30Nov02-7Suf	my	6f	:22 :451 :581 1:113	3↑ⒻAlw 16660N1X	68	1	3	42	33	22½	23¼	Thompson W A	LB116	9.00	86- 15	OuttaLuck1163¼ BeautifulBecke1164¾ BrattleSqure1163¾	Inside, game
4Nov02-6Suf	fst	6f	:222 :464 1:001 1:133	3↑ⒻAlw 16660N1X	25	12	7	86	67	98½	1020¼	Hole T M	LB119	13.50	59- 30	Storybound1196¾ S. S.'s Gold Halo1214¼ Burden Creek1201	Wide tu
20Oct02-7Suf	fst	6f	:223 :47 1:002 1:14	3↑ⒻAlw 16660N1X	44	2	8	84¼	74½	95¾	910	Mascarte Magali	LB116	10.40	67- 23	BllthCt119nk JudyinDsgus1161¾ Lursluckychrm1191¼	Rail-3wd turn, wk
1Jly02-7Rkm	fst	6f	:232 :474 1:003 1:141	3↑ⒻAlw 12544N2L	36	4	2	1hd	1hd	2½	45½	Molinari E	LB114	*1.60	72- 18	Winlocslstduchss1171¾ *TrnquilityBs*1193 PrincssTrlingu119¾	Dueled, tir
17Jun02-7Rkm	fst	6f	:23 :464 :592 1:13	3↑ⒻAlw 12544N1X	62	7	1	1hd	31	33	31¾	Molinari E	LB116	*1.60	82- 16	Wood Lily1141¼ Versaltile119½ Beautiful Becke1164¾	3 wide tu
26May02-5Suf	fst	6f	:223 :471 1:001 1:133	3↑ⒻMd Sp Wt 12k	69	5	3	32	2½	15	19	Molinari E	LB116	2.30	79- 22	BeautifulBecke1169 *MissImagination*118¾ AvilbleDoll1162½	Drew off, dr
12May02-9Suf	my	1 ⊗	:241 :492 1:161 1:42	3↑ⒻMd Sp Wt 12k	44	1	2½	3½	31	22½	211	Molinari E	LB116	*.70	74- 15	Classlylilprincess12311 *BeautifulBecke*1163 *WhirlingCristl*12311¾	No ma
17Apr02-9Suf	fst	1	:251 :494 1:172 1:471	3↑ⒻMd Sp Wt 12k	34	4	1½	11	11	22	24½	Hampshire J F Jr	LB116	*.90	54- 32	*Bolton Nina*1234½ Beautiful Becke116¾ *Alpine Silver*1232¾	2nd b
8Apr02-2Suf	fst	6f	:231 :474 1:011 1:143	3↑ⒻMd Sp Wt 12k	55	3	3	32½	21½	21½	21	Arroyo E N5	LB111	2.60	73- 27	Honour1161 Beautiful Becke1115½ Guestbook1189	Late r
25Mar02-9Suf	fst	6f	:231 :48 1:002 1:13	3↑ⒻMd Sp Wt 12k	45	1	4	1½	2½	23½	211	Arroyo E N5	LB110	*1.60	71- 21	*Conwiss*11911 Beautiful Becke1105 Alpine Silver1231	Rail, easily 2nd b
9Mar02-7Suf	fst	6f	:224 :472 1:012 1:154	ⒻMd Sp Wt 12k	47	3	3	1hd	1hd	12	31¾	Arroyo E N5	LB118	11.20	66- 34	*AfricnPrincess*1241¼ *Honour*123½ BeutifulBecke1185½	Rail, clear, wknd l
26Jan02-6Suf	fst	6f	:223 :474 1:021 1:171	ⒻMd Sp Wt 12k	12	4	1	2½	22	33½	711½	Hampshire J F Jr	LB122	*2.00	50- 33	*Our Resurgence*1225¾ Judge Nancy1223 Early Launch122hd	2wide, stopp
4Jly01-3Rkm	fst	4½f	:222 :482 :553	ⒻMd Sp Wt 11k	18	1	3	12		1½	33	Aguirre E	119	15.00	82- 16	WildRosbud114½ TrnquilityBs1192½ ButifulBck1191¼	Pace, tired, bump

Beautiful Becke not only won her next start, but also improved her Beyer to a 68. The bounce believers took it on the chin that time. (Now, what the heck was she doing running in Fargo, North Dakota, in her next start, carrying 131 pounds?)

That horses are not bouncing as much on synthetic surfaces as they are on dirt tracks is no doubt among the reasons that the synthetic tracks are regularly producing large fields. Horses coming out of big efforts seem to be coming back with fewer aches and pains and are showing signs of life. Trainers see this, which will lead them to run their horses back in less time and run them more frequently over the course of a year.

The fact that racing over synthetic surfaces is easier on horses is surely among the reasons field sizes have been so impressive at the synthetic tracks.

Woodbine averaged 9.2 horses per race in 2006 after Polytrack was installed. The overall average for the year, which included several months of racing on two different dirt tracks, was 8.6 horses per race.

The figures from Turfway are a bit harder to read and were affected by several factors, including the fact that Turfway was running more races after Polytrack was installed because cards were rarely canceled. More racing will ordinarily mean smaller fields.

From Turfway, the easiest meet to compare on an apples-to-apples basis is the holiday meet, where the number of external factors affecting field size is minimal. At the last holiday meet run on the dirt, average field size was 9.9 horses per race. At the first holiday meet run over Polytrack, average field size rose to 10.4 horses per race.

The trend—larger fields for synthetic-surface races—continued. Arlington Park averaged 7.14 horses in 2006 on dirt and 8.19 in 2007 on Polytrack. Del Mar had 8.57 horses per race in 2006 on the dirt and 8.82 in 2007 on Polytrack.

Larger fields produce bigger betting handles, which may be a strong incentive for more tracks to go synthetic in the future. On the other hand, operators of conventional-dirt tracks may decide to wait a while and see how things develop, since some tracks with synthetic surfaces have experienced recent declines in handle. (Average daily all-sources handle—which includes on-track and off-track wagering, as well as full-card simulcasting—was down almost 11 percent at Keeneland's spring 2008 meeting, and Santa

Anita, which had significant weather and track-maintenance issues, was also down.)

I am of the opinion that the way modern trainers pamper their horses is ridiculous and good for no one, be that the horse, the owner or, especially, the sport. Synthetic tracks should help overcome this problem.

In many regards, this has been a case of perception over reality. Trainers don't run horses that often because they have convinced themselves that horses can't handle it. Hopefully, they'll now become convinced that horses can run more often if they've been training over synthetic tracks. It seems to already be happening.

Hall of Famer Bobby Frankel is one of those trainers who seems to tremble in fear at the prospect of running a horse back within six weeks of its last race or more than six times a year. But even Frankel is showing signs that he may change his M.O. in the synthetic era. Frankel ran a horse named Ramsgate three times in a 44-day period during the fall of 2006 at Hollywood Park. No worse for the wear, she won all three of those races.

Ramsgate
Own: Khaled Saud b

Ch. h. 5 (Apr)
Sire: Runaway Groom (Blushing Groom*Fr) $12,500
Dam: Sha Hearah (Dehere)
Br: Palides Investments N. V. Inc (Ky)
Tr: Frankel Robert J(0 0 0 0 .00) 2007:(566 123 .22)

Life	12	4	0	3	$145,496	103	D.Fst	5	1	0	2	$49,880
2007	3	0	0	1	$20,116	103	Wet(402)	1	0	0	1	$4,300
							Synth	5	3	0	0	$90,916
2006	6	3	0	1	$96,680	95	Turf(275)	1	0	0	0	$400
	0	0	0	0	$0	-	Dst(0)	0	0	0	0	$0

12May07-4Hol	fst	6f	◈	:21^{4} :44^{1} :56 1:09	3↑LsAnglsH-G3	72	5	4	5^{7½}	5^{7½}	5^{9½}	5^{13}	Flores D R	LB116	3.00	80-13	SailorsSunset116½ PeaceChant116^{1} NorthernSoldier116^{1}	Off rail, no rally
14Apr07-8Kee	fst	7f	◈	:23^{2} :46^{2} 1:09^{2} 1:21^{1}	3↑CmwlthBC-G2	93	4	7	6^{2¼}	6^{1¾}	6^{4¾}	7^{7}	Flores D R	L118	5.50	94-09	Silent Name118^{4} Lewis Michael118½ Steel Light118½	Between,never fired
17Feb07-9SA	fst	7f		:22^{2} :44^{2} 1:08 1:21	4↑SnCrlosH-G2	103	8	2	6^{4¾}	7^{6¼}	6^{5¼}	3^{2}	Flores D R	LB114	17.90	93-10	LatentHeat118^{nk} ProudTowerToo120^{1¾} Rmsgte114^{1½}	3wd,inside,best rest
17Dec06-8Hol	fst	7f	◈	:22^{3} :45^{3} 1:09^{1} 1:21^{1}	3↑OC 100k/N3x-N	94	1	3	1^{½}	1^{1}	1^{1}	1^{3}	Flores D R	LB122	*1.30	- -	Ramsgate122^{3} SwingYourPartner120^{no} Publiction122½	Inside, ridden out
26Nov06-4Hol	fst	7f	◈	:22 :44 1:08^{3} 1:21^{1}	3↑OC 62k/N2x-N	95	9	3	4^{3¾}	5^{3¾}	2^{1}	1^{1¾}	Flores D R	LB120	*2.00	- -	*Ramsgte*120^{1¾} SevenNtionArmy115^{1¼} Objective119^{nk}	4wd into lane,rallied
3Nov06-7Hol	fst	7f	◈	:23^{2} :46^{4} 1:10^{4} 1:22^{4}	3↑Alw 44948N1x	88	6	1	1^{1½}	1^{1}	1^{1½}	1^{2½}	Flores D R	LB122	*1.50	- -	*Ramsgate*122^{2½} Liver122¾ Will124^{1½}	Bit off rail,handily
30Sep06-8OSA	fm	1	Ⓣ	:22^{4} :46^{4} 1:10^{1} 1:33^{4}	3↑Alw 46000N1x	81	9	4^{1¾}	3^{1½}	4^{1¾}	3^{2}	7^{4½}	Nakatani C S	LB119	6.70	90-12	*Hyperbaric*116^{1} [D]Sea Battle120^{1} Spunky Harry116^{hd}	3wd bid,stdied late
Placed 6th through disqualification																		
20Aug06-9Dmr	fst	7f		:22^{1} :44^{2} 1:09^{1} 1:22^{2}	3↑Alw 83682N1x	79	1	6	1^{hd}	1^{hd}	3^{2}	6^{6¼}	Nakatani C S	LB121	3.30	87-12	*MidnightLute*121^{3½} WinningTctics119^{1¼} Brbrin122^{no}	Inside duel,weakened
28Jly06-7Dmr	fst	6f		:21^{3} :44^{2} :57 1:10	3↑Alw 61800N1x	89	12	2	6^{1¾}	5^{¾}	2^{hd}	3^{½}	Nakatani C S	LB120	16.90	88-17	*Sailors Sunset*118½ *Midnight Lute*120no Ramsgate120¾	5wd bid turn,held 3rd
28Dec05-4SA	fst	1$\frac{1}{16}$		:22^{4} :47^{1} 1:11^{3} 1:44^{2}	Alw 53200N1x	43	5	6^{3}	5^{1¼}	6^{3¼}	7^{13}	7^{24¾}	Desormeaux K J	LB118	*1.60	58-17	WnnRunner120^{1¾} TheFiveJs119^{2¼} SenstionlScore118^{4½}	Bumped brk,tired
12Nov05-7Hol	fst	7f		:22^{3} :45^{3} 1:10^{2} 1:22^{3}	Md Sp Wt 40k	85	6	2	2^{hd}	2^{½}	2^{½}	1^{2¼}	Desormeaux K J	LB120	4.20	90-10	Ramsgate120^{2¼} Presidential Cause120^{1½} Ironstar120^{1¾}	Dueled, drew clear
17Sep05-5Bel	gd	6f		:22^{1} :46 :58^{1} 1:11	Md Sp Wt 43k	76	5	8	9^{15}	9^{8¼}	6^{7}	3^{6½}	Chavez J F	L119	43.25	77-19	High Cotton119¾ Rondo119^{5¾} *Ramsgate*119^{nk}	Going well inside late

"The track at Hollywood at that time was really good and she came out of her races really good," Frankel said in mid-July 2007. "I don't think I could do that with her now because they're having some problems with that track. When the track is right, yes, horses come out of their races better.

"The problem is they're still figuring out how to take care of these tracks. There are a lot of questions that still need to be answered. But when these tracks are at their very best they're very good."

10

Derby Week 2008 and the Lessons It Taught Us

Synthetic surfaces were a big issue leading up to the 2008 Kentucky Derby. There had already been plenty of discussion on the topic the year before, when Keeneland's Blue Grass was run on Polytrack for the first time. Now that Santa Anita's preps also had gone synthetic for the 2008 season, handicappers, more than ever before, had to understand how to evaluate horses that had not only done well on synthetic surfaces but also had never before run on dirt.

Many scratched their heads when trying to deal with Colonel John, the Santa Anita Derby winner. He was a remarkably consistent horse who, coming into the Derby, had never run worse than first or second. But all six of his career starts had come on synthetic tracks.

To his credit, trainer Eoin Harty refused to use the switch to dirt as a possible excuse for Colonel John.

"Dirt is not an issue," the trainer said a few days before the Derby. "I thought he handled it well today. He trained on dirt as a 2-year-old and he handled it well then. I've been confident in him in that regard all along."

Colonel John
Own: WinStar Farm LLC

B. c. 3 (Mar)
Sire: Tiznow (Cee's Tizzy) $30,000
Dam: Sweet Damsel (Turkoman)
Br: WinStar Farm, LLC (Ky)
Tr: Harty Eoin G(0 0 0 0 .00) 2008:(53 7 .13)

Life	6	4	2	0	$825,300	95	D.Fst	0	0	0	0	$0
2008	2	2	0	0	$570,000	95	Wet(399)	0	0	0	0	$0
							Synth	6	4	2	0	$825,300
2007	4	2	2	0	$255,300	93	Turf(254)	0	0	0	0	$0
	0	0	0	0	$0	-	Dst(0)	0	0	0	0	$0

5Apr08-6SA	fst	1⅛ ◈	:47² 1:11³ 1:35² 1:48	SADerby-G1	**95**	5	64½	64	96¼	43	1½	Nakatani C S	LB122	2.60	94-10	ColonelJohn122½ BobBlackJack122¹ CoastGurd122²½	Drifted lane,rallie
1Mar08-7SA	fst	1⅛ ◈	:50 1:14¹ 1:38¹ 1:50	Sham-G3	**86**	4	2½	2hd	2hd	1hd	1½	Gomez G K	LB118	1.50	84-09	*Colonel John*118½ El GatoMalo120³ VictoryPete116¹	Dueled,led,held gam
22Dec07-9Hol	fst	1 1/16 ◈	:22³ :46² 1:10² 1:40⁴	CshClFut-G1	**93**	7	75¼	74¾	64½	42½	21¼	Nakatani C S	LB121	*2.30	103 -	IntoMischief1211¼ *ColonelJohn*121½ MssiveDrm121½	Pulled,split foes la
18Nov07-9Hol	fst	1 1/16 ◈	:24¹ :48 1:12¹ 1:42⁴	RealQuiet105k	**82**	1	63½	63½	53½	11½	13	Nakatani C S	LB119	*.70	94-11	Colonel John119³ Overextended117½ Cafe Tortoni115½	Came out str,cle
7Oct07-3OSA	fst	7f ◈	:23 :45⁴ 1:09⁴ 1:21²	Md Sp Wt 45k	**85**	2	6	41	31	3½	14½	Nakatani C S	LB120	*.40	- -	*Colonel John*120⁴½ *Usurp*120¹ Medjool120²	Re-bid 3wd,ridden o
19Aug07-6Dmr	fst	6f ◈	:23¹ :47³ 1:00² 1:13¹	Md Sp Wt 70k	**74**	12	1	42	32½	1hd	2½	Gomez G K	LB120	2.40	- -	EZsGentlemn120½ *ColonelJohn*120½ Ovrxtndd120³½	3wd bid,bumped,gam

WORKS: ●Apr27 CD 5f fst :57⁴ B *1/62* Apr20 SA ◈5f fst :59² B *3/45* Apr14 SA ◈4f fst :47² H *4/37* Mar31 SA ◈5f fst :58³ H *3/42* Mar25 SA ◈6f fst 1:13³ H *8/13* Mar19 SA ◈5f fst :59³ H *4/36*

Pyro presented still another problem. The Louisiana Derby winner, he was considered one of the top 3-year-olds in the country throughout the spring, but when he got to the Blue Grass at Keeneland, it was as if he had forgotten how to run. A horse who had always shown a powerful closing kick on dirt, he never picked up his feet when racing over Keeneland's Polytrack surface. It was his only career start over anything but dirt.

Pyro
Own: Winchell Thoroughbreds LLC

Dk. b or b. c. 3 (Feb)
Sire: Pulpit (A.P. Indy) $80,000
Dam: Wild Vision (Wild Again)
Br: Winchell Thoroughbreds, LLC (Ky)
Tr: Asmussen Steven M(0 0 0 0 .00) 2008:(889 210 .24)

Life	7	3	2	1	$1,056,718	105	D.Fst	4	3	1	0	$650,018
2008	3	2	0	0	$540,000	95	Wet(398)	2	0	1	1	$406,700
							Synth	1	0	0	0	$0
2007	4	1	2	1	$516,718	105	Turf(319)	0	0	0	0	$0
	0	0	0	0	$0	-	Dst(0)	0	0	0	0	$0

12Apr08-9Kee	fst	1⅛ ◈	:49 1:13 1:37¹ 1:49³	BlueGras-G1	**73**	7	84¾	86½	108¼	108½	1011½	Bridgmohan S X	L123	*1.00	79-10	Monba123nk Cowboy Cal1231¼ Kentucky Bear123¹	Off step slow,6w la
8Mar08-9FG	fst	1 1/16	:24 :48 1:13⁴ 1:44²	LaDerby-G2	**95**	3	44	44½	41¼	2½	13	Bridgmohan S X	L122	*.80	89-08	Pyro122³ My Pal Charlie122½ Yankee Bravo122¹	Awtd rm,splt,clrly b
9Feb08-9FG	fst	1 1/16	:24² :49² 1:14³ 1:44³	RisenStr-G3	**90**	7	105½	115¾	118¾	84¼	12	Bridgmohan S X	L116	*.90	88-08	*Pyro*116² Z Fortune122¾ *Visionaire*118½	Steered out,going aw
27Oct07-5Mth	slyˢ	1 1/16	:22³ :45² 1:09³ 1:42³	BCJuvnle-G1	**105**	6	86¾	811	78½	27	24¾	Bridgmohan S X	L122	4.10	89-07	*War Pass*1224¾ *Pyro*122¹² *Kodiak Kowboy*122¾	Fractious ,bumped b
6Oct07-7Bel	fst	1	:22⁴ :45³ 1:10¹ 1:36	Champagn-G1	**100**	5	88½	87¼	77½	37	21½	Bridgmohan S X	L122	32.00	84-21	*War Pass*1221½ Pyro1221½ Z Humor1225½	Game finish outsi
26Aug07-3Sar	gd	6f	:22¹ :45⁴ :57³ 1:10³	OC 75k/N1X-N	**77**	5	6	57	47	39	36¾	Bridgmohan S X	L120	2.70	80-16	*War Pass*1205½ Fidelio1201¼ Pyro120¹³	Lunged start, stumbl
7Jly07-2CD	fst	6f	:21² :44³ :56³ 1:09³	Md Sp Wt 47k	**81**	8	10	65	66½	22½	1no	Bridgmohan S X	L120	2.60	89-09	Pyro120no Luvandgo120³½ On the Rocks120½	Off rail, closed fa

WORKS: Apr28 CD 4f fst :49⁴ B *29/44* Apr7 Kee ◈4f fst :50³ B *25/28* Mar31 Kee ◈6f fst 1:14³ B *2/3* Mar24 Kee ◈5f fst 1:02² B *16/19* Mar17 FG 4f fst :53¹ B *34/38* Mar3 FG 4f fst :50⁴ B *37/57*

Was this a sign that something had gone amiss with Pyro or was he the type of horse who simply couldn't handle a synthetic surface? Trainer Steve Asmussen argued that, with the return to dirt, the old Pyro would be back for the Kentucky Derby.

"I'm pretty confident it was simply the surface," Asmussen said of Pyro's poor performance in the Blue Grass. "The horse came out of it in good shape. Watching the race, he wasn't going anywhere at any point. He wasn't himself from the first step."

Meanwhile, was Monba's Blue Grass win a sign that he was a viable Derby contender or just an indication that he loved Polytrack?

How about Adriano? He seemed to hate the dirt in the Fountain of Youth but loved the Polytrack in the Lane's End at Turfway. He represented another handicapping conundrum.

riano
Courtlandt Farms

Ch. c. 3 (May)
Sire: A.P. Indy (Seattle Slew) $300,000
Dam: Gold Canyon (Mr. Prospector)
Br: Courtlandt Farm (Ky)
Tr: Motion H. G(0 0 0 0 .00) 2008:(180 37 .21)

Life	7	3	1	0	$387,700	92	D.Fst	1	0	0	0	$0	70
2008	3	2	0	0	$309,300	92	Wet(434)	0	0	0	0	$0	–
2007	4	1	1	0	$78,400	78	Synth	2	1	0	0	$310,000	92
	0	0	0	0	$0	–	Turf(309)	4	2	1	0	$77,700	90
							Dst(0)	0	0	0	0	$0	–

08-12TP fst 1⅛ :47 1:122 1:3741:501 LanesEnd-G2 92 5 45 32 2hd 12 12½ Prado E S L121 4.80 90– 11 Adriano1212½ Halo Najib121¾ Medjool121¾ 4 wide, driving 11
)8–9GP fst 1⅛ :4731:112 1:3611:50 FntnOYth-G2 70 12 85¼ 86¾ 98¼ 1113 917 Castro E L116 14.70 71– 16 CoolColMn118½ ElysiumFlds1165¾ CourtVson1222¼ Steadied into 1st turn 12
)8–5GP fm 1 1/16 ⓣ :223 :454 1:0921:393 Alw 40500N1x 90 7 66 68½ 65¼ 12 16¾ Castro E L118 3.00 92– 15 Adriano1186¾ *Ablaze With Spirit*118no Yes He's Best1221 Drew off, driving 12
07–9Lrl fm 1 1/16 ⓣ :233 :482 1:13 1:424 LrlFuturty105k 75 10 1010108¾ 74½ 38 59¼ Dominguez R A L122 3.00 77– 16 *CowboyCal*1226¼ CasanovJck1222¼ TitnofIndustry122no 5wd 1/4, no factor 13
07–8Kee fst 1 1/16 :24 :493 1:1431:451 BrdrsFut-G1 78 8 105½ 74½ 74¾ 57 45¾ Dominguez R A L121 9.30 76– 22 WickedStyle1213¼ SlewsTiznow121nk OldMnBuck1212¼ 2-3w,mild run late 12
07–4Sar fm 1 1/16 ⓣ :233 :483 1:13 1:43 Md Sp Wt 63k 75 8 84¾ 72¼ 62¼ 1hd 13 Dominguez R A L118 *1.45 82– 10 Adriano1183 Big Al1181½ Celestial Comet118½ Bumped stretch, wide 9
07–6Sar fm 1 1/16 ⓣ :232 :471 1:12 1:43 Md Sp Wt 63k 72 1 65½ 53½ 52¼ 2½ 2¾ Dominguez R A 118 8.80 81– 22 Il Girasole118¾ *Adriano*118¾ Big Al118¾ Good finish outside 10
KS: Apr27 CD 5f fst 1:004 B *21/62* Apr20 CD 5f fst 1:014 B *18/39* Apr13 CD 4f fst :50 B *29/42* Mar14 PmM ⓣ 6f fm 1:12 H *1/3* ●Feb16 PmM 6f fst 1:123 H *1/4* Feb9 PmM 5f fst 1:01 H *3/19*

Colonel John, Adriano, Monba, and Pyro were among the reasons so many handicappers, reporters, and columnists were calling this Derby one of the most mystifying races they had ever tried to analyze. The quirky finish of the Blue Grass, in which several good horses underperformed, also led many to trash synthetic-surface racing, saying the results of the Blue Grass proved just how unpredictable it was.

As far as synthetic surfaces go, the 2008 Derby answered some questions and left others unresolved. But, by and large, it again proved the point that most horses run about the same on synthetic surfaces as they do on dirt tracks.

The two best examples of this were Pyro and Colonel John.

As it turned out, Asmussen and anyone else who liked Pyro in the Derby was wrong about the Blue Grass. Just as he had in the Blue Grass, Pyro turned in another clunker in the Derby, finishing eighth.

Colonel John didn't show much in the Derby, either. Was that because he disliked the dirt surface? It's doubtful. Colonel John was the best of a mediocre lot coming out of California. In fact, the Beyer figure he got for finishing sixth in the Derby, an 88, was better than the 86 Beyer he got for winning the Sham Stakes.

Like the Derby, the Kentucky Oaks presented some handicapping puzzles, thanks to synthetic tracks. In particular, Proud Spell, the 3–1 favorite, was somewhat difficult to gauge. She was coming off a subpar race in the Ashland at Keeneland. Finishing third, she earned an 83 Beyer, 16 points below the figure she earned when winning the Fair Grounds Oaks on the dirt.

Some reasoned that she must have hated the Polytrack at Keeneland. When she romped by five lengths in the Oaks, those people seemed to be proven right. I'm not so sure about that. Unlike Pyro, who was dismal in the Blue Grass, Proud Spell at least ran creditably in the Ashland. Nothing about that race suggested that she had gone seriously off form. Was her defeat there the result of a dislike for Polytrack or simply the case of a horse having an off day? I vote for the latter.

Proud Spell
Own: Jones Brereton C

B. f. 3 (May)
Sire: Proud Citizen (Gone West) $25,000
Dam: Pacific Spell (Langfuhr)
Br: Brereton C. Jones (Ky)
Tr: Jones J. L

Life	8	5	2	1	$1,290,110	99	
2008	4	2	1	1	$681,340	99	
2007	4	3	1	0	$608,770	94	
D.Fst	5	4	1	0	$488,770		
Wet(352)	2	1	1	0	$751,340		
Synth	1	0	0	1	$50,000		
Turf(270)	0	0	0	0	$0		

2May08-10CD	slyS	1⅛	:484 1:124 1:371 1:50	(F)KyOaks-G1	99	7	31	21	21	1½	15	Saez G	L121	*3.40	86-15	Proud Spell1215 Little Belle121¾ Pure Clan121hd Off inside, drivinc
5Apr08-9Kee	fst	1 1/16 ◈	:244 :492 1:132 1:433	(F)Ashland-G1	83	5	42½	3½	42	43½	32¾	Saez G	L121	1.90	87-12	LittleBelle121nk Bsharpsonata1212½ ProudSpell121hd Broke bit awk,dug
8Mar08-8FG	fst	1 1/16	:242 :48 1:124 1:44	(F)FGOaks-G2	99	2	21	21	21½	21	12¼	Saez G	L121	1.90	91-08	Proud Spell1212¼ IndianBlessing12111½ Acacia1219¼ Ranged up, clear late
9Feb08-8FG	fst	1 1/16	:234 :47 1:112 1:433	(F)Slvbltd-G3	97	5	54½	43½	45½	24	21	Saez G	L122	2.30	92-08	IndinBlessing1221 ProudSpell1221¼ HighestClss1164½ Esd ot,rllied,lte gai
27Oct07-4Mth	slyS	1 1/16	:232 :462 1:103 1:443	(F)BCJuvFil-G1	89	10	31	32½	34	36	23½	Saez G	L119	9.40	80-07	IndinBlessing1193½ ProudSpll119½ BckstRhythm1194 Drifted out 3/16 po
15Sep07-6Bel	fst	7f	:222 :454 1:111 1:241	(F)Matron-G2	82	3	1	55¼	53½	2hd	14¼	Saez G	L119	*1.70	80-11	Proud Spell1194¼ Armonk1192¼ Dagger1191½ Came wide, drew away
25Aug07-7Del	fst	6f	:213 :442 :563 1:09	(F)WhtClyCrk57k	94	3	3	32½	31½	11	15	Saez G	L117	*1.00	94-13	ProudSpll1175 ExtrSxyPsychc1197¼ TusclmRd1178¾ Drew off when rous
30Jly07-1Del	fst	5f	:22 :453 :572	(F)Md Sp Wt 41k	76	6	4	43	31	1hd	1½	Saez G	118	5.20	100-11	ProdSpll118½ ShrffsChoc11811¼ KlondkMoon1191¼ Outgamed stablemat

WORKS: Apr27 CD 5f fst :582 B 3/62 Apr20 Kee ◈4f fst :501 B 28/39 Mar30 Kee ◈5f fst 1:003 B 12/23 Mar3 FG 5f fst 1:03 B 12/28 Feb27 FG 4f fst :481 B 2/33

It's also interesting to look at Little Belle, the Ashland winner. She scored an upset in that race at odds of 16–1, winning her first graded stakes race. Did that make her a synthetic sensation? Apparently not. She finished second in the Kentucky Oaks and made a three-point improvement in her Beyer figure, from an 88 to a 91.

Little Belle
Own: Godolphin Racing LLC

B. f. 3 (Apr)
Sire: A.P. Indy (Seattle Slew) $300,000
Dam: Dubai Belle (Mr. Prospector)
Br: Darley (Ky)
Tr: McLaughlin Kiaran P

Life	7	3	2	1	$519,395	91	
2008	5	3	2	0	$511,495	91	
2007	2	M	0	1	$7,900	76	
D.Fst	3	1	1	1	$64,060		
Wet(433)	3	1	1	0	$145,335		
Synth	1	1	0	0	$310,000		
Turf(310)	0	0	0	0	$0		

2May08-10CD	slyS	1⅛	:484 1:124 1:371 1:50	(F)KyOaks-G1	91	6	21	41½	32	32½	25	Maragh R	L121	5.70	81-15	Proud Spell1215 Little Belle121¾ Pure Clan121hd Inside to final 1/16
5Apr08-9Kee	fst	1 1/16 ◈	:244 :492 1:132 1:433	(F)Ashland-G1	88	2	11½	1hd	1½	2hd	1nk	Maragh R	L121	16.10	90-12	LittleBelle121nk Bshrpsont1212½ ProudSpell121hd 2-3w,headed,gamely,d
24Feb08-8Aqu	fst	1 1/16 ⊡	:232 :473 1:122 1:441	(F)Busher81k	88	5	2½	2½	2½	1½	12¾	Maragh R	L116	3.65	90-15	LittleBelle1162¾ SweetVendett11611 DrlingMoniqu116¾ Pressed pace, cle
1Feb08-4Aqu	slyS	170 ⊡	:232 :491 1:152 1:46	(F)Md Sp Wt 49k	76	3	53½	41¼	31½	1½	13½	Maragh R	L120	*1.00	67-37	Little Belle1203½ Serious Vow1206½ Fostoria1201¼ Steadied, wide mo
13Jan08-2Aqu	fst	170 ⊡	:223 :461 1:132 1:434	(F)Md Sp Wt 49k	68	3	410	314	31½	23	21¾	Maragh R	L119	*1.40	76-18	RoughWter1191¾ LittleBelle1193½ SeriousVow1194 Stayed on well stretc
25Nov07-4Aqu	fst	1	:232 :472 1:122 1:372	(F)Md Sp Wt 53k	76	3	73¾	64½	53¼	34	33½	Maragh R	L120	*2.25	71-28	MissStonestreet120nk ColorMeUp1203¼ LittleBell1206 Good finish outsi
28Oct07-2Aqu	gd	6f	:224 :462 :583 1:111	(F)Md Sp Wt 52k	72	1	7	77¾	57	44	42	Garcia Alan	L120	5.10e	84-17	Atash1201½ Timber Trick120½ Game Face120hd Belatedly outsic

WORKS: Apr25 Kee ◈4f fst :461 B 2/42 Apr18 Kee ◈4f fst :472 B 16/43 Mar29 Bel tr.t 4f fst :49 B 30/68 Mar22 Bel tr.t 4f fst :474 H 15/172 Mar14 Bel tr.t 4f fst :49 B 23/54 Feb17 Bel tr.t 4f fst :50 B 24/53

It wasn't just the Oaks and Derby that had horseplayers confused. All week, handicappers were struggling with synthetic-track issues, not uncommon for that time of year, since so many horses come into the Derby off races at Keeneland and Turfway.

Take a look at Forest Attack, who showed up in an allowance race on Derby Day.

rest Attack
: Scarlet Stable

Dk. b or b. c. 4 (Mar)
Sire: Forestry (Storm Cat) $100,000
Dam: Joy Valley*Brz (Ghadeer*Fr)
Br: Aaron U. Jones & Marie D. Jones (Ky)
Tr: Maker Michael J(0 0 0 0 .00) 2008:(98 31 .32)

Life	9	5	2	0	$75,700	98	D.Fst	1	0	0	0	$0	–
2008	4	2	2	0	$51,820	98	Wet(388)	1	0	1	0	$14,200	96
							Synth	7	5	1	0	$61,500	98
2007	5	3	0	0	$23,880	82	Turf(338)	0	0	0	0	$0	–
	0	0	0	0	$0	–	Dst(0)	0	0	0	0	$0	–

y08–3CD	gd	7f		:22 :442 1:083 1:221	3↑OC 80k/N$Y-N	96	8	2	31	31	21	2nk	Leparoux J R	L120 b	4.50	91–08	First Defence120nk Forest Attack1202 Vicarian1223¼	3 wide, slow gain	8
r08–8TP	fst	6½f	◈	:223 :451 1:094 1:161	3↑OC 40k/N2X-N	97	3	3	33½	32	1½	12¾	Lebron V	L118 b	*.70	95–17	Forest Attack1182¾ *Foster*1184½ Sir Hillary1182	Lost footing start	6
b08–8TP	fst	6f	◈	:221 :453 :573 1:093	4↑Alw 22180N1X	98	7	2	52½	1hd	12	17½	Lebron V	L118 b	*1.00	94–18	*Forest Attack*1187½ Jazz Hall1184¾ Flaming Glory1185½	3 wide, driving	7
n08–10TP	fst	5½f	◈	:221 :46 :582 1:044	4↑Alw 23425N1X	76	3	8	55	32½	2½	21	McKee J	L118 b	*1.40	91–14	Foster1181 *Forest Attack*1182¾ Flaming Glory118½	Bothered start	8
c07–4TP	fst	6f	◈	:22 :444 :57 1:094	3↑Clm 15000(15–10)N3L	82	3	4	3nk	21	11	15¾	Hernandez B J Jr	L123 b	*1.50	93–10	Forest Attack1235¾ *My Tune*1193¼ Katzmetic115nk	Fast pace, drew off	7
v07–3TP	fst	6f	◈	:221 :46 :581 1:104	3↑Clm 15000(15–10)N2L	68	5	7	1hd	1hd	1hd	1hd	Hernandez B J Jr	L118 b	*1.50	88–12	*ForestAttack*118hd *MrFrnkieC*1182¼ SwizzleInn1175¼	Batted hard, prevailed	11
v07–7CD	fst	6f		:212 :443 :57 1:094	3↑Clm 30000(30–25)N2L	–0	1	10	1012	812	1025	1042	Mena M	L119 b	*1.50	46–12	D *OneLuckyDevil*1221 MojitoMn1211½ SterlingHt1213½	Clip heels, lost iron	10
laced 9th through disqualification																			
g07–6AP	fst	6f	◈	:23 :454 :572 1:094	3↑Md c-(40–35)	79	1	4	11	13	16	13½	Campbell J M	L121 b	6.20	- -	Forest Attack1213½ DrinkstoGo1215 OneLuckyDevil121½	Clear, ridden out	9
laimed from Jones, Aaron U. and Marie D. for $40,000, Pletcher Todd A Trainer 2007(as of 8/23): (811 201 108 129 0.25)																			
g07–8AP	fst	6f	◈	:214 :442 :562 1:084	3↑Md Sp Wt 34k	62	4	9	67	69	510	414	Douglas R R	L121	6.00	- -	*Shrewd Operator*1218 Thirsty Giant1211 *Exhort*1215	Evenly	9

RKS: ●Apr25 CDT 5f fst 1:002 B *1/4* Apr16 CDT 4f fst :49 B *4/6* Feb25 CDT 3f my :351 B *1/3* ●Feb17 CDT 5f sly 1:022 B *1/5* Feb7 CDT 4f my :482 B *3/7*

His one previous experience on a traditional dirt surface had not been a good one. He was beaten 42 lengths in a $30,000 claimer at Churchill. Was it an indication that he didn't like dirt tracks? Not at all. He ran just fine when entered back on dirt.

"The reason that race looks bad on paper is because he clipped heels that day," trainer Mike Maker said. "The rider lost his stirrups and he's lucky he didn't go down in that race. If you watch the head-on replay, he was probably about three to six inches away from the ground. He had a good winter, had run some strong races, and has the pedigree to be a good one. I wasn't surprised when he ran so well in that race at Churchill."

Another horse who might have caused some problems for handicappers was Lenawee. Out of nowhere, she ran a much-improved race at Keeneland in her synthetic debut, winning a maiden event at odds of 9–1 while improving 30 Beyer points. Was she just a synthetic freak? Her next race proved that wasn't the case.

nawee
: Bloch Randall, Milner, Phil, Basso, K

Gr/ro. f. 3 (Mar)
Sire: Albert the Great (Go for Gin) $4,000
Dam: Butterfield (Unbridled's Song)
Br: Phil Milner & Randy Bloch (Ky)
Tr: Wilkes Ian R(0 0 0 0 .00) 2008:(86 11 .13)

Life	5	2	0	0	$74,432	82	D.Fst	2	0	0	0	$2,000	57
2008	4	2	0	0	$73,244	82	Wet(353)	2	1	0	0	$41,177	82
							Synth	1	1	0	0	$31,255	81
2007	1	M	0	0	$1,188	48	Turf(293)	0	0	0	0	$0	–
	0	0	0	0	$0	–	Dst(0)	0	0	0	0	$0	–

y08–2CD	myS	6f		:204 :44 :563 1:10	ⒻAlw 60910N1X	82	7	8	86¼	54	2½	12½	Theriot H J II	L122	16.30	87–13	Lenawee1222½ Looney Lynda118nk GrandObsession1181	Bold 6 wide move	8
r08–6Kee	fst	6f	◈	:222 :461 :582 1:103	ⒻMd Sp Wt 50k	81	9	7	95¼	51¼	1hd	12½	Theriot H J II	L120	9.40	88–10	*Lenawee*1202½ Happy Point120½ *Pious Ashley*1201	Off slow,6w lane,drv	9
r08–7GP	fst	6f		:221 :451 :573 1:103	ⒻMd Sp Wt 40k	51	2	10	97¾	87	710	612¼	Smith A E	L121	9.20	77–12	Halloween Witch1216½ Nursery Rhyme1211¼ *Shopit*1211¾	Off slowly	10
b08–8GP	fst	6f		:22 :444 :572 1:104	ⒻMd Sp Wt 40k	57	7	4	31	31	55¼	56	Castellano J J	L121	*2.60	82–10	Grand Breeze1212¼ Quiet Harbor121¾ Move It121¾	Steadied early stretch	12
laced 4th through disqualification																			
v07–4CD	gd	6½f		:223 :463 1:114 1:183	ⒻMd Sp Wt 42k	48	7	10	97¾	62¾	44½	59	Borel C H	120	3.70	74–20	*Lady Hillingdon*1206 Raposa120hd Wriggle1201½	Sluggish start,squeeze	10

RKS: Apr27 CD 5f fst 1:022 B *45/62* Apr21 CD 5f fst 1:021 B *12/23* Apr1 CD 5f my 1:013 B *4/9* Mar21 PmM Ⓣ 5f fm 1:04 B(d) *12/15* Mar4 PmM 4f fst :492 B *13/33* Feb26 PmM 5f fst 1:02 B *10/11*

Lenawee also served to validate a point made in Chapter 9—that the bounce factor seems to be reduced by racing on synthetic tracks. She didn't regress after running a big number in the Keeneland maiden win.

As is usually the case, most synthetic shippers don't really throw you curve balls. Showing up on Kentucky Oaks Day, Honest Pursuit was pretty typical of the type of horse a Churchill player has to deal with. She had run well on the dirt, whether it was fast or sloppy. She handled Keeneland with aplomb in her first start over a synthetic surface and she did the same when winning a Churchill allowance race by 1¼ lengths on a dry track. Like most horses out there, her form is pretty much the same on dirt as it is on a synthetic track.

Honest Pursuit
Own: Overbrook Farm

Dk. b or b. f. 3 (Jan)
Sire: Storm Cat (Storm Bird) $300,000
Dam: Honest Lady (Seattle Slew)
Br: Juddmonte Farms Inc. (Ky)
Tr: Stewart Dallas(0 0 0 0 .00) 2008:(194 29 .15)

Life	6	2	2	0	$91,585	83	D.Fst	3	1	1	0	$50,190
2008	4	2	1	0	$81,385	83	Wet(420)	2	0	1	0	$10,140
							Synth	1	1	0	0	$31,255
2007	2	M	1	0	$10,200	62	Turf(357)	0	0	0	0	$0
Cd	2	1	0	0	$42,390	80	Dst(408)	0	0	0	0	$0

2May08–2CD fst 1 1/16 :243 :491 1:134 1:442 3↑ⒻAlw 62970N1x 80 6 43 42 3nk 12 1 1¼ Albarado R J L117 *1.40 84–11 HonestPursuit1171¼ FrenchKiss1162¾ Hndlthtruth1241 4 wide bid, drivin
4Apr08–6Kee fst 1⅛ ◈ :503 1:152 1:391 1:511 ⒻMd Sp Wt 50k 83 7 2½ 41½ 31 12½ 16½ Albarado R J L120 5.00 83–19 *Honest Pursuit*1206½ Splendorella120¾ *Vanquished*1202½ Rated,drew off,dv
22Feb08–8FG slyS 140 :253 :504 1:161 1:422 ⒻMd Sp Wt 39k 71 8 52½ 43½ 42½ 33 2½ Leparoux J R L121 *1.10 84–12 Acacia121½ *Honest Pursuit*121hd *Storm Mesa*1218 Up for second midtrac
26Jan08–3FG slyS 1 ⊗ :241 :49 1:152 1:414 ⒻMd Sp Wt 40k 71 1 32 31½ 41¼ 31½ 15½ Leparoux J R L121 *1.10 76–24 ⒹHonstPursut1215½ VvcosVvn121¾ Rpprnc121hd Angld out,bothered fc
Disqualified and placed 4th
27Dec07–6FG fst 6f :214 :453 :581 1:113 ⒻMd Sp Wt 40k 62 1 7 52½ 42½ 31½ 22½ Albarado R J L120 *1.30 83–13 BrittnsButy1202½ HonstPursuit1203¼ QuitMovr1201 Split foes, up for 2n
9Nov07–7CD fst 6f :211 :451 :571 1:101 ⒻMd Sp Wt 42k 57 12 1 64½ 43 45 49¼ Desormeaux K J L120 4.50 77–14 *Keep the Peace*1204½ *Bella Roja*1202¼ *Pretty Carina*1202½ 4-5w,flattened ou

WORKS: Aug1 CD 4f fst :492 B *13/39* Jly24 CD 3f fst :36 B *3/18* Jly15 CD 3f fst :372 B *3/8* May25 CD 5f fst 1:023 B *25/32* May17 CD 4f fst :493 B *16/52*

11

What's a Polypropylene?

The first time I ever saw a synthetic racing surface was on a visit to Michael Dickinson's farm in the town of North East, Maryland. Dickinson had just finished building a training center to top all training centers—a horse heaven that he felt created every possible advantage for his runners. Nothing had been overlooked. There are Ritz-Carltons that don't have as many amenities.

Of course, Dickinson, a perfectionist, wanted his training center to have the best racing surfaces in the world. His gallops included several turf courses, each one tailored to handle a different type of weather—droughts, deluges, and everything in between. But what Dickinson was most proud of was something he called Tapeta, which is the Latin word for *carpet.*

He told amusing stories about how he had worked long and hard to develop the perfect racing surface. He said his first experiment was so flawed that his employees labeled the track Michael's Mistake. At last, though, he had created a track he was certain was a major improvement over conventional dirt surfaces. It never got wet or sloppy, he said, adding that it would cut down dramatically on the number of injuries his horses might sustain.

To the naked eye, though, the stuff looked ridiculous, like something your 2-year-old might create given a sandbox, a shovel, and some piles of trash.

Tapeta wasn't nearly as dark as a normal track. Instead of being brown, it was grayish. Even stranger were the various things that were in the track. There were cut-up pieces of rubber that looked like parts of old tires. If that weren't odd enough, the mixture also included shreds of what appeared to be pieces of kids' balloons. They were red, yellow, green, blue, and orange.

The people who manufacture synthetic tracks guard their recipes as if they were the formula for Coca-Cola, and Dickinson wouldn't tell me what the deal was with the balloons or anything else that was in the track. For all I knew, there were even parts of a kitchen sink in there. To this day, he still won't reveal the content of the track. He says it is "53 percent sand, 5 percent rubber, and 42 percent secret recipe."

But he did perform a rather impressive demonstration. He took a large chunk of the surface and dumped a bucket of water into it. Within seconds, the stuff was bone dry.

So what is a synthetic surface? More or less, it's sand with a lot of junk thrown in. *Daily Racing Form* writer Jay Privman once joked that synthetic surfaces are racing's version of a toxic-waste dump.

From the Polytrack website, we can see that the mixture includes a "unique blend of polypropylene fibers, recycled rubber and silica sand covered in a wax coating." Some of the synthetic tracks also have something called jelly cable in them, which is the plastic stuff that covers copper wiring. According to one report, Martin Collins, the manufacturer of Polytrack, has used windshield-wiper blades in his tracks.

What, no balloons?

Having gotten a C in Mr. Walsack's 10th-grade chemistry class, I can't tell you what polypropylene is. But Wikipedia can. Here's what it has to say about the stuff: "Polypropylene or polypropene (PP) is a thermoplastic polymer, made by the chemical industry and used in a wide variety of applications, including packaging, textiles (e.g. ropes, thermal underwear and carpets), stationery, plastic parts and reusable containers of various types, laboratory equipment, loudspeakers, automotive components and polymer banknotes. An additional polymer made from the monomer propylene, it is rugged and unusually resistant to many chemical solvents, bases and acids."

Old racetrackers like to say of certain horses that they can run over anything, even "broken bottles." They might now want to say, "My horse can run over anything, even loudspeaker parts."

The basic idea behind all synthetic tracks is to produce a surface that is water-resistant, produces a low amount of kickback, and is safer for horses and, in turn, jockeys, than normal dirt tracks. Among the reasons the synthetic tracks dry out within seconds is because they all have vertical drainage systems. The water flows straight down. On conventional tracks there is a slope, and the water drains toward the inside rail, which is the main reason normal tracks can be uneven and have biases.

As long as synthetic tracks accomplish their goals—and it appears that they do—it doesn't matter what they put in the mixtures. Maybe horses love racing over chewed-up old balloons. Handicappers, however, should be more concerned about the differences between the various *types* of synthetic tracks.

By the end of 2007, there were three different kinds of synthetic tracks in use in North America. Polytrack had been installed at Keeneland, Arlington, Turfway, Woodbine, and Del Mar, and its British-based manufacturer, Martin Collins Surfaces and Footings, had formed a partnership in North America with Keeneland Association, the prestigious, wealthy, and influential racetrack and Thoroughbred-auction company located in Lexington, Kentucky.

Hollywood Park and Santa Anita were using Cushion Track, while Golden Gate Fields in northern California had gone with Tapeta Footings. Presque Isle Downs, a new racetrack in western Pennsylvania that opened during the fall of 2007, had also installed Tapeta. So had the Fair Hill Training Center in Maryland, which was Barbaro's home for much of his life.

As of July 2008, no other North American racetracks had announced plans to go synthetic, although a new player had emerged. When Santa Anita's Cushion Track began to have serious drainage problems earlier that year, the Australian company Pro-Ride was called in to repair the surface. A few months later, Santa Anita announced that the track would undergo a total renovation and was switching to a Pro-Ride mixture.

"The project will include completely removing the existing asphalt base, adding a new grid base material, and treating the entire track with binder and fiber," according to a press release issued June 23. Track president Ron Charles added, "We have all decided this would be the best course of action for Santa Anita to take with the Breeders' Cup committed to coming here over the next two years."

On its website, Pro-Ride boasts that it has "the world's only 2-phase cushioning capability and is backed by an Australian government initiative through AusIndustry." Pro-Ride also claims that the official track condition for its surface will be "good to dead." Apparently, the main difference between Pro-Ride and the other synthetic tracks is that Pro-Ride doesn't use much wax.

"They really run over the top of it, instead of going into it," jockey Aaron Gryder said after riding over Pro-Ride. "It's so different than Cushion Track, Polytrack, or Tapeta."

The Ocala Breeders' Sales Company had announced that it will convert its one-mile track to a synthetic surface called Safetrack, which is manufactured by the English company Andrew Bowens Ltd. Horses preparing for the Ocala 2-year-old sale will work over the synthetic surface, and a day of non-parimutuel races is also held every winter in Ocala for OBS graduates.

In France, all-weather racing is held over a synthetic surface at Deauville that is called ViscoRide, which is manufactured by still another Australian company.

In Australia and New Zealand, synthetic tracks such as Pro-Ride are gaining in favor because of problems with drought conditions and issues of water conservation. (In general, synthetic tracks need to be watered far less than dirt tracks and grass courses, although track officials at Del Mar were planning to water the Polytrack much more at their summer 2008 meeting, hoping to achieve a level of consistency that was missing the previous year when the track was tight and fast in the morning but slow and tiring on hot afternoons. They have also added a new wax to make the track more heat-resistant.)

In June 2007, it was announced that the government of the Australian state of Queensland had earmarked about $10 million to establish three synthetic racetracks.

"Queensland Racing Limited has evaluated the impact of recent drought conditions on our racetracks and the results are poor," Queensland Sports Minister Andrew Fraser told the Australian media. "Drought coupled with limited water use has led to a hardening of racetrack surfaces, and such conditions increase the incidence of soft-tissue damage to horses.

"Unless we act to drastically reduce water use on our racetracks, the risk of injury to both jockeys and horses will be dramatically increased.

"The installation of synthetic tracks would significantly reduce water use by the major Thoroughbred-racing facilities and give the industry the ability to race in all weather conditions."

The list of synthetic-surface manufacturers keeps growing, which can't hurt. There is a lot of money to be made in coming up with the very best synthetic surface and creating one that isn't exorbitantly expensive.

"If 20 years from now the track we have now looks like a Model T Ford, and I think that's possible, I will be thrilled because it's a jet plane compared to the Model T Ford we had before," Keeneland President Nick Nicholson said of Polytrack, comparing it to the track's old surface.

There will always be new twists and new material that will be used. If yesterday's answer to the perfect synthetic surface was balloons, maybe tomorrow's will be crushed-up diapers. With synthetic surfaces, anything is possible.

Is one synthetic surface better than any other? Needless to say, each manufacturer argues that his is superior to the competition's. But, as with so many subjects when it comes to synthetic surfaces, they'll need to run thousands more races over Polytrack, Tapeta, Cushion Track, Pro-Ride, and any other synthetic surface that pops up before anyone knows for sure how similar they are and how different they are.

Once handicappers begin to figure out how to best handicap races run over synthetic tracks, they'll no doubt turn their attention to the differences among synthetic tracks. Should a handicapper treat Cushion Track races differently from Polytrack races, and should Polytrack races be treated differently from Tapeta races?

Some claim that the various types of synthetic surfaces are radically different and that the manufacturers use different recipes with varying amounts of fibers, wax, and rubber. Even the type of fibers used can be different.

Be that as it may, the idea behind all synthetic tracks is essentially the same. They drain vertically instead of horizontally and the materials used in them help create a gentler racetrack that is not as jarring on the horses. Perhaps the day will come when we see some horses who love Tapeta but hate Polytrack, and vice versa. Maybe there will even be sires whose offspring relish Tapeta but can't stand up on Cushion Track. Somehow, though, I doubt it.

Though it will be years before there is enough data to properly evaluate the various synthetic surfaces out there, my guess is that we will eventually come to understand that synthetic is synthetic is synthetic. For now, though, the jury is still out.

12 Synthetic Tracks: Safe at Any Speed?

Whenever horses race and whatever they race over, there will always be injuries. Some will be minor, the type that will keep a horse out of action for two or three months. Some will end their careers. Some will end their lives. It's an ugly part of an otherwise beautiful sport.

Accurate records concerning the number of horses that die each year on the racetrack are hard to find, but the rule of thumb has always been that there will be about 1.5 fatalities per 1,000 starters. That translates to about 700 horses per year, or two deaths every day.

"There are 58 jockeys on the permanently disabled list and we're killing two horses a day on the track," Michael Dickinson said. "That's something that just can't keep happening."

The numbers of catastrophic breakdowns in the afternoon don't take into account horses that die while training. Nor do they include the thousands of horses who are injured while racing, but not fatally. (In June 2008, however, The Jockey Club announced the formation of the first nationwide injury database, so perhaps that will change.) A large percentage of those horses may have suffered career-ending injuries, and that's a blow for the trainer and the owner, who has been footing the bills.

The fragility of the modern Thoroughbred is among the many

reasons racing has fallen so far out of the mainstream when it comes to American sports. Today, racing has become all but invisible, with the exception of the five weeks each spring encompassing the Triple Crown. Even the Breeders' Cup, a two-day celebration of championship-quality racing in the fall, doesn't mean a thing to the average Joe.

There are several reasons why that's so, but the game's inability to develop and cultivate stars that have charisma and name recognition is no doubt part of the problem. Horses that race six or seven times and then get retired are never going to become household names or have a positive and meaningful impact on the sport's popularity.

A lot of good horses have disappeared because they are more valuable as stallions than racehorses, but several others have had their careers shortened by injuries. Horses like Afleet Alex and Smarty Jones might just have become the type of big stars with far-reaching appeal the sport needs. But neither one raced after the Belmont, their careers cut short by injury, as well as pressure to begin generating stud fees.

There are also scores of people who have been turned off to racing by a spate of high-profile injuries and deaths over the last few years. The firestorm that swirled nonstop in the weeks surrounding Eight Belles's death in the 2008 Kentucky Derby was among the sport's darkest periods.

Even those who look at racing as a business and dismiss the Eight Belles situation as "part of the game" have to worry about how the fragility of the modern Thoroughbred hurts the bottom line.

Injured horses can't race, and the sport relies on large fields to fuel betting handle. Every study ever done has shown that the larger the size of the field, the more money will be bet on a particular race. Nothing is less appealing to a gambler than to have a five-horse field with a 3–5 favorite, an 8–5 second choice, and the strong possibility that the winning exacta will pay $8.20.

Small fields are a growing problem that increases every year. The average field size in North American racing was 8.17 in 2007, down significantly from 1985, when it was 9.03. The primary reason for this is that horses don't run nearly as often as they did years ago.

In 1975, the average number of starts per runner was 10.23 per year. That figure is now down to 6.31, a 38.3 percent decline. The number has dropped every year since 1992 and might be headed below the 6.0 mark soon.

It's a puzzling phenomenon, but theories abound. Many believe that the modern Thoroughbred has been weakened by the proliferation of drugs, illegal and otherwise, and by the breeding industry's preference—driven by buyers who want a quick return—for producing fast, precocious horses over stout, late-developing types.

For reasons no one ever seemed to fully comprehend, the conventional dirt track at Arlington contributed to one of the deadliest meets in that track's history, with 22 horses dying during the 2006 stand. There were 11 breakdowns in a period between June 9 and July 1. Del Mar had similar problems. Eight horses broke down on the main track there in 2006 and seven more broke down on the turf. At Bay Meadows, 13 horses suffered fatal injuries during a 48-day meet in 2006, and the California Horse Racing Board jumped in, issuing a mandate that all major tracks in the state install synthetic surfaces by January 1, 2008.

The alarming number of breakdowns at places like Arlington, Del Mar, and Bay Meadows caused serious public-relations problems for an industry that has enough to worry about without having John Q. Public pick up the paper and read about horses dying all over the place.

Whatever the reasons are, the alarming number of injuries, shrinking fields, and the proliferation of horses capable of making no more than four or five starts a year is a serious problem for an industry with a number of serious problems. And it seems to be a problem that grows worse each year.

Synthetic tracks may not be for everyone, and they have their detractors, but they appear to be a major step in the right direction.

"My idea has always been to produce a surface where you can go from A to B in the quickest time, but do so safely. It's all about safety," said Martin Collins, the inventor of Polytrack.

Would synthetic surfaces have saved Ruffian, Go for Wand, Eight Belles, George Washington, Barbaro, or the $6,500 claimer that died on a Thursday afternoon somewhere? No one knows for sure, but some early indications suggest that synthetic tracks are indeed safer than conventional dirt strips.

University of Maine Professor of Mechanical Engineering Michael Peterson probably knows more about the safety aspects of racetrack surfaces than anybody. He has invented a robotic mechanical device that duplicates the action of a horse's hoof hitting a track and he uses it to measure all sorts of factors, including the consistency of a surface and the impact of the force when the hoof strikes the surface.

He has found that the primary reasons tracks can be unsafe is because they are inconsistent, with soft spots in some places and hard spots in others. That can be dangerous, because horses can have problems adapting their gait in the middle of a race, so they need to be running on a surface that is the same from start to finish.

"The dominant characteristic I have seen is variations within a track," Peterson said. "That's huge. One track in particular had unbelievable variations in a couple of areas. There's only one real explanation for that. It had to be due to problems with the base. The problem tracks have is maintaining the base layer.

"What I have seen with the synthetic surfaces is [that] the consistency is much higher than the dirt tracks, and that's why they are safer. There are a couple of dirt tracks out there that have the same level of consistency that the synthetic tracks do, but that assumes that they can control moisture content. We go from a coefficient of variation of 12 to 15 percent, which is not at all uncommon on a dirt track, to 3 or 4 percent on a synthetic track. That's a huge difference."

In the spring of 2008, the racing industry published the most complete data yet compiled about the safety of synthetic tracks and how they compare to regular dirt tracks and to turf courses.

Dr. Mary Scollay, a former track veterinarian at Calder and Gulfstream who is now the equine medical director for the Kentucky Horse Racing Authority, spearheaded an on-track injury-reporting system that was an offshoot of the 2006 Welfare and Safety of the Racehorse Summit. In her report, she collected numbers for the amount of catastrophic breakdowns on each type of North American racetrack—dirt, synthetic, and turf—over a five-month period. Though Scollay was careful to explain that a mere five months' worth of data is not enough to ascertain what surfaces are the safest, her findings were the best proof offered so far that the synthetic tracks are the safest.

Below is the primary data she had collected after roughly five months of study regarding fatal injuries and the type of surface they occurred on:

Fatal Injuries

	Starts	Fatalities	Frequency
All surface (composite)	143,421	237	1/605
Dirt	90,842	163	1/557
Synthetic	22,614	27	1/837
Turf	29,965	47	1/637

Shortly after these numbers were reached, Scollay released a new set of figures, which showed that there were 1.47 fatalities per 1,000 starts on synthetic surfaces versus 2.03 per start on dirt tracks, a difference of 27.59 percent.

When synthetic surfaces debuted in this country, some supporters were optimistic that these new tracks would cause a drastic reduction in fatal injuries. That hasn't happened. But 27.59 percent is a significant number and represents credible ammunition for the pro-synthetic forces.

"We're still early in the project, but I can certainly tell you that the fatal-injury rate on the synthetic surfaces is significantly lower than either dirt tracks or turf courses," Dr. Scollay said.

"I have them all grouped together. We did not separate Tapeta, Polytrack, and Cushion Track because we did not have enough data available to do so. The study so far certainly corresponds well with what we have heard anecdotally, that the catastrophic-injury rate has been reduced over the synthetic surfaces. Again, I don't have 12 months' worth of data, so I'm not sure this will stand up to peer review or scientific scrutiny until I have at least 12 months of data. There needs to be some level of caveat attached to this information."

Scollay was hopeful that someday the industry would also take a close look at other safety factors that relate to use of synthetic tracks.

"The other thing that needs to be looked at is the nonfatal injuries," she said. "If you are a horse owner and your horse bows a tendon, you may be looking at a lost year. That's a lost opportunity so far as completion, not to mention the expense of treatment and recovery and how that horse will be able to return to athletic competition. We need to get a handle on the nonfatal injuries as well. Anecdotally, so far, we're hearing more about soft-tissue injuries with the synthetic tracks than we are about fractures. As far as loss to the industry goes, the nonfatal injuries are just as significant."

Before the Polytrack surface was installed at Turfway Park, the main track there was no safer or more dangerous than just about any other regular dirt track. Racing at Turfway can be a bit on the cheap side, and cheaper horses tend to be a little more infirm than the classier ones. Unsoundness might be one of the reasons a horse is racing in, say, a $5,000 claimer. At the 2004 fall meet at Turfway, which ran from September 8 through October 7, there were six fatal breakdowns. The numbers were a bit better at the 2004 holiday meet, which ran from November 28 through December 31. There were four fatalities. At the winter-spring meet, the last ever run on regular dirt at Turfway, there were 14 fatalities.

That's 24 horses that died in a period of about six months, intolerable numbers by anyone's standards.

In September 2005, Turfway Park became the first North American racetrack to make the switch to a synthetic surface, in this case Polytrack. There was a significant and positive change as the amount of fatal injuries dropped off dramatically. At the 2005 fall meet, the same one at which six horses died a year earlier, not a single horse died as the result of an injury sustained in a race.

"It's even all over," jockey Calvin Borel told *The Cincinnati Enquirer* after riding on the first Polytrack card at Turfway. "It feels good. The horses just seem to bounce along. I can go inside and out. It's like running on a carpet."

There were three fatalities at the holiday meet that followed, but none at the 2005–06 winter-spring meet. A year after 24 horses had died at Turfway, the number for the same period was down to three.

At the same time, it became clear that fewer horses were suffering serious or career-ending injuries, still another win-win situation created by Polytrack. Healthy horses are better for the owners and trainers and a plus for track managements, which strive for large fields. Healthy horses stay in training, which means bigger fields. Bigger fields means bigger handle.

At least in the early days of this new era in racing, tracks featuring synthetic surfaces had an increase in field size and their product was a hit with most bettors. At Turfway Park, all-sources handle rose nearly 62 percent in the first few months after Polytrack was installed.

"It hasn't just been us, it's been Arlington, Hollywood, Keeneland, all the tracks with synthetic surfaces," Turfway President Bob Elliston said, although Keeneland and Santa Anita later experienced significant drops in the spring of 2008. "We have had great meets. Part of it is the media coverage that we've gotten. That's brought the issues to the front and center and everyone has been reading about the benefits of Polytrack.

"But, at the end of the day, I think the real reason people have been betting so much on our racing is the fairness of the racing. The best horse wins. You don't have biases and the racing is more exciting. The big bettors are no longer able to exploit situations like dead rails."

Woodbine was the next track to feature synthetic-track racing, also over a Polytrack surface, which debuted August 30, 2007. The early results at Woodbine were not nearly as encouraging as the ones from Turfway. Four horses suffered fatal breakdowns at Woodbine over Polytrack from September 4, 2006, through November 11, 2006. Things began to look up at Woodbine in 2007, when only two horses suffered fatal injuries over the Polytrack.

Next up was Keeneland. At the inaugural Polytrack meet there, only one horse suffered a fatal breakdown. There were three fatalities at the corresponding meet the year before. At the 2007 spring meet at Keeneland, there was not a single fatality.

At Hollywood Park, where Cushion Track was installed before the 2006 fall meet, there was more good news. Not a single horse suffered a fatal injury during that 36-day meet. At the same meet in 2005, which ran for just 27 days, three horses broke down and died on the track.

But just when everyone figured that synthetic tracks were the be-all and end-all, problems began to surface. As good as the synthetic tracks were, they were not perfect.

At Woodbine, problems continued into the early stages of 2007. Cold temperatures in the early spring in Canada were causing the fibers and wax in the surface to separate. That caused excessive kickback, something that's not supposed to happen with Polytrack.

Martin Collins was called in and he and his staff went to work on the surface. Part of the problem, according to top Canadian trainer Mark Casse, had been that the Woodbine Polytrack did not initially include jelly cable because the material could not be imported into Canada due to government environmental concerns. Eventually, the jelly cable was added and other improvements were made to the surface. Casse said the end result was the best track he has ever seen.

"Since they fixed the problems, this track has been wonderful," Casse said. "Have I had fewer injuries since they put in Polytrack? Absolutely. It used to be that if I went out and breezed 10 horses in a day on the old surface, seven of them would be okay the next day and three of them would be a little off or muscle sore. Now, it's not the least bit unusual for every horse I breeze to come back perfectly fine."

Prior to the start of the 2006 fall meet, Turfway management decided to tweak the Polytrack surface. Some 4,200 tons of new material was put down. The new stuff included plastic cable coating, spandex, and a heavier wax.

They should have left well enough alone. At the fall, holiday, and winter-spring meets combined, 14 horses died due to injuries suffered on the racetrack, a 466 percent increase over the corresponding meets held over Turfway's first Polytrack.

"The first track Turfway had, it was a lot safer," jockey Bill Troilo said. "I'm not so sure about this track. They keep tweaking it, trying to make it perfect. Don't get me wrong, it's a lot better than what we had here before. But it has had its issues. They were worried about the kickback in the beginning and they tweaked the track, hoping that it would resolve problems with kickbacks. What they put down added more wax and sand and the kickback is worse.

"It gets packed in the horse's feet," Troilo explained. "What happens, then, is you have big old clods, like you're riding over a frozen track. It didn't have that before. Last year's track, it kicked up but it would just hit you and fall apart. It doesn't do that this year."

Turfway officials were hopeful that they could make a good track even better and wanted to deal with a few minor problems, primarily the amount of kickback the track was producing. Many of the problems seemed to occur during particularly cold stretches of weather, Elliston said.

"In the latter part of December, we had some issues with the stickiness of the track and the number of breakdowns," Elliston said. "We can't absolutely say that the stickiness caused the breakdowns."

Still, executives from Turfway and Keeneland, a part-owner of Turfway, were quick to point out that even a Polytrack with some apparent problems was safer than a conventional track.

"We're early in the evolution," said Keeneland's Nick Nicholson. "We're not late in the evolution. This will be a theme you'll hear over and over again. When you compare the new surface to the old surface it gets rave reviews. Shortly after the new surface comes in and people get used to it they start comparing the new surface to perfection. That's when the yip-yap starts. That's what happened at Turfway."

The Cushion Track at Hollywood was also less than perfect. There was a breakdown in the wax content, which, trainers said, was resulting in a rash of back injuries. The theory was that horses were having trouble getting traction in their hind ends.

"As for the injury factor, you have soft-tissue injuries and hind-end problems on synthetic surfaces," said trainer John Shirreffs, trainer of 2005 Kentucky Derby winner Giacomo, in the *Los Angeles Times*. "A lot of young horses don't like it because it has the give but not the bounce-back factor."

In the fall of 2006, the Polytrack surface at Wolverhampton Race Course in England was creating serious safety concerns. Five horses in little over a month died on the racetrack. There was speculation that overuse of the course might have created some problems. Said jockey Dale Gibson, "Perhaps there is not enough time between fixtures to properly get the track A 1 and, maybe, something needs looking at to maybe slow it down. For me, bad horses are running exceptional times. There are too many horses going down."

The 2006 meet at Arlington was widely viewed as a disaster because so many horses broke down. To its credit, Arlington management was proactive and had a Polytrack surface installed. The change was notable. Arlington 2006 had 22 fatalities. Arlington 2007 had 13.

The Cushion Track at Santa Anita was another that didn't pass certain tests. The 2008 winter meet there was a nightmare. The Cushion Track did not drain properly, which caused 11 days of cancelations.

The problems with the Cushion Track at Santa Anita are among the reasons not everyone is raving about synthetic surfaces. Another problem might have been that they were overhyped. People seemed to expect that they would end all catastrophic breakdowns. That, of course, was not the case.

"I don't like them," trainer Scott Lake said. Considering that he had a stakes filly named Cantrel break down and die in the first race on opening day at Presque Isle Downs, his opinion is not a surprise.

"They're a great surface to train on but they're a rough surface to run over for horses," Lake continued. "There are horses who don't like it and won't try a little bit over it. I understand the theory is it will be safer for horses. I had the best filly in my barn break her leg the first day at Presque Isle Downs. I'm not blaming the racetrack. But they had three catastrophic breakdowns there and all three were really nice horses.

"A cheaper horse knows how to protect themselves and they will change the way they run and handle things different. A good horse will stride out the best they can no matter what. Most of them are going to try and that's why we saw three good horses break down there and not so much the cheaper ones."

There is another aspect of the safety issue that has nothing to do with rates of injuries and breakdowns on synthetic surfaces. Some people have raised the concern that synthetic tracks, which include all sorts of man-made materials, might turn out to be hazardous to horses and riders who could be ingesting a variety of possibly harmful particles, or that there could be an unforeseen environmental impact. Top Canadian rider Emma Wilson has even started wearing a mosquito net over her face when riding at Woodbine, to keep all the gunk out of her throat.

"I've found that a lot of the kickback is difficult to expel, and it was getting stuck in my sinuses and throat," Wilson told *Daily Racing Form*. "The mosquito net acts as a filter, so any of the Polytrack that's hitting my face gets caught up in the netting and there's no hindrance to my breathing. The only time I didn't wear it was on [front-runner] Friendly Theresa. She's pretty straightforward. When you don't wear it, it's like showing the rest of the guys at the poker table your hand."

Might horses and jockeys racing over synthetic surfaces start coming down with breathing and lung problems? It's highly doubtful. Several tests have already been conducted on synthetic surfaces and each one has indicated that they are perfectly safe.

Before the Polytrack surface could be installed at Del Mar, it had to be approved by the California Coastal Commission. The commission wanted to know if the installation of the synthetic surface would cause any environmental concerns. They ruled that it wouldn't.

According to Michael Dickinson, his Tapeta surface was checked over by Atlantic Environmental Incorporated. "AEI did not find any potentially harmful exposures to respirable dust, total dust, silica, or fibers to the horse and rider on tracks surfaced with the Tapeta Footings material," Dickinson said.

So if synthetic surfaces pose no danger from airborne particles, why did the starting-gate crew at Santa Anita begin wearing surgical masks in 2008? According to California handicapper Bob Ike in his *Notes on a Program* blog, there was a "strong odor emitted by the track since chemicals were added during renovation in early February," and even the track bugler complained that the surface struck a sour note.

"Horn blower Jay Cohen, in perhaps not the best career move ever, told Art Wilson of the *LANG* newspapers, 'I hate the stuff. It smells like kerosene,'" reported Ike. "'It stinks. I hate smelling it, but that's just my opinion. If it's safer for the horses, that's the main thing.'"

It is still early in the synthetic-surface era and obviously there are many questions to be answered. Synthetic surfaces may not be for everyone—but they seem to be safer. That's something the industry can't afford to ignore.

13

What the English Can Teach Us

While synthetic-surface racing might be new and confusing to North American horseplayers, their counterparts in England ("punters") have grown comfortable with the concept. Synthetic tracks, called all-weather tracks in the UK, have been around England for years and have become a major part of racing there.

All-weather tracks now account for some 36 percent of the flat races run each year in the UK. While most of the major races in England are still run on grass at prestigious racecourses such as Ascot and Newmarket during the height of the season (April through October), and nothing more important than a Group 3 is run on an all-weather surface, racing at tracks with synthetic surfaces is getting better and better all the time.

Racing on all-weather surfaces began in 1989 to fill the gap in the winter caused by abandonments of steeplechase meets due to bad weather. All-weather meetings were low-grade fare but kept the betting shops open when the jumpers couldn't compete on the grass.

However, since the Arena Leisure Company took over three all-weather tracks, and since Kempton came on board with an all-weather track of its own, the standard has improved. There was a stigma attached to synthetic surfaces in the early days. Top stables would not run good horses for fear of breaking them down or devaluing them. Today, AW (all-weather) racing has evolved to the point where some high-profile races, including the Group 3 Winter Derby at Lingfield, are run over synthetic tracks.

Such is the quality of the surfaces today that all-weather racing has its own season, November to March, with an official trainers' and jockeys' championship, separate from the turf. However, AW fixtures are run all through the year.

All-weather racing has produced a number of quality horses over the years, perhaps none more notable than Running Stag. He blossomed over the all-weather surfaces in England before coming to the U.S. and winning races such as the Mass Cap and the Brooklyn. AW racing also opened a new avenue to horses in Europe that otherwise might never have been successful. There are plenty of horses out there that don't do well racing on the grass, and many of them have found homes at the English synthetic tracks.

English trainers have become much more accepting of the all-weather tracks, a reason why average field size on the synthetic surfaces has risen from 9.85 in the early years to more than 11.5 horses per race.

But enough from me. There are English handicappers who have a lot more experience dealing with synthetic-surface racing than anyone in North America, and I have turned to one of the best.

Simon Mapletoft might know more about racing on synthetic surfaces than anyone in the world. A commentator on the At The Races racing channel in England, his specialty is AW racing. He annually publishes the *All-Weather Guide*, which features, among other things, "100 Horses to Follow" and "about 30 Trainer Files, Track Facts and other gems of information to keep punters ahead on the sand." Mapletoft has also used his knowledge to build a successful stable of his own, which concentrates on AW racing.

Much of what follows comes straight from Mapletoft, who graciously agreed to share his knowledge of racing on synthetic surfaces in England. I don't expect you to start betting on racing from England, but much of what Mapletoft has to say is relevant to American racing. Because many English tracks look nothing like the standard oval tracks in the U.S. and have what we would consider a lot of unusual twists and turns, post positions are a major handicapping factor in England

and a big part of Mapletoft's handicapping philosophies. For the most part, post positions don't seem to matter on American synthetic tracks, so they will be dealt with here only in minimal detail.

We begin with some nuggets from Mapletoft on each of the four English tracks that have synthetic surfaces.

OVERVIEW

Every season all-weather racing becomes more and more competitive. To make it pay, you need to understand how races at the four tracks–Lingfield, Kempton, Southwell, and Wolverhampton–are likely to unfold. Each surface has its own characteristics, which generally influence the result; the best horse in the race doesn't always win.

LINGFIELD

Before Polytrack was installed here, front-runners prospered around Lingfield's tight turns. Today, horses can win from anywhere, but beware of the draw bias at certain distances.

Beware of falsely run races at this track. Since the arrival of Polytrack in 2001, jockeys have the confidence to sit off the pace and allow their horses to settle, as the kickback is minimal. Also, riders are cagey about committing their mounts before the downhill sweep into the short home straight. Fields often tend to fan out wide off the far turn, giving closers the opportunity to mount their challenge. It is not uncommon for such horses to get a dream run against the fence, though inevitably there can be hard-luck stories, too, when jockeys are competing for the same gaps.

KEMPTON

Kempton's Polytrack circuit, which opened in March 2006, is unique in that it is the only right-handed all-weather track in England, and races take place over an inner and outer loop. The inner loop is used for five-furlong and mile-and-a-quarter races only, with all other races run over the outer course.

Runners in five-furlong sprints encounter two sharp turns, with a home straight of less than two furlongs. The draw bias, therefore, is directly opposite to that at Lingfield and Wolverhampton, in that those drawn high, not low, hold a distinct advantage.

It is, of course, crucial that runners breaking from the outside posts show enough early speed to hold a good racing position. Blow the break and it can be a struggle to get competitive as the race begins to take shape approaching the first bend.

Sprints over six furlongs unfold with a marked difference. These races take place around the outer loop and horses and jockeys have the benefit of a longer straight to mount a challenge. Often closers prevail and it is common to see horses win from far off the pace.

Kempton provides a good test of stamina for a stayer. A generous, even gallop is almost guaranteed and horses can really lengthen and grind out a finish up that nice long straight.

SOUTHWELL

The only track in England with a Fibresand surface, Southwell's long straights and sweeping turns favor relentless gallopers, or "grinders." While it is possible to win from the front, "hold-up horses" have plenty of time to get up a head of steam between the final turn and the winning post.

Remember that Fibresand has a tendency to ride slow at certain times of the year, usually when it has been harrowed deep through the night in the face of a frost. At these times, the testing nature of the surface brings stamina into play and can reduce the advantages of the draw on the round track. For example, horses with seven-furlong form often gain the day in six-furlong races.

It is important to note that the Fibresand surface is more variable than the Polytrack. Significant rainfall often compacts the sand and leads to faster conditions, while frost can slow down the surface considerably. This is because the track is often harrowed through the night to prevent a freeze-up in subzero temperatures, leaving the surface looser and much deeper. While the track can often ride marginally fast in the autumn, and again in the spring, it is common for the going to be slow and testing during the cold weeks of December and January.

WOLVERHAMPTON

Historically, in the days before Polytrack, those breaking from posts 1 through 3 in races up to the extended mile and an eighth had the odds stacked against them. This factor was particularly in evidence in five-furlong sprints, where those drawn close to the fence encountered the deepest, and therefore, slowest, ground.

However, those trends have now been committed firmly to the past with the dawning of a new era of racing on a £3 million Polytrack surface. This new track, which opened in 2005, rides consistently well. Even when it is described as "standard to fast," rather than "standard," the difference on the stopwatch is fractional.

AN ALL-WEATHER TRACKS TIMELINE

All-weather racing in Britain began in 1989 with the opening of a new track at Lingfield Park, Surrey, southeast of London. Lingfield was an existing and well-established turf track. A new Equitrack surface was laid down inside the turf track by Lingfield's then owners and all-weather racing innovators, Ron and Richard Muddle. This father-and-son team later went on to open further all-weather tracks at Southwell and Wolverhampton before selling all three to current owners Arena Leisure.

Equitrack, the surface chosen at Lingfield, was basically a mix of sand and plastic. The plastic helped to prevent the surface from freezing in subzero temperatures. It was a very fast surface, though the downhill run to the final turn also lent itself to fast performances (and still does).

Lingfield's surface was replaced in November 2001 with Polytrack, a more modern, state-of-the-art surface. The investment by then owners Arena Leisure totaled £2.8 million. Polytrack was proven to be able to withstand minus temperatures even more effectively and was considered a more cushioned, sympathetic surface for racing horses on. Equitrack was by comparison much firmer and less forgiving.

Since its inception Lingfield has played a major role in establishing AW racing as a major part of the UK calendar. Such is its credibility now that all of the top trainers run their horses on the all-weather.

Soon after the opening of Lingfield in 1989 came another all-weather track, Southwell, in Nottinghamshire in the East Midlands. Sand racing began there in the same year, again the brainchild of the Muddles, who owned both tracks. Southwell had traditionally been a small National Hunt track, tucked away in the countryside. A new Fibresand circuit was put in, this time outside the turf track.

Fibresand was very different from Equitrack in many ways. Firstly, it was a much slower and testing surface that would equate to soft ground on turf. Fibresand, still in use at Southwell, is a blend of fine silica sand and polypropylene fibers, which help to bind it together. In basic terms, it sits on a tarmacadam base, which in turn covers a lateral drainage system. Over the years, the Fibresand surface has been replaced and replenished.

While Fibresand is not as fashionable and widely accepted as Polytrack, it is popular among many trainers as it offers a very different kind of surface, which suits many horses. Its credibility has been given a boost on a couple of occasions in recent years as top Irish trainer Aidan O'Brien has used Southwell as a Breeders' Cup prep for big names such as Giant's Causeway and Galileo.

The main difference between Fibresand and Polytrack is that Fibresand is softer and therefore produces far more kickback than Polytrack. Polytrack also appears to hold up better in cold temperatures.

Wolverhampton was acquired by the Muddles and was transformed into Britain's third AW track, following the success of Lingfield and Southwell. Formerly a dual-purpose turf track, it was completely knocked down and rebuilt, with a new grandstand and hotel. Fibresand was the chosen surface.

In October 2004, now in the ownership of Arena Leisure, Wolverhampton's surface was replaced and the track slightly reshaped. This time Polytrack was installed at a cost of £3 million, which has played a big part in the further growth in credibility and popularity of AW racing.

Kempton was the latest addition. The flat turf track there was replaced by a right-hand circuit of Polytrack. The new course opened in March 2006. Like Wolverhampton, it is floodlit. This is the only right-handed track and has its own idiosyncrasies, as it has an inner loop. Kempton, in characteristic, is similar to Southwell in that it is a gallopers' track, whereas Lingfield and Wolverhampton are sharper.

A new AW track opened at Great Leighs in Essex in late May 2008. It has a Polytrack circuit and a grass course will be added at a later date.

Great Leighs is the first new racetrack to open in Great Britain in 80 years. That it would include a Polytrack course is a sign of the times. Even in Britain, where grass racing dominates, those looking toward the future are thinking synthetic.

Another AW track opened recently at Dundalk in Ireland. It is Ireland's first AW track. It, too, will be Polytrack.

The safety record for the AW tracks in England has generally been good and the injury rate has been low. This is without doubt due to the

> sympathetic nature of Polytrack. Fibresand, though a much more dated and basic surface, has also served well and injury rates at Southwell are also minimal. There was a spate of fallers at Wolverhampton last winter season but no problems came to light with the track. The theory was that jockeys were riding too tight at a fast pace, as there were several instances of clipping heels—mostly in different parts of the track.
>
> Without doubt, some horses excel on sand while flopping on turf. Equally, many smart turf horses fail to act on sand tracks. It is often more down to the style of racing and profile of the circuits than the surface. Racing on sand is much faster; they race from the gates, pretty much as they do in the United States on dirt. On turf in the UK, races tend to gather momentum and some horses fail to make the transition.

Though Mapletoft was speaking in generalities with that analysis, he could have been talking specifically about Gentleman's Deal, winner of 2007's big AW race, the Group 3 Winter Derby at Lingfield. A group-class runner on Polytrack and Fibresand, he has been unable to make his mark in decent handicaps on turf. After winning four straight on all-weather tracks, he finished 15th as the 7–2 favorite in a handicap race at Newcastle upon his return to the grass. It is interesting to note that he is by Danehill, one of the world's great turf sires.

:ntleman's Deal (Ire)
: Mr Stephen J. Curtis

B. g. 6 (Apr)
Sire: Danehill (Danzig) $39,277
Dam: Sleepytime*Ire (Royal Academy)
Br: C. H. Wacker III (Ire)
Tr: M. W. Easterby

Life	14	6	0	0	$218,886	-	D.Fst	0	0	0	0	$0	-
2007	4	3	0	0	$162,653	-	Wet(394)	0	0	0	0	$0	-
2006	8	2	0	0	$48,486	-	Synth	6	6	0	0	$214,090	-
							Turf(404)	8	0	0	0	$4,796	-

reviously trained by M. W. Easterby r07♦Newcastle (GB) gs 1 Ⓣ 1:46 4↑ acing Post Rating: 51	William Hill Lincoln Hcp 196800	$15^{23\frac{3}{4}}$	Paul Mulrennan	125	*3.50	Very Wise123¹ Rio Riva129⁴ Mutawaffer120ⁿᵏ *Midfield stands side: struggling 3f out: sn btn*	20
reviously trained by M. W. Easterby r07♦Lingfield (GB) ft 1¼ ◈LH 2:04² 4↑ acing Post Rating: 106	Winter Derby (polytrack)-G3 Stk 196000	1^{nk}	Paul Mulrennan	126	*4.00	Gentleman's Deal126ⁿᵏ Grand Passion126ⁿᵏ Illustrious Blue126ⁿᵒ *Slw pc 4f, trckd ldrs, rdn to ld jst ins fnl f, hld on gmly*	12
reviously trained by M. W. Easterby 07♦Kempton (GB) st 1 ◈ 1:36⁴ 4↑ acing Post Rating: 114	Digibet.com Ladybird S. Stk 51200	$1^{1\frac{1}{2}}$	Paul Mulrennan	126	*1.00	Gentleman's Deal126 1½ Grand Passion126 1¼ Party Boss126 1¼ *Trckd ldrs, shkn up to ld jst over 1f out, rdn clr, readily*	8
reviously trained by M. W. Easterby 07♦Southwell (GB) st 1 ◈ 1:40³ 4↑ acing Post Rating: 115	Canvas Prints From Bonusprint.com Hcp 34300	1^{2}	Paul Mulrennan	128	*.70	Gentleman's Deal128² Speedy Sam116¹ Uhoomagoo116³ *Dwlt: sn chsng ldrs: lft in ld over 4f out: hdd over 3f out: led*	8
reviously trained by M. W. Easterby 06♦Southwell (GB) st 1 ◈ 1:41¹ 3↑ acing Post Rating: 108	Southwell-racecourse.co.uk H. Hcp 35600	1^{6}	Paul Mulrennan	127	*1.75	Gentleman's Deal127⁶ Wessex129 1¼ Nevada Desert118ⁿᵒ *A.p: hdwy to ld wl over 1f out: rdn clr ent last: sn clr*	9
reviously trained by M. W. Easterby 06♦Windsor (GB) gs 1¼ Ⓣ RH 2:09¹ 3↑ acing Post Rating: 93	Tote Text Betting Handicap Hcp 38000	$7^{1\frac{1}{4}}$	Paul Mulrennan	121	12.00	Folio118ⁿᵒ Rampallion124ʰᵈ Ofaraby131½ *Wl in tch: urged along and looked to be struggling over 2f out: r*	18
reviously trained by M. W. Easterby :t06♦Newmarket (GB) sf 1 Ⓣ Str 1:38² 3↑ acing Post Rating: 93	Bet365 Handicap Hcp 56900	$4^{4\frac{3}{4}}$	Robert Francis Wins	133	7.00	Arm Candy117³ Rio Riva130 1¾ Rain Stops Play122ⁿᵒ *Racd far side: hld up in tch: rdn over 2f out: hung rt over 1f ou*	15
reviously trained by M. W. Easterby 06♦York (GB) sf 1 Ⓣ 1:42² 3↑ acing Post Rating: 90	TSG H. Hcp 33800	$5^{5\frac{3}{4}}$	Robert Francis Wins	132	20.00	Army of Angels135 1½ Wavertree Warrior121 1¾ Collateral Damage116 1½ *Stdd s and bhd: hdwy 3f out: rdn 2f out: styd on appr last: nrst*	12
reviously trained by M. W. Easterby p06♦Haydock (GB) gd 1⁴⁰ Ⓣ LH 1:45¹ 3↑ acing Post Rating: 93	Griffiths & Armour Hcp (1m,30y) Hcp 28500	$4^{2\frac{3}{4}}$	Dale Gibson	134	14.00	Abbey Cat117ⁿᵒ Skidrow127 1¾ Ingratitude122¹ *Midfield: hdwy 3f out: rdn wl over 1f out: styd on ins last: nrst*	16
reviously trained by M. W. Easterby 06♦York (GB) gd 1 5/16 Ⓣ 2:12² 3↑ acing Post Rating: 90	Symphony Group Chamossaire S. Hcp 46600	$9^{6\frac{3}{4}}$	Dale Gibson	125	10.00	Rohaani130¹ Topatoo123¾ Kahlua Kiss121ʰᵈ *T.k.h in mid-field: effrt over 3f out: wknd over 1f out*	11
reviously trained by M. W. Easterby ar06♦Redcar (GB) sf 1 Ⓣ 1:44¹ 4↑ acing Post Rating: 51	William Hill Lincoln Hcp 174300	$21^{26\frac{3}{4}}$	Dale Gibson	121	10.00	Blythe Knight122¾ Royal Island126 3½ Capable Guest121ⁿᵏ *Swtchd lft s: in rr: effrt over 3f out: hung lft: nvr a factor*	30
reviously trained by M. W. Easterby 06♦Southwell (GB) ft 1 ◈ 1:40³ 4↑ acing Post Rating: 95	Bet Direct Freephone 0800 211 222 Hcp 34400	1^{3}	Dale Gibson	119	7.00	Gentleman's Deal119³ Waterside119⁴ Moayed133⁶ *Hld up: hdwy over 2f out: led over 2f out: r.o wl*	7
:t04♦Wolverhampton (GB) st 1 3/16 ◈ 2:01¹	Sponsor A Race At Dunstall P Hcp 10700	1^{3}	Ahern E	135	*1.75	Gentleman's Deal135³ Miss Polaris134¾ Hazewind130ⁿᵏ *Trckd ldrs: led over 2f out: sn hung rt: r.o wl*	13
y04♦Newmarket (GB) gd 1 Ⓣ Str 1:40³	Hugo and the Huguenotes Maiden St Maiden 16100	4^{4}	Hughes R	126	16.00	Hermitage Court126ʰᵈ Kauri Forest126½ Arctic Silk121 3½ *Racd far side: trckd ldrs: swtchd rt and continued to hang rt fr*	20

There are other synthetic-surface specialists, horses who clearly show a preference for the sand tracks and struggle over the turf. It should be noted that, just as in the U.S., turf form often does not translate to synthetic surfaces. Take a look at Orchard Supreme, a useful handicap horse on synthetic tracks and a hopeless bum on turf. Note how poorly he ran in his one start on turf in 2007. But put him on synthetic surfaces and he is a different horse.

Orchard Supreme (GB)
Own: Mr Brian C. Oakley

Ch. c. 4 (Apr)
Sire: Titus Livius*Fr (Machiavellian)
Dam: Bogus Penny*Ire (Pennekamp)
Br: Mrs M. H. Goodrich (GB)
Tr: R. Hannon

Life	21	4	1	3	$129,932	-	D.Fst	0	0	0	0	$0
							Wet(358*)	1	1	0	0	$21,167
2007	7	1	0	1	$69,871	-	Synth	14	4	1	3	$128,826
2006	12	3	1	2	$60,061	-	Turf(286*)	7	0	0	0	$1,106

Date / Track	Cond	Dist	Surf	Time	Race / Class	Fin	Jockey	Wt	Odds	Top finishers / Comment	Racing Post Rating	Previously trained by
4May07♦Lingfield (GB)	st	1¼	◈	2:05^{1} 4↑	Betdirectpoker.com Get Involved H, Hcp 37800	5^{8}	Richard Hughes	130	9.00	Tabadul124^{1¼} Vacation111^{nk} Queen's Best116^{3} — Hld up in rr: effrt 3f out: outpcd 2f out: no ch	95	R. Hannon
28Apr07♦Sandown Park (GB)	gd	1	Ⓣ	1:41^{3} 4↑	Text Betfred To 83080 For Mobile, Hcp 40000	$8^{25¾}$	Pat Dobbs	121	4.50	Capable Guest119^{2½} Humungous127^{4} DH Red Somerset120 — V scratchy to post: hld up: gng wl enough over 2f out: rdn ar	41	R. Hannon
29Mar07♦Lingfield (GB)	st	1	◈	1:37^{1} 4↑	Doncaster Mile, Stk 51000	3^{2}	Jimmy Fortune	126	*2.00	Banknote126^{½} Chicken Soup126^{1½} Orchard Supreme126^{no} — T.k.h, sn stdd in rr, efrt ov 2f out kpt on to take 3rd o	99	R. Hannon
24Mar07♦Lingfield (GB)	ft	1¼	◈LH	2:04^{2} 4↑	Winter Derby (polytrack)-G3, Stk 196000	$8^{1½}$	Richard Hughes	126	20.00	Gentleman's Deal126^{nk} Grand Passion126^{nk} Illustrious Blue126^{no} — Hld up in rr, rdn & r.o fnl 2f, nt rc	102	R. Hannon
10Mar07♦Wolverhampton (GB)	st	1$\frac{1}{16}$	◈	1:47^{1} 4↑	William Hill Lincoln Trial S., Hcp 96600	$1^{½}$	Richard Hughes	134	9.00	Orchard Supreme134^{½} Bomber Command129^{¾} Tanzanite126^{nk} — Hld up and bhd: hdwy on ins wl over 1f out: rdn to ld 1f out	108	R. Hannon
24Feb07♦Lingfield (GB)	st	7f	◈	1:23^{1} 4↑	Bonusprint.com H., Hcp 35300	$4^{½}$	Dane O'Neill	128	6.50	Wavertree Warrior116^{nk} Bomber Command115^{nk} Waterside130^{no} — Hld up: hdwy over 2f out: rdn over 1f out: chsd ldr wl ins	103	R. Hannon
17Feb07♦Lingfield (GB)	st	1	◈	1:35^{4} 4↑	Pontinsbingo.com Conditions S., Alw 35100	4^{4}	Richard Hughes	126	*1.35	Party Boss138^{1} Ceremonial Jade129^{½} Red Spell129^{2¼} — Stdd s: hld up in last: nt clr run and swtchd rt over 1f ou	88	R. Hannon
22Dec06♦Lingfield (GB)	st	1	◈	1:35^{4} 3↑	Pontins.com H., Hcp 34900	$1^{¾}$	Richard Hughes	129	3.00	Orchard Supreme129^{¾} Secret Night121^{nk} Bomber Command127^{¾} — T.k.h, hld up, shkn up & hdwy 1f out, led insd fnl f, re	103	R. Hannon
3Dec06♦Lingfield (GB)	ft	7f	◈LH	1:23 3↑	Racing Post Hcp (polytrack), Hcp 35600	$5^{2¾}$	Dane O'Neill	121	7.00	Areyoutalkingtome130^{no} Marajaa114^{1½} Vortex122^{1} — Dwlt: sn in tch: rdn over 2f out: kpt on sam	96	R. Hannon
18Nov06♦Lingfield (GB)	st	7f	◈	1:22^{4} 3↑	Ibetx.com Betting Exchange H., Hcp 34100	$2^{½}$	Stephane Breux^{3}	113	10.00	Areyoutalkingtome125^{½} Orchard Supreme113^{1¼} Qadar121^{1½} — Sn last: prog but v wd bnd 2f out: gd hdwy over 1f out: clsc	99	R. Hannon
26Oct06♦Lingfield (GB)	st	7f	◈	1:23^{1} 3↑	Weatherbys Bank H., Hcp 23500	$6^{1½}$	Richard Hughes	121	10.00	Areyoutalkingtome127^{1¼} Viking Spirit129^{no} Secret Night118^{no} — Hld up in rr: prog 3f out: effrt on inner and nrly on term.	94	R. Hannon
15Oct06♦Lingfield (GB)	ft	1	◈LH	1:36^{4} 3↑	Book Online for a Discount Hcp(po, Hcp 24100	$3^{1¼}$	Richard Hughes	130	9.00	Zato130^{nk} Cross The Line131^{1} Orchard Supreme130^{no} — Hld up in rr: hdwy over 2f out: swtchd rt over 1f out: r.o	95	R. Hannon
15Sep06♦Newbury (GB)	gd	7f	Ⓣ Str	1:25^{2} 3↑	Dubai Duty Free Handicap, Hcp 18800	6^{4}	Richard Hughes	132	25.00	Carnivore124^{nk} DH Millennium Force126 DH Grizedale127^{1¾} — Bhd: hdwy over 2f out: swtchd lft and rdn over 1f out: kpt or	82	R. Hannon
3Aug06♦Goodwood (GB)	gf	7f	Ⓣ RH	1:24^{4}	De Boer Handicap, Hcp 75000	$15^{25¾}$	Ryan L Moore	118	20.00	Dream Theme118^{nk} High Curragh120^{1½} Heaven Sent120^{½} — A wl in rr: wknd over	27	R. Hannon
26Jly06♦Sandown Park (GB)	gf	7f	Ⓣ RH	1:27^{2}	Lord McGowan Handicap, Hcp 23000	$4^{2½}$	Ryan L Moore	130	25.00	Ans Bach133^{no} Scrummage115^{2½} Alfie Tupper129^{no} — Bhd: stl plenty to do over 2f out: hdwy on outside over 1f	87	R. Hannon
6Jun06♦Windsor (GB)	gf	1^{70}	Ⓣ RH	1:44^{4}	K&LNG Challenge Us Handicap, Hcp 31800	$11^{18¼}$	Richard Hughes	133	20.00	La Mottie133^{2½} Queen's Best121^{1} Cactus King128^{no} — Bhd: sme hdwy fr 3f out but nvr in contention and sn bhd	65	R. Hannon
23May06♦Lingfield (GB)	gd	7f	◈LH	1:24^{2}	Oxted Veterinary Clinic H (dirt), Hcp 33900	1^{hd}	Richard Hughes	119	5.50	Orchard Supreme119^{hd} Easy Air122^{1½} Dark Islander130^{1½} — T.k.h: hld up in 5th: effrt 2f out: shkn up to ld last 150y	92	R. Hannon
21Feb06♦Lingfield (GB)	st	7f	◈	1:25^{1}	Betdirect Freephone 0800 211 222, Hcp 8700	$1^{¾}$	Richard Hughes	130	*2.25	Orchard Supreme130^{¾} Didn't We130^{7} The London Gang126^{1½} — Towards rr: hdwy 2f out: chsd ldr over 1f out: r.o to ld f	88	R. Hannon
1Feb06♦Lingfield (GB)	st	7f	◈	1:24^{4}	Over 60 Games At Littlewoodscasin, Hcp 8900	$3^{2½}$	Richard Hughes	130	*2.25	Kingsgate Prince136^{¾} Didn't We127^{1½} Orchard Supreme130^{3½} — Led: set stdy pce 1st 3f: pressed 2f out: hdd over 1f out: o	79	R. Hannon
4Nov05♦Yarmouth (GB)	hy	1	Ⓣ Str	1:46^{4}	Crystal Cleaning Nursery Hcp, Hcp 12900	$9^{22¼}$	Ryan L Moore	124	7.00	Risk Runner124^{3½} Snake Skin111^{1} At The Money116^{1} — Chsd ldrs: rdn and hung lft over 3f out: hung rt and wknd o	29	R. Hannon
23Jly05♦Salisbury (GB)	gf	6f	Ⓣ Str	1:14^{1}	Famous Grouse Maiden Stks, Maiden 12700	$11^{10¾}$	Dane O'Neill	126	100.00	Stratham126^{no} Loyal Royal126^{2½} Go Figure126^{1½} — Led, ridden & headed ovr 2f out, weakened just ovr	46	Richard M. Hannon

Running Stag was another horse who struggled on the grass, but was a top horse on both all-weather surfaces and conventional dirt tracks in the U.S. He lost 15 races on the grass in Europe before winning at Deauville, but he was never worse than second in five tries on all-weather tracks in England.

He went on to great success in the U.S. racing over dirt, where he became a Grade 2 winner. Based on his pedigree, Running Stag was another horse that figured to like turf better than dirt or all-weather. He is by Cozzene, a horse who did his best running on the grass and won the 1985 Breeders' Cup Mile on the turf at Aqueduct. Running Stag won only once in 20 lifetime starts on the grass.

unning Stag
n: Cohen Richard J

B. h. 13 (Jun)
Sire: Cozzene (Caro*Ire) $35,000
Dam: Fruhlingstag*Fr (Orsini II)
Br: Juddmonte Farms (Ky)
Tr: Mitchell Philip

Life	40	7	11	2	$1,663,227	118	D.Fst	13	4	2	1	$1,037,215	118
2000	7	2	1	0	$524,975	117	Wet(316)	2	0	0	0	$105,000	105
1999	9	2	4	0	$837,782	118	Synth	5	2	3	0	$90,275	-
							Turf(313)	20	1	6	1	$430,737	97

ug00- 9AP yl 1¼ Ⓣ :473 1:114 1:3712:011 3+ ArlMilln-G1 97 6 25 23 2½ 21 66 Sellers S J L126 10.90 95- 04 Chester House1263¼ Manndar126½ Mula Gula1261 Stalked, tired late 7
ug00- 9Sar gd 1⅛ :463 1:101 1:35 1:481 3+ WhitneyH-G1 105 5 63¾ 63 63 45 47¾ Sellers S J L120 10.40 92 - Lemon Drop Kid1232 Cat Thief1174¼ Behrens1221½ Steadied first turn 6
un00- 8Bel fst 1⅛ :47 1:114 1:3711:494 3+ BroklynH-G2 102 6 1hd 2½ 1hd 22½ 67¾ Sellers S J L121 *1.45 74- 29 LemonDropKid1207¼ Lger114hd DowntheAisle112hd Between foes, gave way 7
un00-13Suf fst 1⅛ :462 1:103 1:3611:492 3+ MassH-G2 117 8 41½ 31½ 21 1hd 11¼ Velazquez J R LB116 *1.60 89- 17 Running Stag1161¼ Out of Mind1161¼ David113¾ Wide 1st, driving 8
ay00- 8Bel fst 1⅛ :451 1:091 1:3431:48 4+ Alw 59000N$Y 107 2 33½ 32 21 1½ 11½ Sellers S J L123 *1.60 91- 16 RunningStg1231½ ErlyWrning1173½ WldImgnton1143¼ With something left 6

Previously trained by Mitchell Philip
ar00 ♦ Nad Al Sheba (UAE) ft *1¼ LH 1:592 4+ Dubai World Cup-G1 Stk 6000000 717¾ Sellers S J 126 - Dubai Millennium1266 Behrens1265½ Public Purse126hd 13
Racing Post Rating: 109 *Tracked in 4th,3rd 3f out,weakened 1-1/2f out.Puerto Madero 4th*

Previously trained by Mitchell Philip
ar00 ♦ Nad Al Sheba (UAE) ft *7½f LH 1:29 4+ Al Futtaim Trophy Alw 19100 21¼ Ryan W 121 - Blue Snake1191¼ Running Stag121no Jila1191¾ 5
Racing Post Rating: 107 *Wide in 4th,dueled 170y out,headed 50y out.No betting*

Previously trained by Mitchell Philip
ec99 ♦ Sha Tin (HK) gd *1¼ Ⓣ RH 2:012 3+ Hong Kong Cup-G1 Stk 1286000 23¾ Sellers S 126 25.00 Jim and Tonic1263¾ Running Stag1261½ Lear Spear1261¼ 12
Racing Post Rating: 117 *Tracked leader,led briefly over 1f out,second best.Kabool 4th*

Previously trained by Mitchell Philip
ov99 ♦ Lingfield (GB) ft 1¼ ◈LH 2:043 3+ Ind Prchsng Asso Cndtn S(dirt) Alw 25600 2nk Eddery P 126 *.30 Brilliant Red126nk Running Stag1261¼ Pas de Memoires1311¼ 11
Racing Post Rating: 97+ *Rated in 7th,close 3rd 3f out,led 1f out,caught near line*

ep99- 9Bel fst 1⅛ :454 1:094 1:3421:464 3+ Woodward-G1 114 6 72½ 62¾ 41 3nk 41¾ Sellers S J L126 *.95 95- 14 RiverKeen126no Almutwkel1261½ StephnGotEvn121nk Rated, 4 wide move 7
ug99- 8Sar fst 1¼ :474 1:114 1:3622:01 3+ SarBCH-G2 116 7 31 3½ 1hd 12 1½ Sellers S J L122 *1.00 103- 16 RunningStag122½ Ctienus115½ GoldenMissile1158½ Stalked 3 wide,driving 8

Previously trained by Mitchell Philip
y99 ♦ Sandown Park (GB) gd 1¼ Ⓣ RH 2:062 3+ Eclipse Stakes-G1 Stk 465100 54¾ Cochrane R 133 9.00 Compton Admiral122nk Xaar133½ Fantastic Light1221½ 8
Racing Post Rating: 115 *Tracked leader,weakened over 1f out.Insatiable 6th,Croco Rouge7th*

un99- 8Bel fst 1⅛ :461 1:10 1:34 1:461 3+ BroklynH-G2 118 6 63¾ 64¼ 52¼ 13 17¼ Sellers S J L117 3.95 100- 08 RunningStag1177¼ DeputyDiamond1132¼ SirBear1193¼ Quick 5 wide burst 8
ay99-13Suf fst 1⅛ :472 1:11 1:36 1:49 3+ MassH-G2 116 1 1½ 11 1½ 1½ 2½ Sellers S J LB113 8.20 90- 16 Behrens118½ Running Stag1132¾ Real Quiet1214½ Off rail, faltered 6

Previously trained by Mitchell Philip
y99 ♦ Goodwood (GB) gd 1⅛ Ⓣ RH 2:074 4+ Shergar Cup Classic Alw 163100 2½ Cochrane R 124 10.00 Handsome Ridge124½ Running Stag1242 Border Arrow1242½ 10
Racing Post Rating: 120 *Rated in 7th,bid over 1f out,held by winner.Happy Valentine 4th*

Previously trained by Mitchell Philip
ar99 ♦ Nad Al Sheba (UAE) ft *1¼ LH 2:003 4+ Dubai World Cup-G1 Stk 5000000 714½ Cochrane R 126 b - Almutawakel126¾ Malek126¾ Victory Gallop1261½ 8
Racing Post Rating: 100 *Rank at rear,wide 6th 3f out,never threatened.Silver Charm 6th*

ov98-11CD fst 1⅛ :472 1:112 1:3611:49 3+ ClarkH-G2 110 8 53¾ 41½ 51¾ 42 41½ Velazquez J R L116 13.20 97- 14 Silver Charm124hd Littlebitlively1131 Wild Rush117½ Lacked room 3/16s 8
ov98-10CD fst 1¼ :473 1:12 1:3712:02 3+ BCClasic-G1 107 7 62¾ 73¾ 63¼ 74¼ 76¼ Velazquez J R L126 104.70 89- 07 Awesome Again126¾ Silver Charm126nk Swain126no Steadied early 10
Oct98-10Bel sly 1¼ :462 1:093 1:3412:003 3+ JkyClbGC-G1 94 1 58½ 37½ 37 46½ 414¼ Cochrane R 126 f 19.80 77- 14 Wagon Limit1265½ Gentlemen1264¾ Skip Away1264 Rail run second turn 6
Sep98- 9Bel fst 1⅛ :452 1:09 1:3411:474 3+ Woodward-G1 106 1 52¾ 52 52¾ 34½ 37¾ Cochrane R 126 48.50 83- 18 Skip Away1261¾ Gentlemen1266 Running Stag1269 Determinedly on rail 5
ug98 ♦ Deauville (Fr) yl *1¼ Ⓣ RH 2:052 4+ Prix Gontaut-Biron-G3 Stk 60300 13 Cochrane R 123 28.30 Running Stag1233 Garuda1231½ Lord of Men121½ 11
Racing Post Rating: 119 *Rated at rear,rail bid to lead ovr 1f out,ridden clear.Sasuru 5th*

un98 ♦ Longchamp (Fr) sf *1¼ Ⓣ RH 2:032 4+ La Coupe-G3 Stk 60500 34½ Day N 123 14.00 Public Purse1232 Farasan1232½ Running Stag1231½ 11
Racing Post Rating: 103 *Rated in 7th,steady progress,5th 2-1/2f out,gained 3rd 100y out*

n98 ♦ Epsom (GB) gd 1½ Ⓣ LH 2:333 4+ Vodafone International Rated H Hcp 70800 918¾ Cochrane R 133 20.00 Hajr119no Sabadilla1261½ Tough Leader1192 15
Racing Post Rating: 87 *Never a factor*

pr98 ♦ Cologne (Ger) sf *1½ Ⓣ RH 2:361 4+ Gerling-Preis-G2 Stk 69800 65¼ Swinburn W R 126 24.10 Ferrari1262 Asolo126½ Ungaro1301 10
Racing Post Rating: 105 *Rated in 7th,lacked room 2f out,outfinished*

r98 ♦ Gelsenkirchen (Ger) hy *1¼ Ⓣ RH 2:154 4+ GP Gelsenkirchner-Wirtschaft-G3 Stk 55200 58½ Cochrane R 126 6.80 Eden Rock1284 Sambakoenig126½ Orsuno1212 10
Racing Post Rating: 95 *Trailed to 3f out,some late progress.Ferrari 4th*

ar98 ♦ Lingfield (GB) ft 1¼ ◈LH 2:054 3+ Winter Derby (dirt) Alw 90500 13½ Cochrane R 132 4.50 Running Stag1323½ Refuse to Lose1327 Fayik132½ 14
Racing Post Rating: 118 *Rated towards rear,long drive to lead over 1f out,ridden clear*

c97 ♦ Wolverhampton (GB) ft 1³⁄₁₆ ◈LH 2:003 3+ Wulfrun Stakes (Listed) Stk 89900 2½ Clark A 123 4.50 Farmost125½ Running Stag1237 Puzzlement123hd 7
Settled in 6th,bid 2f out,drifted left,2nd best.Centre Stalls 7th

ov97 ♦ Lingfield (GB) ft 1¼ ◈LH 2:032 3+ Faucets Conditions Stks (dirt) Alw 8800 2nk Clark A 127 *.80 Unconditional Love121nk Running Stag12713 Acharne1262½ 6
Tracked in 4th,bid 2f out,dueled 1f out,outgamed

ep97 ♦ Goodwood (GB) gd 1¼ Ⓣ RH 2:092 3+ ROA Foundation Stakes (Listed) Stk 43600 41¼ Clark A 120 4.50 Danish Rhapsody126½ Proper Blue126no Sandstone120¾ 5
Tracked in 3rd,2nd and drifted left over 1f out,outfinished

ep97 ♦ Longchamp (Fr) sf *1⅜ Ⓣ RH 2:152 Prix du Lion d'Angers (Listed) Stk 43500 25 Clark A 128 35.00 Majorien1285 Running Stag128no Kaizen1281 7
Rated in 6th,prevailed in duel for 2nd.Tavildaran 5th,Rate Cut6th

p97 ♦ Saint-Cloud (Fr) yl *1 Ⓣ RH 1:403 Prix Ridgway (Listed) Stk 42500 44 Clark A 128 4.50 Such Charisma1283 Stingy128½ Blue Sky128½ 7
Tracked in 3rd,dueled briefly 2f out,gradually weakened

g97 ♦ Goodwood (GB) gd 1 Ⓣ RH 1:37 Conditions Stakes Alw 37800 43 Eddery P 124 10.00 Cape Cross1242½ Dragonada123nk Kenmist119nk 6
Rated in 5th,mild bid over 1f out,one-paced late

un97 ♦ Ascot (GB) gd 1 Ⓣ RH 1:39 St James's Palace Stakes-G1 Stk 373400 714 Fallon K 126 66.00 Starborough1261 Air Express1264 Daylami126½ 8
Tracked in 3rd,weakened 2f out.Desert King 4th

ay97 ♦ Goodwood (GB) gd 1¼ Ⓣ RH 2:123 Predominate Stakes (Listed) Stk 57700 22½ Fallon K 120 12.00 Grapeshot1232½ Running Stag1201 Shii-Take1201¼ 6
Tracked in 4th,progress halfway,chased winner home last quarter

pr97 ♦ Newmarket (GB) gd 1 Ⓣ Str 1:38 Craven Stakes-G3 Stk 54800 52¾ Fallon K 121 33.00 Desert Story124¾ Grapeshot121hd Cape Cross1211½ 8
Squeezed back start,rated in last,mild late gain.Air Express 4th

ar97 ♦ Kempton (GB) gd 1¼ Ⓣ RH 2:07 Stanmore Conditions Stakes Alw 12800 21¾ Clark A 125 3.00 Palio Sky1221¾ Running Stag1259 Drive Assured1221 5
Rank in 4th,ridden into lead 2f out,headed 1f out

eb97 ♦ Lingfield (GB) ft 1¼ ◈LH 2:073 Atlanta Maiden Stakes (dirt) Maiden 8400 17 Clark A 126 *1.40 Running Stag1267 Around Fore Alliss1262 Solar Dawn1218 6
Rated in 4th,led over 2f out,quickly clear

Previously trained by Maurice Zilber
ep96 ♦ Maisons-Laffitte (Fr) gd *7½f Ⓣ Str 1:323 Prix Aethelstan-EBF Alw 27100 2½ Vion V 118 17.00 With Fire123½ Running Stag118¾ Alekos1181½ 9
Led to 1f out,dueled,gave ground grudgingly

ep96 ♦ Saint-Cloud (Fr) gd *1 Ⓣ LH 1:413 Prix Hauban-EBF Alw 27200 11 Guignard G 123 b 3.75e Catfriend123nk Babalover123hd Point Proven1231 16
Never a factor

ug96 ♦ Deauville (Fr) gd *1 Ⓣ RH 1:48 Prix des Roches Noires-EBF Alw 35300 67 Guignard G 121 2.25 Peintre Celebre1212 New Frontier121no Safarid1211½ 6
Pressed pace,led 3f out,weakened 1-1/2f out

The cases of Running Stag, Gentleman's Deal, and others lend further credence to my theory that grass form and synthetic-surface form are two very different things. You will come across many grass horses who won't run a lick on synthetic surfaces, just as they won't run a lick on conventional dirt.

The English all-weather tracks do have biases and idiosyncrasies, but they vary from course to course.

Front-runners do well at Southwell. This is probably due to the severe kickback that closers have to face. It is a true gallopers' track and often horses who hit the front and have the ability to maintain their run from the turn are very hard to wear down. Wolverhampton favors front-runners when the track is riding fast. At Lingfield, closers stack up on the decline to the home turn and front-runners often get swallowed up. This is because jockeys often ride a patient race to the home turn. It is not uncommon to get hard-luck stories there—strong-traveling closers often encounter traffic problems. Kempton has a long straight on the outer loop, like Southwell, and races tend to change complexion readily. Closers are definitely favored there

You have to handicap each of the four AW tracks in England differently. It is generally a matter of horses for courses. Few horses are versatile enough to act on all tracks. The draw factor is a massive influence in finding a winner on the all-weathers, especially in races up to seven furlongs. The difference between being drawn low or on the outer can be nine to 10 strides, which in a five-furlong sprint makes it very hard to claw back.

14

The Future of Synthetic Surfaces

Perhaps you've gotten to this point in the book and have had it with synthetic surfaces. Considering the additional challenges they bring to the already difficult task of handicapping, that wouldn't be an irrational conclusion. You might even be tempted to ignore racing at places with synthetic tracks and concentrate on good old-fashioned dirt, at tracks such as Belmont, Saratoga, and Churchill Downs.

Don't do it.

There are already nine synthetic tracks in North America, including Keeneland, Del Mar, Hollywood, and Santa Anita, four of the biggest tracks in the sport. Anyone hoping to have a clue about future Kentucky Derbies or Breeders' Cups is going to have to know something about synthetic surfaces. The road to the Derby includes numerous preps run on synthetic tracks, such as the Lexington, the Blue Grass, the Santa Anita Derby, the Lane's End, the San Felipe, the San Rafael, the Sham, and the Robert B. Lewis. The 2008 Breeders' Cup at Santa Anita will be run on its brand-new synthetic track, Pro-Ride, and numerous Breeders' Cup preps will be run on other synthetic surfaces.

In the short term, it doesn't look like any other tracks have plans to convert to synthetic surfaces. The great Cushion Track debacle of 2008 at Santa Anita all but guaranteed that no one else is going to go synthetic in the near future.

After getting through the Oak Tree meeting in the fall of 2007 without serious problems, Santa Anita's Cushion Track turned into a nightmare at the meet that began a few months later in late December. Track crews couldn't get the surface to drain properly in the wake of heavy rains. Paul Harper, technical director of Cushion Track Footings, said that creating a surface that was resistant to high temperatures had ended up compromising the drainage. A synthetic surface, which is never supposed to be wet under any conditions, turned into a pond of sorts. The water just sat on top of the track. Things got so bad that Santa Anita had to cancel 11 cards, taking a huge financial hit.

And even on some days when the track was usable, the racing turned out to be farcical. For a period of time, the surface was so fast that a world record was set, and even allowance horses were cracking the 1:07 mark for six furlongs.

Finally, they got things under control and Santa Anita finished out the meet without any further serious problems, but only after a Cushion Track competitor, the Australian firm Pro-Ride, had to be called in to fix things.

Santa Anita's problems caused racing executives to take a completely different look at synthetic surfaces. No longer were they the cure-all, but an unproven surface that very well could lead you down the road to ruin.

"I can't imagine that any track is talking about switching to synthetic right now," Oaklawn Park General Manager Eric Jackson said shortly before the 2008 Kentucky Derby. "I wouldn't want to be the GM who recommends it at the moment."

The death of Eight Belles in the 2008 Kentucky Derby brought the thorny issue of horse safety back into the limelight, leading many to call for more tracks to convert to synthetic surfaces in the hope that they would be safer. But no one among track management seemed ready to budge. Those who ran tracks with dirt surfaces still had Santa Anita's problems fresh in their minds.

Another deterrent to putting in a synthetic racing surface is the expense involved. Depending upon the size of the track and the type of surface installed, the ballpark figure for the changeover is about $10 million.

Clearly, some track managements, especially those at smaller tracks, have come to the conclusion that they cannot afford to go synthetic. In California, they didn't have a choice.

The California Horse Racing Board took the decision out of the hands of tracks in its state. In 2006, it ruled that all Thoroughbred tracks in the state that race for four weeks or more (which gives the northern California fairs an exemption) had to install a synthetic racing surface by January 1, 2008. The CHRB based its decision on the safety factor, citing synthetic surfaces as a way of cutting back on horse injuries and deaths.

"While it is not just racing surfaces causing the problem, it certainly is a contributing factor," CHRB Chairman Richard Shapiro said when announcing the edict. "I think it is clear, given Turfway Park's experience, that California needs to move forward and continue our progress."

While safety issues are a compelling reason for tracks to go synthetic, whether or not more tracks will make the switch will ultimately come down to economics. Will the benefits outweigh the costs? On that, the jury is still out.

For a track to invest upward of $10 million on a new racing surface, it will have to be convinced that it will see a substantial return on its investment.

Now that the first wave of the synthetic era has come and gone, track operators are sure to sit back and watch where the money goes. Will bettors gravitate toward synthetic tracks, or, uncomfortable with their idiosyncrasies, stick to the dirt tracks? Should synthetic surfaces prove to increase betting handle, then many racetrack executives will be convinced that the investment is well worth it.

Like many issues concerning synthetic tracks, it may be too soon to tell. The early returns were promising, as bettors seemed more than willing to give the Polytracks of the world a try.

The first Polytrack meet at Keeneland produced terrific numbers. When Hollywood concluded its 2007 fall meet, the numbers were also good. All-sources handle was up by about 5 percent. One of the reasons clearly was field size. Southern California tracks had been notorious for their small fields, but Hollywood was able to boast of having an average of 8.6 starters per race, clearly a benefit of Cushion Track and a big reason why handle was so good at the meet.

Then, things turned.

The 2008 Keeneland spring meet was a disaster from a business standpoint. Total all-sources handle was off by nearly 11 percent. Keeneland's Nick Nicholson admitted that bettors' discomfort with Polytrack might have been part of the problem.

"As someone said to me, there's been a learning curve with Polytrack for trainers and jockeys, and it's the same for handicappers," he told *Daily Racing Form.*

Keeneland's poor meet came on the heels of a bad meet at Turfway, where all-sources handle was down $9.6 million at the 2008 winter-spring meet.

"I can't bet on that stuff," one bettor, who handles about $2 million per year, told me. "I can't even put my finger on it. There's just something about racing on Polytrack that I don't like. It's just strange racing, and I'm uncomfortable with it."

Were the poor numbers at Turfway and Keeneland a sign that bettors had had enough of synthetic surfaces or just an aberration? Stay tuned.

Even if the betting on synthetic-surface venues does decline, tracks will have other incentives to go artificial. Maintenance costs are much less for synthetic tracks, which require little in the way of management, than they are for dirt tracks. It has been estimated that Turfway Park's Polytrack surface will pay for itself in five years due to the decline in maintenance costs. David Willmott, the president of Woodbine Entertainment Group, estimates that there will be an annual savings of $750,000 at Woodbine from the reduced costs of caring for Polytrack versus the conventional dirt track.

It's also reasonable to expect that the cost of synthetic surfaces will come down in the future, just as has happened with so many other new products on the market. Enough companies are spending significant amounts of money on research and development that someone is sure to come up with a synthetic surface that can be constructed out of less-expensive materials than the ones being used today.

The same synthetic surface that now costs $10 million could conceivably cost $6 million someday. At that price, more tracks would be able to afford a synthetic track if they chose to install one.

There may even be still another phase to this story—synthetic turf racing. Artificial turf is far from a new concept. It has been used in many sports stadiums for decades. For myriad reasons, 100 percent fake grass will not work when it comes to horse racing. But the sport has already made great strides when it comes to grass courses that have synthetically reinforced root zones. Such tracks are already in use in Hong Kong, Singapore, and Australia.

"The grass courses here are unbelievably good," said former New York Racing Association executive Bill Nader, who now works for the Hong Kong Jockey Club. "This is really one of those situations where you have to see it to believe it. We got six inches of rain in less than 24 hours prior to a race day with 10 turf races. No problem. The turf was listed as good to firm and the running times were less than one second off the par times. We have a number of 11-race programs at Sha Tin when all races are on turf. Happy Valley is all turf; there is no dirt track. The turf courses in Hong Kong are ridiculously good."

The leading manufacturer of such courses is the Australian company StrathAyr. Much like the case with synthetic dirt tracks, the StrathAyr courses hold up to any kind of weather and appear to be much safer than conventional grass courses.

According to Dr. George Mundy, formerly the chief veterinarian for the Kentucky Racing Commission, the fatality rate over Hong Kong's grass surface is just 0.3 per 1,000 starters. That makes Hong Kong racing about 80 percent safer than U.S. racing.

"Why don't we add this natural turf option to our arsenal in the fight to increase the safety of our racehorses?" Mundy wrote in an Internet post. "The answer is obvious—let's get to work!"

It doesn't matter how much it rains; these tracks don't get wet and races do not have to be switched off the turf.

"Where it is different from U.S. turf courses is that we've got a proven track record of being all-weather," said StrathAyr Chairman Bill Casimaty. "In fact, it is more 'all-weather' than some of the synthetics. We've had occasions when our tracks have been in use and even the synthetic-surface races have been canceled.

"We believe that statistics will prove that we have the absolute safest racing surface there is. That comes from the fact that you have a cushion root zone. You never wind up with a hard track. We are safer because we have high drainage. That takes away the variation between wet and dry. If we put a semi-trailer tractor over our turf track you will see the indentation made by the track's wheels. But come back a few hours later or the next morning and they are gone. The mesh elements we use in the root zone cause the track to spring back up. The actual horse is helping the grass grow because it compresses the turf and as it slowly springs back up it sucks air into the root zone. It's never hard and it has a springing effect. We strongly believe it's the safest of all our surfaces."

Because dirt races make up the bulk of this country's racing cards, all-weather grass courses might not be as important to American tracks as they are to tracks in other parts of the world that race primarily—or exclusively—on grass, but a U.S. track that installs such a course could put itself at a huge advantage over its rivals when it comes to attracting betting dollars and offering the safest racing possible.

Turf races universally attract bigger fields and more betting dollars than dirt races. The reason there aren't more of them in the U.S. is that turf courses get chewed up and can't be overused. A semi-synthetic turf course couldn't be used for 10 races a day, five days a week, but it could be used far more often than a conventional grass course. A StrathAyr course in Singapore is currently used for more than 600 races a year, an unheard-of amount for a U.S. course. If a U.S. track could conduct 600 turf races a year it would guarantee itself a healthy increase in handle.

"We're probably not talking about a huge number of tracks going with this, the way it has been with the synthetics, because there is not that much racing on the turf in the U.S.," Casimaty said. "But turf is regarded as the Rolls-Royce of horse racing. People I have talked to in the U.S. tell me that there will be a lot of interest in new turf tracks after this wave of synthetics has passed.

This general focus and attention on tracks and safety issues could lead to that. It will help us."

Casimaty's one fear is that U.S. racetracks will be reluctant to go with synthetic grass after the problems Santa Anita had in the late 1980s when it spent about $3 million on a new turf course. Called Netlon, it had a mesh base and was supposed to be the wave of the future.

Netlon was nothing but trouble. It turned out to be so fast that ordinary horses were running in near-world-record times. The course was extremely hard and several horses were injured when racing over it. Among them was 1988 Breeders' Cup Turf winner Great Communicator, who broke down when running over Netlon in the Burke Handicap and had to be destroyed.

Nelton lasted less than two years before Santa Anita was forced to tear it out.

Here's another prediction: There will be a day when harness races are run on synthetic surfaces. Harness racing doesn't have nearly the problem Thoroughbred racing has when it comes to injuries or wet tracks, but there are a few places, such as the Meadowlands, that race both breeds. There could be significant cost savings involved if the tracks did not have to be converted each time the switch was made from Standardbreds to Thoroughbreds and vice versa. Meadowlands officials have already looked into going synthetic for both breeds and sent prominent harness trainer Jimmy Takter to take a few test drives over the synthetic Tapeta surface at Michael Dickinson's Maryland farm with a trotter. Takter told Meadowlands officials he thought that Tapeta, with a few modifications, would work fine for Standardbreds.

Will there be a Hambletonian on Polytrack? Why not? The world of horse racing is rapidly changing and synthetic tracks are going to be a big part of the sport. The handicapper is going to have no choice but to change with the times.